Functional Programming Using F#

This introduction to the principles of functional programming using F# shows how to apply theoretical concepts to produce succinct and elegant programs. The book shows how mainstream computer science problems can be solved using functional programming. It introduces a model-based approach exploiting the rich type system of F#. It also demonstrates the role of functional programming in a wide spectrum of applications including databases and systems that engage in a dialogue with a user. Coverage also includes advanced features in the .NET library, the imperative features of F# and topics such as sequences, computation expressions and asynchronous computations.

With a broad spectrum of examples and exercises, the book is intended for courses in functional programming as well as for self-study. Enhancing its use as a text is a website with downloadable programs, lecture slides, mini-projects and links to further F# sources.

Michael R. Hansen is an Associate Professor in Computer Science at the Technical University of Denmark. He is the author of *Introduction to Programming Using SML* (with Hans Rischel) and *Duration Calculus: A Formal Approach to Real-Time Systems* (with Zhou Chaochen).

Hans Rischel is a former Associate Professor in Computer Science at the Technical University of Denmark. He is the author of *Introduction to Programming Using SML* (with Michael R. Hansen).

Functional Programming Using F#

MICHAEL R. HANSEN
Technical University of Denmark, Lyngby

HANS RISCHEL
Technical University of Denmark, Lyngby

CAMBRIDGE
UNIVERSITY PRESS

University Printing House, Cambridge CB2 8BS, United Kingdom

One Liberty Plaza, 20th Floor, New York, NY 10006, USA

477 Williamstown Road, Port Melbourne, VIC 3207, Australia

314-321, 3rd Floor, Plot 3, Splendor Forum, Jasola District Centre, New Delhi - 110025, India

79 Anson Road, #06-04/06, Singapore 079906

Cambridge University Press is part of the University of Cambridge.

It furthers the University's mission by disseminating knowledge in the pursuit of education, learning and research at the highest international levels of excellence.

www.cambridge.org
Information on this title: www.cambridge.org/9781107684065

First published 2013
3rd printing 2016

A catalogue record for this publication is available from the British Library

Library of Congress Cataloging in Publication data
Hansen, Michael R., author.
Functional programming Using F# / Michael R. Hansen, Technical University of Denmark,
Lyngby, Hans Rischel, Technical University of Denmark, Lyngby.
    pages cm
Includes bibliographical references and index.
ISBN 978-1-107-01902-7 (hardback) – ISBN 978-1-107-68406-5 (paperback)
1. Functional programming (Computer science)   2. F# (Computer program language)
I. Rischel, Hans, author.   II. Title.
QA76.62.H37   2013
005.1′14–dc23   2012040414

ISBN 978-1-107-01902-7 Hardback
ISBN 978-1-107-68406-5 Paperback

Additional resources for this publication at http://www.cambridge.org/9781107019027

Contents

v

Preface

The purpose of this book is to introduce a wide range of readers – from the professional programmer to the computer science student – to the rich world of functional programming using the F# programming language. The book is intended as the textbook in a course on functional programming and aims at showing the role of functional programming in a wide spectrum of applications ranging from computer science examples over database examples to systems that engage in a dialogue with a user.

Why functional programming using F#?

Functional programming languages have existed in academia for more than a quarter of a century, starting with the untyped Lisp language, followed by strongly typed languages like Haskell and Standard ML.

The penetration of functional languages to the software industry has, nevertheless, been surprisingly slow. The reason is probably lack of support of functional languages by commercial software development platforms, and software development managers are reluctant to base software development on languages living in a non-commercial environment.

This state of affairs has been changed completely by the appearance of F#, an opensource, full-blown functional language integrated in the Visual Studio development platform and with access to all features in the .NET program library. The language is also supported on Linux and MAC systems using the Mono platform.

The background

The material in this book has been developed in connection with courses taught at the Technical University of Denmark, originating from the textbook *Introduction to Programming Using SML* by Hansen and Rischel (Addison-Wesley, 1999).

It has been an exciting experience for us to learn the many elegant and useful features of the F# language, and this excitement is hopefully transferred to the reader of this book.

The chapters

- Chapter 1: The basic concepts of F#, including values, types and recursive functions, are introduced in a manner that allows readers to solve interesting problems from the start.
- Chapter 2: A thorough introduction to the basic types in F# is given, together with a gentle introduction to the notion of higher-order functions.
- Chapter 3: The simplest composite types of F#, tuples and records, are introduced. They allow several values to be grouped together into one component. Furthermore, tagged values are introduced.

- Chapter 4: A list is a finite sequence of values with the same type. Standard recursions on lists are studied and examples illustrating a model-based approach to functional programming are given.

- Chapter 5: The concepts of sets and maps are introduced and the powerful F# collection libraries for lists, sets and maps are studied and applied in connection with a model-based approach.

- Chapter 6: The concept of finite tree is introduced and illustrated through a broad selection of examples.

- Chapter 7: It is shown how users can make their own libraries by means of modules consisting of signature and implementation files. Furthermore, object-oriented features of F# are mentioned.

- Chapter 8: Imperative features of F# are introduced, including the array part of the collection library and the imperative sets and maps from the .NET framework.

- Chapter 9: The memory management concepts, stack, heap and garbage collection, are described. Tail-recursive functions are introduced and two techniques for deriving such functions are presented: one using accumulating parameters, the other continuations. Their efficiency advantages are illustrated.

- Chapter 10: A variety of facilities for processing text are introduced, including regular expressions, file operations, web-based operations and culture-dependent string ordering. The facilities are illustrated using a real-world example.

- Chapter 11: A sequence is a, possibly infinite, collection of elements that are computed on-demand only. Sequence functions are expressed using library functions or sequence expressions that provide a step-by-step method for generating elements. Database tables are viewed as sequences (using a type provider) and operations on databases are expressed using query expressions.

- Chapter 12: The notion of computation expression, which is based on the theory of monads, is studied and used to hide low-level details of a computation from its definition. Monadic parsing is used as a major example to illustrate the techniques.

- Chapter 13: This last chapter describes how to construct asynchronous reactive programs, spending most of their time awaiting a request or a response from an external agent, and parallel programs, exploiting the multi-core processor of the computer.

The first six chapters cover a standard curriculum in functional programming, while the other chapters cover more advanced topics.

Further material

The book contains a large number of exercises, and further material is available at the book's homepage. A link to this homepage is found at:

```
http://www.cambridge.org/9781107019027
```

This material includes a complete set of slides for a course in functional programming plus a collection of problems and descriptions of topics to be used in student projects.

Acknowledgments

Special thanks go to Peter Sestoft, Don Syme and Anh-Dung Phan. The idea to make a textbook on functional programming on the basis of F# originates from Peter, who patiently commented on the manuscript during its production and helped with advice and suggestions. From the very start of this project we had the support of Don. This is strongly appreciated and so is the help, clarifications and constructive comments that we received throughout this project. Phan helped with many comments, suggestions and insights about the platform. We are grateful for this help, for many discussions and for careful comments on all the chapters.

Furthermore, we are grateful to Nils Andersen, Mary E. Böker, Diego Colombo and Niels Hallenberg for reading and commenting on the complete manuscript.

Earlier versions of this manuscript have been used in connection with courses at the Technical University of Denmark and the IT-University of Copenhagen. The comments we received from the students in these courses are greatly appreciated.

Lyngby, July 31, 2012
Michael R. Hansen and Hans Rischel

1

Getting started

In this chapter we will introduce some of the main concepts of functional programming languages. In particular we will introduce the concepts of value, expression, declaration, recursive function and type. Furthermore, to explain the meaning of programs we will introduce the notions: binding, environment and evaluation of expressions.

The purpose of the chapter is to acquaint the reader with these concepts, in order to address interesting problems from the very beginning. The reader will obtain a thorough knowledge of these concepts and skills in applying them as we elaborate on them throughout this book.

There is support of both compilation of F# programs to executable code and the execution of programs in an interactive mode. The programs in this book are usually illustrated by the use of the interactive mode.

The interface of the interactive F# compiler is very advanced as, for example, structured values like tuples, lists, trees and functions can be communicated directly between the user and the system without any conversions. Thus, it is very easy to experiment with programs and program designs and this allows us to focus on the main structures of programs and program designs, that is, the core of programming, as input and output of structured values can be handled by the F# system.

1.1 Values, types, identifiers and declarations

In this section we illustrate how to use an F# system in interactive mode.

The interactive interface allows the user to enter, for example, an arithmetic expression in a line, followed by two semicolons and terminated by pressing the return key:

```
2*3 + 4;;
```

The answer from the system contains the value and the type of the expression:

```
val it : int = 10
```

The system will add some leading characters in the input line to make a distinction between input from the user and output from the system. The dialogue may look as follows:

```
> 2*3 + 4;;
val it : int = 10
>
```

The leading string "> " is output whenever this particular system is awaiting input from the user. It is called the *prompt*, as it "prompts" for input from the user. The input from the user is ended by a double semicolon "; ;" while the next line contains the answer from the system.

In the following we will distinguish between user input and answer from the system by the use of different type fonts:

```
2*3 + 4;;
val it : int = 10
```

The input from the user is written in `typewriter` font while the answer from the system is written in *`italic typewriter`* font.

The above answer starts with the *reserved word* `val`, which indicates that a value has been computed, while the special *identifier* `it` is a name for the computed value, that is, 10. The *type* of the result is `int`, denoting the subset of the integers $\{\ldots, -2, -1, 0, 1, 2, \ldots\}$ that can be represented using the system.

The user can give a name to a value by entering a *declaration*, for instance:

```
let price = 125;;
```

where the reserved word `let` starts the declarations. In this case the system answers:

```
val price : int = 125
```

The *identifier* `price` is now a name for the integer value 125. We also say that the identifier `price` is *bound* to 125.

Identifiers which are bound to values can be used in expressions:

```
price * 20;;
val it : int = 2500
```

The identifier `it` is now bound to the integer value 2500, and this identifier can also be used in expressions:

```
it / price = 20;;
val it : bool = true
```

The operator `/` is the quotient operator on integers. The expression `it/price = 20` is a question to the system and the identifier `it` is now bound to the answer `true` of type `bool`, where `bool` is a type denoting the two-element set $\{\text{true}, \text{false}\}$ of truth values. Note that the equality sign in the input is part of an expression of type `bool`, whereas the equality sign in the answer expresses a binding of the identifier `it` to a value.

1.2 Simple function declarations

We now consider the declaration of functions. One can name a *function*, just as one can name an integer constant. As an example, we want to compute the area of a circle with given radius r, using the well known area function: $\text{circleArea}(r) = \pi r^2$.

Circle with radius r and area πr^2.

The constant π is found in the Library under the name `System.Math.PI`:

```
System.Math.PI;;
val it : float = 3.141592654
```

The type `float` denotes the subset of the real numbers that can be represented in the system, and `System.Math.PI` is bound to a value of this type.

We choose the name `circleArea` for the circle area function, and the function is then declared using a `let`-declaration:

```
let circleArea r = System.Math.PI * r * r;;
val circleArea : float -> float
```

The answer says that the identifier `circleArea` now denotes a value, as indicated by the reserved word `val` occurring in the answer. This value is a *function* with the type `float -> float`, where the symbol `->` indicates a function type and the argument as well as the value of the function has type `float`. Thus, the answer says that `circleArea` is bound to a value that is some function of type `float -> float`.

The function `circleArea` can be *applied* to different *arguments*. These arguments must have the type `float`, and the result has type `float` too:

```
circleArea 1.0;;
val it : float = 3.141592654

circleArea (2.0);;
val it : float = 12.56637061
```

Brackets around the argument `1.0` or `(2.0)` are optional, as indicated here.

The identifier `System.Math.PI` is a composite identifier. The identifier `System` denotes a *namespace* where the identifier `Math` is defined, and `System.Math` denotes a namespace where the identifier `PI` is defined. Furthermore, `System` and `System.Math` denote parts of the .NET Library. We encourage the reader to use program libraries whenever appropriate. In Chapter 7 we describe how to make your own program libraries.

Comments

A string enclosed within a matching pair (`*` and `*`) is a *comment* which is ignored by the F# system. Comments can be used to make programs more readable for a human reader by explaining the intention of the program, for example:

```
(* Area of circle with radius r *)
let circleArea r = System.Math.PI * r * r;;
val circleArea : float -> float
```

Two slash characters // can be used for one-line comments:

```
// Area of circle with radius r
let circleArea r = System.Math.PI * r * r;;
val circleArea : float -> float
```

A comment line can also begin with three slash characters ///. The tool XMLDocs can produce program documentation from such comment, but we will not pursue this any further in this book.

Comments can be very useful, especially in large programs, but long comments should be avoided as they tend to make it more difficult for the reader to get an overview of the program.

1.3 Anonymous functions. Function expressions

A function can be created in F# without getting any name. This is done by evaluating a *function expression*, that is an expression where the *value* is a *function*. This section introduces simple function expressions and function expressions with patterns.

A nameless, anonymous function can be defined by a *simple function expression*, also called a *lambda expression*,[1] for example:

```
fun r -> System.Math.PI * r * r;;
val it : float -> float = <fun:clo@10-1>
it 2.0;;
val it : float = 12.56637061
```

The expression fun r -> System.Math.PI * r * r denotes the circle-area function and it reads: "the function of r given by $\pi \cdot r^2$". The reserved word fun indicates that a function is defined, the identifier r occurring to the left of -> is a pattern for the argument of the function, and System.Math.PI * r * r is the expression for the value of the function.

The declaration of the circle-area function could be made as follows:

```
let circleArea = fun r ->  System.Math.PI * r * r;;
val circleArea : float -> float
```

but it is more natural in this case to use a let-declaration let circleArea r = ... with an argument pattern. We shall later see many uses of anonymous functions.

Function expressions with patterns

It is often convenient to define a function in terms of a number of cases. Consider, for example, a function giving the number of days in a month, where a month is given by its number, that is, an integer between 1 and 12. Suppose that the year of consideration is not a leap year. This function can thus be expressed as:

---

[1] Lambda calculus was introduced by Alonzo Church in the 1930s. In this calculus an expression of the form $\lambda x.e$ was used to denote the function of x given by the expression e. The fun-notation in F# is a direct translation from λ-expressions.

```
function
| 1  -> 31  // January
| 2  -> 28  // February
| 3  -> 31  // March
| 4  -> 30  // April
| 5  -> 31  // May
| 6  -> 30  // June
| 7  -> 31  // July
| 8  -> 31  // August
| 9  -> 30  // September
| 10 -> 31  // October
| 11 -> 30  // November
| 12 -> 31;;// December
  function
   ^
```

stdin(17,1): warning FS0025: Incomplete pattern matches on
this expression. For example, the value '0' may indicate a
case not covered by the pattern(s).
val it : int -> int = <fun:clo@17-2>

The last part of the answer shows that the computed value, named by it, is a function with
the type int -> int, that is, a function from integers to integers. The answer also shows
the internal name for that function. The first part of the answer is a warning that the set
of patterns used in the function-expression is incomplete. The expression enumerates a
value for every legal number for a month $(1, 2, \ldots, 12)$. At this moment we do not care
about other numbers.

The function can be applied to 2 to find the number of days in February:

```
it 2;;
val it : int = 28
```

This function can be expressed more compactly using a *wildcard pattern* "_":

```
function
| 2  -> 28  // February
| 4  -> 30  // April
| 6  -> 30  // June
| 9  -> 30  // September
| 11 -> 30  // November
| _  -> 31;;// All other months
```

In this case, the function is defined using six clauses. The first clause 2 -> 28 consists
of a pattern 2 and a corresponding expression 28. The next four clauses have a similar
explanation, and the last clause contains a wildcard pattern. Applying the function to a value
v, the system finds the clause containing the first pattern that matches v, and returns the
value of the corresponding expression. In this example there are just two kinds of matches
we should know:

- A constant, like 2, matches itself only, and
- the wildcard pattern _ matches any value.

For example, applying the function to 4 gives 30, and applying it to 7 gives 31.

An even more succinct definition can be given using an *or*-pattern:

```
function
| 2         -> 28  // February
| 4|6|9|11 -> 30  // April, June, September, November
| _         -> 31  // All other months
;;
```

The or-pattern $4 \mid 6 \mid 9 \mid 11$ matches any of the values $4, 6, 9, 11$, and no other values.

We shall make extensive use of such a case splitting in the definition of functions, also when declaring named functions:

```
let daysOfMonth = function
    | 2         -> 28  // February
    | 4|6|9|11 -> 30  // April, June, September, November
    | _         -> 31  // All other months
;;
val daysOfMonth : int -> int

daysOfMonth 3;;
val it : int = 31

daysOfMonth 9;;
val it : int = 30
```

1.4 Recursion

This section introduces the concept of recursion formula and recursive declaration of functions by an example: the factorial function $n!$. It is defined by:

$$
\begin{aligned}
0! &= 1 \\
n! &= 1 \cdot 2 \cdot \ldots \cdot n \quad \text{for } n > 0
\end{aligned}
$$

where n is a non-negative integer. The dots $\cdots$ indicate that all integers from 1 to n should be multiplied. For example:

$$4! = 1 \cdot 2 \cdot 3 \cdot 4 = 24$$

Recursion formula

The underbraced part of the below expression for $n!$ is the expression for $(n-1)!$:

$$n! = \underbrace{1 \cdot 2 \cdot \ldots \cdot (n-1)}_{(n-1)!} \cdot n \quad \text{for } n > 1$$

so we get the formula:

$$n! = n \cdot (n-1)! \quad \text{for } n > 1$$

This formula is actually correct also for $n = 1$ as:

$$0! = 1 \quad \text{and} \quad 1 \cdot (1 - 1)! = 1 \cdot 0! = 1 \cdot 1 = 1$$

so we get:

$$
\begin{array}{llll}
0! & = & 1 & \text{(Clause 1)} \\
n! & = & n \cdot (n - 1)! \quad \text{for } n > 0 & \text{(Clause 2)}
\end{array}
$$

This formula is called a *recursion formula* for the factorial function ($\_!$) as it expresses the value of the function for some argument n in terms of the value of the function for some other argument (here: $n - 1$).

Computations

This definition has a form that can be used in the computation of values of the function. For example:

$$
\begin{array}{ll}
& 4! \\
= & 4 \cdot (4 - 1)! \\
= & 4 \cdot 3! \\
= & 4 \cdot (3 \cdot (3 - 1)!) \\
= & 4 \cdot (3 \cdot 2!) \\
= & 4 \cdot (3 \cdot (2 \cdot (2 - 1)!)) \\
= & 4 \cdot (3 \cdot (2 \cdot 1!)) \\
= & 4 \cdot (3 \cdot (2 \cdot (1 \cdot (1 - 1)!))) \\
= & 4 \cdot (3 \cdot (2 \cdot (1 \cdot 0!))) \\
= & 4 \cdot (3 \cdot (2 \cdot (1 \cdot 1))) \\
= & 24
\end{array}
$$

The clauses of the definition of the factorial function are applied in a purely "mechanical" way in the above computation of 4!. We will now take a closer look at this mechanical process as the system will compute function values in a similar manner:

Substitution in clauses

The first step is obtained from Clause 2, by *substituting* 4 for n. The condition for using the second clause is satisfied as $4 > 0$. This step can be written in more detail as:

$$
\begin{array}{ll}
& 4! \\
= & 4 \cdot (4 - 1)! \quad \text{(Clause 2, } n = 4\text{)}
\end{array}
$$

Computation of arguments

The new argument $(4 - 1)$ of the factorial function in the expression $(4 - 1)!$ is computed in the next step:

$$
\begin{array}{ll}
& 4 \cdot (4 - 1)! \\
= & 4 \cdot 3! \quad \text{(Compute argument of !)}
\end{array}
$$

Thus, the principles used in the first two steps of the computation of 4! are:

- Substitute a value for n in Clause 2.
- Compute argument.

These are the only principles used in the above computation until we arrive at the expression:

$$4 \cdot (3 \cdot (2 \cdot (1 \cdot 0!)))$$

The next computation step is obtained by using Clause 1 to obtain a value of 0!:

$$
\begin{aligned}
& 4 \cdot (3 \cdot (2 \cdot (1 \cdot 0!))) \\
= \ & 4 \cdot (3 \cdot (2 \cdot (1 \cdot 1))) \qquad \text{(Clause 1)}
\end{aligned}
$$

and the multiplications are then performed in the last step:

$$
\begin{aligned}
& 4 \cdot (3 \cdot (2 \cdot (1 \cdot 1))) \\
= \ & 24
\end{aligned}
$$

This recursion formula for the factorial function is an example of a general pattern that will appear over and over again throughout the book. It contains a clause for a *base case* "0!", and it contains a clause where a more general case "n!" is reduced to an expression "$n \cdot (n-1)$!" involving a "smaller" instance "$(n-1)$!" of the function being characterized. For such recursion formulas, the computation process will terminate, that is, the computation of n! will terminate for all $n \geq 0$.

Recursive declaration

We name the factorial function `fact`, and this function is then declared as follows:

```
let rec fact = function
    | 0 -> 1
    | n -> n * fact(n-1);;
val fact : int -> int
```

This declaration corresponds to the recursion formula for n!. The reserved word `rec` occurring in the `let`-declaration allows the identifier being declared (`fact` in this case) to occur in the defining expression.

This declaration consists of two clauses

$$0 \text{ -> } 1 \qquad \text{and} \qquad n \text{ -> } n \text{ * } \text{fact}(n-1)$$

each initiated by a vertical bar. The *pattern* of the first clause is the constant 0, while the pattern of the second clause is the identifier n.

The patterns are *matched* with integer arguments during the *evaluation* of function values as we shall see below. The only value matching the pattern 0 is 0. On the other hand, every value matches the pattern n, as an identifier can name any value.

Evaluation

The system uses the declaration of `fact` to evaluate function values in a way that resembles the above computation of 4!.

Substitution in clauses

To evaluate `fact 4`, the system searches for a clause in the declaration of `fact`, where 4 matches the pattern of the clause.

The system starts with the first clause of the declaration: `0 -> 1`. This clause is skipped as the value 4 does not match the pattern 0 of this clause.

Then, the second clause: `n -> n * fact (n-1)` is investigated. The value 4 matches the pattern of this clause, that is, the identifier n. The value 4 is bound to n and then substituted for n in the right-hand side of this clause thereby obtaining the expression: `4 * fact (4-1)`.

We say that the expression `fact 4` *evaluates to* `4 * fact (4-1)` and this evaluation is written as:

```
      fact 4
  ⤳   4 * fact (4-1)
```

where we use the symbol ⤳ for a step in the evaluation of an expression. Note that the symbol ⤳ is not part of any program, but a symbol used in explaining the evaluation of expressions.

Evaluation of arguments

The next step in the evaluation is to evaluate the argument `4-1` of `fact`:

```
      4 * fact (4-1)
  ⤳   4 * fact 3
```

The evaluation of the expression `fact 4` proceeds until a value is reached:

```
      fact 4
  ⤳   4 * fact (4-1)                          (1)
  ⤳   4 * fact 3                              (2)
  ⤳   4 * (3 * fact (3-1))                    (3)
  ⤳   4 * (3 * fact 2)                        (4)
  ⤳   4 * (3 * (2 * fact (2-1)))              (5)
  ⤳   4 * (3 * (2 * fact 1))                  (6)
  ⤳   4 * (3 * (2 * (1 * fact (1-1))))        (7)
  ⤳   4 * (3 * (2 * (1 * fact 0)))            (8)
  ⤳   4 * (3 * (2 * (1 * 1)))                 (9)
  ⤳   4 * (3 * (2 * 1))                      (10)
  ⤳   4 * (3 * 2)                            (11)
  ⤳   4 * 6                                  (12)
  ⤳   24                                     (13)
```

The argument values 4, 3, 2 and 1 do not match the pattern 0 in the first clause of the declaration of `fact`, but they match the second pattern n. Thus, the second clause is chosen for further evaluation in the evaluation steps (1), (3), (5) and (7).

The argument value 0 does, however, match the pattern 0, so the first clause is chosen for further evaluation in step (9). The steps (2), (4), (6) and (8) evaluate argument values to `fact`, while the last steps (10) - (13) reduce the expression built in the previous steps.

Unsuccessful evaluations

The evaluation of `fact` n may not evaluate to a value, because

- the system will run out of memory due to long expressions,
- the evaluation may involve bigger integers than the system can handle, or
- the evaluation of an expression may not terminate.[2]

For example, applying `fact` to a negative integer leads to an *infinite evaluation*:

```
       fact -1
  ~>   -1 * fact (-1 - 1)
  ~>   -1 * fact -2
  ~>   -1 * (-2 * fact (-2 - 1))
  ~>   -1 * (-2 * fact -3)
  ~>   ...
```

A remark on recursion formulas

The above recursive function declaration was motivated by the recursion formula:

$$0! \;=\; 1$$
$$n! \;=\; n \cdot (n-1)! \quad \text{for } n > 0$$

which gives a unique characterization of the factorial function.

The factorial function may, however, be characterized by other recursion formulas, for example:

$$0! \;=\; 1$$
$$n! \;=\; \frac{(n+1)!}{n+1} \quad \text{for } n \ge 0$$

This formula is *not* well-suited for computations of values, because the corresponding function declaration based on this formula (where / denotes integer division):

```
let rec f = function
    | 0 -> 1
    | n -> f(n+1)/(n+1);;
val f : int -> int
```

gives an infinite evaluation of `f` k when $k > 0$. For example:

```
         f 2
  ~>   f (2+1) / (2+1)
  ~>   f (3) / 3
  ~>   f (3+1) / (3+1)
  ~>   ...
```

---

[2] Note that a text like `fact` n is *not* part of F#. It is a *schema* where one can obtain a program piece by replacing the *meta symbol* n with a suitable F# entity. In the following we will often use such schemas containing meta symbols in *italic font*.

Thus, in finding a declaration of a function, one has to look for a *suitable* recursion formula expressing the computation of function values. This declaration of f contains a base case "f 0". However, the second clause does not reduce the general case "f(n)" to an instance which is closer to the base case, and the evaluation of f(n) will not terminate when $n > 0$.

1.5 Pairs

Consider the function:

$$x^n = x \cdot x \cdot \ldots \cdot x \qquad n \text{ occurrences of } x, \text{ where } n \geq 0$$

where x is a real number and n is a natural number.

The under-braced part of the expression below for x^n is the expression for x^{n-1}:

$$x^n = x \cdot \underbrace{x \cdot \ldots \cdot x}_{x^{n-1}} \qquad n \text{ occurrences of } x, \text{ where } n > 0$$

Using the convention: $x^0 = 1$, the function can be characterized by the recursion formula:

$$\begin{aligned} x^0 &= 1 \\ x^n &= x \cdot x^{n-1} \quad \text{for } n > 0 \end{aligned}$$

In mathematics x^n is a function of two variables x and n, but it is treated differently in F# using the concept of a *pair*:

> If a_1 and a_2 are values of types τ_1 and τ_2 then (a_1, a_2) is a value of type $\tau_1 * \tau_2$

For example:

```
let a = (2.0,3);;
val a = (2.0, 3) : float * int
```

Furthermore, given patterns pat_1 and pat_2 there is a *composite* pattern (pat_1, pat_2). It matches a pair (a_1, a_2) exactly when pat_1 matches a_1 and pat_2 matches a_2, for example:

```
let (x,y) = a;;
val y : int = 3
val x : float = 2.0
```

The concept of a pair is a special case of tuples that are treated in Section 3.1.

Using these concepts we represent x^n as a function power with a pair (x, n) as the argument. The following declaration is based on the above recursion formula, using composite patterns (x, 0) and (x, n):

```
let rec power = function
    | (x,0) -> 1.0                     //  (1)
    | (x,n) -> x * power(x,n-1);; //  (2)
val power : float * int -> float
```

The type of power is float * int -> float. The argument of power is therefore a pair of type float * int while the value of the function is of type float.

The power function can be applied to pairs of type float * int:

```
power a;;
val it : float = 8.0

power(4.0,2);;
val it : float = 16.0
```

A function in F# has *one* argument and *one* value. In this case the argument is a pair (u, i) of type float * int, while the value of the function is of type float.

The system evaluates the expression power(4.0,2) as follows:

```
      power(4.0,2)
   ~  4.0 * power(4.0,2-1)         (Clause 2, x is 4.0, n is 2)
   ~  4.0 * power(4.0,1)
   ~  4.0 * (4.0 * power(4.0,1-1))  (Clause 2, x is 4.0, n is 1)
   ~  4.0 * (4.0 * power(4.0,0))
   ~  4.0 * (4.0 * 1.0)            (Clause 1, x is 4.0)
   ~  16.0
```

Notes on pattern matching

Note that the *order* of the *clauses* in the declaration of power is significant. The following declaration will *not* work:

```
let rec powerNo = function
    | (x, n) -> x * powerNo(x,n-1)    // This does NOT work
    | (x, 0) -> 1.0
;;
```

The first pattern (x, n) will match any pair of form (u, i) and the second clause will consequently never come into use. The F# compiler actually discovers this and issues a warning:

```
    | (x, 0) -> 1.0
    ----^^^^^^
... warning FS0026: This rule will never be matched
```

The function can be applied to an argument (despite the warning), but that would give an infinite evaluation since the base case (x, 0) -> 1.0 is never reached.

A similar remark on the order of clauses applies to the declaration of fact.

One should also note that a prior binding of an identifier used in a pattern has no effect on the pattern matching.[3] Hence, the following will also *not* work:

```
let zero = 0;;

let rec powerNo = function
    | (x,zero) -> 1.0                    // This does NOT work
    | (x,n)    -> x * powerNo(x,n-1)
;;
```

The first pattern `(x,zero)` will match any pair of form (u, i), binding x to u and zero to i so the second clause will again never come into use. The F# compiler issues a warning like in the previous example.

1.6 Types and type checking

The examples in the previous sections show that types like `float * int -> float` or `int` form an integral part of the responses from the system.

In fact, F# will try to *infer* a *type* for each value, expression and declaration entered. If the system can infer a type for the input, then the input is accepted by the system. Otherwise the system will reject the input with an error message.

For example, the expression `circleArea 2.0` is accepted, because

- `circleArea` has the type `float -> float`, and
- `2.0` has the type `float`.

Furthermore, the result of evaluating `circleArea 2.0`, that is `12.5663706144`, has type `float`.

On the other hand, the system will reject the expression `circleArea 2` with an error message since 2 has type `int` while the argument for `circleArea` must be of type `float`:

```
circleArea 2;;
  circleArea 2;;
  -----------^

stdin(95,12): error FS0001: This expression was expected to
have type
    float
but here has type
    int
```

The above type consideration for *function application* $f(e)$ is a special case of the general type rule for function application:

> if f has type $\tau_1 \; -> \; \tau_2$ and e has type τ_1
> then $f(e)$ has type τ_2.

---

[3] Identifiers that are *constructors* are, however, treated in a special way (cf. Section 3.8).

Using the notation $e : \tau$ to assert that the expression e has type τ, this rule can be presented more succinctly as follows:

> if $f : \tau_1 \rightarrow \tau_2$ and $e : \tau_1$
> then $f(e) : \tau_2$.

Consider, for example, the function power with type float * int -> float. In this case, τ_1 is float * int and τ_2 is float. Furthermore, the pair (4.0, 2) has type float * int (which is τ_1). According to the above rule, the expression power(4.0, 2) hence has type float (which is τ_2).

1.7 Bindings and environments

In the previous sections we have seen that identifiers can be bound to denote an integer, a floating-point value, a pair or a function. The notions of *binding* and *environment* are used to explain that entities are bound by identifiers.

The *execution* of a declaration, say let $x = e$, causes the identifier x to be bound to the value of the expression e. For example, the execution of the declaration:

```
let a = 3;;
val a : int = 3
```

causes the identifier a to be bound to 3. This binding is denoted by a $\mapsto$ 3.

Execution of further declarations gives extra bindings. For example, execution of

```
let b = 7.0;;
val b : float = 7.0
```

gives a further binding b $\mapsto$ 7.0.

A collection of bindings is called an *environment*, and the environment env_1 obtained from execution of the above two declarations is denoted by:

$$env_1 = \begin{bmatrix} a & \mapsto & 3 \\ b & \mapsto & 7.0 \end{bmatrix}$$

Note that this notation is *not* part of any program. Bindings and environments are mathematical objects used to explain the meaning of programs.

The execution of an additional declaration causes an extension of env_1. For example

```
let c = (2, 8);;
val c : int * int = (2, 8)

let circleArea r = System.Math.PI * r * r;;
val circleArea : float -> float
```

adds bindings of the identifiers c and circleArea to the environment env_1 giving the environment env_2:

$$env_2 = \begin{bmatrix} a & \mapsto & 3 \\ b & \mapsto & 7.0 \\ c & \mapsto & (2,8) \\ circleArea & \mapsto & \text{"the circle area function"} \end{bmatrix}$$

The value of an expression is always evaluated in the *actual environment*, that contains the bindings of identifiers that are valid at evaluation time. When the F# system is activated, the actual environment is the *Basis Environment* that gives meanings to `/`, `+`, `-`, `sqrt`, for example. When using environments we will usually not show bindings from the Basis Environment. We will usually also omit bindings of identifiers like `System.Math.PI` from the Library.

1.8 Euclid's algorithm

This section presents the famous algorithm of Euclid for computing the greatest common divisor of two natural numbers.

For a given integer n, an integer d is called a *divisor* of n (written $d|n$) if there exists an integer q such that $n = q \cdot d$. Hence, the number 1 is a divisor of any integer. Any integer $n \neq 0$ has a finite number of divisors as each divisor has absolute value $\leq |n|$, while 0 has infinitely many divisors as any integer is a divisor of 0. Thus, integers m, n have at least one common divisor (namely 1), and if either $m \neq 0$ or $n \neq 0$, then the set of common divisors of m and n is finite.

The *GCD theorem of Euclid* states that for any integers m, n there exists an integer $\gcd(m, n)$ such that $\gcd(m, n) \geq 0$, and such that the *common divisors* of m and n are precisely the *divisors* of $\gcd(m, n)$.

Note that if $m \neq 0$ or $n \neq 0$ then $\gcd(m, n)$ is the *greatest* common divisor of m and n. For $m = 0$ and $n = 0$ we have $\gcd(0, 0) = 0$, as the common divisors for 0 and 0 are precisely the divisors of 0, but 0 and 0 have no *greatest* common divisor as any number is a divisor of 0.

Euclid gave an algorithm for computing $\gcd(m, n)$ for arbitrary integers m and n and this algorithm gives at the same time a proof of the theorem.

Division with remainder. The / *and* % *operators*

Euclid's algorithm is based on the concept of *integer division with remainder*. Let m and n be integers with $m \neq 0$. An identity with integers q and r of the form:

$$n = q \cdot m + r$$

is then called a division with quotient q and remainder r. There are infinite many possible remainders (corresponding to different quotients q):

$$\ldots, n - 3 \cdot |m|, \ n - 2 \cdot |m|, \ n - |m|, \ n, \ n + |m|, \ n + 2 \cdot |m|, \ n + 3 \cdot |m|, \ \ldots$$

It follows that there are two possibilities concerning remainders r with $-|m| < r < |m|$:

1. The integer 0 is a remainder and any other remainder r satisfies $|r| \geq |m|$.
2. There are two remainders r_{neg} and r_{pos} such that $-|m| < r_{neg} < 0 < r_{pos} < |m|$.

The F# operators / and % (quotient and remainder) are defined (for $m \neq 0$) such that:

$$n = (n \; / \; m) \cdot m + (n \; \% \; m) \tag{1.1}$$

$$|n \; \% \; m| < |m| \tag{1.2}$$

$$n \; \% \; m \geq 0 \text{ when } n \geq 0 \tag{1.3}$$

$$n \; \% \; m \leq 0 \text{ when } n < 0 \tag{1.4}$$

so $n \; \% \; m = 0$ when m is a divisor of n, otherwise r_{pos} is used if $n > 0$ and r_{neg} if $n < 0$.

Note that the corresponding operators in other programming languages may use different conventions for negative integers.

Euclid's algorithm in F#

Euclid's algorithm is now expressed in the following declaration

```
let rec gcd = function
  | (0,n) -> n
  | (m,n) -> gcd(n % m,m);;
val gcd : int * int -> int
```

For example:

```
gcd(12,27);;
val it : int = 3

gcd(36, 116);;
val it : int = 4
```

Termination of Euclid's algorithm

It is not obvious that the evaluation of $\gcd(m, n)$ will terminate with a result for all integers m and n. We will now prove that the second clause in the declaration is in fact used at most $|m|$ times in the evaluation of $\gcd(m, n)$. It follows that the evaluation always terminates.

Consider an evaluation with at least $k \; (> 0)$ steps using the second clause:

$$
\begin{array}{lll}
& \gcd(m, n) & m \neq 0 \\
\rightsquigarrow & \gcd(m_1, n_1) & m_1 \neq 0 \\
\rightsquigarrow & \gcd(m_2, n_2) & m_2 \neq 0 \\
& \cdots & \\
\rightsquigarrow & \gcd(m_{k-1}, n_{k-1}) & m_{k-1} \neq 0 \\
\rightsquigarrow & \gcd(m_k, n_k) & \\
\rightsquigarrow & \cdots &
\end{array}
$$

The right-hand side of the second clause gives the identities:

$$
\begin{array}{llllll}
m_1 & = & n \; \% \; m & \qquad n_1 & = & m \\
m_2 & = & n_1 \; \% \; m_1 & \qquad n_2 & = & m_1 \\
& \cdots & & \qquad & \cdots & \\
m_k & = & n_{k-1} \; \% \; m_{k-1} & \qquad n_k & = & m_{k-1}
\end{array}
$$

Using $|n \ \% \ m| < |m|$ when $m \neq 0$, we get:

$$|m| > |m_1| > \cdots > |m_k| \geq 0$$

It follows that

$$k \leq |m|$$

because $|m_1|, |m_2|, \ldots, |m_k|$ are k mutually different integers among the $|m|$ integers $|m|-1, |m|-2, \ldots, 1, 0$.

The evaluation of $\mathrm{gcd}(m, n)$ will hence involve at most $|m|$ uses of the second clause.

Proof of Euclid's theorem

The key to prove Euclid's theorem is that the following holds when $m \neq 0$:

The integers $n \ \% \ m$ and m have the same common divisors as the integers n and m

This follows from the identities:

$$n \ \% \ m + q \cdot m = n \quad \text{and} \quad n - q \cdot m = n \ \% \ m \quad \text{(with integer } q = n/m)$$

which show that any common divisor of $(n \ \% \ m)$ and m is also a divisor of n, and hence a common divisor of n and m – and conversely – any common divisor of n and m is also a divisor of $(n \ \% \ m)$, and hence a common divisor of $(n \ \% \ m)$ and m.

Using the above integers $n_1, n_2, \ldots$ and $m_1, m_2, \ldots$ we hence get:

m_1 and n_1	have same common divisors as	m and n
m_2 and n_2	have same common divisors as	m_1 and n_1
$\ldots$	$\ldots$	$\ldots$
m_p and n_p	have same common divisors as	m_{p-1} and n_{p-1}

where the evaluation terminates with an index p where $m_p = 0$ and $n_p = \mathrm{gcd}\,(m, n)$.

The common divisors of 0 and n_p are, however, exactly the divisors of $n_p = \mathrm{gcd}\,(m, n)$ as any integer is a divisor of 0. It follows by induction that the common divisors of m and n are exactly the divisors of $\mathrm{gcd}\,(m, n)$.

1.9 Evaluations with environments

During the evaluation of expressions the system may create and use temporary bindings of identifiers. This is, for example, the case for function applications like $\mathrm{gcd}(36, 116)$ where the function gcd is applied to the argument $(36, 116)$. We will study such bindings as it gives insight into how recursive functions are evaluated.

The declaration:

```
let rec gcd = function
    | (0,n) -> n
    | (m,n) -> gcd(n % m,m);;
val gcd : int * int -> int
```

contains two clauses: One with pattern $(0, n)$ and expression n and another with pattern (m, n) and expression gcd $(n \% m, m)$. There are hence two cases in the evaluation of an expression $gcd(x, y)$ corresponding to the two clauses:

1. $gcd(0, y)$: The argument $(0, y)$ matches the pattern $(0, n)$ in the first clause giving the binding $n \mapsto y$, and the system will evaluate the corresponding right-hand side expression n using this binding:

$$gcd(0, y) \rightsquigarrow (n, [n \mapsto y]) \rightsquigarrow y$$

2. $gcd(x, y)$ with $x \neq 0$: The argument (x, y) does not match the pattern $(0, n)$ in the first clause but it matches the pattern (m, n) in the second clause giving the bindings $m \mapsto x$, $n \mapsto y$, and the system will evaluate the corresponding right-hand side expression gcd $(n \% m, m)$ using these bindings:

$$gcd(x, y) \rightsquigarrow (gcd (n \% m, \ m), [m \mapsto x, n \mapsto y]) \rightsquigarrow \ldots$$

Consider, for example, the expression gcd $(36, 116)$. The value $(36, 116)$ does not match the pattern $(0, n)$, so the first evaluation step is based on the second clause:

$$
\begin{aligned}
&gcd(36, 116) \\
\rightsquigarrow \ &(gcd (n \% m, \ m), [m \mapsto 36, n \mapsto 116])
\end{aligned}
$$

The expression gcd $(n \% m, m)$ will then be further evaluated using the bindings for m and n. The next evaluation steps evaluate the argument expression $(n \% m, m)$ using the bindings:

$$
\begin{aligned}
&(gcd (n \% m, \ m), [m \mapsto 36, n \mapsto 116]) \\
\rightsquigarrow \ &gcd (116 \% 36, \ 36) \\
\rightsquigarrow \ &gcd (8, 36),
\end{aligned}
$$

The evaluation continues evaluating the expression gcd $(8, 36)$ and this proceeds in the same way, but with different values bound to m and n:

$$
\begin{aligned}
&gcd(8, 36) \\
\rightsquigarrow \ &(gcd (n \% m, \ m), [m \mapsto 8, n \mapsto 36]) \\
\rightsquigarrow \ &gcd (36 \% 8, \ 8) \\
\rightsquigarrow \ &gcd (4, 8)
\end{aligned}
$$

The evaluation will in the same way reduce the expression gcd $(4, 8)$ to gcd $(0, 4)$, but the evaluation of gcd $(0, 4)$ will use the first clause in the declaration of gcd, and the evaluation terminates with result 4:

$$
\begin{aligned}
&gcd(4, 8) \\
\rightsquigarrow \ &\ldots \\
\rightsquigarrow \ &gcd (0, 4) \\
\rightsquigarrow \ &(n, [n \mapsto 4]) \\
\rightsquigarrow \ &4
\end{aligned}
$$

Note that different bindings for m and n occur in this evaluation and that all these bindings have disappeared when the result of the evaluation (that is, 4) is reached.

1.10 Free-standing programs

A free-standing program contains a *main* function of type:

```
string[] -> int
```

preceded by the *entry point attribute*:

```
. . .
[<EntryPoint>]
let main (param: string[]) =
. . .
```

The type `string[]` is an array type (cf. Section 8.10) and the argument `param` consists of k strings (cf. Section 2.3):

$$param.[0], \ param.[1], \ \dots, param.[k-1]$$

The following is a simple, free-standing "hello world" program:

```
open System;;
[<EntryPoint>]
let main(param: string[]) =
  printf "Hello %s\n" param.[0]
  0;;
```

It uses the `printf` function (cf. Section 10.7) to make some output. The zero result signals normal termination of the program. The program source file `Hello.fsx` compiles to an `exe`-file using the F# batch compiler:

```
fsc Hello.fsx -o Hello.exe
```

and the program can now be called from a command prompt:

```
>Hello Peter
Hello Peter

>Hello "Sue and Allan"
Hello Sue and Allan
```

Using the `fsc` command requires that the directory path of the F# compiler (with file name `fsc.exe` or `Fsc.exe`) is included in the `PATH` environment variable.

Summary

The main purpose of this chapter is to familiarize the reader with some of the main concepts of F# to an extent where she/he can start experimenting with the system. To this end, we have introduced the F# notions of values, expressions, types and declarations, including recursive function declarations.

The main concepts needed to explain the meaning of these notions are: integers and floating-point numbers, bindings and environments, and step by step evaluation of expressions.

Exercises

1.1 Declare a function g: `int -> int`, where $g(n) = n + 4$.

1.2 Declare a function h: `float * float -> float`, where $h(x, y) = \sqrt{x^2 + y^2}$. Hint: Use the function `System.Math.Sqrt`.

1.3 Write function expressions corresponding to the functions g and h in the exercises 1.1 and 1.2.

1.4 Declare a recursive function f: `int -> int`, where

$$f(n) = 1 + 2 + \cdots + (n - 1) + n$$

for $n \geq 0$. (Hint: use two clauses with 0 and n as patterns.)

State the recursion formula corresponding to the declaration.

Give an evaluation for $f(4)$.

1.5 The sequence $F_0, F_1, F_2, \ldots$ of Fibonacci numbers is defined by:

$$\begin{aligned} F_0 &= 0 \\ F_1 &= 1 \\ F_n &= F_{n-1} + F_{n-2} \end{aligned}$$

Thus, the first members of the sequence are $0, 1, 1, 2, 3, 5, 8, 13, \ldots$.

Declare an F# function to compute F_n. Use a declaration with three clauses, where the patterns correspond to the three cases of the above definition.

Give an evaluations for F_4.

1.6 Declare a recursive function sum: `int * int -> int`, where

$$\text{sum}(m, n) = m + (m + 1) + (m + 2) + \cdots + (m + (n - 1)) + (m + n)$$

for $m \geq 0$ and $n \geq 0$. (Hint: use two clauses with $(m, 0)$ and (m, n) as patterns.)

Give the recursion formula corresponding to the declaration.

1.7 Determine a type for each of the expressions:

```
(System.Math.PI, fact -1)
fact(fact 4)
power(System.Math.PI, fact 2)
(power, fact)
```

1.8 Consider the declarations:

```
let a = 5;;
let f a = a + 1;;
let g b = (f b) + a;;
```

Find the environment obtained from these declarations and write the evaluations of the expressions f 3 and g 3.

2

Values, operators, expressions and functions

The purpose of this chapter is to illustrate the use of values of basic types: numbers, characters, truth values and strings by means of some examples. The concepts of operator overloading and type inference are explained. Furthermore, the chapter contains a gentle introduction to higher-order functions. It is explained how to declare operators, and the concepts of equality and ordering in F# are introduced. After reading the chapter the reader should be able to construct simple programs using numbers, characters, strings and truth values.

2.1 Numbers. Truth values. The `unit` type

From mathematics we know the set of natural numbers as a subset of the set of integers, which again is a subset of the rational numbers (i.e., fractions), and so on. In F#, however, the set of values with the type: `int`, for the integers, is considered to be disjoint from the set of values with the type: `float`, for floating-point numbers, that is, the part of the real numbers that are representable in the computer. The reason is that the encodings of integer and float values in the computer are different, and that the computer has different machine instructions for adding integer values and for adding float values, for example.

A value of type `int` is written as a sequence of digits possibly prefixed with the minus sign "−". Real numbers are written using decimal point notation or using exponential notation, or using both:

```
0;;
val it : int = 0

0.0;;
val it : float = 0.0

0123;;
val it : int = 123

-7.235;;
val it : float = -7.235

-388890;;
val it : int = -388890
```

```
1.23e-17;;
val it : float = 1.23e-17
```

where `1.23e-17` denotes $1.23 \cdot 10^{-17}$.

Operators

We will use the term *operator* as a synonym for function and the components of the argument of an operator will be called *operands*. Furthermore, a *monadic* operator is an operator with one operand, while a *dyadic* operator has two operands. Most monadic operators are used in *prefix* notation where the operator is written in front of the operand.

Examples of operators on numbers are monadic minus -, and the dyadic operators addition +, subtraction -, multiplication * and division /. Furthermore, the relations: =, <> (denoting inequality $\neq$), >, >= (denoting $\geq$), < and <= (denoting $\leq$), between numbers are considered to be operators on numbers computing a truth value.

The symbol "−" is used for three purposes in F# as in mathematics. In number constants like "−2" it denotes the sign of the constant, in expressions like "− 2" and "−(2+1)" it denotes an application of the monadic minus operator, and in the expression "1−2" it denotes the dyadic subtraction operator.

Consider, as a strange example:

```
2 - - -1;;
val it : int = 1
```

Starting from the right, −1 denotes the the integer "minus one", the expression − −1 denotes monadic minus applied to minus one, and the full expression denotes the dyadic operation two minus one.

Division is *not* defined on integers, but we have instead the operators / for quotient and % for remainder as described on Page 15, for example:

```
13 / -5;;
val it : int = -2

13 % -5;;
val it : int = 3
```

Truth values

There are two values `true` and `false` of the type `bool`:

```
true;;
val it : bool = true

false;;
val it : bool = false
```

Logical operators	
not	(unary) negation
&&	logical and (conjunction)
||	logical or (disjunction)

Table 2.1 *Operators on truth values*

Functions can have truth values as results. Consider, for example, a function `even` determining whether an integer n is even (i.e., $n \% 2 = 0$). This function can be declared as follows:

```
let even n = n % 2 = 0;;
val even : int -> bool
```

A truth-valued function such as `even` is called a *predicate*.

Functions on truth values are often called *logical operators*, and some of the main ones are shown in Table 2.1. The *negation* operator `not` applies to truth values, and the comparison operators = and <> are defined for truth values. For example:

```
not true <> false;;
val it : bool = false
```

Furthermore, there are expressions $e_1 \mathbin{||} e_2$ and $e_1 \mathbin{\&\&} e_2$ corresponding to the disjunction and conjunction operators of propositional logic. The expression $e_1 \mathbin{||} e_2$ is true if either e_1 or e_2 (or both) are true; otherwise the expression is false. The expression $e_1 \mathbin{\&\&} e_2$ is true if both e_1 and e_2 are true; otherwise the expression is false.

Evaluations of $e_1 \mathbin{||} e_2$ and $e_1 \mathbin{\&\&} e_2$ will only evaluate the expression e_2 when needed, that is, the expression e_2 in $e_1 \mathbin{||} e_2$ is not evaluated if e_1 evaluates to `true`, and the expression e_2 in $e_1 \mathbin{\&\&} e_2$ is not evaluated if e_1 evaluates to `false`. For example:

```
1 = 2 && fact -1 = 0;;
val it : bool = false
```

Thus, `1 = 2 && fact -1 = 0` evaluates to `false` without attempting to evaluate the expression `fact -1 = 0`, which would result in a non-terminating evaluation.

The `unit` *type*

There is only one value, written `()`, of type `unit`. It is mentioned here as it belongs to the basic types in F#. It is used in the imperative part of F# as a "dummy" result of a computation consisting solely of side-effects like input-output or modification of mutable data. There are no operators on the value `()` of type `unit`.

2.2 Operator precedence and association

The monadic operator – is written in front of the argument (like other function names), while the dyadic operators are written in *infix* notation, where the operator is placed between the operands. Table 2.2 shows the arithmetic operators.

+	unary plus
–	unary minus
+	addition
–	subtraction
*	multiplication
/	division
%	modulo (remainder)
**	exponentiation

Table 2.2 *Arithmetic operators*

Usual rules for omitting brackets in mathematical expressions also apply to F# expressions. These rules are governed by two concepts: operator *precedence* and operator *association* for dyadic operators as shown in Table 2.3. The operators occurring in the same row have same precedence, which is higher than that of operators occurring in succeeding rows. For example, * and / have the same precedence. This precedence is higher than that of +.

Operator	Association
**	Associates to the right
* / %	Associates to the left
+ –	Associates to the left
= <> > >= < <=	No association
&&	Associates to the left
||	Associates to the left

Table 2.3 *Operator precedence and association*

Furthermore, a monadic operator (including function application) has higher precedence than any dyadic operator. The idea is that higher (larger) precedence means earlier evaluation. For example:

$$- \ 2 \ - \ 5 \ * \ 7 \ > \ 3 \ - \ 1 \ \ \text{means} \ \ ((-\ 2) \ - \ (5{*}7)) \ > \ (3 \ - \ 1)$$

and

```
fact 2 - 4 means (fact 2) - 4
```

The dyadic operators for numbers and truth values (except **) *associate* to the *left*, which means that operators of the same precedence are applied starting from the left, so the evaluation of an expression will proceed as if the expression was fully bracketed. For example:

$$1 \ - \ 2 \ - \ 3 \ \ \text{means} \ \ (1 \ - \ 2) \ - \ 3$$

2.3 Characters and strings

A character is a letter, a digit or a special character (i.e., a punctuation symbol like comma or semicolon or a control character). Characters are encoded in the computer as integer values using the *Unicode alphabet*, which is an international standard for encoding characters.

A character value is written as the character c enclosed in apostrophes. Examples of values of type char are:

```
'a';;
val it : char = 'a'

' ';;
val it : char = ' '
```

where the last one denotes the space character.

The new line, apostrophe, quote and backslash characters are written by means of the *escape sequences* shown in Table 2.4. Functions on characters are found in the System.Char library.

Sequence	Meaning
\'	Apostrophe
\"	Quote
\\	Backslash
\b	Backspace
\n	Newline
\r	Carriage return
\t	Horizontal tab

Table 2.4 *Character escape sequences*

The operators ||, && and not are convenient when declaring functions with results of type bool, like in the following declarations of the functions isLowerCaseConsonant and isLowerCaseVowel determining whether a character is a lower-case consonant or vowel, respectively:

```
let isLowerCaseVowel ch =
    ch='a' || ch='e' || ch='i' || ch='o' || ch='u';;
val isLowerCaseVowel : char -> bool

let isLowerCaseConsonant ch =
    System.Char.IsLower ch && not (isLowerCaseVowel ch);;
val isLowerCaseConsonant : char -> bool

isLowerCaseVowel 'i' && not (isLowerCaseConsonant 'i');;
val it : bool = true

isLowerCaseVowel 'I' || isLowerCaseConsonant 'I';;
val it : bool = false

not (isLowerCaseVowel 'z') && isLowerCaseConsonant 'z';;
val it : bool = true
```

where we use the function IsLower from the library System.Char to check whether ch is a lower-case letter. This library contains predicates IsDigit, IsSeparator, and so on, expressing properties of a character.

Strings

A *string* is a sequence of *characters*. Strings are values of the type `string`. A string is written inside enclosing quotes that are *not* part of the string. Quote, backslash or control characters in a string are written by using the escape sequences. Comments cannot occur inside strings as comment brackets ((* or *)) inside a string simply are interpreted as parts of the string. Examples of values of type `string` are:

```
"abcd---";;
val it : string = "abcd---"

"\"1234\"";;
val it : string = "\"1234\""

"";;
val it : string = ""
```

The first one denotes the 7-character string "abcd---", the second uses escape sequences to get the 6-character string ""1234"" including the quotes, while the last denotes the *empty string* containing no characters.

Strings can also be written using the *verbatim* string notation where the character @ is placed in front of the first quote:

$$@"c_0\ c_1\ \ldots\ c_{n-1}"$$

It denotes the string of characters $c_0\ c_1\ \ldots\ c_{n-1}$ *without* any conversion of escape sequences. Hence @"\\\\" denotes a string of four backslash characters:

```
@"\\\\";;
val it : string = "\\\\"
```

while the escape sequence \\ for backslash is converted in the string "\\\\":

```
"\\\\";;
val it : string = "\\"
```

Verbatim strings are useful when making strings containing backslash characters. Note that it is not possible to make a verbatim string containing a quote character because \" is interpreted as a backslash character followed by the terminating quote character.

Functions on strings

The `String` library contains a variety of functions on strings. In this section we will just illustrate the use of a few of them by some examples.

The `length` function computes the number of characters in a string:

```
String.length "1234";;
val it : int = 4

String.length "\"1234\"";;
val it : int = 6
```

```
String.length "";;    // size of the empty string
val it : int = 0
```

The concatenation function + joins two strings together forming a new string by placing the two strings one after another. The operator + is used in infix mode:

```
let text = "abcd---";;
val text : string = "abcd---"

text + text;;
val it: string = "abcd---abcd---"

text + " " = text;;
val it : bool = false

text + "" = text;;
val it : bool = true

"" + text = text;;
val it : bool = true
```

The last two examples show that the empty string is the *neutral element* for concatenation of strings just like the number 0 is the neutral element for addition of integers.

Note that the *same* operator symbol + is used for integer addition and string concatenation. This *overloading* of operator symbols is treated in Section 2.5.

A string s with length n is given by a sequence of n characters $s = \text{``}c_0 c_1 \cdots c_{n-1}\text{''}$, where the convention in F# is that the numbering starts at 0. For any such string s there is a function, written $s.[i]$, to extract the i'th character in s for $0 \leq i \leq n - 1$. The integer i used in $s.[i]$ is called an *index*. For example:

```
"abc".[0];;
val it : char = 'a'

"abc".[2];;
val it : char = 'c'

"abc".[3];;
System.IndexOutOfRangeException: ...
Stopped due to error
```

where the last example shows (a part of) the error message which will occur when the index is out of bounds.

If we want to concatenate a string and a character, we need to use the `string` function to convert the character to a string, for example

```
"abc" + string 'd';;
val it : string = "abcd"
```

as the operator + in this case denotes string concatenation, and this operator cannot concatenate a string with a character.

Conversion of integer, real or Boolean values to their string representations are done by using the function `string`, for example:

```
string -4;;
val it : string = "-4"

string 7.89;;
val it : string = "7.89"

string true;;
val it : string = "True"
```

A simple application of this conversion function is the declaration of the function `nameAge`:

```
let nameAge(name,age) =
    name + " is " + (string age) + " years old";;
```

It converts the integer value of the age to the corresponding string of digits and builds a string containing the string for the name and the age. For example:

```
nameAge("Diana",15+4);;
val it : string = "Diana is 19 years old"

nameAge("Philip",1-4);;
val it : string = "Philip is -3 years old"
```

The `string` function can actually give a string representation of every value, including values belonging to user-defined types. We shall return to this in Section 7.7. Examples of string representations are:

```
string (12, 'a');;
val it : string = "(12, a)"

string nameAge;;
val it : string = "FSI_0022+it@29-4"
```

where the pair (`12`, `'a'`) has a natural string representation in contrast to that of the user-defined `nameAge` function.

2.4 If-then-else expressions

An `if-then-else` expression has form:

> if exp_1 then exp_2 else exp_3

where exp_1 is an expression of type `bool` while exp_2 and exp_3 are expressions of the same type. The `if-then-else` expression is evaluated by first evaluating exp_1. If exp_1 evaluates to `true` then the expression exp_2 is evaluated; otherwise, if exp_1 evaluates to `false` then the expression exp_3 is evaluated. Note that at most one of the expressions exp_2

and exp_3 will be evaluated (none of them will be evaluated if the evaluation of exp_1 does not terminate).

An if-then-else expression is used whenever one has to express a splitting into cases that cannot be expressed conveniently by use of patterns. As an example we may declare a function on strings that adjusts a string to even size by putting a space character in front of the string if the size is odd. Using the function even on Page 23 and if-then-else for the splitting into cases gives the following declaration:

```
let even n = n % 2 = 0;;
val even : int -> bool

let adjString s = if even(String.length s)
                    then s else " " + s;;
val adjString : string -> string

adjString "123";;
val it : string = " 123"

adjString "1234";;
val it : string = "1234"
```

One may, of course, use an if-then-else expression instead of splitting into clauses by pattern matching. But pattern matching is to be preferred, as illustrated by the following (less readable) alternative declaration of the gcd function (cf. Page 16):

```
let rec gcd(m,n) = if m=0 then n
                      else gcd(n % m,m);;
val gcd : int * int -> int
```

One should also avoid expressions of the forms:

```
if e₁ then true else e₂
if e₁ then e₂ else false
```

for defining Boolean combinations of expressions and instead use the shorter, equivalent forms:

```
e₁ || e₂
e₁ && e₂
```

2.5 Overloaded functions and operators

A name or symbol for a function or operator is *overloaded* if it has different meanings when applied to arguments or operands of different types. We have already seen that the plus operator + denote addition for integers but concatenation for strings.

A (mathematical) function on real numbers is considered different from the corresponding function on integers, as they are implemented in F# by different machine instructions. An operator of this kind is hence overloaded: it denotes different functions depending on the context, and it depends on the types of the operands whether, for example, the operator * denotes multiplication on integers (of type `int`) or multiplication on real numbers (of type `float`). The F# system tries to resolve these ambiguities in the following way:

- If the type can be inferred from the context, then an overloaded operator symbol is interpreted as denoting the function on the inferred type.
- If the type cannot be inferred from the context, then an overloaded operator symbol with a default type will default to this type. The default type is `int` if the operator can be applied to integers.

For example, the obvious declaration of a squaring function yields the function on integers:

```
let square x = x * x;;
val square : int -> int
```

Declaring a squaring function on reals can be done either by specifying the type of the argument:

```
let square (x:float) = x * x;;
val square : float -> float
```

or by specifying the type of the result:

```
let square x : float = x * x;;
val square : float -> float
```

or by specifying the type of the expression for the function value:

```
let square x = x * x : float;;
val square : float -> float
```

or by choosing any mixture of the above possibilities.

abs, acos, atan, atan2, ceil, cos, cosh, exp, floor, log log10, pow, pown, round, sin, sinh, sqrt, tan, tanh

Table 2.5 *Mathematical functions*

There are many overloaded operators in F#, in particular mathematical functions that can be applied to integers as well as to real numbers. Some of them can be found in Table 2.5. The function `abs`, for example, computes the absolute value of a number that can be of type `int`, `float` or any of the number types in Table 2.6, for example, `float32`:

```
abs -1;;
val it : int = 1

abs -1.0;;
val it : float = 1.0

abs -3.2f;;
val it : float32 = 3.20000000f
```

Overloading is extensively used in the .NET library and typing of arguments is frequently needed to resolve ambiguities. The user may declare overloaded operators and functions inside a type declaration as explained in Section 7.3.

2.6 Type inference

When an expression is entered, the F# system will try to determine a unique type using so-called *type inference*. If this does not succeed then the expression is not accepted and an error message is issued.

Consider once more the declaration of the function power (cf. Section 1.5):

```
let rec power = function
    | (x, 0) -> 1.0                    (* 1 *)
    | (x, n) -> x * power(x,n-1)       (* 2 *);;
val power : float * int -> float
```

The F# system deduces that power has the type: float * int -> float. We can see how F# is able to infer this type of power by arguing as follows:

1. The keyword function indicates that the type of power is a function type $\tau \rightarrow \tau'$, for some types τ and τ'.
2. Since power is applied to a pair (x, n) in the declaration, the type τ must have the form $\tau_1 * \tau_2$ for some types τ_1 and τ_2.
3. We have $\tau_2 = $ int, since the pattern of the first clause is (x, 0), and 0 has type int.
4. We have that $\tau' = $ float, since the expression for the function value in the first clause: 1.0 has type float.
5. We know that power (x, n-1) has the type float since $\tau' = $ float. Thus, the overloaded operator symbol * in x * power (x, n-1) resolves to float multiplication and x must be of type float. We hence get $\tau_1 = $ float.

The above declaration of the power function has been used for illustrating the declaration of recursive functions and the type inference performed by the system. As described above there is already a power operator ** in F# and this should of course be used in programs. In general we recommend to inspect the F# and .NET libraries and use available library functions when appropriate.

2.7 Functions are first-class citizens

In functional languages, and F# is no exception, functions are what is called *first-class citizens*. An implication of this is that a function can be argument of another function and that the value of a function can again be a function. In this section we shall give a first, gentle introduction to this concept, which also is known as *higher-order* functions.

The value of a function can be a function

As a first example we shall consider the infix operator +. There is a version of this operator that is not written between the operands. This *non-fix* version is written (+), and we shall now study its type:

```
(+);;
val it : (int -> int -> int) = <fun:it@1>
```

The type operator "->" *associates* to the *right*, so (+) has the type:

```
(+) : int -> (int -> int)
```

This type shows that the value of the function (+) is another function with type int -> int. Applying (+) to an integer n thus gives a function:

$$(+) \ n: \text{int} \ -> \ \text{int}$$

For example:

```
let plusThree = (+) 3;;
val plusThree : (int -> int)

plusThree 5;;
val it : int = 8

plusThree -7;;
val it : int = -4
```

The sum of two integers m and n can be computed as $((+) \ m) \ n$. The brackets can be omitted because *function application associates to the left*. For example:

```
(+) 1 3;;
val it : int = 4
```

The argument of a function can be a function

Function composition $f \circ g$ is defined in mathematics by: $(f \circ g)(x) = f(g(x))$. This operator on functions is well-defined when domains and ranges of f and g match:

If $f : A \to B$ and $g : C \to A$, then $f \circ g : C \to B$

For example, if $f(y) = y + 3$ and $g(x) = x^2$, then $(f \circ g)(z) = z^2 + 3$.

We want to construe the function composition $\circ$ as a function, and this function will obviously take functions as arguments. There is actually an infix operator << in F# denoting function composition, and the above example can hence be paraphrased as follows:

```
let f = fun y -> y+3;;          // f(y) = y+3
val f : int -> int

let g = fun x -> x*x;;          // g(x) = x*x
val g : int -> int
```

```
let h = f << g;;                    // h = (f o g)
val h : int -> int
```

```
h 4;;                              // h(4) = (f o g)(4)
val it : int = 19
```

Using function expressions instead of named functions f, g and h, the example looks as follows:

```
((fun y -> y+3) << (fun x -> x*x)) 4;;
val it : int = 19
```

Declaration of higher-order functions

So far we have seen higher-order built-in functions like (+) and (<<). We shall now illustrate ways to declare such functions by means of a simple example.

Suppose that we have a cube with side length s, containing a liquid with density ρ. The weight of the liquid is then given by $\rho \cdot s^3$. If the unit of measure of ρ is kg/m^3 and the unit of measure of s is m then the unit of measure of the weight will be kg.

Consider the following declaration of the weight function:

```
let weight ro = fun s -> ro * s ** 3.0;;
val weight : float -> float -> float
```

where we use the operator $**$ to compute x^y for floating-point numbers x and y. A function value weight ρ is again a *function* as the expression on the right-hand side of the declaration is a fun-expression. This property of the function value is also visible in the type of weight.

We can make *partial evaluations* of the function weight to define functions for computing the weight of a cube of either water or methanol (having the densities 1000kg/m^3 and 786.5kg/m^3 respectively under "normal" pressure and temperature):

```
let waterWeight = weight 1000.0;;
val waterWeight : (float -> float)
```

```
waterWeight 1.0;;
val it : float = 1000.0
```

```
waterWeight 2.0;;
val it : float = 8000.0
```

```
let methanolWeight = weight 786.5;;
val methanolWeight : (float -> float)
```

```
methanolWeight 1.0;;
val it : float = 786.5
```

```
methanolWeight 2.0;;
val it : float = 6292.0
```

Higher-order functions may alternatively be defined by supplying the arguments as follows in the `let`-declaration:

```
let weight ro s = ro * s ** 3.0;;
val weight : float -> float -> float
```

and this is normally the preferred way of defining higher-order functions.

2.8 Closures

A *closure* gives the means of explaining a value that is a function. A closure is a triple:

$$(x, \ exp, \ env)$$

where x is an argument identifier, *exp* is the expression to evaluate to get a function value, while *env* is an environment (cf. Section 1.7) giving bindings to be used in such an evaluation.

Consider as an example the evaluation of `weight 786.5` in the previous example. The result is the closure:

$$\left(s,\ \texttt{ro*s**3.0},\ \begin{bmatrix} \texttt{ro} & \mapsto & 786.5 \\ \texttt{*} & \mapsto & \textit{"the product function"} \\ \texttt{**} & \mapsto & \textit{"the power function"} \end{bmatrix} \right)$$

The environment contains bindings of all identifiers in the expression `ro*s**3.0` except the argument `s`.

Note that a closure is a *value* in F# – functions are first-class citizens.

The following simple example illustrates the role of the environment in the closure:

```
let pi = System.Math.PI;;
let circleArea r = pi * r * r;;
val circleArea : float -> float
```

These declarations bind the identifier `pi` to a `float` value and `circleArea` to a closure:

$$\begin{array}{ll} \texttt{pi} & \mapsto \quad 3.14159\ldots \\ \texttt{circleArea} & \mapsto \quad (\texttt{r},\ \texttt{pi*r*r},\ [\texttt{pi} \mapsto 3.14159\ldots]) \end{array}$$

A fresh binding of `pi` does not affect the meaning of `circleArea` that uses the binding of `pi` in the closure:

```
let pi = 0;;
circleArea 1.0;;
val it : float = 3.141592654
```

This feature of F# is called *static binding* of identifers occurring in functions.

2.9 Declaring prefix and infix operators

Expressions containing functions on pairs can often be given a more readable form by using infix notation where the function symbol is written between the two components of the argument. Infix form is used for the dyadic arithmetic operators +, −, %, /, for example. This allows us to make expressions more readable by use of rules for omission of brackets. For example: $x-y-z$ means $(x-y)-z$ and $x+y*z$ means $x+(y*z)$. These rules for omitting brackets are governed by *precedence* and *association* for the operators (see Section 2.2).

Operators are written using special character strings which cannot be used as "normal" identifiers. Infix operators are sequences of the following symbols[1]

```
!  %  &  *  +  -  .  /  <  =  >  ?  @  ^  |  ~
```

while prefix operators are one of

```
+   -   +.  -.  &  &&  %  %%
~   ~~  ~~~  ~~~~            (tilde characters)
```

The *bracket notation* converts from infix or prefix operator to (prefix) function:

- The corresponding (prefix) function for an infix operator *op* is denoted by (*op*).
- The corresponding (prefix) function for a prefix operator *op* is denoted by (~*op*).

An infix operator is declared using the bracket notation as in the following declaration of an infix exclusive-or operator .||. on truth values:

```
let (.||.) p q = (p || q) && not(p && q);;
val ( .||. ) : bool -> bool -> bool

(1 > 2) .||. (2 + 3 < 5);;
val it : bool = false
```

The system determines the precedence and association of declared operators on the basis of the characters in the operator. In the case of .||. the periods have no influence on this, so the precedence and association of .||. will be the same as those of ||. Therefore,

```
true .||. false && true;;
```

is equivalent to

```
true .||. (false && true);;
```

as && has higher precedence than || and .||..

A prefix operator is declared using a leading tilde character. We may, for example, declare a prefix operator %% to calculate the reciprocal value of a float as follows:

```
let (~%%) x = 1.0 / x;;
val ( ~%% ) : float -> float

%% 0.5;;
val it : float = 2.0
```

---

[1] This description of legal operators in F# is incomplete. The precise rules are complicated.

Remark: When defining an operator starting or ending in an asterisks "∗" a space must be inserted after " (" or before ") " to avoid a conflict with the comment convention using " (∗" and "∗) ".

2.10 Equality and ordering

The *equality* and *inequality* operators = and <> are defined on any basic type and on strings:

```
3.5 = 2e-3;;
val it : bool = false

"abc" <> "ab";;
val it : bool = true
```

It is not defined on functions (closures):

```
cos = sin;;
stdin(5,1): error FS0001: The type '( ^a ->  ^a) ...
does not support the 'equality' constraint because
it is a function type
```

No type containing a function type can support equality as F# has no means to decide whether two functions are equal: It is a fundamental fact of theoretical computer science that there exists no (always terminating) algorithm to determine whether two arbitrary programs f and g (i.e., two closures) denote the same function.

The equality function is automatically extended by F# whenever the user defines a new type – in so far as the type does not contain function types.

The type of the function eqText declared by:

```
let eqText x y =
    if x = y then "equal" else "not equal";;
val eqText : 'a -> 'a -> string when 'a : equality
```

contains a *type variable* ' a with the *constraint*: when ' a : equality.

This means that eqText will accept parameters x and y of any type τ equipped with equality:

```
eqText 3 4;;
val it : string = "not equal"

eqText ' ' (char 32);;
val it : string = "equal"
```

Ordering

The *ordering* operators: >, >=, <, and <= are defined on values of basic types and on strings. They correspond to the usual ordering of numbers. The ordering of characters is given by the ordering of the Unicode values, while true > false in the ordering of truth values.

Strings are ordered in the *lexicographical* ordering. That is, for two strings s_1 and s_2 we have that $s_1 < s_2$ if s_1 would occur before s_2 in a lexicon. For example:

```
                  // Upper case letters precede
'A' < 'a';;       // lower case letters
val it : bool = true


"automobile" < "car";;
val it : bool = true


"" < " ";;
val it : bool = true
```

Thus, the empty string precedes the string containing a space character, and the empty string precedes any other string in the lexicographical ordering. Ordering is automatically extended by F# whenever the user defines a new type, in so far as the type does not contain functions.

Using the comparison operators one may declare functions on values of an arbitrary type equipped with an ordering:

```
let ordText x y = if x > y then "greater"
                  else if x = y then "equal"
                  else "less";;
val ordText : 'a -> 'a -> string when 'a : comparison
```

The type of x and y contains a *type variable* ' a with the *constraint*

```
when 'a : comparison
```

indicating that x and y can be of any type equipped with an ordering.

The library function `compare` is defined such that:

$$\text{compare } x\, y \;=\; \begin{cases} > 0 & \text{if } x > y \\ 0 & \text{if } x = y \\ < 0 & \text{if } x < y \end{cases}$$

where the precise value of `compare` x y depends on the structure of the values x and y.

It may be convenient to use *pattern matching with guards* when declaring functions using the `compare` function, for instance:

```
let ordText x y = match compare x y with
                  | t when t > 0 -> "greater"
                  | 0            -> "equal"
                  | _            -> "less";;
val ordText : 'a -> 'a -> string when 'a : comparison
```

The *guard* "when t > 0" restricts the matching, while the pattern "t" would otherwise match any value.

Type	Description	Constant
bool	Logical value	true, false
unit	Void	()
char	Character	*'char'*
byte	8-bit unsigned integer	*digits* uy or 0x *hexdigits* uy
sbyte	8-bit signed integer	{−}*digits* y or {−}0x *hexdigits* y
int16	16-bit signed integer	{−}*digits* s or {−}0x *hexdigits* s
uint16	16-bit unsigned integer	*digits* us or 0x *hexdigits* us
int (or int32)	32-bit signed integer	{−}*digits* or {-}0x *hexdigits*
uint32	32-bit unsigned integer	*digits* u or 0x *hexdigits* u
int64	64-bit signed integer	{−}*digits* L or {−}0x *hexdigits* L
uint64	64-bit unsigned integer	*digits* UL or 0x *hexdigits* UL
nativeint	Machines integer	{−}*digits* n or {−}0x *hexdigits* n
unativeint	Machines unsigned integer	*digits* un or 0x *hexdigits* un
float32 (or single)	32-bit IEEE floating-point	{−} *digits* . *digits* f or {−}*digits*{. *digits*} e {−} *digits* f
float (or double)	64-bit IEEE floating-point	{−}*digits* . *digits* or {−}*digits*{. *digits*} e{−}*digits*
decimal	High-precision decimal	*digits* M or {−}*digits* . *digits* M
bigint	Arbitrary integer	{−}*digits* I
bignum	Arbitrary rational number	{−}*digits* N

Table 2.6 *Basic Types*

2.11 Function application operators |> and <|

The operator |> means "send the value as argument to the function on the right" while <| means "send the value as argument to the function on the left," that is:

$$arg \; |> \; fct \quad \text{means} \quad fct \; arg$$
$$fct \; <| \; arg \quad \text{means} \quad fct \; arg$$

These operators are sometimes useful to make expressions more readable. There are two reasons for that:

- The operator |> allows you to write the argument to the *left* of the function.
- The operators |> and <| have lower precedence than the arithmetic operators.

Both expressions a+b |> sin and sin <| a+b do hence mean sin(a+b). The operator |> has precedence over <| so 2 |> (−) <| 3 means (2 |> (−)) <| 3.

Both operators associate to the left. The parentheses in 2 |> (3 |> (−)) are hence needed to get the rightmost |> operator applied before the leftmost.

2.12 Summary of the basic types

The F# system supports a number of basic types not addressed previously in this chapter. Table 2.6 depicts the basic types, where the column "Constant" describes how constants are written. The meta symbols *digits*, *hexdigits*, *char*, and {...} have the following meanings:

digits: One or more decimal digits: 0, 1, ... , 9

hexdigits: One or more hex digits: 0, 1, . . . , 9, A, B, . . . , F, a, b, . . . , f

char: A character or an escape sequence denoting a character.

{. . .}: The part between the brackets is optional. The brackets are not part of the string.

Hence 33e-8 is a constant of type float and -0x1as is a constant of type int16 while 32f is not accepted by F#.

Each type name denotes an overloaded conversion function converting to a value of the type in question (in so far as this is possible).

Summary

In this chapter we have described values and functions belonging to the basic F# types: integers, reals, characters, truth values and strings. Furthermore, we have discussed evaluation of infix operators with precedences, and the typing of arithmetic expressions where some operators may be overloaded. The concept of higher-order functions was introduced and the concept of a closure was used to explain the meaning of a function in F#. It was explained how to declare operators, and finally, the concepts of equality and ordering were explained.

Exercises

2.1 Declare a function f: int -> bool such that $f(n)$ = true exactly when n is divisible by 2 or divisible by 3 but not divisible by 5. Write down the expected values of f(24), f(27), f(29) and f(30) and compare with the result. Hint: n is divisible by q when $n\%q = 0$.

2.2 Declare an F# function pow: string * int -> string, where:

$$\text{pow}(s, n) = \underbrace{s \cdot s \cdots \cdot s}_{n}$$

where we use · to denote string concatenation. (The F# representation is +.)

2.3 Declare the F# function isIthChar: string * int * char -> bool where the value of isIthChar(str, i, ch) is true if and only if ch is the i'th character in the string str (numbering starting at zero).

2.4 Declare the F# function occFromIth: string * int * char -> int where

$$\text{occFromIth}(str, i, ch) = \quad \text{the number of occurrences of character } ch$$
$$\text{in positions } j \text{ in the string } str \text{ with } j \geq i.$$

Hint: the value should be 0 for $i \geq$ size str.

2.5 Declare the F# function occInString: string * char -> int where

$$\text{occInString}(str, ch) = \quad \text{the number of occurrences of character } ch$$
$$\text{in the string } str.$$

2.6 Declare the F# function notDivisible: int * int -> bool where

$$\text{notDivisible}(d, n) \text{ is true if and only if } d \text{ is not a divisor of } n.$$

For example notDivisible(2,5) is true, and notDivisible(3,9) is false.

2.7 1. Declare the F# function `test`: `int * int * int -> bool`. The value of $\text{test}(a, b, c)$, for $a \leq b$, is the truth value of:

$$\text{notDivisible}(a, c)$$
$$\text{and} \quad \text{notDivisible}(a + 1, c)$$
$$\vdots$$
$$\text{and} \quad \text{notDivisible}(b, c)$$

2. Declare an F# function `prime`: `int -> bool`, where $\text{prime}(n) = \text{true}$, if and only if n is a prime number.
3. Declare an F# function `nextPrime`: `int -> int`, where $\text{nextPrime}(n)$ is the smallest prime number $> n$.

2.8 The following figure gives the first part of Pascal's triangle:

$$1$$
$$1 \ 1$$
$$1 \ 2 \ 1$$
$$1 \ 3 \ 3 \ 1$$
$$1 \ 4 \ 6 \ 4 \ 1$$

The entries of the triangle are called *binomial* coefficients. The k'th binomial coefficient of the n'th row is denoted $\binom{n}{k}$, for $n \geq 0$ and $0 \leq k \leq n$. For example, $\binom{2}{1} = 2$ and $\binom{4}{2} = 6$. The first and last binomial coefficients, that is, $\binom{n}{0}$ and $\binom{n}{n}$, of row n are both 1. A binomial coefficient inside a row is the sum of the two binomial coefficients immediately above it. These properties can be expressed as follows:

$$\binom{n}{0} = \binom{n}{n} = 1$$

and

$$\binom{n}{k} = \binom{n-1}{k-1} + \binom{n-1}{k} \quad \text{if } n \neq 0, k \neq 0, \text{ and } n > k.$$

Declare an F# function `bin`: `int * int -> int` to compute binomial coefficients.

2.9 Consider the declaration:

```
let rec f = function
  | (0,y) -> y
  | (x,y) -> f(x-1, x*y);;
```

1. Determine the type of `f`.
2. For which arguments does the evaluation of `f` terminate?
3. Write the evaluation steps for `f(2,3)`.
4. What is the mathematical meaning of $f(x, y)$?

2.10 Consider the following declaration:

```
let test(c,e) = if c then e else 0;;
```

1. What is the type of `test`?
2. What is the result of evaluating `test(false, fact(-1))`?
3. Compare this with the result of evaluating

```
if false then fact -1 else 0
```

2.11 Declare a function VAT: int -> float -> float such that the value VAT n x is obtained by increasing x by n percent.

Declare a function unVAT: int -> float -> float such that

$$\text{unVAT n (VAT n x) = x}$$

Hint: Use the conversion function float to convert an int value to a float value.

2.12 Declare a function min of type (int -> int) -> int. The value of min(f) is the smallest natural number n where $f(n) = 0$ (if it exists).

2.13 The functions curry and uncurry of types

```
curry   : ('a * 'b -> 'c) -> 'a -> 'b -> 'c
uncurry : ('a -> 'b -> 'c) -> 'a * 'b -> 'c
```

are defined in the following way:

curry f is the function g where $g\,x$ is the function h where $h\,y = f(x, y)$.

uncurry g is the function f where $f(x, y)$ is the value $h\,y$ for the function $h = g\,x$.

Write declarations of curry and uncurry.

3

Tuples, records and tagged values

Tuples, records and tagged values are compound values obtained by combining values of other types. Tuples are used in expressing "functions of several variables" where the argument is a tuple, and in expressing functions where the result is a tuple. The components in a record are identified by special identifiers called labels. Tagged values are used when we group together values of different kinds to form a single set of values. Tuples, records and tagged values are treated as "first-class citizens" in F#: They can enter into expressions and the value of an expression can be a tuple, a record or a tagged value. Functions on tuples, records or tagged values can be defined by use of patterns.

3.1 Tuples

An ordered collection of n values $(v_1, v_2, \ldots, v_n)$, where $n > 1$, is called an *n-tuple*. Examples of *n*-tuples are:

```
(10, true);;
val it : int * bool = (10, true)

(("abc",1),-3);;
 val it : (string * int) * int = (("abc", 1), -3)
```

A 2-tuple like `(10,true)` is also called a *pair*. The last example shows that a pair, for example, `(("abc",1),-3)`, can have a component that is again a pair `("abc",1)`. In general, tuples can have arbitrary values as components. A 3-tuple is called a *triple* and a 4-tuple is called a *quadruple*. An expression like `(true)` is *not* a tuple but just the expression `true` enclosed in brackets, so there is *no* concept of 1-tuple. The symbol `()` denotes the only value of type `unit` (cf. Page 23).

The *n*-tuple $(v_1, v_2, \ldots, v_n)$ represents the graph:

The tuples `(true,"abc",1,-3)` and `((true,"abc"),1,-3)` contain the same values `true`, `"abc"`, `1` and `-3`, but they are different because they have a different structure. This difference is easily seen from the structure of the corresponding graphs in Figure 3.1, where the 4-tuple `(true,"abc",1,-3)` represents the graph with four branches

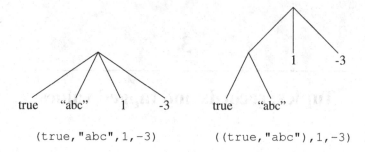

(true,"abc",1,-3)   ((true,"abc"),1,-3)

Figure 3.1 Graphs for tuple values

while the 3-tuple ((true,"abc"),1,-3) represents the graph with three branches and a sub-graph with two branches.

Tuple expressions

A *tuple expression* $(expr_1, expr_2, \dots, expr_n)$ is obtained by enclosing n expressions $expr_1, expr_2, \dots, expr_n$ in parentheses. It has the type $\tau_1 * \tau_2 * \cdots * \tau_n$ when $expr_1, expr_2, \dots, expr_n$ have types $\tau_1, \tau_2, \dots, \tau_n$. For example:

(1<2,"abc",1,1-4)	has type	bool * string * int * int
(true,"abc")	has type	bool * string
((2>1,"abc"),3-2,-3)	has type	(bool * string) * int * int

Remark: The tuple type $\tau_1 * \tau_2 * \cdots * \tau_n$ corresponds to the *Cartesian Product*

$$A = A_1 \times A_2 \times \cdots \times A_n$$

of n sets $A_1, A_2, \dots, A_n$ in mathematics. An element a of the set A is a tuple $a = (a_1, a_2, \dots, a_n)$ of elements $a_1 \in A_1, a_2 \in A_2, \dots, a_n \in A_n$.

A tuple expression $(expr_1, expr_2, \dots, expr_n)$ is *evaluated* from left to right, that is, by first evaluating $expr_1$, then $expr_2$, and so on. Tuple expressions can be used in declarations whereby an identifier is bound to a tuple value, for example:

```
let tp1 = ((1<2, "abc"), 1, 1-4);;
val tp1 : (bool * string) * int * int = ((true, "abc"), 1, -3)

let tp2 = (2>1, "abc", 3-2, -3);;
val tp2 : bool * string * int * int = (true, "abc", 1, -3)
```

Tuples are individual values

A tuple expression may contain identifiers that are already bound to tuples, for example:

```
let t1 = (true,"abc");;
val t1 : bool * string = (true, "abc")
```

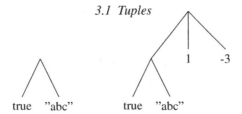

Figure 3.2 Graphs for tuples (`true`, `"abc"`) and (`(true`, `"abc")`, `1`, `-3`)

```
let t2 = (t1,1,-3);;
val t2 : (bool * string) * int * int = ((true, "abc"), 1, -3)
```

The value bound to the identifier `t1` is then found as a subcomponent of the value bound to `t2` as shown in Figure 3.2. A fresh binding of `t1` is, however, *not* going to affect the value of `t2`:

```
let t1 = -7 > 2;;
val t1 : bool = false
```

```
t2;;
val it : (bool * string) * int * int = ((true, "abc"), 1, -3)
```

The subcomponent (true,"abc") is a value in its own right and it depends in no way on possible future bindings of `t1` once the value of the expression (`t1,1,-3`) has been evaluated.

Equality

Equality is defined for n-tuples of the same type, provided that equality is defined for the components. The equality is defined componentwise, that is, $(v_1, v_2, \ldots, v_n)$ is equal to $(v'_1, v'_2, \ldots, v'_n)$ if v_i is equal to v'_i for $1 \leq i \leq n$. This corresponds to equality of the graphs represented by the tuples. For example:

```
("abc", 2, 4, 9) = ("ABC", 2, 4, 9);;
val it : bool = false
```

```
(1, (2,true)) = (2-1, (2,2>1));;
val it : bool = true
```

```
(1, (2,true)) = (1, 2, 2>1);;
   (1, (2,true)) = (1, 2, 2>1);;
   ------------------^^^^^^^^^^
stdin(25,18): error FS0001: Type mismatch. Expecting a
     int * (int * bool)
but given a
     int * (int * bool) * 'a
The tuples have differing lengths of 2 and 3
```

An error message occurs in the last example. The pair (`1, (2,true)`) on the left-hand side of the equality has type int * (int * bool) while the tuple on the right-hand side has type int * int * bool. The system recognizes that these types are different and issues an error message.

Ordering

The *ordering* operators: >, >=, <, and <=, and the `compare` function are defined on n-tuples of the same type, provided ordering is defined for the components. Tuples are ordered lexicographically:

$$(x_1, x_2, \ldots, x_n) < (y_1, y_2, \ldots, y_n)$$

exactly when, for some k, where $1 \le k \le n$, we have:

$$x_1 = y_1 \wedge x_2 = y_2 \wedge \ldots \wedge x_{k-1} = y_{k-1} \wedge x_k < y_k$$

For example:

```
(1, "a") < (1, "ab");;
val it : bool = true

(2, "a") < (1, "ab");;
val it : bool = false
```

since "a" < "ab" holds while 2 < 1 does not.

The other comparison operators and the `compare` function can be defined in terms of = and < as usual, for example:

```
('a', ("b",true), 10.0) >= ('a', ("b",false), 0.0);;
val it : bool = true

compare ("abcd", (true, 1)) ("abcd", (false, 2));;
val it : int = 1
```

Tuple patterns

A tuple pattern represents a graph. For example, the pattern (x,n) is a *tuple pattern*. It represents the graph shown to the left containing the identifiers x and n:

The graph represented by the value (3,2) (shown to the right) *matches* the graph for the pattern in the sense that the graph for the value is obtained from the graph for the pattern by substituting suitable values for the identifiers in the pattern – in this case the value 3 for the identifier x and the value 2 for the identifier n. Hence, the pattern matching gives the bindings x ↦ 3 and n ↦ 2.

Patterns can be used on the left-hand side in a `let` declaration which binds the identifiers in the pattern to the values obtained by the pattern matching, for example:

```
let (x,n) = (3,2);;
val x : int = 3
val n : int = 2
```

Patterns may contain constants like the pattern (x,0), for example, containing the constant 0. It matches any pair (v_1, v_2) where $v_2 = 0$, and the binding x $\mapsto v_1$ is then obtained:

```
let (x,0) = ((3,"a"),0);;
val x : int * string = (3, "a")
```

This example also illustrates that the pattern matching may bind an identifier (here: x) to a value which is a tuple.

The pattern (x, 0) is *incomplete* in the sense that it just matches pairs where the second component is 0 and there are other pairs of type $\tau * \text{int}$ that do not match the pattern. The system gives a warning when an incomplete pattern is used:

```
let (x,0) = ((3,"a"),0);;
----^^^^^

stdin(46,5): warning FS0025: Incomplete pattern matches on
this expression. For example, the value '(_,1)' may indicate a
case not covered by the pattern(s).
```

The warning can be ignored since the second component of ((3,"a"),0) is, in fact, 0. By contrast the declaration:

```
let (x,0) = (3,2);;
  let (x,0) = (3,2);;
----^^^^^

stdin(49,5): warning FS0025: Incomplete pattern matches on
this expression. For example, the value '(_,1)' may indicate a
case not covered by the pattern(s).
Microsoft.FSharp.Core.MatchFailureException: The match cases
   were incomplete at <StartupCode$FSI_0036>.$FSI_0036.main@()
Stopped due to error
```

generates an error message because the constant 0 in the pattern does not match the corresponding value 2 on the right-hand side. The system cannot generate any binding in this case.

The wildcard pattern can be used in tuple patterns. Every value matches this pattern, but the matching provides no bindings. For example:

```
let ((_,x),_,z) = ((1,true), (1,2,3), false);;
val z : bool = false
val x : bool = true
```

A pattern cannot contain multiple occurrences of the same identifier, so (x, x), for example, is an illegal pattern:

```
let (x,x) = (1,1);;
  let (x,x) = (1,1);;
-------^

... error FS0038: 'x' is bound twice in this pattern
```

3.2 Polymorphism

Consider the function `swap` interchanging the components of a pair:

```
let swap (x,y) = (y,x);;
val swap : 'a * 'b -> 'b * 'a

swap ('a',"ab");;
val it : string * char = ("ab", 'a')

swap ((1,3),("ab",true));;
val it : (string*bool) * (int*int) = (("ab", true), (1, 3))
```

The examples show that the function applies to all kinds of pairs. This is reflected in the type of the function: `'a * 'b -> 'b * 'a`.

The type of `swap` expresses that the argument (type `'a * 'b`) must be a pair, and that the value will be a pair (type `'b * 'a`) such that the first/second component of the value is of same type as the second/first component of the argument.

The type of `swap` contains two *type variables* `'a` and `'b`. A type containing type variables is called a *polymorphic type* and a function with polymorphic type like `swap` is called a *polymorphic function*. Polymorphic means "of many forms": In our case the F# compiler is able to generate a *single* F# function `swap` working on any kind of pairs and which is hence capable of handling data of many forms.

Polymorphism is related to overloading (cf. Section 2.5) as we in both cases can apply the same function name or operator to arguments of different types, but an overloaded operator denotes *different* F# functions for different argument types (like + denoting integer addition when applied to `int`'s and floating-point addition when applied to `float`'s).

There are two predefined, polymorphic functions

$$\text{fst: } 'a * 'b -> 'a \quad \text{and} \quad \text{snd: } 'a * 'b -> 'b$$

on pairs, that select the first and second component, respectively. For example:

```
fst((1,"a",true), "xyz");;
val it : int * string * bool = (1, "a", true)

snd('z', ("abc", 3.0));;
val it : string * float = ("abc", 3.0)
```

3.3 Example: Geometric vectors

A proper vector in the plane is a direction in the plane together with a non-negative length. The null vector is any direction together with the length 0. A vector can be *represented* by its set of Cartesian coordinates which is a pair of real numbers. A vector might instead be represented by its polar coordinates, which is also a pair of real numbers for the length and the angle. These two representations are different, and the operators on vectors (addition of vectors, multiplication by a scalar, etc.) are expressed by different functions on the representing pairs of numbers.

In the following we will just consider the Cartesian coordinate representation, where a vector in the plane will be represented by a value of type `float * float`.

We will consider the following operators on vectors:

Vector addition:	$(x_1, y_1) + (x_2, y_2)$	$=$	$(x_1 + x_2, y_1 + y_2)$
Vector reversal:	$-(x, y)$	$=$	$(-x, -y)$
Vector subtraction:	$(x_1, y_1) - (x_2, y_2)$	$=$	$(x_1 - x_2, y_1 - y_2)$
		$=$	$(x_1, y_1) + -(x_2, y_2)$
Multiplication by a scalar:	$\lambda (x_1, y_1)$	$=$	$(\lambda x_1, \lambda y_1)$
Dot product:	$(x_1, y_1) \cdot (x_2, y_2)$	$=$	$x_1 x_2 + y_1 y_2$
Norm (length):	$\|(x_1, y_1)\|$	$=$	$\sqrt{x_1^2 + y_1^2}$

We cannot use the operator symbols $+$, $-$, $*$, and so on, to denote the operations on vectors, as this would overwrite their initial meaning. But using $+.$ for vector addition, $-.$ for vector reversal and subtraction, $*.$ for product by a scalar and $\&.$ for dot product, we obtain operators having a direct resemblance to the mathematical vector operators and having the associations and precedences that we would expect.

The prefix operator for vector reversal is declared by (cf. Section 2.9):

```
let (~-.) (x:float,y:float) = (-x,-y);;
val ( ~-. ) : float * float -> float * float
```

and the infix operators are declared by:

```
let (+.) (x1, y1) (x2,y2) = (x1+x2,y1+y2): float*float;;
val ( +. ) : float * float -> float * float -> float * float

let (-.) v1 v2 = v1 +. -. v2;;
val ( -. ) : float * float -> float * float -> float * float

let ( *.) x (x1,y1) = (x*x1, x*y1): float*float;;
val ( *. ) : float -> float * float -> float * float

let (&.) (x1,y1) (x2,y2) = x1*x2 + y1*y2: float;;
val ( &. ) : float * float > float * float -> float
```

The norm function is declared using the `sqrt` function (cf. Table 2.5) by:

```
let norm(x1:float,y1:float) = sqrt(x1*x1+y1*y1);;
val norm : float * float -> float
```

These functions allow us to write vector expressions in a form resembling the mathematical notation for vectors. For example:

```
let a = (1.0,-2.0);;
val a : float * float = (1.0, -2.0)

let b = (3.0,4.0);;
val b : float * float = (3.0, 4.0)
```

```
let c = 2.0 *. a -. b;;
val c : float * float = (-1.0, -8.0)

let d = c &. a;;
val d : float = 15.0

let e = norm b;;
val e : float = 5.0
```

3.4 Records

A *record* is a generalized tuple where each component is identified by a *label* instead of the position in the tuple.

The record type must be declared before a record can be made. We may for example declare a type person as follows:

```
type Person = {age : int; birthday : int * int;
               name : string; sex : string};;
```

The keyword type indicates that this is a *type declaration* and the braces { and } indicate a record type. The (distinct) identifiers age, birthday, name and sex are called *record labels* and they are considered part of the type.

A value of type Person is entered as follows:

```
let john = {name =  "John"; age = 29;
            sex = "M"; birthday = (2,11)}};;
val john : Person = {age = 29;
                     birthday = (2, 11);
                     name = "John";
                     sex = "M";}
```

This record contains the following *fields*: The string "John" with label name, the integer 29 with label age, the string "M" with label sex, and the integer pair (2,11) with label birthday.

The declaration creates the following binding of the identifier john:

$$\text{john} \mapsto \{\, \text{age} \mapsto 29 \,,\, \text{birthday} \mapsto (2,11) \,,\, \text{name} \mapsto \text{"John"} \,,\, \text{sex} \mapsto \text{"M"} \,\}$$

A record is hence a *local environment* packaged in a certain way. It contains a binding of each record label to the corresponding value.

A field in the record denoted by john is obtained by suffixing the identifier john with the corresponding record label:

```
john.birthday;;
val it : int * int = (2, 11)
john.sex;;
val it : string = "M"
```

Equality and ordering

The equality of two records with the same type is defined componentwise from the equality of values associated with the same labels, so the ordering of the components in the record is of no importance when entering values. For example

```
john = {age = 29; name = "John";
        sex = "M"; birthday = (2,11)};;
val it : bool = true
```

Hence two records are equal if they are of the same type and contain the same local bindings of the labels.

Ordering of records is based on a lexicographical ordering using the ordering of the labels in the record type declaration. Consider, for example:

```
type T1 = {a:int; b:string};;
let v1 = {a=1; b="abc"};;
let v2 = {a=2; b="ab"};;
v1<v2;;
val it : bool = true

type T2 = {b:string; a:int};;
let v1' = {T2.a=1; b="abc"};;
let v2' = {T2.a=2; b="ab"};;
v1'>v2';;
val it : bool = true
```

The value v1 is smaller than the value v2 because the label a occurs first in the record type T1 and v1.a = 1 is smaller than v2.a = 2 – while the value v1' is larger than the value v2' because the label b occurs first in the record type T2 and v1'.b = "abc" is larger than v2'.b = "ab".

The composite identifier T2.a consists of the record label a prefixed with the record type T2. It is used in order to resolve the ambiguity created by reuse of record labels.

Note that the values v1 and v1' cannot be compared as they are of different types.

Record patterns

A *record pattern* is used to decompose a record into its fields. The pattern

```
{name = x; age = y; sex = s; birthday =(d,m)}
```

denotes the graph shown in Figure 3.3. It generates bindings of the identifiers x, y, s, d and m when matched with a person record:

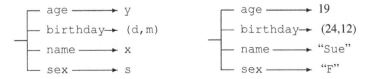

Figure 3.3 Record pattern and record

```
let sue = {name="Sue"; age = 19; sex="F";
            birthday = (24,12)};;
let {name = x; age = y; sex = s; birthday = (d,m) } = sue;;
val y : int = 19
val x : string = "Sue"
val s : string = "F"
val m : int = 12
val d : int = 24
```

Record patterns are used when defining functions. Consider, for example, the declaration of a function `age` where the argument is a record of type `Person`:

```
let age {age = a; name = _; sex=_; birthday=_} = a;;
val age : Person -> int
```

```
let isYoungLady {age=a; sex=s; name=_; birthday=_}
                                      = a < 25 && s = "F";;
val isYoungLady : Person -> bool
```

```
age john;;
val it : int = 29
```

```
isYoungLady john;;
val it : bool = false
```

```
isYoungLady sue;;
val it : bool = true
```

The type of the above functions can be inferred from the context since `name`, `age`, and so on are labels of the record type `Person` only.

3.5 Example: Quadratic equations

In this section we consider the problem of finding solutions to quadratic equations

$$ax^2 + bx + c = 0$$

with real coefficients a, b, c.

The equation has no solution in the real numbers if the *discriminant* $b^2 - 4ac$ is negative; otherwise, if $b^2 - 4ac \geq 0$ and $a \neq 0$, then the equation has the solutions x_1 and x_2 where:

$$x_1 = \frac{-b + \sqrt{b^2 - 4ac}}{2a} \quad \text{and} \quad x_2 = \frac{-b - \sqrt{b^2 - 4ac}}{2a}$$

Note that $x_1 = x_2$ if $b^2 - 4ac = 0$.

We may represent the equation $ax^2 + bx + c = 0$ by the triple (a, b, c) of real numbers and the solutions x_1 and x_2 by the pair (x_1, x_2) of real numbers. This representation is captured in the type declarations:

```
type Equation = float * float * float;;
type Equation = float * float * float
```

```
type Solution = float * float;;
type Solution = float * float
```

A function:

```
solve: Equation -> Solution
```

for computing the solutions of the equation should then have the indicated type. Note that type declarations like the ones above are useful in program documentation as they communicate the intention of the program in a succinct way. The system does, however, just treat the identifiers `Equation` and `Solution` as shorthand for the corresponding types.

Error handling

The function `solve` must give an error message when $b^2 - 4ac < 0$ or $a = 0$ as there is no solution in these cases. Such an error message can be signalled by using an *exception*. An exception is named by an *exception declaration*. We may, for example, name an exception `Solve` by the declaration:

```
exception Solve;;
exception Solve
```

The declaration of the function `solve` is:

```
let solve(a,b,c) =
    if b*b-4.0*a*c < 0.0 || a = 0.0 then raise Solve
    else ((-b + sqrt(b*b-4.0*a*c))/(2.0*a),
          (-b - sqrt(b*b-4.0*a*c))/(2.0*a));;
val solve : float * float * float -> float * float
```

The `then` branch of this declaration contains the expression: `raise Solve`. An evaluation of this expression terminates with an error message. For example:

```
solve(1.0, 0.0, 1.0);;
FSI_0015+Solve: Exception of type 'FSI_0015+Solve' was thrown.
   at FSI_0016.solve(Double a, Double b, Double c)
   at <StartupCode$FSI_0017>.$FSI_0017.main@()
Stopped due to error
```

We say that the exception `Solve` is *raised*. Note that the use of the exception does not influence the type of `solve`.

Other examples of the use of `solve` are:

```
solve(1.0, 1.0, -2.0);;
val it : float * float = (1.0, -2.0)

solve(2.0, 8.0, 8.0);;
val it : float * float = (-2.0, -2.0)
```

An alternative to declaring your own exception is to use the built-in function:

```
failwith: string -> 'a
```

that takes a string as argument. An application `failwith` s raises the exception `Faiure` s and the argument string s is shown on the console. The function can be applied in any context because the function value has a polymorphic type. For example:

```
let solve(a,b,c) =
    if b*b-4.0*a*c < 0.0 || a = 0.0
    then failwith "discriminant is negative or a=0.0"
    else ((-b + sqrt(b*b-4.0*a*c))/(2.0*a),
          (-b - sqrt(b*b-4.0*a*c))/(2.0*a));;

solve(0.0,1.0,2.0);;
System.Exception: discriminant is negative or a=0.0
   at FSI_0037.solve(Double a, Double b, Double c)
   at <StartupCode$FSI_0038>.$FSI_0038.main@()
Stopped due to error
```

We shall on Page 63 study how raised exceptions can be caught.

3.6 Locally declared identifiers

It is often convenient to use *locally declared* identifiers in function declarations. Consider for example the above declaration of the function `solve`. The expression `b*b-4.0*a*c` is evaluated three times during the evaluation of `solve(1.0,1.0,-2.0)` and this is not satisfactory from an efficiency point of view. Furthermore, the readability of the declaration suffers from the repeated occurrences of the same subexpression.

These problems are avoided using a locally declared identifier d:

```
let solve(a,b,c) =
    let d = b*b-4.0*a*c
    if d < 0.0 || a = 0.0
    then failwith "discriminant is negative or a=0.0"
    else ((-b + sqrt d)/(2.0*a),(-b - sqrt d)/(2.0*a));;
val solve : float * float * float -> float * float
```

There is room for improvement in the above declaration as the expression `sqrt d` is evaluated twice during the evaluation of a function value. This leads to yet another declaration of `solve` with a further locally declared identifier `sqrtD`:

```
let solve(a,b,c) =
    let sqrtD =
        let d = b*b-4.0*a*c
        if d < 0.0 || a = 0.0
        then failwith "discriminant is negative or a=0.0"
        else sqrt d
    ((-b + sqrtD)/(2.0*a),(-b - sqrtD)/(2.0*a));;
 val solve : float * float * float -> float * float
```

The evaluation of `solve(1.0,1.0,-2.0)` proceeds as follows, where *env* denotes the environment:

$$env = [a \mapsto 1.0, \ b \mapsto 1.0, c \mapsto -2.0]$$

obtained by binding the parameters a, b and c to the actual values 1.0, 1.0 and -2.0:

Expression	Environment	Note
`solve(1.0,1.0,-2.0)`		
$\leadsto$ `let sqrtD = ...,`	*env*	(1)
$\leadsto$ Start evaluating subexpression		
`let d=b*b-4.0...,`	*env*	(2)
$\leadsto$ `if d < 0...,`	*env* plus $d \mapsto 9.0$	(3)
$\leadsto$ 3.0	*env* plus $d \mapsto 9.0$	(4)
End evaluating subexpression		(5)
$\leadsto$ `((-b + sqrtD...`	*env* plus $sqrtD \mapsto 3.0$	(6)
$\leadsto$ $(1.0, -2.0)$		(7)

1. The binding of `sqrtD` can only be established when the value of the subexpression has been evaluated.

2. The evaluation of the subexpression starts with the declaration `let b = ...`.

3. The expression `b*b-4.0*a*c` evaluates to 9.0 using the bindings in *env*. A binding of d to this value is added to the environment.

4. The evaluation of `if d < 0.0 ... else sqrt d` gives the value 3.0 using the bindings in the environment *env* plus $d \mapsto 9.0$.

5. The evaluation of the subexpression is completed and the binding of d is removed from the environment.

6. A binding of `sqrtD` to the value 3.0 is added to the environment, and the expression `((-b + sqrtD ...` is evaluated in this environment.

7. The bindings of a, b, c and `sqrtD` are removed and the evaluation terminates with result $(1.0, -2.0)$.

Note the role of *indentation* in F#. The `let`-expression:

```
let d = b*b-4.0*a*c
if d < 0.0 || a = 0.0
then failwith "discriminant is negative or a=0.0"
else sqrt d
```

is terminated by the occurrence of a less indented line:

```
((-b + sqrtD)/(2.0*a),(-b - sqrtD)/(2.0*a));;
```

and this also ends the lifetime of the binding of d. One says that the `let`-expression constitutes the *scope* of the declaration of d.

The surrounding `let`-expression

```
let sqrtD =
    let d = b*b-4.0*a*c
    if d < 0.0 || a = 0.0
    then failwith "discriminant is negative or a=0.0"
    else sqrt d
((-b + sqrtD)/(2.0*a),(-b - sqrtD)/(2.0*a))
```

is terminated by the double semicolon. Note that the expression `((-b + ...` must be on the same indentation level as `let sqrtD =`.

A `let`-expression may contain more than one local declaration as shown in yet another version of `solve` (probably the most readable):

```
let solve(a,b,c) =
    let d = b*b-4.0*a*c
    if d < 0.0 || a = 0.0
    then failwith "discriminant is negative or a=0.0"
    else let sqrtD = sqrt d
         ((-b + sqrtD)/(2.0*a),(-b - sqrtD)/(2.0*a));;
val solve : float * float * float -> float * float
```

The evaluation of `solve(1.0,1.0,-2.0)` in this version of the function will add the binding of d to the environment *env*. Later the binding of `sqrtD` is further added without removing the binding of b. Finally the expression in the last line is evaluated and the bindings of a, b, c, d and `sqrtD` are all removed at the same time.

3.7 Example: Rational numbers. Invariants

A *rational* number q is a fraction $q = \frac{a}{b}$, where a and b are integers with $b \neq 0$.

Ideas to express the operations on rational numbers by function declarations come easily from the following well-known rules of arithmetic, where a, b, c and d are integers such that $b \neq 0$ and $d \neq 0$:

$$\frac{a}{b} + \frac{c}{d} = \frac{ad + bc}{bd}$$

$$\frac{a}{b} - \frac{c}{d} = \frac{a}{b} + \frac{-c}{d} = \frac{ad - bc}{bd}$$

$$\frac{a}{b} \cdot \frac{c}{d} = \frac{ac}{bd} \tag{3.1}$$

$$\frac{a}{b} / \frac{c}{d} = \frac{a}{b} \cdot \frac{d}{c} \quad \text{where} \quad c \neq 0$$

$$\frac{a}{b} = \frac{c}{d} \quad \text{exactly when} \quad ad = bc$$

Representation. Invariant

We use the *representation* (a, b), where $b > 0$ and where the fraction $\frac{a}{b}$ is irreducible, that is, $\gcd(a, b) = 1$, to represent the rational number $\frac{a}{b}$. Thus, a value (a, b) of type `int * int` represents a rational number if $b > 0$ and $\gcd(a, b) = 1$, and we name this condition the *invariant* for pairs representing rational numbers. Any rational number has a unique *normal form* of this kind. This leads to the type declaration:

```
type Qnum = int*int;;     // (a,b) where b > 0 and gcd(a,b) = 1
```

where the invariant is stated as a comment to the declaration. (The declaration of `gcd` is found on Page 15.)

Operators

It is convenient to declare a function `canc` that cancels common divisors and thereby reduces any fraction with non-zero denominator to the normal form satisfying the invariant:

```
let canc(p,q) =
   let sign = if p*q < 0 then -1 else 1
   let ap = abs p
   let aq = abs q
   let d  = gcd(ap,aq)
   (sign * (ap / d), aq / d);;
```

In the below declarations for the other functions, `canc` is applied to guarantee that the resulting values satisfy the invariant.

When a rational number is generated from a pair of integers, we must check for division by zero and enforce that the invariant is established for the result. The function `mkQ` does that by the use of `canc`:

```
let mkQ = function
   | (_,0)  -> failwith "Division by zero"
   | pr     -> canc pr;;
```

The operators on rational numbers are declared below. These declarations follow the rules (3.1) for rational numbers. We assume that the arguments are legal representations of rational numbers, that is, they respect the invariant. Under this assumption, the result of any of the functions must respect the invariant. This is enforced by the use of `canc` and `mkQ`:

```
let (.+.) (a,b) (c,d) = canc(a*d + b*c, b*d);;     // Addition

let (.-.) (a,b) (c,d) = canc(a*d - b*c, b*d);;   // Subtraction

let (.*.) (a,b) (c,d) = canc(a*c, b*d);;       // Multiplication

let (./.) (a,b) (c,d) = (a,b) .*. mkQ(d,c);;      // Division

let (.=.) (a,b) (c,d) = (a,b) = (c,d);;          // Equality
```

Note that the definition of equality assumes the invariant. Equality should be declared by
a*d=b*c if we allow integer pairs *not* satisfying the invariant as there would then be *many different* integer pairs representing the *same* rational number.

It is straightforward to convert a rational number representation to a string:

```
let toString(p:int,q:int) = (string p) + "/" + (string q);;
```

as the representation is unique. We can operate on rational numbers in a familiar manner:

```
let q1 = mkQ(2,-3);;
val q1 : int * int = (-2, 3)
let q2 = mkQ(5,10);;
val q2 : int * int = (1, 2)
let q3 = q1 .+. q2;;
val q3 : int * int = (-1, 6)


toString(q1 .-. q3 ./. q2);;
val it : string = "-1/3"
```

3.8 Tagged values. Constructors

Tagged values are used when we group together values of different kinds to form a single set of values.

For example, we may represent a circle by its radius r, a square by its side length a, and a triangle by the triple (a, b, c) of its side lengths a, b and c. Circles, squares, and triangles may then be grouped together to form a *single* collection of *shapes* if we put a *tag* on each representing value. The tag should be Circle, Square, or Triangle depending on the kind of shape. The circle with radius 1.2, the square with side length 3.4 and the triangle with side lengths 3.0, 4.0 and 5.0 are then represented by the tagged values shown in the following graphs:

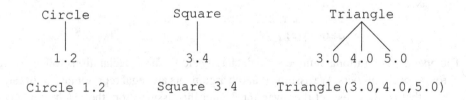

In F#, a collection of tagged values is declared by a *type* declaration. For example, a type for shapes is declared by:

```
type Shape = | Circle of float
             | Square of float
             | Triangle of float*float*float;;
type Shape =
  | Circle of float
  | Square of float
  | Triangle of float * float * float
```

Constructors and values

The response from F# indicates that `Shape` names a type, and that `Circle`, `Square` and `Triangle` are bound to *value constructors*. These value constructors are functions and they give a *tagged value* of type `Shape` when applied to an argument.

For example, `Circle` is a value constructor with type `float -> Shape`. This means that `Circle` r denotes a value of type `Shape`, for every float r. For example, `Circle 1.2` denotes the leftmost graph in the above figure and `Circle 1.2` is an example of a *tagged value*, where `Circle` is the tag.

We can observe that `Circle 1.2` is a value which is not evaluated further by F#:

```
Circle 1.2;;
val it : Shape = Circle 1.2
```

as the value in the answer is equal to the expression being evaluated, that is, `Circle 1.2`.

Values can be constructed using `Square` and `Triangle` in a similar way.

Since constructors are functions in F#, `Circle` can be applied to an expression of type `float`:

```
Circle(8.0 - 2.0*3.4);;
val it : Shape = Circle 1.2
```

Thus, the declaration of `Shape` allows one to write tagged values like `Circle 1.2`, `Square 3.4` and `Triangle(3.0,4.0,5.0)` using the constructors, and any value of type `Shape` has one of the forms:

```
Circle r
Square a
Triangle (a, b, c)
```

for some float value r, float value a, or triple (a, b, c) of float values.

Equality and ordering

Equality and ordering are defined for tagged values provided they are defined for their components. Two tagged values are equal if they have the same constructor and their components are equal. This corresponds to equality of the graphs represented by the tagged values. For example:

```
Circle 1.2 = Circle(1.0 + 0.2);;
val it : bool = true

Circle 1.2 = Square 1.2;;
val it : bool = false
```

The sequence in which the tags occur in the declaration is significant for the ordering. For example, any circle is smaller than any square, which again is smaller than any triangle due to the order in which the corresponding tags are declared. For example:

```
Circle 1.2 < Circle 1.0;;
val it : bool = false
```

```
Circle 1.2 < Square 1.2;;
val it : bool = true

Triangle(1.0,1.0,1.0) > Square 4.0;;
val it : bool = true
```

Constructors in patterns

Constructors can be used in patterns. For example, an area function for shapes is declared by:

```
let area = function
    | Circle r           -> System.Math.PI * r * r
    | Square a           -> a * a
    | Triangle(a,b,c) ->
           let s = (a + b + c)/2.0
           sqrt(s*(s-a)*(s-b)*(s-c));;
val area : Shape -> float
```

The pattern matching treats constructors differently from other identifiers:

> A constructor matches itself only in a pattern match while other identifiers match any value.

For example, the value `Circle 1.2` will match the pattern `Circle r`, but not the other patterns in the function declaration. The matching binds the identifier r to the value `1.2`, and the expression `Math.pi * r * r` is evaluated using this binding:

$$\text{area (Circle 1.2)}$$
$$\rightsquigarrow \text{(Math.PI } * \text{ r } * \text{ r, } [r \mapsto 1.2])$$
$$\rightsquigarrow \dots$$

The value `Triangle(3.0,4.0,5.0)` will in a similar way only match the pattern in the third clause in the declaration, and we get bindings of a, b and c to `3.0`, `4.0` and `5.0`, and the `let` expression is evaluated using these bindings:

$$\text{area (Triangle(3.0,4.0,5.0))}$$
$$\rightsquigarrow \text{(let s = } \dots, [a \mapsto 3.0, b \mapsto 4.0, c \mapsto 5.0])$$
$$\rightsquigarrow \dots$$

Invariant for the representation of shapes

Some values of type `Shape` do not represent geometric shapes. For example, `Circle -1.0` does not represent a circle, as a circle cannot have a negative radius, `Square -2.0` does not represent a square, as a square cannot have a negative side length, and

```
Triangle(3.0, 4.0, 7.5)
```

does not represent a triangle, as $7.5 > 3.0 + 4.0$ and, therefore, one of the triangle inequalities is not satisfied.

Therefore, there is an *invariant* for this representation of shapes: the real numbers have to be positive, and the triangle inequalities must be satisfied. This invariant can be declared as a predicate isShape:

```
let isShape = function
    | Circle r          -> r > 0.0
    | Square a          -> a > 0.0
    | Triangle(a,b,c) ->
        a > 0.0 && b > 0.0 && c > 0.0
        && a < b + c && b < c + a && c < a + b;;
val isShape : Shape -> bool
```

We consider now the declaration of an area function for geometric shapes that raises an exception when the argument of the function does not satisfy the invariant. If we try to modify the above area function:

```
let area x = if not (isShape x)
             then failwith "not a legal shape"
             else ...
```

then the else-branch must have means to select the right area-expression depending on the form of x. This is done using a match ... with ... expression:

```
let area x =
    if not (isShape x)
    then failwith "not a legal shape" raise
    else match x with
        | Circle r          -> System.Math.PI * r * r
        | Square a          -> a * a
        | Triangle(a,b,c) ->
            let s = (a + b + c)/2.0
            sqrt(s*(s-a)*(s-b)*(s-c));;
val area : Shape -> float
```

The modified area function computes the area of legal values of the type Shape and terminates the evaluation raising an exception for illegal values:

```
area (Triangle(3.0,4.0,5.0));;
val it : float = 6.0

area (Triangle(3.0,4.0,7.5));;
System.Exception: not a legal shape
  ...
```

3.9 Enumeration types

Value constructors need not have any argument, so we can make special type declarations like:

```
type Colour = Red | Blue | Green | Yellow | Purple;;
type Colour =
  | Red
  | Blue
  | Green
  | Yellow
  | Purple
```

Types like `Colour` are called *enumeration types*, as the declaration of `Colour` just enumerates five constructors:

Red, Blue, Green, Yellow, Purple

where each constructor is a value of type `Colour`, for example:

```
Green;;
val it : Colour = Green
```

Functions on enumeration types may be declared by pattern matching:

```
let niceColour = function
    | Red  -> true
    | Blue -> true
    | _    -> false;;
val niceColour : Colour -> bool

niceColour Purple;;
val it : bool = false
```

The days in a month example on Page 4 can be nicely expressed using an enumeration type:

```
type Month = January | February | March | April
             | May | June | July | August | September
             | October | November | December;;

let daysOfMonth = function
    | February                                    -> 28
    | April | June | September | November         -> 30
    | _                                           -> 31;;
```

The Boolean type is actually a predefined enumeration type:

```
type bool = false | true
```

where the order of the constructors reflects that `false` < `true`. Notice that user-defined constructors must start with uppercase letters.

3.10 Exceptions

Exceptions have already been used in several examples earlier in this chapter. In this section we give a systematic account of this subject.

Raising an exception terminates the evaluation of a call of a function as we have seen for the `solve` function on Page 53 that raises the exception `Solve` when an error situation is encountered. In the examples presented so far the exception propagates all the way to top level where an error message is issued.

It is possible to *catch* an exception using a `try...with` expression as in the following `solveText` function:

```
let solveText eq =
    try
        string(solve eq)
    with
    | Solve -> "No solutions";;
val solveText : float * float * float -> string
```

It calls `solve` with a float triple `eq` representing a quadratic equation and returns the string representation of the solutions of the equation:

```
solveText (1.0,1.0,-2.0);;
val it : string = "(1, -2)"
```

The string "`No solutions`" is returned if the equation has no solutions:

```
solveText (1.0, 0.0, 1.0);;
val it : string = "No solutions"
```

An application of the function `failwith` *s* will raise the exception `Failure` *s* and this exception can also be caught. Application of the function `mkQ` (see Page 57), for example, will call `failwith` in the case of a division by zero:

```
try
    toString(mkQ(2,0))
with
| Failure s -> s;;
val it : string = "Division by zero"
```

A `try...with` expression has the general form:

```
try e with match
```

where *e* is an expression (possibly extending over several lines) and *match* is a construct of the form:

```
| pat_1 -> e_1
| pat_2 -> e_2
...
| pat_n -> e_n
```

with patterns $pat_1, \ldots pat_n$ and expressions $e_1, \ldots, e_n$.

A try *e* with *match* expression is evaluated as follows:

- Evaluate the expression *e*. If this evaluation terminates normally with a value *v* then return *v* as the result of evaluating the try ... with ... expression.
- If the evaluation raises an exception *Exc* then evaluate *match* by matching *Exc* to the patterns $pat_1, \ldots pat_n$. If *Exc* matches a pattern pat_k then evaluate the corresponding expression e_k. If *Exc* matches none of the patterns then propagate the exception as a result of evaluating the try ... with ... expression.

The exception mechanism in F# and .NET is *not* intended for use in the "normal case" in a program but for *error handling only*.

Library functions (e.g., for performing I/O) may raise exceptions that can only be captured using a *match on type* (cf. Section 7.7).

3.11 Partial functions. The option type

A function f is a *partial* function on a set A if the domain of f is a proper subset of A. For example, the factorial function is a partial function on the set of integers because it is undefined on negative integers.

In declaring a partial function, F# offers the programmer three ways of handling argument values where the function is *undefined*:

1. The evaluation of the function value does not terminate.
2. The evaluation of the function value is terminated by raising an exception.
3. The evaluation of the function value gives a special result, indicating that the function is undefined for the actual argument.

The first choice was used in the declaration of the factorial function fact, where, for example, the evaluation of fact -1 never terminates.

The second choice was selected for the improved area function (cf. Page 61).

The third choice uses the predefined option type:

```
type 'a option = None | Some of 'a
```

where None is used as result for arguments where the function is undefined while Some *v* is used when the function has value *v*.

The constructor Some is polymorphic and can be applied to values of any type:

```
Some false;;
val it : bool option = Some false

Some (1, "a");;
val it : (int * string) option = Some (1, "a")
```

The value None is a polymorphic value of type 'a option:

```
None;;
val it : 'a option = None
```

The library function

```
Option.get : 'a option -> 'a
```

"removes the Some", that is, Option.get(Some n) $= n$. It raises an exception when applied to None. For example:

```
Option.get(Some (1,"a"));;
val it : int * string = (1, "a")

Option.get(Some 1);;
val it : int = 1

Option.get None + 1;;
System.ArgumentException: The option value was None ...
```

We may, for instance, declare a modified factorial function optFact(n) with value Some $n!$ for $n \geq 0$ and None for $n < 0$:

```
let optFact n = if n < 0 then None else Some(fact n);;
val optFact : int -> int option
```

The function application optFact n always gives a result:

```
optFact 5;;
val it : int option = Some 120

optFact -2;;
val it : int option = None
```

The declaration of optFact presumes that fact has already been declared. An independent declaration of optFact is achieved using the Option.get function:

```
let rec optFact = function
  | 0              -> Some 1
  | n when n > 0 -> Some(n * Option.get(optFact(n-1)))
  | _              -> None;;
val optFact : int -> int option
```

Note the use of guarded patterns in this declaration (cf. Section 2.10).

Summary

This chapter introduces the notions of tuples and tuple types, the notions of records and record types, and the notions of tagged values and tagged-value types. Tuples and records are composite values, and we have introduced the notion of patterns that is used to decompose a composite value into its parts. Tagged values are used to express disjoint unions.

An operator can be given infix mode and precedence, and this feature was exploited in writing the operators on geometric vectors in the same way as they are written in mathematical notation.

The notion of exceptions was introduced for handling errors and let expressions were introduced for having locally declared identifiers.

Exercises

3.1   A time of day can be represented as a triple $(hours, minutes, f)$ where f is either AM or PM – or as a record. Declare a function to test whether one time of day comes before another. For example, $(11, 59, \text{"AM"})$ comes before $(1, 15, \text{"PM"})$. Make solutions with triples as well as with records. Declare the functions in infix notation.

3.2   The former British currency had 12 pence to a shilling and 20 shillings to a pound. Declare functions to add and subtract two amounts, represented by triples $(pounds, shillings, pence)$ of integers, and declare the functions when a representation by records is used. Declare the functions in infix notation with proper precedences, and use patterns to obtain readable declarations.

3.3   The set of *complex numbers* is the set of pairs of real numbers. Complex numbers behave almost like real numbers if addition and multiplication are defined by:

$$
\begin{aligned}
(a, b) + (c, d) &= (a + c, b + d) \\
(a, b) \cdot (c, d) &= (ac - bd, bc + ad)
\end{aligned}
$$

1. Declare suitable infix functions for addition and multiplication of complex numbers.
2. The inverse of (a, b) with regard to addition, that is, $-(a, b)$, is $(-a, -b)$, and the inverse of (a, b) with regard to multiplication, that is, $1/(a, b)$, is $(a/(a^2 + b^2), -b/(a^2 + b^2))$ (provided that a and b are not both zero). Declare infix functions for subtraction and division of complex numbers.
3. Use let-expressions in the declaration of the division of complex numbers in order to avoid repeated evaluation of identical subexpressions.

3.4   A straight line $y = ax + b$ in the plane can be represented by the pair (a, b) of real numbers.

1. Declare a type StraightLine for straight lines.
2. Declare functions to mirror straight lines around the x and y-axes.
3. Declare a function to give a string representation for the equation of a straight line.

3.5   Make a type Solution capturing the three capabilities for roots in a quadratic equation: two roots, one root and no root (cf. Section 3.5). Declare a corresponding solve function.

3.6   Solve Exercise 3.1 using tagged values to represent AM and PM.

3.7   Give a declaration for the area function on Page 61 using guarded patterns rather than an if...then...else expression.

4

Lists

Lists are at the core of functional programming. A large number of applications can be modelled and implemented using lists. In this chapter we introduce the list concept, including list values, patterns and basic operations, and we study a collection of recursion schemas over lists. We end the chapter introducing a model-based approach to functional programming on the basis of two examples. The concept of a list is a special case of a collection. In the next chapter, when we consider collections more generally, we shall see that the F# library comprises a rich collection of powerful functions on lists.

4.1 The concept of a list

A *list* is a finite sequence of values

$$[v_0;\ v_1;\ \ldots;\ v_{n-1}]$$

of the same type. For example, [2], [3; 2], and [2; 3; 2] are lists of integers. A list can contain an arbitrary number of elements.

A list $[v_0;\ v_1;\ \ldots;\ v_{n-1}]$ is either empty (when $n = 0$), or it is a non-empty list and can be characterized by the first element v_0 called its *head*, and the rest $[v_1;\ \ldots;\ v_{n-1}]$ called its *tail*.

Figure 4.1 shows the graphs for the lists [2; 3; 2] and [2]. The list [2; 3; 2] is

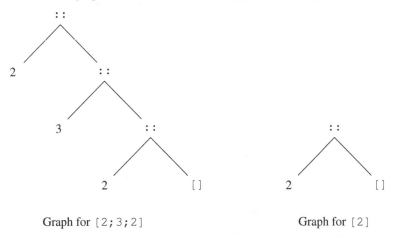

Graph for [2; 3; 2]   Graph for [2]

Figure 4.1 Graphs for two lists

67

hence a tagged pair with tag : : where the first component, the head of the list, is the integer 2, while the second component, the tail of the list, is the list [3; 2] with just two elements. This list is again a tagged pair with tag : :, head 3 and tail [2]. Finally the head of the list [2] is the integer 2, while the tail is the empty list [].

List constants in F#

Lists can be entered as values:

```
let xs = [2;3;2];;
val xs : int list = [2; 3; 2]

let ys = ["Big"; "Mac"];;
val ys  : string list = ["Big"; "Mac"]
```

The types int list and string list, containing the *type constructor* list, indicate that the value of xs is a list of integers and that the value of ys is a list of strings.

We may have lists with any element type, so we can, for example, build lists of pairs:

```
[("b",2);("c",3);("e",5)];;
val it : (string * int) list = [("b", 2);("c", 3);("e", 5)]
```

lists of records:

```
type P = {name: string; age: int}
[{name = "Brown"; age = 25}; {name = "Cook";  age = 45}];;
val it : P list =
   [{name = "Brown"; age = 25}; {name = "Cook"; age = 45}]
```

lists of functions:

```
[sin; cos];;
val it : (float -> float) list = [<fun:it@7>; <fun:it@7-1>]
```

or even lists of lists:

```
[[2;3];[3];[2;3;3]];;
val it : int list list = [[2; 3]; [3]; [2; 3; 3]]
```

Furthermore, lists can be components of other values. We can, for example, have pairs containing lists:

```
("bce", [2;3;5]);;
val it : string * int list = ("bce", [2; 3; 5])
```

The type constructor list

The type constructor list has higher *precedence* than * and -> in *type expressions*, so the type string * int list means string * (int list). The type constructor list is used in postfix notation like the factorial function _! in 3! and associates to the left, so `int list list` means `(int list) list`. Note that `int (list list)` would not make sense.

All elements in a list must have the same type. For example, the following is *not* a legal value in F#:

```
["a";1];;
-----^
stdin(8,6): error FS0001:
This expression was expected to have type
    string
but here has type
    int
```

Equality of lists

Two lists $[x_0; x_1; \ldots; x_{m-1}]$ and $[y_0; y_1; \ldots, y_{n-1}]$ (of the same type) are *equal* when $m = n$ and $x_i = y_i$, for all i such that $0 \leq i < m$. This corresponds to equality of the graphs represented by the lists. Hence, the order of the elements as well as repetitions of the same value are significant in a list.

The equality operator = of F# can be used to test equality of two lists provided that the elements of the lists are of the same type and provided that the equality operator can be used on values of that element type.

For example:

```
[2;3;2] = [2;3];;
val it : bool = false

[2;3;2] = [2;3;3];;
val it : bool = false
```

The differences are easily recognized from the graphs representing `[2; 3; 2]`, `[2; 3]` and `[2; 3; 3]`.

Lists containing functions cannot be compared because F# equality is not defined for functions.

For example:

```
[sin; cos] = [];;
_^^^
... The type '( ^a ->  ^a ) when
^a : (static member Sin :   ^a ->  ^a)' does not support
the 'equality' constraint because it is a function type
```

Ordering of lists

Lists of the same type are ordered *lexicographically*, provided there is an ordering defined on the elements:

$$[x_0; x_1; \ldots; x_{m-1}] < [y_0; y_1; \ldots; y_{n-1}]$$

exactly when

$$
\begin{array}{ll}
[x_0; x_1; \ldots; x_k] \\
= [y_0; y_1; \ldots; y_k]
\end{array}
\quad \text{and} \quad
\left(
\begin{array}{l}
k = m - 1 < n - 1 \\
\text{or} \quad k < \min\{m - 1, n - 1\} \text{ and } x_{k+1} < y_{k+1}
\end{array}
\right)
$$

for some k, where $0 \le k < \min\{m - 1, n - 1\}$.

There are two cases in this definition of $xs < ys$:

1. The list xs is a *proper prefix* of ys:

   ```
   [1; 2; 3] < [1; 2; 3; 4];;
   val it : bool = true
   ```

   ```
   ['1'; '2'; '3'] < ['1'; '2'; '3'; '4'];;
   val it : bool = true
   ```

   The examples illustrate comparisons of integer lists and character lists. Furthermore, the empty list is smaller than any non-empty list:

   ```
   [] < [1; 2; 3];;
   val it : bool = true
   ```

   ```
   [] < [[]; [(true,2)]];;
   val it : bool = true
   ```

2. The lists agree on the first k elements and $x_{k+1} < y_{k+1}$. For example:

   ```
   [1; 2; 3; 0; 9; 10] < [1; 2; 3; 4];;
   val it : bool = true
   ```

   ```
   ["research"; "articles"] < ["research"; "books"];;
   val it : bool = true
   ```

   because 0 < 4 and "articles" < "books".

The other comparison relations can be defined in terms of = and < as usual. For example:

```
[1; 1; 6; 10] >= [1; 2];;
val it : bool = false
```

The compare function is defined for lists, provided it is defined for the element type. For example:

```
compare [1; 1; 6; 10] [1; 2];;
val it : int = -1
```

```
compare [1;2] [1; 1; 6; 10];;
val it : int = 1
```

4.2 Construction and decomposition of lists

The cons *operator*

The infix operator : : (called "cons") builds a list from its head and its tail as shown in Figures 4.2 and 4.3 so it adds an element at the front of a list:

```
let x = 2::[3;4;5];;
val x : int list = [2; 3; 4; 5]

let y = ""::[];;
val y : string list = [""]
```

Figure 4.2 Graph for the list $x::xs$

The operator *associates* to the *right*, so $x_0::x_1::xs$ means $x_0::(x_1::xs)$ where x_0 and x_1 have the same type and xs is a list with elements of that same type (cf. Figure 4.3) so we get, for example:

```
let z = 2::3::[4;5];;
val z : int list = [2; 3; 4; 5]
```

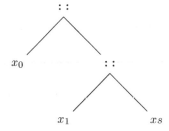

Figure 4.3 Graph for the list $x_0::(x_1::xs)$

List patterns

While the cons operator can be used to construct a list from a (head) element and a (tail) list, it is also used in *list patterns*. List patterns and pattern matching for lists are used in the subsequent sections to declare functions on lists by using the bindings of identifiers in a list pattern obtained by matching a list to the pattern.

There is the list pattern [ ] for the empty list while patterns for non-empty lists are constructed using the cons operator, that is, x : : xs matches a non-empty list.

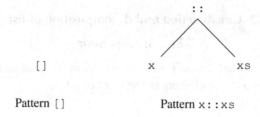

Pattern []   Pattern x::xs

Figure 4.4 Graphs for list patterns

The patterns [] and x::xs denote the graphs in Figure 4.4. The pattern [] matches the empty list only, while the pattern x::xs matches any non-empty list $[x_0; x_1; \ldots; x_{n-1}]$. The latter matching gives the bindings $x \mapsto x_0$ and $xs \mapsto [x_1; \ldots; x_{n-1}]$ of the identifiers x and xs, as the list $[x_0; x_1; \ldots; x_{n-1}]$ denotes the graph in Figure 4.5.

x_0 $[x_1; \ldots; x_{n-1}]$

Figure 4.5 Graph for the list $[x_0; x_1; \ldots; x_{n-1}]$

For example, the execution of the declarations:

```
let x::xs = [1;2;3];;
val xs : int list = [2; 3]
val x : int = 1
```

will simultaneously bind x to the value 1 and xs to the value [2;3] by matching the value [1;2;3] to the pattern x::xs.

A list pattern for a list with a fixed number of elements, for example, three, may be written as x0::x1::x2::[] or in the shorter form [x0;x1;x2]. This pattern will match any list with precisely three elements $[x_0; x_1; x_2]$, and the matching binds x0 to x_0, x1 to x_1, and x2 to x_2. For example:

```
let [x0;x1;x2] = [(1,true); (2,false); (3, false)];;
  let [x0;x1;x2] = [(1,true); (2,false); (3, false)];;
  ----^^^^^^^^^^^
stdin(1,5): warning FS0025: Incomplete pattern matches on this
expression. For example, the value '[_;_;_;_]' may indicate a
case not covered by the pattern(s).
val x2 : int * bool = (3, false)
val x1 : int * bool = (2, false)
val x0 : int * bool = (1, true)
```

This generalizes to any fixed number of elements. (The F# compiler issues a warning because list patterns with a fixed number of elements are in general not recommended, but the bindings are, nevertheless, made.)

List patterns may have more structure than illustrated above. For example, we can construct list patterns that match lists with two or more elements (e.g., x0::x1::xs), and list patterns matching only non-empty lists of pairs (e.g., (y1,y2)::ys), and so on. For example:

```
let x0::x1::xs = [1.1; 2.2; 3.3; 4.4; 5.5];;
val xs : float list = [3.3; 4.4; 5.5]
val x1 : float = 2.2
val x0 : float = 1.1

let (y1, y2)::ys = [(1,[1]); (2, [2]); (3, [3]); (4,[4])];;
val ys : (int * int list) list =
        [(2, [2]); (3, [3]); (4, [4])]
val y2 : int list = [1]
val y1 : int = 1
```

We shall see examples of more involved patterns in this chapter and throughout the book.

Note the different roles of the operator symbol :: in patterns and expressions. It denotes decomposing a list into smaller parts when used in a pattern like x0::x1::xs, and it denotes building a list from smaller parts in an expression like 0::[1; 2].

Simple list expressions

In F# there are special constructs that can generate lists. In this section we will just introduce the two simple forms of expressions called *range expressions*:

$$[b \ .. \ e] \qquad\qquad [b \ .. \ s \ .. \ e]$$

where b, e and s are expressions having number types.

The range expression $[b \ .. \ e]$, where $e \geq b$, generates the list of consecutive elements:

$$\lfloor b; \ b+1; \ b+2; \ldots; \ b+n \rfloor$$

where n is chosen such that $b + n \leq e < b + n + 1$. The range expression generates the empty list when $e < b$.

For example, the list of integers from -3 to 5 is generated by:

```
[ -3 .. 5 ];;
val it : int list = [-3; -2; -1; 0; 1; 2; 3; 4; 5]
```

and a list of floats is, for example, generated by:

```
[2.4 .. 3.0 ** 1.7];;
val it : float list = [2.4; 3.4; 4.4; 5.4; 6.4]
```

Note that 3.0 ** 1.7 = 6.47300784.

The expression s in the range expression $[b \mathrel{..} s \mathrel{..} e]$ is called the step. It can be positive or negative, but not zero:

$$[b \mathrel{..} s \mathrel{..} e] = [b; b+s; b+2s; \ldots; b+ns]$$
$$\text{where} \quad \begin{cases} b+ns \le e < b + (n+1)s & \text{if } s \text{ is positive} \\ b+ns \ge e > b + (n+1)s & \text{if } s \text{ is negative} \end{cases}$$

The generated list will be either ascending or descending depending on the sign of s. For example, the descending list of integers from 6 to 2 is generated by:

```
[6 .. -1 .. 2];;
val it : int list = [6; 5; 4; 3; 2]
```

and the float-based representation of the list consisting of $0, \pi/2, \pi, \frac{3}{2}\pi, 2\pi$ is generated by:

```
[0.0 .. System.Math.PI/2.0 .. 2.0*System.Math.PI];;
val it : float list =
    [0.0; 1.570796327; 3.141592654; 4.71238898; 6.283185307]
```

An exception is raised if the step is 0:

```
> [0 .. 0 .. 0];;
System.ArgumentException: The step of a range cannot be zero.
Parameter name: step
  ......
Stopped due to error
```

4.3 Typical recursions over lists

In this section we shall consider a collection of archetypical recursive function declarations on lists.

Function declarations with two clauses

Let us consider the function `sum1` that computes the sum of a list of integers:

$$\texttt{sum1}\ [x_0; x_1; \ldots; x_{n-1}] = \sum_{i=0}^{n-1} x_i = x_0 + x_1 + \cdots + x_{n-1} = x_0 + \sum_{i=1}^{n-1} x_i$$

We get the recursion formula:

$$\texttt{sum1}\ [x_0; x_1; \ldots; x_{n-1}] = x_0 + \texttt{sum1}\ [x_1; \ldots; x_{n-1}]$$

We define the value of the "empty" sum, that is, `sum1 []`, to be 0 and we arrive at a recursive function declaration with two clauses:

```
let rec sum1 = function
    | []    -> 0
    | x::xs -> x + sum1 xs;;
val sum1 : int list -> int
```

In evaluating a function value for `suml` xs, F# scans the clauses and selects the first clause where the argument matches the pattern. Hence, the evaluation of `suml [1;2]` proceeds as follows:

```
    suml [1;2]
~→  1 + suml [2]          (x::xs matches [1;2] with x ↦ 1 and xs ↦ [2])
~→  1 + (2 + suml [])     (x::xs matches [2] with x ↦ 2 and xs ↦ [])
~→  1 + (2 + 0)           (the pattern [] matches the value [])
~→  1 + 2
~→  3
```

This example shows that patterns are convenient in order to split up a function declaration into clauses covering different forms of the argument. In this example, one clause of the declaration gives the function value for the empty list, and the other clause reduces the computation of the function value for a non-empty list `suml`$(x::xs)$ to a simple operation (addition) on the head x and the value of `suml` on the tail xs (i.e., `suml` xs), where the length of the argument list has been reduced by one.

It is easy to see that an evaluation for `suml` $[x_0; \ldots; x_{n-1}]$ will terminate, as it contains precisely $n + 1$ recursive calls of `suml`.

The above declaration is an example of a typical recursion schema for the declaration of functions on lists.

Function declarations with several clauses

One can have function declarations with any number (≥ 1) of clauses. Consider, for example, the alternate sum of an integer list:

$$\texttt{altsum } [x_0; x_1; \ldots; x_{n-1}] = x_0 - x_1 + x_2 - \cdots + (-1)^{n-1} x_{n-1}$$

In declaring this function we consider three different forms of the argument:

1. empty list: `altsum []` $= 0$
2. list with one element: `altsum` $[x_0] = x_0$
3. list with two or more elements:

$$\texttt{altsum } [x_0; x_1; x_2; \ldots; x_{n-1}] = x_0 - x_1 + \texttt{altsum } [x_2; \ldots; x_{n-1}]$$

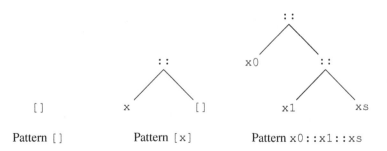

Pattern `[]`　　　Pattern `[x]`　　　Pattern `x0::x1::xs`

Figure 4.6 List patterns for `altsum` declaration

These cases are covered by the patterns in Figure 4.6. Thus, the function can be declared by:

```
let rec altsum = function
    | []          -> 0
    | [x]         -> x
    | x0::x1::xs -> x0 - x1 + altsum xs;;
val altsum : int list -> int

altsum [2; -1; 3];;
val it : int = 6
```

It is left as an exercise to give a declaration for altsum containing only two clauses.

Layered patterns

We want to define a function succPairs such that:

$$
\begin{aligned}
\text{succPairs } [] &= [] \\
\text{succPairs } [x] &= [] \\
\text{succPairs } [x_0; x_1; \ldots; x_{n-1}] &= [(x_0, x_1); (x_1, x_2); \ldots; (x_{n-2}, x_{n-1})]
\end{aligned}
$$

Using the pattern x0::x1::xs as in the above example we get the declaration

```
let rec succPairs = function
    | x0 :: x1 :: xs -> (x0,x1) :: succPairs(x1::xs)
    | _              -> [];;
val succPairs : 'a list -> ('a * 'a) list
```

This works OK, but we may get a smarter declaration avoiding the cons expression x1::xs in the recursive call in the following way:

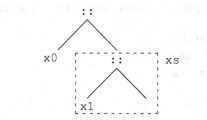

Figure 4.7 A pattern x0::(x1::_ as xs) containing a layered sub-pattern x1::_ as xs

```
let rec succPairs = function
    | x0::(x1::_ as xs) -> (x0,x1) :: succPairs xs
    | _                 -> [];;
val succPairs : 'a list -> ('a * 'a) list

succPairs [1;2;3];;
val it : (int * int) list = [(1, 2); (2, 3)]
```

The pattern x1::_ as xs is an example of a *layered pattern*. It is part of the pattern shown in Figure 4.7. A layered pattern has the general form:

$$pat \text{ as } id$$

with pattern *pat* and identifier *id*. A value *val* matches this pattern exactly when the value matches the pattern *pat*. The matching binds identifiers in the pattern *pat* as usual with the addition that the identifier *id* is bound to *val*. Matching the list $[x_0; x_1; \ldots]$ with the pattern x0::(x1::_ as xs) will hence give the following bindings:

$$
\begin{array}{rcl}
\text{x0} & \mapsto & x_0 \\
\text{x1} & \mapsto & x_1 \\
\text{xs} & \mapsto & [x_1; \ldots]
\end{array}
$$

which is exactly what is needed in this case.

Pattern matching on result of recursive call

The following example illustrates the use of pattern matching to split the result of a recursive call into components. The function sumProd computes the pair consisting of the sum and the product of the elements in a list of integers, that is:

sumProd $[x_0; x_1; \ldots; x_{n-1}]$
$$= \quad (x_0 + x_1 + \ldots + x_{n-1} \ , \ x_0 \star x_1 \star \ldots \star x_{n-1})$$
sumProd [] $= \quad (0,1)$

The declaration is based on the recursion formula:

$$\text{sumProd } [x_0; x_1; \ldots; x_{n-1}] = (x_0 + \text{rSum}, x_0 \star \text{rProd})$$

where

$$(\text{rSum}, \text{rProd}) = \text{sumProd } [x_1; \ldots; x_{n-1}]$$

This gives the declaration:

```
let rec sumProd = function
    | []     -> (0,1)
    | x::rest ->
          let (rSum,rProd) = sumProd rest
          (x+rSum,x*rProd);;
val sumProd : int list -> int * int

sumProd [2;5];;
val it : int * int = (7, 10)
```

Another example is the unzip function that maps a list of pairs to a pair of lists:

$$\text{unzip}([(x_0, y_0) ; (x_1, y_1) ; \ldots ; (x_{n-1}, y_{n-1})])$$
$$= ([x_0; x_1; \ldots; x_{n-1}], [y_0; y_1; \ldots; y_{n-1}])$$

The declaration of `unzip` looks as follows:

```
let rec unzip = function
    | []               -> ([],[])
    | (x,y)::rest ->
        let (xs,ys) = unzip rest
        (x::xs,y::ys);;
val unzip : ('a * 'b) list -> 'a list * 'b list

unzip [(1,"a");(2,"b")];;
val it : int list * string list = ([1; 2], ["a"; "b"])
```

The `unzip` function is found as `List.unzip` is the F# library.

Pattern matching on pairs of lists

We want to declare a function `mix` that mixes the elements of two lists with the same length:

$$\text{mix} \; ([x_0; \; x_1; \; \ldots; \; x_{n-1}], \; [y_0; \; y_1; \; \ldots; \; y_{n-1}])$$
$$= [x_0; \; y_0; \; x_1; \; y_1; \; \ldots; \; x_{n-1}; \; y_{n-1}]$$

It is declared using pattern matching on the pair of lists:

```
let rec mix = function
    | (x::xs,y::ys) -> x::y::(mix (xs,ys))
    | ([],[])       -> []
    | _             -> failwith "mix: parameter error";;
val mix : 'a list * 'a list -> 'a list

mix ([1;2;3],[4;5;6]);;
val it : int list = [1; 4; 2; 5; 3; 6]
```

The corresponding higher-order function is defined using a `match` expression:

```
let rec mix xlst ylst =
    match (xlst,ylst) with
    | (x::xs,y::ys) -> x::y::(mix xs ys)
    | ([],[])       -> []
    | _             -> failwith "mix: parameter error";;
val mix : 'a list -> 'a list -> 'a list

mix [1;2;3] [4;5;6];;
val it : int list = [1; 4; 2; 5; 3; 6]
```

4.4 Polymorphism

In this section we will study some general kinds of polymorphism, appearing frequently in connection with lists. We will do that on the basis of three useful list functions that all can be declared using the same structure of recursion as shown in Section 4.3.

List membership

The member function for lists determines whether a value x is equal to one of the elements in a list $[y_0; y_1; \ldots; y_{n-1}]$, that is:

$$\begin{aligned} &\text{isMember } x \ [y_0; y_1; \ldots; y_{n-1}] \\ = \ &(x = y_0) \text{ or } (x = y_1) \text{ or } \cdots \text{ or } (x = y_{n-1}) \\ = \ &(x = y_0) \text{ or } (\text{isMember } x \ [y_1; \ldots; y_{n-1}]) \end{aligned}$$

Since no x can be a member of the empty list, we arrive at the declaration:

```
let rec isMember x = function
    | y::ys -> x=y || (isMember x ys)
    | []    -> false;;
val isMember : 'a -> 'a list -> bool when 'a : equality
```

The function `isMember` can be useful in certain cases, but it is not included in the F# library.

The annotation `'a : equality` indicates that `'a` is an *equality type variable*; see Section 2.10. The equality type is inferred from the expression x=y. It implies that the function `isMember` will only allow an argument x where the equality operator = is defined for values of the type of x. A type such as `int * (bool * string) list * int list` is an equality type, and the function can be applied to elements of this type.

Append and reverse. Two built-in functions

The infix operator @ (called 'append') joins two lists of the same type:

$$[x_0; x_1; \ldots; x_{m-1}] \text{ @ } [y_0; y_1; \ldots; y_{n-1}] = [x_0; x_1; \ldots; x_{m-1}; y_0; y_1; \ldots; y_{n-1}]$$

and the function `List.rev` (called "reverse") reverses a list:

$$\text{List.rev } [x_0; x_1; \ldots; x_{n-1}] = [x_{n-1}; \ldots; x_1; x_0]$$

These functions are predefined in F#, but their declarations reveal important issues and are therefore discussed here. The operator @ is actually the infix operator corresponding to the library function `List.append`.

The declaration of the (infix) function @ is based on the recursion formula:

$$\begin{aligned} [] \text{ @ } ys &= ys \\ [x_0; x_1; \ldots; x_{m-1}] \text{ @ } ys &= x_0 :: ([x_1; \ldots; x_{m-1}] \text{ @ } ys) \end{aligned}$$

This leads to the declaration:

```
let rec (@) xs ys =
    match xs with
    | []      -> ys
    | x::xs' -> x::(xs' @ ys);;
val (@) : 'a list -> 'a list -> 'a list
```

The evaluation of append decomposes the left-hand list into its elements, that are afterwards 'cons'ed' onto the right-hand list:

$$
\begin{aligned}
&\texttt{[1;2]@[3;4]}\\
\rightsquigarrow\ &\texttt{1::([2]@[3;4])}\\
\rightsquigarrow\ &\texttt{1::(2::([]@[3;4]))}\\
\rightsquigarrow\ &\texttt{1::(2::[3;4])}\\
\rightsquigarrow\ &\texttt{1::[2;3;4]}\\
\rightsquigarrow\ &\texttt{[1;2;3;4]}
\end{aligned}
$$

The evaluation of xs @ ys comprises $m + 1$ pattern matches plus m cons'es where m is the length of xs.

The notion of polymorphism is very convenient for the programmer because one need not write a special function for appending, for example, integer lists and another function for appending lists of integer lists, as the polymorphic append function is capable of both:

```
[1;2] @ [3;4];;
val it : int list = [1; 2; 3; 4]

[[1];[2;3]] @ [[4]];;
val it : int list list = [[1]; [2; 3]; [4]]
```

The operators :: and @ have the same precedence (5) and both associate to the *right*. A mixture of these operators also associates to the right, so [1]@2::[3], for example, is interpreted as [1]@(2::[3]), while 1::[2]@[3] is interpreted as 1::([2]@[3]):

```
[1] @ 2 :: [3];;
val it : int list = [1; 2; 3]

1 :: [2] @ [3];;
val it : int list = [1; 2; 3]
```

For the reverse function rev, where

$$\texttt{rev } [x_0; x_1; \ldots; x_{n-1}] = [x_{n-1}; \ldots; x_1; x_0]$$

we have the recursion formula:

$$\texttt{rev } [x_0; x_1; \ldots; x_{n-1}] = (\texttt{rev } [x_1; \ldots; x_{n-1}]) \text{ @ } [x_0]$$

because

$$\texttt{rev } [x_1; \ldots; x_{n-1}] = [x_{n-1}; \ldots; x_1]$$

This leads immediately to a naive declaration of a reverse function:

```
let rec naiveRev xls  =
    match xls with
    | []    -> []
    | x::xs -> naiveRev xs @ [x];;
val naiveRev : 'a list -> 'a list
```

This declaration corresponds directly to the recursion formula for `rev`: the tail list `xs` is reversed and the head element `x` is inserted at the end of the resulting list — but it may be considered naive as it gives a very inefficient evaluation of the reversed list:

```
       naiveRev[1;2;3]
   ⤳   naiveRev[2;3] @ [1]
   ⤳   (naiveRev[3] @ [2]) @ [1]
   ⤳   ((naiveRev[] @ [3]) @ [2]) @ [1]
   ⤳   (([] @ [3]) @ [2]) @ [1]
   ⤳   ([3] @ [2]) @ [1]
   ⤳   (3::([] @ [2])) @ [1]
   ⤳   (3::[2]) @ [1]
   ⤳   [3,2] @ [1]
   ⤳   3::([2] @ [1])
   ⤳   3 :: (2 :: ([] @ [1]))
   ⤳   3 :: (2 :: [1])
   ⤳   3 :: [2;1]
   ⤳   [3;2;1]
```

We will make a much more efficient declaration of the reverse function in a later chapter (Page 208). The library function `List.rev` is, of course, implemented using an efficient declaration.

4.5 The value restrictions on polymorphic expressions

The type system and type inference of F# is very general and flexible. It has, however, been necessary to make a *restriction* on the *use of polymorphic expressions* in order to ensure type correctness in all situations.

The formulation of this restriction is based on the concept of *value expressions*. A value expression is an expression that is not reduced further by an evaluation, that is, it has already the same form as its value. The following expressions are hence value expressions:

```
[]        Some []        (5,[])        (fun x -> [x])
```

while

```
List.rev []        [] @ []
```

do not qualify as a value expression as they can be further evaluated. Note that a function expression (a closure) is considered a value expression because it is only evaluated further when applied to an argument.

The restriction applies to the expression *exp* in declarations

```
let id = exp
```

and states the following

> At top level, polymorphic expressions are allowed only if they are value expressions. Polymorphic expressions can be used freely for intermediate results.

Hence F# allows *values* of polymorphic types, such as the empty list [ ], the pair (5, [[ ]]) or the function (fun x -> [x]):

```
let z = [];;
val z : 'a list

(5,[[]]);;
val it : int * 'a list list = (5, [[]]

let p = (fun x -> [x]);;
val p : 'a -> 'a list
```

On the other hand, the following is refused at top level:

```
List.rev [];;
^^^^^^^^^^

stdin(86,1): error FS0030: Value restriction.
The value 'it' has been inferred to have generic type
```

The restriction on polymorphic expressions may be paraphrased as follows:

- All monomorphic expressions are OK, even non-value expressions,
- all value expressions are OK, even polymorphic ones, and
- at top-level, polymorphic non-value expressions are forbidden,

where the type of a *monomorphic expression* does not contain type variables, that is, it is a *monomorphic type*.

The rationale for these restrictions will only become clear much later when imperative features of F# are introduced in Chapter 8. In the meantime, we just have to accept the restrictions, and they will really not do us much harm.

Remark: A list expression $a_0 :: a_1 :: \cdots :: a_k :: [a_{k+1}, \ldots, a_{n-1}]$ containing values $a_0, a_2, \ldots, a_{n-1}$ is considered a value expression with the value $[a_0, a_1, \ldots, a_{n-1}]$.

4.6 Examples. A model-based approach

In this section we will introduce a model-based approach to functional programming by means of two examples. The goal is to get a program directly reflecting the problem formulation. An important step in achieving this goal is to identify names denoting key concepts in the problem and to associate F# types with these names. We shall return to these two examples in the next chapter when we have a richer set of collection types with associated library functions.

Example: Cash register

Consider an electronic cash register that contains a data register associating the name of the article and its price to each valid article code. A purchase comprises a sequence of items, where each item describes the purchase of one or several pieces of a specific article.

The task is to construct a program that makes a bill of a purchase. For each item the bill must contain the name of the article, the number of pieces, and the total price, and the bill must also contain the grand total of the entire purchase.

Article code and article name are central concepts that are named and associated with a type:

```
type ArticleCode = string;;
type ArticleName = string;;
```

where the choice of the `string` type for `ArticleCode` is somewhat arbitrary. An alternative choice could be the `int` type.

The register associates article name and article price with each article code, and we model a register by a list of pairs. Each pair has the form:

$$(ac, (aname, aprice))$$

where ac is an article code, $aname$ is an article name, and $aprice$ is an article price. We choose (non-negative) integers to represent prices (in the smallest currency unit):

```
type Price       = int;;            // pr  where  pr >= 0
```

and we get the following type for a register:

```
type Register    = (ArticleCode * (ArticleName*Price)) list;;
```

The following declaration names a register:

```
let reg = [("a1",("cheese",25));
           ("a2",("herring",4));
           ("a3",("soft drink",5)) ];;
```

A purchase comprises a list of items, where each item comprises a pair:

$$(np, ac)$$

describing a number of pieces np (that is a non-negative integer) purchased of an article with code ac:

```
type NoPieces    = int;;            // np  where np >= 0
type Item        = NoPieces * ArticleCode;;
type Purchase    = Item list;;
```

The following declaration names a purchase:

```
let pur = [(3,"a2"); (1,"a1")];;
```

A bill comprises an information list *infos* for the individual items and the grand total *sum*, and this composite structure is modelled by a pair:

$$(infos, sum)$$

where each element in the list *infos* is a triple

$$(np, aname, tprice)$$

of the number of pieces *np*, the name *aname*, and the total price *tprice* of a purchased article:

```
type Info        = NoPieces * ArticleName * Price;;
type Infoseq     = Info list;;
type Bill        = Infoseq * Price;;
```

The following value is an example of a bill:

```
([(3,"herring",12);  (1,"cheese",25)],37)
```

The function makeBill computes a bill given a purchase and a register and it has the type:

```
makeBill: Register -> Purchase -> Bill
```

In this example, it is convenient to declare a auxiliary function:

```
findArticle: ArticleCode -> Register -> ArticleName * Price
```

to find the article name and price in the register for a given article code. This will make the declaration for the function makeBill easier to comprehend. An exception is raised when no article with the given code occurs in the register:

```
let rec findArticle ac = function
    | (ac',adesc)::_ when ac=ac' -> adesc
    | _::reg                     -> findArticle ac reg
    | _                          ->
            failwith(ac + " is an unknown article code");;
val findArticle : string -> (string * 'a) list -> 'a
```

Then the bill is made by the function:

```
let rec makeBill reg = function
  | []                -> ([],0)
  | (np,ac)::pur -> let (aname,aprice) = findArticle ac reg
                    let tprice         = np*aprice
                    let (billtl,sumtl) = makeBill reg pur
                    ((np,aname,tprice)::billtl,tprice+sumtl);;
val makeBill :
  (string * ('a * int)) list -> (int * string) list
                -> (int * 'a * int) list * int

makeBill reg pur;;
val it : (int * string * int) list * int =
  ([(3, "herring", 12); (1, "cheese", 25)], 37)
```

The declaration of makeBill uses the pattern introduced in Section 4.3 to decompose the value of the recursive call.

Note that the F# system infers a more general type for the makeBill function than the type given in our model. This is, however, no problem as the specified type is an instance of the inferred type – makeBill has the specified type (among others).

Example: Map colouring

We shall now consider the problem of colouring a map in a way so that neighbouring countries get different colours. We will provide a model using named types, similar to what we did in the previous example. But the map colouring problem is more complex than the cash register example, and we use it to illustrate *functional decomposition* by devising a collection of simple well-understood functions that can be composed to solve the problem.

This problem is a famous mathematical problem and it has been proved that any (reasonable) map can be coloured by using at most four different colours. We will not aim for an "optimal" solution. Neither will we consider the trivial solution where each country always gets its own separate colour. We will assume that each country is connected. This is an oversimplification as Alaska and Kaliningrad, for example, are not connected to other regions of the United States and Russia, respectively.

A *country* is represented by its name, that is a string, and a *map* is represented by a *neighbour relation*, that is represented by a list of pairs of countries with a common border:

```
type Country = string;;
type Map     = (Country * Country) list;;
```

Consider the map in Figure 4.8 with four countries "a", "b", "c", and "d", where the country "a" has the neighbouring countries "b" and "d", the country "b" has the neighbouring country "a", and so on. The F# value for this map is given by the declaration of exMap.

```
let exMap = [("a","b"); ("c","d"); ("d","a")];;
```

Figure 4.8 Colouring problem with 4 countries

A *colour* on a map is represented by the set of countries having this colour, and a *colouring* is described by a list of mutually disjoint colours:

```
type Colour    = Country list;;
type Colouring = Colour list;;
```

The countries of the map in Figure 4.8 may hence be coloured by the colouring:

```
[["a";"c"]; ["b"; "d"]]
```

This colouring has two colours ["a";"c"] and ["b"; "d"], where the countries "a" and "c" get one colour, while the countries "b" and "d" get another colour.

An overview of the model is shown in Figure 4.9 together with sample values. This figure also contains meta symbols used for the various types, as this helps in achieving a consistent naming convention throughout the program.

Meta symbol: Type	Definition	Sample value
c: Country	string	"a"
m: Map	(Country*Country) list	[("a","b"); ("c","d");("d","a")]
col: Colour	Country list	["a";"c"]
cols: Colouring	Colour list	[["a";"c"];["b";"d"]]

Figure 4.9 A Data model for map colouring problem

Our task is to declare a function:

```
colMap: Map -> Colouring
```

that can generate a colouring of a given map. We will express this function as a composition of simple functions, each with a well-understood meaning. These simple functions arise from the *algorithmic idea* behind the solutions to the problem. The idea we will pursue here is the following: We start with the empty colouring, that is, the empty list containing no colours. Then we will gradually extend the actual colouring by adding one country at a time.

	country	old colouring	new colouring
1.	"a"	[]	[["a"]]
2.	"b"	[["a"]]	[["a"];["b"]]
3.	"c"	[["a"];["b"]]	[["a";"c"];["b"]]
4.	"d"	[["a";"c"];["b"]]	[["a";"c"];["b";"d"]]

Figure 4.10 Algorithmic idea

We illustrate this algorithmic idea on the map in Figure 4.8, with the four countries: "a", "b", "c" and "d". The four main algorithmic steps (one for each country) are shown in Figure 4.10. We give a brief comment to each step:

1. The colouring containing no colours is the empty list.
2. The colour ["a"] cannot be *extended* by "b" because the countries "a" and "b" *are neighbours*. Hence the colouring should be extended by a new colour ["b"].
3. The colour ["a"] can be extended by "c" because "a" and "c" are not neighbours.
4. The colour ["a","c"] can not be extended by "d" while the colour ["b"] can be extended by "d".

The task is now to make a program where the main concepts of this algorithmic idea are directly represented. The concepts emphasized in the above discussion are:

- Test whether a colour can be extended by a country for a given map.
- Test whether two countries are neighbours in a given map.
- Extend a colouring by a country for a given map.

The function specification of each of the main concepts documents the algorithmic idea. These specifications are shown in Figure 4.11. We have added the specification of a function countries for extracting the list of countries occurring in a given map and the specification of a function colCntrs which gives the colouring for given country list and map.

Type
Meaning
`areNb`: `Map -> Country -> Country -> bool`
Decides whether two countries are neighbours
`canBeExtBy`: `Map -> Colour -> Country -> bool`
Decides whether a colour can be extended by a country
`extColouring`: `Map -> Colouring -> Country -> Colouring`
Extends a colouring by an extra country
`countries`: `Map -> Country list`
Computes a list of countries in a map
`colCntrs`: `Map -> Country list -> Colouring`
Builds a colouring for a list of countries

Figure 4.11 Functional break-down for map colouring problem

We now give a declaration for each of the functions specified in Figure 4.11.

1. First we declare a predicate (i.e., a truth-valued function) `areNb` to determine for a given map whether two countries are neighbours:

```
let areNb m c1 c2 =
    isMember (c1,c2) m || isMember (c2,c1) m;;
```

This declaration makes use of the `isMember`-function declared in Section 4.4.

2. Next we declare a predicate to determine for a given map whether a colour can be extended by a country:

```
let rec canBeExtBy m col c =
    match  col with
    | []        -> true
    | c'::col' -> not(areNb m c' c) && canBeExtBy m col' c;;

canBeExtBy exMap ["c"] "a";;
val it : bool = true

canBeExtBy exMap ["a"; "c"] "b";;
val it : bool = false
```

3. Our solution strategy is to insert the countries of a map one after the other into a colouring, starting with the empty one. To this end we declare a function `extColouring` that for a given map extends a partial colouring by a country:

```
let rec extColouring m cols c =
    match cols with
    | []          -> [[c]]
    | col::cols' -> if canBeExtBy m col c
                        then (c::col)::cols'
                        else col::extColouring m cols' c;;


extColouring exMap [] "a";;
val it : string list list = [["a"]]
```

```
extColouring exMap [["c"]] "a";;
val it : string list list = [["a"; "c"]]

extColouring exMap [["b"]] "a";;
val it : string list list = [["b"]; ["a"]]
```

Note that the first of the three examples exercises the base case of the declaration, the second example the `then`-branch, and the last example the `else`-branch (the recursion and the base case).

4. In order to complete our task, we declare a function to extract a list of countries without repeated elements from a map and a function to colour a list of countries given a map:

```
let addElem x ys = if isMember x ys then ys else x::ys;;

let rec countries = function
    | []               -> []
    | (c1,c2)::m -> addElem c1 (addElem c2 (countries m));;

let rec colCntrs m = function
    | []        -> []
    | c::cs -> extColouring m (colCntrs m cs) c;;
```

The function giving a colouring for a given map is declared by combination of the functions `colCntrs` and `countries`.

```
let colMap m = colCntrs m (countries m);;

colMap exMap;;
val it : string list list = [["c"; "a"]; ["b"; "d"]]
```

Comments

In these two examples we have just used types introduced previously in this book, and some comments could be made concerning the adequacy of the solutions. For example, modelling a data register by a list of pairs does not capture that each article has a unique description in the register, and modelling a colour by a list of countries does not capture the property that the sequence in which countries occur in the list is irrelevant. The same applies to the property that repeated occurrences of a country in a colour are irrelevant.

In Chapter 5 we shall introduce maps and sets and we shall give more suitable models and solutions for the two examples above.

Summary

In this chapter we have introduced the notions of lists and list types, and the notion of list patterns. A selection of typical recursive functions on lists were presented, and the notions of polymorphic types and values were studied. Furthermore, we have introduced a model-based approach to functional programming, where important concepts are named and types are associated with the names.

Exercises

4.1 Declare function `upto`: `int -> int list` such that `upto` $n = [1; 2; \ldots; n]$.

4.2 Declare function `downto1`: `int -> int list` such that the value of `downto1` n is the list $[n; n-1; \ldots; 1]$.

4.3 Declare function `evenN`: `int -> int list` such that `evenN` n generates the list of the first n non-negative even numbers.

4.4 Give a declaration for `altsum` (see Page 76) containing just two clauses.

4.5 Declare an F# function `rmodd` removing the odd-numbered elements from a list:

$$\text{rmodd } [x_0; x_1; x_2; x_3; \ldots] = [x_0; x_2; \ldots]$$

4.6 Declare an F# function to remove even numbers occurring in an integer list.

4.7 Declare an F# function `multiplicity` x xs to find the number of times the value x occurs in the list xs.

4.8 Declare an F# function `split` such that:

$$\text{split } [x_0; x_1; x_2; x_3; \ldots; x_{n-1}] = ([x_0; x_2; \ldots], [x_1; x_3; \ldots])$$

4.9 Declare an F# function `zip` such that:

$$\text{zip}([x_0; x_1; \ldots; x_{n-1}], [y_0; y_1; \ldots; y_{n-1}])$$
$$= [(x_0, y_0); (x_1, y_1); \ldots; (x_{n-1}, y_{n-1})]$$

The function should raise an exception if the two lists are not of equal length.

4.10 Declare an F# function `prefix`: `'a list -> 'a list -> bool` when a : equality. The value of the expression `prefix` $[x_0; x_1; \ldots; x_m]$ $[y_0; y_1; \ldots; y_n]$ is `true` if $m \leq n$ and $x_i = y_i$ for $0 \leq i \leq m$, and `false` otherwise.

4.11 A list of integers $[x_0; x_1; \ldots; x_{n-1}]$ is *weakly ascending* if the elements satisfy:

$$x_0 \leq x_1 \leq x_2 \leq \ldots \leq x_{n-2} \leq x_{n-1}$$

or if the list is empty. The problem is now to declare functions on weakly ascending lists.

1. Declare an F# function `count`: `int list * int -> int`, where `count`(xs, x) is the number of occurrences of the integer x in the weakly ascending list xs.

2. Declare an F# function `insert`: `int list * int -> int list`, where the value of `insert`(xs, x) is a weakly ascending list obtained by inserting the number x into the weakly ascending list xs.

3. Declare an F# function `intersect`: `int list * int list -> int list`, where the value of `intersect`(xs, xs') is a weakly ascending list containing the common elements of the weakly ascending lists xs and xs'. For instance:

$$\text{intersect}([1;1;1;2;2], [1;1;2;4]) = [1;1;2]$$

4. Declare an F# function `plus`: `int list * int list -> int list`, where the value of `plus`(xs, xs') is a weakly ascending list, that is the union of the weakly ascending lists xs and xs'. For instance:

$$\text{plus}([1;1;2], [1;2;4]) = [1;1;1;2;2;4]$$

5. Declare an F# function `minus`: `int list * int list -> int list`, where the value of `minus`(xs, xs') is a weakly ascending list obtained from the weakly ascending list xs by removing those elements, that are also found in the weakly ascending list xs'. For instance:

$$\text{minus}([1;1;1;2;2], [1;1;2;3]) = [1;2]$$
$$\text{minus}([1;1;2;3], [1;1;1;2;2]) = [3]$$

4.12 Declare a function sum(p, xs) where p is a predicate of type int -> bool and xs is a list of integers. The value of sum(p, xs) is the sum of the elements in xs satisfying the predicate p. Test the function on different predicates (e.g., $p(x) = x > 0$).

4.13 Naive sort function:

1. Declare an F# function finding the smallest element in a non-empty integer list.

2. Declare an F# function delete: int * int list -> int list, where the value of delete(a, xs) is the list obtained by deleting one occurrence of a in xs (if there is one).

3. Declare an F# function that sorts an integer list so that the elements are placed in weakly ascending order.

Note that there is a much more efficient sort function List.sort in the library.

4.14 Declare a function of type int list -> int option for finding the smallest element in an integer list.

4.15 Declare an F# function revrev working on a list of lists, that maps a list to the reversed list of the reversed elements, for example:

```
revrev [[1;2];[3;4;5]] = [[5;4;3];[2;1]]
```

4.16 Consider the declarations:

```
let rec f = function
    | (x, [])    -> []
    | (x, y::ys) -> (x+y)::f(x-1, ys);;

let rec g = function
    | []         -> []
    | (x,y)::s -> (x,y)::(y,x)::g s;;

let rec h = function
    | []      -> []
    | x::xs -> x::(h xs)@[x];;
```

Find the types for f, g and h and explain the value of the expressions:

1. f$(x, [y_0, y_1, \ldots, y_{n-1}]), n \geq 0$
2. g$[(x_0, y_0), (x_1, y_1), \ldots, (x_{n-1}, y_{n-1})], n \geq 0$
3. h$[x_0, x_1, \ldots, x_{n-1}], n \geq 0$

4.17 Consider the declaration:

```
let rec p q = function
    | []      -> []
    | x::xs -> let ys = p q xs
               if q x then x::ys else ys@[x];;
```

Find the type for p and explain the value of the expression:

$$\text{p } q \ [x_0; x_1; x_3; \ldots; x_{n-1}]$$

4.18 Consider the declaration:

```
let rec f g = function
  | []      -> []
  | x::xs -> g x :: f (fun y -> g(g y)) xs;;
```

Find the type for `f` and explain the value of the expression:

$$\text{f } g \,[x_0; x_1; x_2; \ldots; x_{n-1}]$$

4.19 Evaluation of the expression $\text{areNb } m\, c_1\, c_2$ may traverse the map m twice. Explain why and give an alternative declaration for `areNb` which avoids this problem.

4.20 Most of the auxiliary functions for the map-colouring program just assume an arbitrary, but fixed, map. The function `canBeExtBy`, for example, just passes m on to `areNb`, which again passes m on to `isMember`. The program can therefore be simplified by declaring (most of) the auxiliary functions locally as sketched here:

```
  . . .
let colMap m =
      let areNb c1 c2 = ...
      let canBeExtBy col c = ...
      . . .
```

Revise the program by completing this skeleton.

4.21 Revise the map-colouring program so that it can cope with countries which are islands (such as Iceland) having no neighbours.

4.22 We represent the polynomial $a_0 + a_1 \cdot x + \ldots + a_n \cdot x^n$ with integer coefficients $a_0, a_1, \ldots, a_n$ by the list $[a_0, a_1, \ldots, a_n]$. For instance, the polynomial $x^3 + 2$ is represented by the list $[2, 0, 0, 1]$.

1. Declare an F# function for multiplying a polynomial by a constant.
2. Declare an F# function for multiplying a polynomial $Q(x)$ by x.
3. Declare infix F# operators for addition and multiplication of polynomials in the chosen representation. The following recursion formula is useful when defining the multiplication:

$$0 \cdot Q(x) \;\; = 0$$
$$(a_0 + a_1 \cdot x + \ldots + a_n \cdot x^n) \cdot Q(x)$$
$$= a_0 \cdot Q(x) + x \cdot \left((a_1 + a_2 \cdot x + \ldots + a_n \cdot x^{n-1}) \cdot Q(x)\right)$$

4. Declare an F# function to give a textual representation for a polynomial.

4.23 A dating bureau has a file containing name, telephone number, sex, year of birth and themes of interest for each client. You may make a request to the bureau stating your own sex, year of birth and themes of interest and get a response listing all matching clients, that is, clients with different sex, a deviation in age less than 10 years and with at least one common theme of interest. The problem is to construct a program for generating the responses from the dating bureau.

5

Collections: Lists, maps and sets

Functional languages make it easy to express standard recursion patterns in the form of higher-order functions. A collection of such higher-order functions on lists, for example, provides a powerful library where many recursive functions can be obtained directly by application of higher-order library functions. This has two important consequences:

1. The functions in the library correspond to natural abstract concepts and conscious use of them supports high-level program design, and
2. these functions support code reuse because you can make many functions simply by applying library functions.

In this chapter we shall study libraries for lists, sets and maps, which are parts of the collection library of F#. This part of the collection library is studied together since:

- It constitutes the *immutable part* of the collection library. The list, set and map collections are finite collections programmed in a functional style.
- There are many similarities in the corresponding library functions.

This chapter is a natural extension of Chapter 4 since many of the patterns introduced in that chapter correspond to higher-order functions for lists and since more natural program designs can be given for the two examples in Section 4.6 using sets and maps.

We will focus on the main concepts and applications in this book, and will deliberately not cover the complete collection library of F#. The functions of the collection library do also apply to (mutable) arrays. We address this part in Section 8.10.

5.1 Lists

This section describes the library functions `map`, various library functions using a predicate on list elements plus the functions `fold` and `foldBack`. Each description aims to provide the following:

1. An intuitive understanding of the objective of the function.
2. Examples of use of the function.

The actual declarations of the library functions are not considered as we want to concentrate on how to *use* these functions in problem solving. Declarations of `fold` and `foldBack` are, however, of considerable theoretical interest and are therefore studied in the last part of the section. An overview of the `List`-library functions considered in this section is found in Table 5.1.

Operation
Meaning
`map: ('a -> 'b) -> 'a list -> 'b list`, where $\quad$ map f $xs = [f(x_0); f(x_1); \ldots; f(x_{n-1})]$
`exists: ('a -> bool) -> 'a list -> bool`, where $\quad$ exists p $xs = \exists x \in xs.p(x)$
`forall: ('a -> bool) -> 'a list -> bool`, where $\quad$ forall p $xs = \forall x \in xs.p(x)$
`tryFind: ('a -> bool) -> 'a list -> 'a option`, where $\quad$ tryFind p xs is Some x for some $x \in xs$ with $p(x) =$ true or None if no such x exists
`filter: ('a -> bool) -> 'a list -> 'a list`, where $\quad$ filter p $xs = ys$ where ys is obtained from xs by deletion of elements $x_i : p(x_i) =$ false
`fold: ('a -> 'b -> 'a) -> 'a -> 'b list -> 'a`, where $\quad$ fold f a $[b_0; b_1; \ldots; b_{n-2}; b_{n-1}] = f(f(f(\cdots f(f(a, b_0), b_1), \ldots), b_{n-2}), b_{n-1})$
`foldBack: ('a -> 'b -> 'b) -> 'a list -> 'b -> 'b`, where $\quad$ foldBack f $[a_0; a_1; \ldots; a_{n-2}; a_{n-1}]$ $b = f(a_0, f(a_1, f(\ldots, f(a_{n-2}, f(a_{n-1}, b)) \cdots)))$
`collect: ('a -> 'b list) -> 'a list -> 'b list`, where $\quad$ collect f $[a_0; a_1; \ldots; a_{n-1}] = (f\, a_0)@(f\, a_1)@ \cdots @(f\, a_{n-1})$

These operations are found under the names: `List.map`, `List.exists`, and so on.
We assume that $xs = [x_0; x_1; \ldots; x_{n-2}; x_{n-1}]$.

Table 5.1 *A selection of functions from the* `List` *library*

The map *function*

The library function

```
List.map: ('a -> 'b) -> 'a list -> 'b list
```

works as follows:

$$\text{List.map } f\ [x_0; x_1; \cdots ; x_{n-1}]\ =\ [f\, x_0; f\, x_1; \cdots ; f\, x_{n-1}]$$

In words:

> The function application `List.map` f is the function that applies the function f
> to each element $x_0, x_1, \ldots, x_{n-1}$ in a list $[x_0; x_1; \cdots ; x_{n-1}]$

It is easy to use `List.map`:

- The function `addFsExt` adds the F# file extension ".fs" to every string in a list of file names.
- The function `intPairToRational` converts every integer pair in a list to the string of a rational number on the basis of the declarations in Section 3.7.
- The function `areaList` computes the area of every shape in a list on the basis of the declarations in Section 3.8.

```
let addFsExt = List.map (fun s -> s + ".fs");;
val addFsExt : (string list -> string list)

let intPairToRational = List.map (toString << mkQ);;
val intPairToRational : ((int * int) list -> string list)
```

```
let areaList = List.map area;;
val areaList : (shape list -> float list)
```

since

- addFsExt applies the function that concatenates the suffix ".fs" to a string, to every element in a string list,
- intPairToRational applies the function that converts an integer pair to the string representation of the corresponding rational number to every element in a list of integer pairs, and
- areaList applies the area function to every element in a shape list.

The functions work as follows:

```
addFsExt ["ListPrograms"; "AuxiliaryPrograms"];;
val it : string list =
      ["ListPrograms.fs"; "AuxiliaryPrograms.fs"]

intPairToRational [(2,6); (20,-8); (-12,-4)];;
val it : string list = ["1/3"; "-5/2"; "3/1"]

areaList [Circle 2.0; Square 2.0; Triangle(2.0, 3.0, 4.0)];;
val it : float list = [12.56637061; 4.0; 2.90473751]
```

Alternative ways of declaring intPairToRational using List.map are

```
let intPairToRational = List.map (fun p -> toString(mkQ p));;

let intPairToRational ps =
    List.map (fun p -> toString(mkQ p)) ps;;
```

where fun p -> toString(mkQ p) is an expansion of the function composition operator in toString << mkQ and ps is used as explicit list argument in the last declaration. Explicit list arguments could also be used in declarations of addFsExt and areaList.

Functions using a predicate on the list elements

The F# library contains a large number of functions using a predicate of type 'a -> bool on elements in a list of type 'a list.

We consider some of these functions here, namely (cf. Table 5.1):

```
List.exists  : ('a -> bool) -> 'a list -> bool
List.forall  : ('a -> bool) -> 'a list -> bool
List.tryFind : ('a -> bool) -> 'a list -> 'a option
List.filter  : ('a -> bool) -> 'a list -> 'a list
```

The value of the expression

$$\text{List.exists } p \ [x_0; x_1; \ldots; x_{n-1}]$$

is true, if $p(x_k) = $ true holds for some list element x_k, and false otherwise.

The value of the expression

$$\text{List.forall } p \; [x_0; x_1; \ldots; x_{n-1}]$$

is true, if $p(x_k) = $ true holds for all list elements x_k, and false otherwise.

The value of the expression

$$\text{List.tryFind } p \; [x_0; x_1; \ldots; x_{n-1}]$$

is Some x_k for a list element x_k with $p(x_k) = $ true, or None if no such element exists.

The value of the expression

$$\text{List.filter } p \; [x_0; x_1; \ldots; x_{n-1}]$$

is the list of those list elements x_k where $p(x_k) = $ true.

Note that the evaluation of the expression

$$\text{List.exists } p \; [x_0, x_1, \ldots x_{i-1}, x_i, \ldots, x_{n-1}]$$

does not terminate if the evaluation of the expression $p(x_k)$ does not terminate for some k, where $0 \leq k \leq n - 1$ and if $p(x_j) = $ false for all j where $1 \leq j < k$. A similar remark will apply to the other functions using a predicate on list elements.

Simple applications of the functions are:

```
List.exists (fun x -> x>=2) [1;3;1;4];;
val it : bool = true

List.forall (fun x -> x>=2) [1;3;1;4];;
val it : bool = false

List.tryFind (fun x -> x>3) [1;5;-2;8];;
val it : int option = Some 5

List.filter (fun x -> x>3) [1;5;-2;8];;
val it : int list = [5; 8]
```

The function isMember (cf. Section 4.4) can be declared using List.exists:

```
let isMember x xs = List.exists (fun y -> y=x) xs;;
val isMember : 'a -> 'a list -> bool when 'a : equality

isMember (2,3.0) [(2, 4.0) ; (3, 7.0)];;
val it : bool = false

isMember "abc" [""; "a"; "ab"; "abc"];;
val it : bool = true
```

The functions fold *and* foldBack

The library functions List.fold and List.foldBack are very powerful and rather useful in many circumstances, but they are somewhat difficult to understand at first glance. To ease the understanding we use a rather naive, almost grotesque, example to convey the ideas behind these functions.

We consider small cheeses and a round package to contain small cheeses:

cheese   package

Cheeses and packages are considered elements of type cheese and package. A package may contain zero or more cheeses.

The function

```
packCheese: package -> cheese -> package
```

packs an extra cheese into a package:

The function List.fold can be applied to the function packCheese, a start package and a list of cheeses. It uses packCheese to pack the elements of the list (the cheeses) into the package one after the other – starting with the given start package:

This is a special case of the general formula:

$$\text{List.fold } f\ e\ [x_0; x_1; \ldots; x_{n-1}] = f\,(\ldots(f\,(f\,e\,x_0)\,x_1)\ldots)\,x_{n-1}$$

with

$$f = \text{packCheese} \qquad e = \qquad x_0 = \qquad x_1 = \qquad x_2 =$$

because we can identify the sub-expressions on the right-hand side of the general formula in our special case:

$$f\,e\,x_0 = \qquad f\,(f\,e\,x_0)\,x_1 =$$

and

$$f\,(f\,(f\,e\,x_0)\,x_1)\,x_2 =$$

The function of List.fold can be expressed in words as follows:

> The evaluation of List.fold f e $[x_0; x_1; \ldots; x_{n-1}]$ accumulates the list
> elements $x_0, x_1, \ldots, x_{n-1}$ using the accumulation function f and the start value e

One also says that the function f is folded over the list $[x_0; x_1; \ldots; x_{n-1}]$ starting with the value e.

The type of List.fold is:

```
List.fold: ('a -> 'b -> 'a) -> 'a -> 'b list -> 'a
```

with list element type 'b and accumulator type 'a.

When applying List.fold one has to look for the following entities:

List element type 'b	corresponding to cheese in the example
Accumulator type 'a	corresponding to package in the example
Accumulator function f	corresponding to packCheese in the example
Start value e	corresponding to the empty package in the example

and we have to arrange the parameters in the accumulator function to suit the type of List.fold.

As an example we consider a list $vs = [v_0; \ldots; v_{n-1}]$ of geometric vectors in the plane (see Section 3.3), where v_i is a pair (x_i, y_i) of floats, for $0 \le i < n$. We want to compute the sum of the norms of the vectors in vs using the norm function declared as follows in Section 3.3:

```
let norm(x:float,y:float) = sqrt(x*x+y*y);;
val norm : float * float -> float
```

This is a case for applying List.fold with:

List element type:	float * float
Accumulator type:	float
Accumulator function:	fun s (x,y) -> s + norm(x,y)
Start value:	0.0

This leads to the declaration:

```
let sumOfNorms vs =
   List.fold (fun s (x,y) -> s + norm(x,y)) 0.0 vs;;
val sumOfNorms : (float * float) list -> float

let vs = [(1.0,2.0); (2.0,1.0); (2.0, 5.5)];;
val vs : (float * float) list =
           [(1.0, 2.0); (2.0, 1.0); (2.0, 5.5)]

sumOfNorms vs;;
val it : float = 10.32448591
```

The `length` function on lists can be defined using `List.fold` with

List element type:	`'a`
Accumulator type:	`int`
Accumulator function:	`fun e _ -> e + 1`
Start value:	`0`

This leads to the declaration:

```
let length lst = List.fold (fun e _ -> e+1) 0 lst;;
val length : 'a list -> int

length [[1;2];[];[3;5;8];[-2]];;
val it : int = 4
```

Applying `fold` to the following version of "cons":

$$\text{fun rs x -> x::rs}$$

where the parameters are interchanged, gives a declaration of the reverse function for lists:

```
let rev xs = List.fold (fun rs x -> x::rs) [] xs;;
val rev : 'a list -> 'a list

rev [1;2;3];;
val it : int list = [3; 2; 1]
```

The function `List.foldBack` is similar to `List.fold` but the list elements are accumulated in the opposite order. The type of `List.foldBack` is:

```
List.foldBack: ('a -> 'b -> 'b) -> 'a list -> 'b -> 'b
```

and the general formula is:

$$\text{List.foldBack}\, g\, [x_0; x_1; \ldots; x_{n-1}]\, e \;=\; g\, x_0\, (g\, x_1\, (\ldots (g\, x_{n-1}\, e)\ldots))$$

We may use our "cheese" example also in this case with a modified accumulation function:

```
cheesePack: cheese -> package -> package
```

where

cheesePack ... = ...

The function `List.foldBack` can be applied to the function `cheesePack`, a list of cheeses and a start package. It uses `cheesePack` to pack the elements of the list (the cheeses) taken in reverse order into the package:

List.foldBack cheesePack $[\,\cdot\,;\,\cdot\,;\,\cdot\,]$ ... = ...

This is a special case of the general formula with:

$$g = \texttt{cheesePack} \quad x_0 = \boxed{0} \quad x_1 = \boxed{1} \quad x_2 = \boxed{2} \quad e = \bigcirc$$

because we can identify the sub-expressions in the right-hand side of the general formula in our special case:

$$g\, x_2\, e = \bigcirc \qquad g\, x_1\, (g\, x_2\, e) = \bigcirc$$

and

$$g\, x_0\, (g\, x_1\, (g\, x_2\, e)) = \bigcirc$$

The function of `List.foldBack` can be expressed in words as follows:

> The evaluation of `List.foldBack` g $[x_0; x_1; \ldots; x_{n-1}]$ e accumulates the list elements in reverse order $x_{n-1}, \ldots, x_1, x_0$ using the accumulation function g and the start value e

When applying `List.foldBack` one has to look for the following entities:

List element type `'a`   corresponding to `cheese` in the example
Accumulator type `'b`   corresponding to `package` in the example
Accumulator function g corresponding to `cheesePack` in the example
Start value e corresponding to the empty package in the example

and we have to arrange the parameters in the accumulator function to suit the type of `List.foldBack`.

Using `List.foldBack` we may define an alternative "sum of norms" function. Element and accumulator types can be used unchanged, but the parameters in the accumulator function must be interchanged. This gives the following declaration:

```
let backSumOfNorms vs =
  List.foldBack (fun (x,y) s -> s + norm(x,y)) vs 0.0;;
val backSumOfNorms : (float * float) list -> float
```

This function will work like the previous `sumOfNorms` but the norms are added in the opposite order, starting with the norm of the last vector in the list.

Applying `List.foldBack` on the "cons" operator:

$$\texttt{fun x xs -> x::xs}$$

gives the append function:

```
let app ys zs = List.foldBack (fun x xs -> x::xs) ys zs;;
val app : 'a list -> 'a list -> 'a list
app [1;2;3] [4;5;6];;
val it : int list = [1; 2; 3; 4; 5; 6]
```

The `unzip` function on Page 77 can be obtained using `foldBack` with the following data:

List element type	`'a * 'b`
Accumulator type	`'a list * 'b list`
Accumulator function	`fun (x,y) (xs,ys) -> (x::xs,y::ys)`
Start value	`([],[])`

This gives the declaration

```
let unzip zs = List.foldBack
                (fun (x,y) (xs,ys) -> (x::xs,y::ys))
                zs
                ([],[]);;
val unzip : ('a * 'b) list -> 'a list * 'b list

unzip [(1,"a");(2,"b")];;
al it : int list * string list = ([1; 2], ["a"; "b"])
```

A similar construction using `List.fold` gives a `revUnzip` function where the resulting lists are reversed:

```
let revUnzip zs =
  List.fold (fun (xs,ys) (x,y) -> (x::xs,y::ys)) ([],[]) zs;;
val revUnzip : ('a * 'b) list -> 'a list * 'b list

revUnzip [(1,"a");(2,"b")];;
val it : int list * string list = ([2; 1], ["b"; "a"])
```

The prefix version of an *infix operator* can be used as argument in `fold` and `foldBack`:

```
List.fold (+) 0 [1; 2; 3];;
val it : int = 6

List.foldBack (+) [1; 2; 3] 0;;
val it : int = 6
```

These expression compute $((0 + 1) + 2) + 3$ and $1 + (2 + (3 + 0))$, but the results are equal because $+$ is a *commutative* operator: $a + b = b + a$.

A difference in using `fold` or `foldBack` shows up when using a non-commutative operator, that is:

```
List.fold (-) 0 [1; 2; 3];;
val it : int = -6

List.foldBack (-) [1; 2; 3] 0;;
val it : int = 2
```

These expressions use the functions:

```
fun e x -> e - x
fun x e -> x - e
```

and we get

```
List.fold (-) 0 [1;2;3]      =  ((0 - 1) - 2) - 3  =  -6
List.foldBack (-) [1;2;3] 0  =  1 - (2 - (3 - 0))  =  2
```

The map function can be declared using `foldBack`:

```
let map f xs = List.foldBack (fun x rs -> f x :: rs) xs [];;
val map : ('a -> 'b) -> 'a list -> 'b list

map (fun x -> x+1) [0; 1; 2];;
val it : int list = [1; 2; 3]
```

Remark

A function declared by means of `fold` or `foldBack` will always scan the whole list. Thus, the following declaration for the `exists` function

```
let existsF p =
    List.fold (fun b -> (fun x -> p x || b)) false;;
val existsF : ('a -> bool) -> ('a list -> bool)
```

will not behave like the function `List.exists` with regard to non-termination: It will give a non-terminating evaluation if the list contains any element where the evaluation of the predicate p does not terminate, while the library function `List.exists` may terminate in this case as it does not scan the list further when an element satisfying the predicate has been found. So it is not considered a good idea to use `fold` or `foldBack` to declare functions like `exists` or `find` (cf. Page 95) as these functions need not scan the whole list in all cases.

Declarations of `fold` and `foldBack`

The list functions `fold` and `foldBack` are defined on Pages 97 and 99 by the formulas:

$$\text{fold } f\, e\ [x_0; x_1; \ldots; x_{n-1}] \quad = \quad f\left(\ldots(f\,(f\,e\,x_0)\,x_1)\ldots\right)x_{n-1}$$
$$\text{foldBack } g\ [x_0; x_1; \ldots; x_{n-1}]\, e \quad = \quad g\,x_0\left(g\,x_1\left(\ldots(g\,x_{n-1}\,e)\ldots\right)\right)$$

A recursion formula for `fold` is obtained by observing that:

$$f\left(\ldots(f\,(f\,e\,x_0)\,x_1)\ldots\right)x_{n-1} = f\left(\ldots(f\,e'\,x_1)\ldots\right)x_{n-1}$$

where $e' = f\,e\,x_0$. The expression on the right-hand side is equal to:

$$\text{fold } f\, e'\ [x_1; \ldots; x_{n-1}]$$

and we get the recursion formula:

$$\text{fold } f\, e\ [x_0; x_1; \ldots; x_{n-1}] = \text{fold } f\,(f\,e\,x_0)\ [x_1; \ldots; x_{n-1}]$$

A recursion formula for `foldBack` is obtained by observing that the subexpression:

$$(g\,x_1\left(\ldots(g\,x_{n-1}\,e)\ldots\right))$$

on the right-hand side of the formula for foldBack is equal to:

$$\text{foldBack } g \; [x_1; \ldots; x_{n-1}] \; e$$

and we get the recursion formula:

$$\text{foldBack } g \; [x_0; x_1; \ldots; x_{n-1}] \; e = g \; x_0 \; (\text{foldBack } g \; [x_1; \ldots; x_{n-1}] \; e)$$

These recursion formulas lead to the declarations:

```
let rec fold f e = function
    | x::xs -> fold f (f e x) xs
    | []     -> e;;

let rec foldBack g xlst e =
    match xlst with
    | x::xs -> g x (foldBack g xs e)
    | []     -> e;;
```

The evaluation of a function value fold f e $[x_0; x_1; \ldots; x_{n-1}]$ proceeds as follows applying f in each evaluation step without building any large expression:

$$
\begin{array}{lll}
& \text{fold } f \; e \; [x_0; x_1; \ldots; x_{n-1}] & \\
\rightsquigarrow & \text{fold } f \; e_1 \; [x_1; x_2; \ldots; x_{n-1}] & e_1 = f \; e \; x_0 \\
\rightsquigarrow & \text{fold } f \; e_2 \; [x_2; x_3; \ldots; x_{n-1}] & e_2 = f \; e_1 \; x_1 \\
& \cdots & \\
\rightsquigarrow & \text{fold } f \; e_{n-1} \; [x_{n-1}] & e_{n-1} = f \; e_{n-2} \; x_{n-2} \\
\rightsquigarrow & \text{fold } f \; e_n \; [] & e_n = f \; e_{n-1} \; x_{n-1} \\
\rightsquigarrow & e_n &
\end{array}
$$

The evaluation of foldBack g $[x_0; x_1; \ldots; x_{n-1}]$ e first builds a large expression:

$$
\begin{array}{ll}
& \text{foldBack } g \; [x_0; x_1; \ldots; x_{n-1}] \; e \\
\rightsquigarrow & g \; x_0 \; (\text{foldBack } g \; [x_1; x_2; \ldots; x_{n-1}] \; e) \\
\rightsquigarrow & g \; x_0 \; (g \; x_1 \; (\text{foldBack } g \; [x_1; x_2; \ldots; x_{n-1}] \; e)) \\
& \cdots \\
\rightsquigarrow & g \; x_0 \; (g \; x_1 \; (g \; x_2 \; (\ldots (g \; x_{n-2} \; (\text{foldBack } g \; [x_{n-1}] \; e)) \ldots))) \\
\rightsquigarrow & g \; x_0 \; (g \; x_1 \; (g \; x_2 \; (\ldots (g \; x_{n-2} \; (g \; x_{n-1} \; (\text{foldBack } g \; [] \; e)) \ldots))) \\
\rightsquigarrow & g \; x_0 \; (g \; x_1 \; (g \; x_2 \; (\ldots (g \; x_{n-2} \; (g \; x_{n-1} \; e)) \ldots)))
\end{array}
$$

and this expression is then evaluated "inside-out" using repeated calls of g:

$$
\begin{array}{lll}
& g \; x_0 \; (g \; x_1 \; (g \; x_2 \; (\ldots (g \; x_{n-2} \; (g \; x_{n-1} \; e)) \ldots))) & \\
\rightsquigarrow & g \; x_0 \; (g \; x_1 \; (g \; x_2 \; (\ldots (g \; x_{n-2} \; e'_1))) \ldots))) & e'_1 = g \; x_{n-1} \; e \\
& \cdots & \\
\rightsquigarrow & g \; x_0 \; (g \; x_1 \; e'_{n-2}) & e'_{n-2} = g \; x_2 \; e'_{n-3} \\
\rightsquigarrow & g \; x_0 \; e'_{n-1} & e'_{n-1} = g \; x_1 \; e'_{n-2} \\
\rightsquigarrow & e'_n & e'_n = g \; x_0 \; e'_{n-1}
\end{array}
$$

The evaluation of fold is obviously much more efficient than the evaluation of foldBack, so fold should be preferred whenever possible. The List.foldBack function in the library is more efficient than the above foldBack but List.fold is still more efficient.

5.2 Finite sets

In solving programming problems it is often convenient to use values that are *finite sets* of form $\{a_1, a_2, \ldots, a_n\}$ with elements $a_1, \ldots, a_n$ from some set A. The notion of a set provides a useful abstraction in cases where we have an unordered collection of elements where repetitions among the elements are of no concern.

This section introduces the set concept and operations on sets in F# on the basis of the library `Set`. The focus is on the principal issues so just a small part of the available operations will be covered. Please consult the on-line documentation (in [9]) for an overview of the complete `Set` library.

The mathematical set concept

A *set* (in mathematics) is a collection of elements like

$$\{\text{Bob}, \text{Bill}, \text{Ben}\} \quad \text{and} \quad \{1, 3, 5, 7, 9\}$$

where it is possible to decide whether a given value is in the set. For example, Alice is not in the set $\{\text{Bob}, \text{Bill}, \text{Ben}\}$ and 7 is in the set $\{1, 3, 5, 7, 9\}$, also written:

$$\text{Alice} \notin \{\text{Bob}, \text{Bill}, \text{Ben}\} \quad \text{and} \quad 7 \in \{1, 3, 5, 7, 9\}$$

The empty set containing no element is written $\{\}$ or $\emptyset$.

Since the order in which elements are enumerated in a set is of no concern, and repetitions among members of a set is of no concern either, the following expressions denote the same set:

$$\{\text{Bob}, \text{Bill}, \text{Ben}\} \quad \{\text{Bob}, \text{Bill}, \text{Ben}, \text{Bill}\} \quad \{\text{Bill}, \text{Ben}, \text{Bill}, \text{Bob}\}$$

The above examples are all finite sets; but sets may be infinite and examples are the set of all natural numbers $\mathbb{N} = \{0, 1, 2, \ldots\}$ and the set of all real numbers $\mathbb{R}$.

A set A is a *subset* of a set B, written $A \subseteq B$, if all the elements of A are also elements of B, for example

$$\{\text{Ben}, \text{Bob}\} \subseteq \{\text{Bob}, \text{Bill}, \text{Ben}\} \quad \text{and} \quad \{1, 3, 5, 7, 9\} \subseteq \mathbb{N}$$

Furthermore, two sets A and B are equal, if they are both subsets of each other:

$$A = B \quad \text{if and only if} \quad A \subseteq B \text{ and } B \subseteq A$$

that is, two sets are equal if they contain exactly the same elements.

The subset of a set A that consists of those elements satisfying a predicate p can be expressed using a *set-comprehension* $\{x \in A \mid p(x)\}$. For example, the set $\{1, 3, 5, 7, 9\}$ consists of the odd natural numbers that are smaller than 11:

$$\{1, 3, 5, 7, 9\} = \{x \in \mathbb{N} \mid \text{odd}(x) \text{ and } x < 11\}$$

If it is clear from the context from which set A the elements of the set-comprehension originate, then we use the simplified notation: $\{x \mid p(x)\}$.

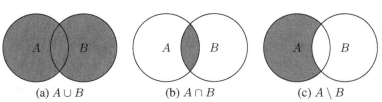

(a) $A \cup B$ (b) $A \cap B$ (c) $A \setminus B$

Figure 5.1 Venn diagrams for (a) union, (b) intersection and (c) difference

Some of the standard operations on sets are *union*: $A \cup B$, *intersection* $A \cap B$ and *difference* $A \setminus B$:

$$A \cup B = \{x \mid x \in A \text{ or } x \in B\}$$
$$A \cap B = \{x \mid x \in A \text{ and } x \in B\}$$
$$A \setminus B = \{x \in A \mid x \notin B\}$$

that is, $A \cup B$ is the set of elements that are in at least one of the sets A and B, $A \cap B$ is the set of elements that are in both A and B, and $A \setminus B$ is the subset of the elements from A that are not in B. These operations are illustrated using Venn diagrams in Figure 5.1. For example:

$$\{\text{Bob, Bill, Ben}\} \cup \{\text{Alice, Bill, Ann}\} = \{\text{Alice, Ann, Bob, Bill, Ben}\}$$
$$\{\text{Bob, Bill, Ben}\} \cap \{\text{Alice, Bill, Ann}\} = \{\text{Bill}\}$$
$$\{\text{Bob, Bill, Ben}\} \setminus \{\text{Alice, Bill, Ann}\} = \{\text{Bob, Ben}\}$$

Sets in F#

The `Set` library of F# supports finite sets of elements of a type where ordering is defined, and provides efficient implementations for a rich collection of set operations. The implementation is based on a balanced binary tree representation of a set and this is why an ordering of the elements is required (but we will not consider such implementation details in this section).

Consider the following example of a set in F#:

```
set ["Bob"; "Bill"; "Ben"];;
val it : Set<string> = set ["Ben"; "Bill"; "Bob"]
```

Hence, a set can be given in a manner similar to a list using the "set-builder" function `set`. The resulting value is of type `Set<string>`, that is, a set of strings, and we can see from the F# answer that the elements occur according to a lexicographical ordering. A standard number ordering is used for sets of integers, for example:

```
set [3; 1; 9; 5; 7; 9; 1];;
val it : Set<int> = set [1; 3; 5; 7; 9]
```

Equality of two sets is tested in the usual manner:

```
set ["Bob";"Bill";"Ben"] = set ["Bill";"Ben";"Bill";"Bob"];;
val it : bool = true
```

and sets are ordered on the basis of a similar kind of lexicographical ordering as used for lists. (See Section 4.1.) For example, {Ann, Jane} is smaller than {Bob, Bill, Ben} (in the F# representation) since Ann is smaller than every element in {Bob, Bill, Ben} using the string representation:

```
compare (set ["Ann";"Jane"]) (set ["Bill";"Ben"; "Bob"]);;
val it : int = -1
```

Operation
Meaning
ofList: 'a list -> Set<'a>, where ofList $[a_0;\ldots;a_{n-1}] = $ set $[a_0;\ldots;a_{n-1}]$
toList: Set<'a> -> 'a list, where toList $\{a_0,\ldots,a_{n-1}\} = [a_0;\ldots;a_{n-1}]$
add: 'a -> Set<'a> -> Set<'a>, where add $a\ A = \{a\} \cup A$
remove: 'a -> Set<'a> -> Set<'a>, where remove $a\ A = A \setminus \{a\}$
contains: 'a -> Set<'a> -> bool, where contains $a\ A = a \in A$
isSubset: Set<'a> -> Set<'a> -> bool, where isSubset $A\ B = A \subseteq B$
minElement: Set<'a> -> 'a, where
minElement $\{a_0, a_1, \ldots, a_{n-2}, a_{n-1}\} = a_0$ when $n > 0$
maxElement: Set<'a> -> 'a, where
maxElement $\{a_0, a_1, \ldots, a_{n-2}, a_{n-1}\} = a_{n-1}$ when $n > 0$
count: Set<'a> -> int, where
count $\{a_0, a_1, \ldots, a_{n-2}, a_{n-1}\} = n$

These operations are found under the names: Set.add, Set.contains, and so on. It is assumed that the enumeration $\{a_0, a_1, \ldots, a_{n-2}, a_{n-1}\}$ respects the ordering of elements.

Table 5.2 *A selection of basic operations from the* Set *library*

Basic properties and operations on sets

We shall now describe the basic properties of sets and the operations on sets in F# as shown in Table 5.2. The functions Set.ofList and Set.toList are conversion functions between lists and sets:

```
let males = Set.ofList ["Bob"; "Bill"; "Ben"; "Bill"];;
val males : Set<string> = set ["Ben"; "Bill"; "Bob"]

Set.toList males;;
val it : string list = ["Ben"; "Bill"; "Bob"]
```

Note that the resulting list is ordered and contains no repeated elements.

An element can be inserted in a set with the function Set.add:

```
Set.add "Barry" males;;
val it : Set<string> = set ["Barry"; "Ben"; "Bill"; "Bob"]
```

and removed from a set with the function Set.remove:

```
Set.remove "Bill" males;;
val it : Set<string> = set ["Ben"; "Bob"]
```

The add and remove operations do not change the original set, that is, they have no side effect. The same observation applies for all other operations in the Set library. For example, the add and remove operations above did not change the value of males:

```
males;;
val males : Set<string> = set ["Ben"; "Bill"; "Bob"]
```

Containment in a set is tested using Set.contains and a subset relationship is tested using Set.isSubset:

```
Set.contains "Barry" males;;
val it : bool = false

Set.isSubset males (set ["Bob"; "Bill"; "Ann"]);;
val it : bool = false

Set.isSubset males (Set.add "Ben" (set ["Bob";"Bill";"Ann"]));;
val it : bool = true
```

Due to the ordering required for set elements, every non-empty set has a minimal and a maximal element:

```
Set.minElement (set ["Bob"; "Bill"; "Ben"]);;
val it : string = "Ben"
Set.maxElement (set ["Bob"; "Bill"; "Ben"]);;
val it : string = "Bob"
```

Furthermore, the cardinality of a finite set is in F# given by the function Set.count:

```
Set.count (set ["Bob"; "Bill"; "Ben"]);;
val it : int = 3
Set.count (Set.empty);;
val it : int = 0
```

which also shows that the cardinality of the empty set (denoted by Set.empty) is 0.

Fundamental operations on sets

We shall now consider the selection of fundamental operations from the Set library in F# shown in Table 5.3.

We illustrate set operations for union, intersection and difference using an example where males are supposed to be all the males at a golf club, and boardMembers are the members of the board for that club:

```
let boardMembers = Set.ofList [ "Alice"; "Bill"; "Ann"];;
val boardMembers : Set<string> = set ["Alice"; "Ann"; "Bill"]

Set.union males boardMembers;;
val it : Set<string> = set ["Alice";"Ann";"Ben";"Bill";"Bob"]
```

Operation
Meaning
union: Set<'a> -> Set<'a> -> Set<'a>, where union $A\,B = A \cup B$
intersect: Set<'a> -> Set<'a> -> Set<'a>, where intersect $A\,B = A \cap B$
difference: Set<'a> -> Set<'a> -> Set<'a>, where difference $A\,B = A \setminus B$
filter: ('a -> bool) -> Set<'a> -> Set<'a>, where filter $p\,A = \{x \in A \mid p(x)\}$
exists: ('a -> bool) -> Set<'a> -> bool, where exists $p\,A = \exists x \in A.p(x)$
forall: ('a -> bool) -> Set<'a> -> bool, where forall $p\,A = \forall x \in A.p(x)$
map: ('a -> 'b) -> Set<'a> -> Set<'b>, where map $f\,A = \{f(x) \mid x \in A\}$
fold: ('a -> 'b -> 'a) -> 'a -> Set<'b> -> 'a, where
$\quad$ fold $f\,a\,\{b_0,b_1,\ldots,b_{n-2},b_{n-1}\} = f(f(f(\cdots f(f(a,b_0),b_1),\ldots),b_{n-2}),b_{n-1})$
foldBack: ('a -> 'b -> 'b) -> Set<'a> -> 'b -> 'b, where
$\quad$ foldBack $f\,\{a_0,a_1,\ldots,a_{n-2},a_{n-1}\}\,b = f(a_0,f(a_1,f(\ldots,f(a_{n-2},f(a_{n-1},b))\cdots)))$

It is assumed that the enumerations in the sets $\{a_0, a_1, \ldots, a_{n-2}, a_{n-1}\}$ and $\{b_0, b_1, \ldots, b_{n-2}, b_{n-1}\}$ respect the ordering of the respective types.

Table 5.3 *A selection of operations from the* Set *library*

```
Set.intersect males boardMembers;;
val it : Set<string> = set ["Bill"]

Set.difference males boardMembers;;
val it : Set<string> = set ["Ben"; "Bob"]
```

where, for example, the set of males being board members is obtained using intersections and the set of those who are not board members is obtained using difference.

A function can be applied to every member of a set using Set.map in the same manner it can be applied to every element of a list using List.map. The following function, that transforms a set of sets $S = \{s_0, \ldots, s_{n-1}\}$ to the set $\{|s_0|, \ldots, |s_{n-1}|\}$ containing the cardinalities of the elements of S, is, for example, defined using Set.map in a natural manner:

```
let setOfCounts s = Set.map Set.count s;;
val setOfCounts: Set<Set<'a>> -> Set<int> when 'a: comparison
```

Consider the F# value for the set of sets $\{\{1, 3, 5\}, \{2, 4\}, \{7, 8, 9\}\}$:

```
let ss = set [set [1;3;5]; set [2;4]; set [7;8;9] ];;
val it : Set<Set<int>>
        = set [set [1; 3; 5]; set [2; 4]; set [7; 8; 9]]

setOfCounts ss;;
val it : Set<int> = set [2; 3]
```

The functions: Set.exists, Set.forall and Set.filter, work in a similar manner to their List siblings:

```
Set.exists (fun x -> x>=2) (set [1;3;1;4]);;
val it : bool = true
```

```
Set.forall (fun x -> x>=2) (set [1;3;1;4]);;
val it : bool = false

Set.filter (fun x -> x>3) (set [1;5;-2;8]);;
val it : Set<int> = set [5; 8]
```

The functions `Set.fold` and `Set.foldBack` also correspond to their list siblings. This is illustrated in the following evaluations:

$$\text{Set.fold } (-) \; 0 \; (\text{set } [1;2;3]) \;=\; ((0-1)-2)-3 \;=\; -6$$
$$\text{Set.foldBack } (-) \; (\text{set } [1;2;3]) \; 0 \;=\; 1-(2-(3-0)) \;=\; 2$$

where the ordering on the set elements is exploited.

The functions `sumSet` and `setOfCounts` can be succinctly declared using `foldBack`:

```
let sumSet s = Set.foldBack (+) s 0;;
val sumSet : Set<int> -> int

let setOfCounts s = Set.foldBack
                         (fun se sn -> Set.add (Set.count se) sn)
                         s
                         Set.empty;;
setOfCounts : Set<Set<'a>> -> Set<int> when 'a : comparison

sumSet (set [1 .. 5]);;
val it : int = 15

setOfCounts (set [set [1;3;5]; set [2;4]; set [7;8;9] ]);;
val it : Set<int> = set [2; 3]
```

Declarations of these functions could also be based on `Set.fold`:

```
let sumSet s = Set.fold (+) 0 s;;

let setOfCounts s = Set.fold
                         (fun sn se -> Set.add (Set.count se) sn)
                         Set.empty
                         s;;
```

Notice that is is more natural to base a declaration of `setOfCounts` on `Set.map` as done above, rather than basing it on one of the fold functions.

Recursive functions on sets

The functions `Set.map`, `Set.filter`, `Set.fold` and `Set.foldBack` will traverse the complete set before they terminate, unless the evaluation is aborted by raising an exception, and this may be undesirable in some situations. Consider, for example, the function that finds the least element in a set satisfying a given predicate:

```
tryFind: ('a -> bool) -> Set<'a> -> 'a option
         when 'a : comparison
```

This function can be declared by repeated extraction of the minimal element from a set until an element satisfying the predicate is found:

```
let rec tryFind p s =
    if Set.isEmpty s then None
    else let minE = Set.minElement s
             if p minE then Some minE
             else tryFind p (Set.remove minE s);;
```

For example, the least three-element set from a set of sets is extracted as follows:

```
let ss = set [set [1;3;5]; set [2;4]; set [7;8;9] ];;

tryFind (fun s -> Set.count s = 3) ss;;
val it : Set<int> option = Some (set [1; 3; 5])
```

A declaration of this function that is based on `Set.fold` will always traverse the entire set leading to a linear best-case running time, while the function declared above will terminate as soon as an element satisfying the predicate is found, and the best-case execution time is dominated by the time required for finding the minimal element in a set, and that execution time is logarithmic in the size of the set when it is represented by a balanced binary tree. Note however, that the worst-case execution time of traversing a set S using `Set.fold` or `Set.foldBack` is $O(|S|)$, that is linear in the size $|S|$ of the set, while it is $O(|S| \cdot \log(|S|))$ for a function based on a recursion schema like that for `tryFind`, due to the logarithmic operations for finding and removing the minimal element of a set.

A more efficient implementation of the function `tryFind` using an enumerator is given on Page 191, and the efficiency of different methods for traversal of collections is analyzed in Exercise 9.14. Enumerators for collections (to be introduced in Section 8.12) provide a far more efficient method than the above used recursion schema for `tryFind`.

Example: Map colouring

The solution of the map-colouring problem from Section 4.6 shall now be improved using sets. The basic algorithmic idea for the solution below using sets is basically the same as that for using lists. But the model using sets is a more natural one. Furthermore, we shall take advantage of the higher-order library functions.

A map is mathematically modelled as a binary relation of countries, that is, as a set of country pairs. Furthermore, since the order in which countries occur in a colour is not relevant and since repetition among the countries in a colour is of no concern, the natural model of a colour is a country set. A similar observation applies to a colouring:

```
type Country   = string;;
type Map       = Set<Country*Country>;;
type Colour    = Set<Country>;;
type Colouring = Set<Colour>;;
```

Two countries c_1, c_2 are neighbors in a map m, if either $(c_1, c_2) \in m$ or $(c_2, c_1) \in m$. In F# this is expressed as follows:

```
let areNb c1 c2 m =
    Set.contains (c1,c2) m || Set.contains (c2,c1) m;;
```

A colour *col* can be extended by a country *c* for a given map *m*, if for every country *c′* in *col*, we have that *c* and *c′* are not neighbours in *m*. This can be directly expressed using `Set.forall`:

```
let canBeExtBy m col c =
    Set.forall (fun c' -> not (areNb c' c m)) col;;
```

The function

```
extColouring: Map -> Colouring -> Country -> Colouring
```

is declared as a recursive function over the colouring:

```
let rec extColouring m cols c =
    if Set.isEmpty cols
    then Set.singleton (Set.singleton c)
    else let col = Set.minElement cols
         let cols' = Set.remove col cols
         if canBeExtBy m col c
         then Set.add (Set.add c col) cols'
         else Set.add col (extColouring m cols' c);;
```

This recursive declaration is preferred to using a declaration based on either `Set.fold` or `Set.foldBack`, since the recursive version terminates as soon as a colour that can be extended by the country is found, whereas a declaration based on one of the fold functions always will iterate through the entire colouring.

A set of countries is obtained from a map by the function:

```
countries: Map -> Set<Country>
```

The declaration of this function is based on repeated insertion (using `Set.fold`) of the countries in the map into a set:

```
let countries m =
    Set.fold
      (fun set (c1,c2) -> Set.add c1 (Set.add c2 set))
      Set.empty
      m;;
```

The function

```
colCntrs: Map -> Set<Country> -> Colouring
```

that creates a colouring for a set of countries in a given map, can be declared by repeated insertion of countries in colourings using the `extColouring` function:

```
let colCntrs m cs = Set.fold (extColouring m) Set.empty cs;;
```

The function that creates a colouring from a map is declared using function composition and used as follows:

```
let colMap m = colCntrs m (countries m);;

let exMap = Set.ofList [("a","b"); ("c","d"); ("d","a")];;

colMap exMap;;
val it: Set<Set<string>> = set [set ["a";"c"]; set ["b";"d"]]
```

Comparing this set-based solution with the list-based one in Section 4.6 we can first observe that the set-based model is more natural, due to the facts that a map is a binary relation of countries and a colouring is a partitioning of the set of countries in a map. For most of the functions there is even an efficiency advantage with the set-based functions. This advantage is due to the following

- the worst-case execution time for testing for membership of a set (represented by a balanced binary tree) is logarithmic in the size of the set, while this operation is linear when the set is represented by a list, and
- the worst-case execution time for inserting an element into a set (represented by a balanced binary tree) is logarithmic in the size of the set, while this operation is linear when the set is represented by a list without duplicated elements.

The use of lists has an advantage in the case of the recursive function extColouring since the pattern matching for lists yields a more readable declaration and since the worst-case execution time of this list-based version is linear in the size $|S|$ of the colouring S, while it is $O(|S| \cdot \log(|S|))$ for the set-based one. (See remark on Page 110.)

An improved version is therefore based on the following type declaration:

```
type Country   = string;;
type Map       = Set<Country*Country>;;
type Colour    = Set<Country>;;
type Colouring = Colour list;;
```

Just two functions extColouring and colCntrs are affected by this change of the type for colouring while the remaining functions are as above. The new declarations are:

```
let rec extColouring m cols c =
    match cols with
    | []          -> [Set.singleton c]
    | col::cols' -> if canBeExtBy m col c
                    then (Set.add c col)::cols'
                    else col::(extColouring m cols' c);;

let colCntrs m cs = Set.fold (extColouring m) [] cs;;

colMap exMap;;
val it : Set<string> list = [set ["a"; "c"]; set ["b"; "d"]]
```

5.3 Maps

In the modelling and solution for many problems it is often convenient to use finite functions to uniquely associate *values* with *keys*. Such finite functions from keys to values are called *maps*. This section introduces the map concept and some of the main operations on maps in the F# Map library. Please consult the on-line documentation in [9] for an overview of the complete Map library.

The mathematical concept of a map

A *map* from a set A to a set B is a *finite* subset A' of A together with a *function* m defined on A':

$$m : A' \to B$$

The set A' is called the *domain* of m and we write dom $m = A'$.

A map m can be described in a tabular form as shown below. The left column contains the elements $a_0, a_1, \ldots, a_{n-1}$ of the set A', while the right column contains the corresponding values $m(a_0) = b_0, m(a_1) = b_1, \ldots, m(a_{n-1}) = b_{n-1}$:

a_0	b_0
a_1	b_1
$\vdots$	
a_{n-1}	b_{n-1}

An element a_i in the set A' is called a *key* for the map m. A pair (a_i, b_i) is called an *entry*, and b_i is called the *value* for the key a_i. Note that the order of the entries is of no significance, as the map only expresses an association of values to keys. Note also that any two keys a_i and a_j in different entries are different, as there is only one value for each key. Thus, a map may be represented as a finite set of its entries. We use

$$\text{entriesOf}(m) = \{(a_0, b_0), \ldots, (a_{n-1}, b_{n-1})\}$$

to denote the sets of entries of a map.

The cash register example in Chapter 4.6 comprises an article register associating name and price to article codes, and this register can be viewed as a map. A key in the map is an article code and the corresponding value is the pair with the name and price of the article.

A particular article register is given by the following map:

reg_1 :	a1	(cheese, 25)
	a2	(herring, 4)
	a3	(soft drink, 5)

It associates the value (cheese, 25) with the key a1, the value (herring, 4) with the key a2, and the value (soft drink, 5) with the key a3. Hence, it has the domain $\{a1, a2, a3\}$.

Operation
Meaning
`ofList: ('a*'b) list -> Map<'a,'b>`, where
`ofList` $[(a_0, b_0); \ldots; (a_{n-1}, b_{n-1})] = m$
`toList: Map<'a,'b> -> ('a*'b) list`, where
`toList` $m = [(a_0, b_0); \ldots; (a_{n-1}, b_{n-1})]$
`add: 'a -> 'b -> Map<'a,'b> -> Map<'a,'b>`, where
`add` $a\, b\, m = m'$, where m' is obtained by overriding m with the entry (a, b)
`containsKey: 'a -> Map<'a,'b> -> bool`, where `containsKey` $a\, m = a \in \text{dom } m$
`find: 'a -> Map<'a,'b> -> 'b`, where
`find` $a\, m = m(a)$, if $a \in \text{dom } m$; otherwise an exception is raised
`tryFind: 'a -> Map<'a,'b> -> 'b option`, where
`tryFind` $a\, m = $ `Some` $(m(a))$, if $a \in \text{dom } m$; `None` otherwise
`filter: ('a -> 'b -> bool) -> Map<'a,'b> -> Map<'a,'b>`, where `filter` $p\, m$
is obtained from m by deletion of entries (a_i, b_i) where $p\, a_i\, b_i = $ `false`
`exists: ('a -> 'b -> bool) -> Map<'a,'b> -> bool`, where
`exists` $p\, m = \exists (a, b) \in \text{entriesOf}(m).p\, a\, b$
`forall: ('a -> 'b -> bool) -> Map<'a,'b> -> bool`, where
`forall` $p\, A = \forall (a, b) \in \text{entriesOf}(m).p\, a\, b$
`map: ('a -> 'b -> 'c) -> Map<'a,'b> -> Map<'a,'c>`, where
`map` $f\, m = $ `ofList` $[(a_0, f\, a_0\, b_0); \ldots; (a_{n-1}, f\, a_{n-1}\, b_{n-1})]$
`fold: ('a -> 'b -> 'c -> 'a) -> 'a -> Map<'b,'c> -> 'a`, where
`fold` $f\, a\, m_{bc} = f(\cdots(f(f\, a\, b_0\, c_0)\, b_1\, c_1)\ldots)\, b_{n-1}\, c_{n-1}$
`foldBack: ('a -> 'b -> 'c -> 'c) -> Map<'a,'b> -> 'c -> 'c`, where
`foldBack` $f\, m\, c = f\, a_0\, b_0\, (f\, a_1\, b_1\, (f \ldots (f\, a_{n-1}\, b_{n-1}\, c)\cdots))$

It is assumed that m and m_{bc} are maps with types `Map<'a,'b>` and `Map<'b,'c>`, that

$$
\begin{aligned}
\text{entriesOf}(m) &= \{(a_0, b_0), \ldots, (a_{n-1}, b_{n-1})\} \\
\text{entriesOf}(m_{bc}) &= \{(b_0, c_0), \ldots, (b_{n-1}, c_{n-1})\}
\end{aligned}
$$

and that the enumerations $\{a_0, a_1, \ldots, a_{n-2}, a_{n-1}\}$ and $\{b_0, b_1, \ldots, b_{n-2}, b_{n-1}\}$ respect the ordering of the respective types.

Table 5.4 *A selection of operations from the* `Map` *library*

Maps in F#

The `Map` library of F# supports maps of polymorphic types `Map<'a,'b>`, where `'a` and `'b` are the types of the keys and values, respectively, of the map. The `Map` is implemented using balanced binary trees, and requires therefore that an ordering is defined on the type `'a` of keys. Some of the functions of the `Map` library are specified in Table 5.4.

A map in F# can be generated from a list of its entries. For example:

```
let reg1 = Map.ofList [("a1",("cheese",25));
                       ("a2",("herring",4));
                       ("a3",("soft drink",5))];;
val reg1 : Map<string,(string * int)> =
  map [("a1", ("cheese", 25)); ("a2", ("herring", 4));
       ("a3", ("soft drink", 5))]
```

is an F# map for the register reg_1, where keys are strings and values are pairs of the type string*int. If the list contains multiple entries for the same key, then the last occurring entry is the significant one:

```
Map.ofList [(1,"a"); (2,"b"); (2,"c"); (1,"d")];;
val it : Map<int,string> = map [(1, "d"); (2, "c")]
```

The list of entries of a map is achieved using the Map.toList function:

```
Map.toList reg1;;
val it : (string * (string * int)) list =
  [("a1", ("cheese", 25)); ("a2", ("herring", 4));
   ("a3", ("soft drink", 5))]
```

An entry can be added to a map using add while the value for a key in a map is retrieved using either find or tryFind:

```
let reg2 = Map.add "a4" ("bread", 6) reg1;;
val reg2 : Map<string,(string * int)> =
  map [("a1", ("cheese", 25)); ("a2", ("herring", 4));
       ("a3", ("soft drink", 5)); ("a4", ("bread", 6))]

Map.find "a2" reg1;;
val it : string * int = ("herring", 4)

Map.tryFind "a2" reg1;;
val it : (string * int) option = Some ("herring", 4)

Map.containsKey "a4" reg1;;
val it : bool = false

Map.find "a4" reg1;;
System.Collections.Generic.KeyNotFoundException: The given key
was not present in the dictionary.
...
Stopped due to error

Map.tryFind "a4" reg1;;
val it : (string * int) option = None
```

where find raises an exception if the key is not in the domain of the map and tryFind returns None in that case.

The old entry is overridden if you add an entry for an already existing key. The entry for a given key can be deleted using the remove function:

```
let reg3 = Map.add "a4" ("bread", 8) reg1;;
val reg3 : Map<string,(string * int)> =
  map [("a1", ("cheese", 25)); ("a2", ("herring", 4));
       ("a3", ("soft drink", 5)); ("a4", ("bread", 8))]
```

```
let reg4 = Map.remove "a2" reg3;;
val reg4 : Map<string,(string * int)> =
  map [("a1", ("cheese", 25)); ("a3", ("soft drink", 5));
       ("a4", ("bread", 8))]
```

The `Map` functions `exists`, `forall`, `map`, `fold` and `foldBack` are similar to their `List` and `Set` siblings. These functions are specified with type and meaning in Table 5.4, so we just give some illustrative examples below.

The following expression tests whether there are expensive articles, for which the price exceeds 100, in a register:

```
Map.exists (fun _ (_,p) -> p > 100) reg1;;
val it : bool = false
```

The natural requirement that every price occurring in a register must be positive is expressed by:

```
Map.forall (fun _ (_,p) -> p > 0) reg1;;
val it : bool = true
```

The part of a register with articles having a price smaller than 7 is extracted as follows:

```
Map.filter (fun _ (_,p) -> p < 7) reg3;;
val it : Map<string,(string * int)> =
  map [("a2", ("herring", 4)); ("a3", ("soft drink", 5))]
```

A new register, where a 15% discount is given on all articles, can be computed as follows:

```
Map.map
  (fun ac (an,p) -> (an,int(round(0.85*(float p))))) 
  reg3;;
val it : Map<string,(string * int)> =
  map [("a1", ("cheese", 21)); ("a2", ("herring", 3));
       ("a3", ("soft drink", 4)); ("a4", ("bread", 7))]
```

We can extract the list of article codes and prices for a given register using the fold functions for maps:

```
Map.foldBack (fun ac (_,p) cps -> (ac,p)::cps) reg1 [];;
val it: (string*int) list = [("a1",25); ("a2",4); ("a3",5)]

Map.fold (fun cps ac (_,p) -> (ac,p)::cps) [] reg1;;
val it: (string*int) list = [("a3",5); ("a2",4); ("a1",25)]
```

where these two examples show that the entries of a map are ordered according to the keys.

Example: Cash register

We give a solution to the cash register example discussed in Section 4.6. Article codes and names, number of pieces and prices are modelled just like in Section 4.6:

```
type ArticleCode = string;;
type ArticleName = string;;
type NoPieces    = int;;
type Price       = int;;
```

The natural model of a register, associating article name and price with each article code, is using a map:

```
type Register = Map<ArticleCode, ArticleName*Price>;;
```

since an article code is a unique identification of an article.

The information concerning a bill is also modelled as in Section 4.6:

```
type Info   = NoPieces * ArticleName * Price;;
type Infoseq = Info list;;
type Bill   = Infoseq * Price;;
```

For the remaining parts we give three versions.

Version 1

In the first version we model a purchase just as in Section 4.6:

```
type Item     = NoPieces * ArticleCode;;
type Purchase = Item list;;
```

The function makebill1: Register -> Purchase -> Bill makes the bill for a given register and purchase and it can be defined by a recursion following the structure of a purchase:

```
let rec makeBill1 reg = function
    | []                -> ([],0)
    | (np,ac)::pur ->
        match Map.tryFind ac reg with
        | Some(aname,aprice) ->
            let tprice          = np*aprice
            let (infos,sumbill) = makeBill1 reg pur
            ((np,aname,tprice)::infos, tprice+sumbill)
        | None                  ->
            failwith(ac + " is an unknown article code");;
```

where an exception signals an undefined article code in a register. We use the function Map.tryFind in order to detect when this exception should be raised. A simple application of the program is:

```
let pur = [(3,"a2"); (1,"a1")];;

makeBill1 reg1 pur;;
val it : (int * string * int) list * int =
  ([(3, "herring", 12); (1, "cheese", 25)], 37)
```

where reg1 is declared on Page 114.

Version 2

The recursion pattern of `makeBill1` is the same as that of `List.foldBack`, and the explicit recursion can be replaced by application of that function. Furthermore, it may be acceptable to use the exception from the `Map` library instead of using `failwith`. This leads to the following declaration:

```
let makeBill2 reg pur =
    let f (np,ac) (infos,billprice) =
        let (aname, aprice) = Map.find ac reg
        let tprice          = np*aprice
        ((np,aname,tprice)::infos, tprice+billprice)
    List.foldBack f pur ([],0);;

makeBill2 reg1 pur;;
val it : (int * string * int) list * int =
  ([(3, "herring", 12); (1, "cheese", 25)], 37)
```

where `Map.find` will raise an exception if an article code is not found in a register.

Version 3

A purchase is so far just modelled as a list of items, each item consisting of a count and an article code. The order of appearance in the list may represent the sequence in which items are placed on the counter in the shop. One may, however, argue that a purchase of the following three items: three herrings, one piece of cheese, and two herrings, is the same as a purchase of one piece of cheese and five herrings. Furthermore, the latter form is more convenient if we have to model a discount on five herrings, as the discount applies independently of the order in which the items are placed on the counter. Thus one could model a purchase as a map, where article codes are keys and number of pieces are values of a map.

```
type Purchase = Map<ArticleCode,NoPieces>;;
```

With this model, the `makeBill3: Register -> Purchase -> Bill` function is declared and used as follows:

```
let makeBill3 reg pur =
    let f ac np (infos,billprice) =
        let (aname, aprice) = Map.find ac reg
        let tprice          = np*aprice
        ((np,aname,tprice)::infos, tprice+billprice)
    Map.foldBack f pur ([],0);;
```

where we use `Map.foldBack` to fold the function `f` over a purchase.

An example showing the use of this function is:

```
let purMap = Map.ofList [("a2",3); ("a1",1)];;
val purMap : Map<string,int> = map [("a1", 1); ("a2", 3)]

makeBill3 reg1 purMap;;
val it : (int * string * int) list * int =
  ([(1, "cheese", 25); (3, "herring", 12)], 37)
```

We leave the generation of a map for a purchase on the basis of a list of items for Exercise 5.9. Furthermore, it is left for Exercise 5.10 to take discounts for certain articles into account.

Summary

In this chapter we have introduced the list, set and map parts from the collection library of F#. These three libraries are efficient implementations of such finite, immutable collections. Notice that this chapter just covers a small part of the libraries. Furthermore, in many applications these collections provide a natural data model and we strongly encourage to use these libraries whenever it is appropriate.

In Chapter 11 we introduce sequences, which is another part of the collection library. Sequences are (possibly infinite) list-like structures, where just a finite part of the sequence is computed at any stage of a computation.

Exercises

5.1   Give a declaration for `List.filter` using `List.foldBack`.

5.2   Solve Exercise 4.15 using `List.fold` or `List.foldBack`.

5.3   Solve Exercise 4.12 using `List.fold` or `List.foldBack`.

5.4   Declare a function `downto1` such that:

$$\begin{aligned} \texttt{downto1}\ f\ n\ e &= f(1, f(2, \ldots, f(n-1, f(n, e))\ldots)) \quad &&\text{for } n > 0 \\ \texttt{downto1}\ f\ n\ e &= e \quad &&\text{for } n \leq 0 \end{aligned}$$

Declare the factorial function by use of `downto1`.

Use `downto1` to declare a function that builds the list $[g(1), g(2), \ldots, g(n)]$ for a function g and an integer n.

5.5   Consider the map colouring example in Section 4.6. Give declarations for the functions `areNb` `canBeExtBy`, `extColouring`, `countries` and `colCntrs` using higher-order list functions. Are there cases where the old declaration from Section 4.6 is preferable?

5.6   We define a *relation* from a set A to a set B as a subset of $A \times B$. A relation r' is said to be *smaller* than r, if r' is a subset of r, that is, if $r' \subseteq r$. A relation r is called *finite* if it is a finite subset of $A \times B$. Assuming that the sets A and B are represented by F# types `'a` and `'b` allowing comparison we can represent a finite relation r by a value of type `set<'a * 'b>`.

1. The domain dom r of a relation r is the set of elements a in A where there exists an element b in B such that $(a, b) \in r$. Write an F# declaration expressing the domain function.

2. The range rng r of a relation r is the set of elements b in B where there exists an element a in A such that $(a, b) \in r$. Write an F# declaration expressing the range function.

3. If r is a finite relation from A to B and a is an element of A, then the application of r to a, apply $r\ a$, is the set of elements b in B such that $(a, b) \in r$. Write an F# declaration expressing the apply function.

4. A relation r from a set A to the same set is said to be *symmetric* if $(a_1, a_2) \in r$ implies $(a_2, a_1) \in r$ for any elements a_1 and a_2 in A. The symmetric closure of a relation r is the smallest symmetric relation containing r. Declare an F# function to compute the symmetric closure.

5. The relation composition $r \circ\circ s$ of a relation r from a set A to a set B and a relation s from B to a set C is a relation from A to C. It is defined as the set of pairs (a, c) where there exist an element b in B such that $(a, b) \in r$ and $(b, c) \in s$. Declare an F# function to compute the relational composition.

6. A relation r from a set A to the same set A is said to be *transitive* if $(a_1, a_2) \in r$ and $(a_2, a_3) \in r$ implies $(a_1, a_3) \in r$ for any elements a_1, a_2 and a_3 in A. The transitive closure of a relation r is the smallest transitive relation containing r. If r contains n elements, then the transitive closure can be computed as the union of the following n relations:

$$r \cup (r \circ\circ r) \cup (r \circ\circ r \circ\circ r) \cup \cdots \cup (r \circ\circ r \circ\circ \cdots \circ\circ r)$$

Declare an F# function to compute the transitive closure.

5.7 Declare a function `allSubsets` such that `allSubsets n k` is the set of all subsets of $\{1, 2, \ldots, n\}$ containing exactly k elements. Hint: use ideas from Exercise 2.8. For example, $\binom{n}{k}$ is the number of subsets of $\{1, 2, \ldots, n\}$ containing exactly k elements.

5.8 Give declarations for `makeBill3` using `map.fold` rather than `map.foldBack`.

5.9 Declare a function to give a purchase map (see Version 3 on Page 118) on the basis of a list of items (from the Versions 1 and 2).

5.10 Extend the cash register example to take discounts for certain articles into account. For example, find a suitable representation of discounts and revise the function to make a bill accordingly.

5.11 Give a solution for Exercise 4.23 using the `Set` and `Map` libraries.

6

Finite trees

This chapter is about trees, which are structures that may contain subcomponents of the same type. A list is an example of a tree. The list $1::[2;3;4]$, for example, contains a subcomponent $[2;3;4]$ that is also a list. In this chapter we will introduce the concept of a tree through a variety of examples.

In F# we use a *recursive* type declaration to represent a set of values which are trees. The constructors of the type correspond to the rules for building trees, and patterns containing constructors are used when declaring functions on trees.

We motivate the use of finite trees and recursive types by a number of examples: Chinese boxes, symbolic differentiation, expression trees, search trees, file systems, trees with different kinds of nodes and electrical circuits.

6.1 Chinese boxes

A *Chinese box* is a coloured cube that contains a coloured cube that ... that contains a coloured cube that contains nothing. More precisely, a Chinese box is either *Nothing* or a *Cube* characterised by its *side length*, *colour* and the *contained* Chinese box. This characterization can be considered as stating rules for generating Chinese boxes, and it is used in the following definition of Chinese boxes as *trees*:

The set Cbox of *Chinese boxes* can be represented as the set of trees generated by the rules:

Rule 1: The tree Nothing is in Cbox.

Rule 2: If r is a float number, if c is a colour, and if cb is in Cbox, then the tree:

is also in Cbox.

Rule 3: The set Cbox contains no other values than the trees generated by repeated use of Rule 1 and Rule 2.

The following example shows how this definition can be used to generate elements of Cbox.

Step a: The void tree `Nothing` is a member of Cbox by Rule 1.
Step b: The following tree is a member of Cbox by Step a and Rule 2:

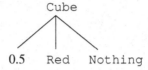

Step c: The following tree is a member of Cbox by Step b and Rule 2:

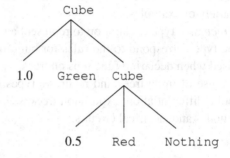

Step d: The following tree is a member of Cbox by Step c and Rule 2:

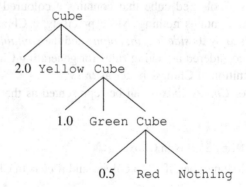

Type declaration

Using the following type `Colour`:

```
type Colour = Red | Blue | Green | Yellow | Purple;;
```

we declare a type Cbox representing the set of Chinese boxes as follows:

```
type Cbox = | Nothing                          // 1.
            | Cube of float * Colour * Cbox;; // 2.
```

The declaration is recursive, because the declared type Cbox occurs in the argument type of the constructor Cube. The constructors Nothing and Cube correspond to the above rules 1 and 2 for generating trees, so we can redo the above steps a through d with values of type Cbox:

Step a': The constructor Nothing is a value of type Cbox.

Step b': The value Cube(0.5,Red,Nothing) of type Cbox represents the tree generated in Step b.

Step c': The value Cube(1.0,Green,Cube(0.5,Red,Nothing)) of type Cbox represents the tree generated in Step c.

Step d': The value:

```
Cube(2.0,Yellow,Cube(1.0,Green,Cube(0.5,Red,Nothing)))
```

of type Cbox represents the tree generated in Step d.

These examples show the relationship between trees and values of type Cbox, and we note the following statements where the last one follows from Rule 3 for generating trees:

- Different values of type Cbox represent different trees.
- Any tree is represented by a value of type Cbox.

Hence, a value of type Cbox is just a way of writing a tree instead of drawing it. F# does not draw trees when printing values of type Cbox – the interactive F# system prints the textual form of the value:

```
let cb1 = Cube(0.5, Red, Nothing);;
val cb1 : Cbox = Cube (0.5,Red,Nothing)

let cb2 = Cube(1.0, Green, cb1);;
val cb2 : Cbox = Cube (1.0,Green,Cube (0.5,Red,Nothing))

let cb3 = Cube(2.0, Yellow, cb2);;
val cb3 : Cbox = Cube (2.0,Yellow,Cube (1.0,Green,
                     Cube (0.5,Red,Nothing)))
```

Patterns

In Section 3.8 we have seen declarations containing patterns for tagged values. Constructors for trees can occur in patterns just like constructors for tagged values. An example of a *tree pattern* is Cube(r,c,cb), containing identifiers r, c and cb for the components. This pattern denotes the tree in Figure 6.1.

This pattern will, for example, match the tree shown in Figure 6.2 corresponding to the value Cube(1.0,Green,Cube(0.5,Red,Nothing)) with bindings

$$r \mapsto 1.0$$
$$c \mapsto Green$$
$$cb \mapsto Cube(0.5,Red,Nothing)$$

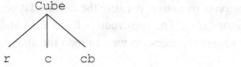

Figure 6.1 Tree for pattern Cube (r, c, cb)

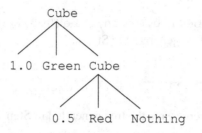

Figure 6.2 Tree for value cb2

where cb is bound to a value of type cbox corresponding to the tree shown in Step b on Page 122.

The *inductive* definition of the trees implies that any tree will either match the empty tree corresponding to the pattern:

```
Nothing
```

according to Rule 1 in the definition of trees, or the tree pattern for a cube in Figure 6.1 corresponding to:

```
Cube(r,c,cb)
```

according to Rule 2 in the definition of trees.

Function declarations

We give a declaration of the function:

```
count: Cbox -> int
```

such that the value of the expression: count (*cb*) is the number of cubes of the Chinese box *cb*:

```
let rec count = function
    | Nothing          -> 0
    | Cube(r,c,cb)     -> 1 + count cb;;
val count : Cbox -> int
```

The declaration divides into two cases, one with pattern Nothing and the other with pattern Cube (r, c, cb). Thus, the declaration follows the inductive definition of Chinese boxes.

This function can be applied to the above values cb2 and cb3:

```
count cb2 + count cb3;;
val it : int = 5
```

Invariant for Chinese boxes

A Chinese box must satisfy the invariant that the length of its sides is a positive floating-point number, which is larger than the side length of any cube it contains. The above four Chinese boxes in steps a to d satisfy this invariant, but using the generation process for trees one can construct the tree in Figure 6.3 that violates the invariant (i.e., it does not correspond to any Chinese box).

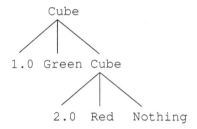

Figure 6.3 A tree violating the invariant

When declaring a function on Chinese boxes by the use of the type Cbox we must ensure that the function respects the invariant, that is, the function will only compute values of type Cbox satisfying the invariant when applied to values satisfying the invariant.

Insertion function

We can declare an insertion function on Chinese boxes:

```
insert: float * Colour * Cbox -> Cbox
```

The value of the expression insert (r, c, cb) is the Chinese box obtained from cb by inserting an extra cube with side length r and colour c at the proper place among the cubes in the box. The function insert is a partial function, that raises an exception in case the insertion would violate the invariant for Chinese boxes:

```
let rec insert(r,c,cb) =
  if r <= 0.0 then failwith "ChineseBox"
  else match cb with
       | Nothing          -> Cube(r,c,Nothing)
       | Cube(r1,c1,cb1) ->
             match compare r r1 with
             | t when t > 0 -> Cube(r,c,cb)
             | 0            -> failwith "ChineseBox"
             | _            -> Cube(r1,c1,insert(r,c,cb1));;
```

```
insert(2.0,Yellow,insert(1.0,Green,Nothing));;
val it : Cbox = Cube (2.0,Yellow,Cube (1.0,Green,Nothing))

insert(1.0,Green,insert(2.0,Yellow,Nothing));;
val it : Cbox = Cube (2.0,Yellow,Cube (1.0,Green,Nothing))

insert(1.0,Green,Cube(2.0,Yellow,Cube(1.0,Green,Nothing)));;
System.Exception: ChineseBox
Stopped due to error
```

Note, that any legal Chinese box can be generated from the box Nothing by repeated use of insert.

Other F# representations of Chinese Boxes

One may argue that the type cbox is unnecessarily complicated as Chinese boxes may simply be modelled using lists:

```
type Cbox = (float * Colour) list
```

This is, however, essentially the same as the above Cbox type of trees, as the list type is a special case of the general concept of recursive types (cf. Section 6.3).

One may also argue that it is strange to have a constructor Nothing denoting a non-existing Chinese box, and one might rather discard the empty box and divide the Chinese boxes into those consisting of a single cube and those consisting of multiple cubes, as expressed in the following declaration:

```
type Cbox1 = | Single of float * Colour
             | Multiple of float * Colour * Cbox1;;
```

Using this type, we get the following declarations of the functions count and insert:

```
let rec count1 = function
  | Single _          -> 1
  | Multiple(_,_,cb) -> 1 + count1 cb;;

let rec insert1 (r1,c1,cb2) =
  if r1 <= 0.0 then failwith "insert1: Chinese box"
  else match cb2 with
       | Single (r2,c2)      ->
         match compare r1 r2 with
         | t when t < 0 -> Multiple(r2,c2,Single(r1,c1))
         | 0            -> failwith "ChineseBox"
         | _            -> Multiple(r1,c1,cb2)
       | Multiple (r2,c2,cb3) ->
         match compare r1 r2 with
         | t when t < 0 -> Multiple(r2,c2,insert1(r1,c1,cb3))
         | 0            -> failwith "ChineseBox"
         | _            -> Multiple(r1,c1,cb2);;
```

We have now suggested several representations for Chinese boxes. The preferable choice of representation will in general depend on which functions we have to define. The clumsy declaration of the `insert1` function contains repeated sub-expressions and this indicates that the first model for Chinese boxes with a `Nothing` value is to be preferred.

6.2 Symbolic differentiation

We want to construct a program for computing the derivative of a real function of one variable. The program should, for example, compute the derivative $f'(x) = 2x \cdot \cos(x^2)$ of the function $f(x) = \sin(x^2)$. The concept of *function* in F# cannot be used for this purpose, as such a function declaration just gives the means of computing values of the function. For example:

```
let f x = sin(x * x);;
val f : float -> float

f 2.0;;
val it : float = -0.7568024953
```

The differentiation is a manipulation of the *expression* denoting a function, so we need a *representation* of the *structure* of such expressions. This can be done using expression trees.

We restrict our attention to expressions constructed from real-valued constants and the variable x, using the arithmetic functions: addition, subtraction, multiplication and division, and the real functions sin, cos, log and exp. We use the symbols `Add`, `Sub`, `Mul` and `Div` to represent the arithmetic operators, and the symbols `Sin`, `Cos`, `Log` and `Exp` to represent the special functions. The expressions $\sin(x \cdot x)$ and $(\sin x) \cdot x$ will then be represented by the expression trees shown in Figure 6.4.

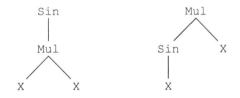

Figure 6.4 Trees for $\sin(x \cdot x)$ and $(\sin x) \cdot x$

The different order of the operators in these expressions is reflected in the trees: the tree for $\sin(x \cdot x)$ contains a sub-tree for the sub-expression $x \cdot x$, which again contains two sub-trees for the sub-expressions x and x, while the tree for $(\sin x) \cdot x$ contains sub-trees for the sub-expressions $\sin x$ and x.

The set of finite expression trees Fexpr is generated inductively by the following rules:

Rule 1: For every float number r, the tree for the constant r shown in Figure 6.5 is a member of Fexpr.

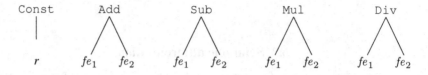

Figure 6.5 Tree for the constant r and trees for dyadic operators

Rule 2: The tree X is in Fexpr.

Rule 3: If fe_1 and fe_2 are in Fexpr, then the trees for the dyadic operators for addition, subtraction, multiplication and division shown in Figure 6.5 are members of Fexpr.

Rule 4: If fe is in Fexpr, then the trees for the special functions shown in Figure 6.6 are in Fexpr.

Figure 6.6 Trees for special functions

Rule 5: The set Fexpr contains no other values than the trees generated by rules 1. to 4.

Type declaration

Expression trees can be represented in F# by values of a recursively defined type. We get the following declaration of the type Fexpr:

```
type Fexpr = | Const of float
             | X
             | Add of Fexpr * Fexpr
             | Sub of Fexpr * Fexpr
             | Mul of Fexpr * Fexpr
             | Div of Fexpr * Fexpr
             | Sin of Fexpr
             | Cos of Fexpr
             | Log of Fexpr
             | Exp of Fexpr;;
```

For instance, the expression trees for $\sin(x \cdot x)$ and $(\sin x) \cdot x$ are represented by the values Sin(Mul(X,X)) and Mul(Sin X,X) of type Fexpr.

Patterns

The following patterns correspond to values of type `Fexpr`:

```
Const r           X
Add(fe1,fe2)      Sub(fe1,fe2)      Mul(fe1,fe2)      Div(fe1,fe2)
Sin fe            Cos fe            Log fe            Exp fe
```

These patterns can be used in function declarations with a division into clauses according to the structure of expression trees.

$g'(x) = 0$ when $g(x) = c$, for $c \in \mathbb{R}$	Constant
$f'(x) = 1$ when $f(x) = x$	Identity
$(f(x) + g(x))' = f'(x) + g'(x)$	Addition
$(f(x) - g(x))' = f'(x) - g'(x)$	Subtraction
$(f(x) \cdot g(x))' = f'(x) \cdot g(x) + f(x) \cdot g'(x)$	Multiplication
$(f(x)/g(x))' = (f'(x) \cdot g(x) - f(x) \cdot g'(x))/(g(x))^2$	Division
$f(g(x))' = f'(g((x))) \cdot g'(x)$	Composition
$(\sin x)' = \cos x$ and $(\cos x)' = -\sin x$	Trigonometry
$(\log x)' = 1/x$	Logarithmic
$(\exp x)' = \exp x$	Exponential

Table 6.1 *Differentiation rules*

Function declaration

We are now in a position to declare a function

```
D: Fexpr -> Fexpr
```

such that D(fe) is a representation of the derivative with respect to x of the function represented by fe. The declaration for D has a clause for each constructor generating a value of type `Fexpr`, and each clause is a direct translation of the corresponding mathematical differentiation rule (see Tables 6.1 and 6.2):

```
let rec D = function
  | Const _     -> Const 0.0
  | X           -> Const 1.0
  | Add(fe,ge)  -> Add(D fe, D ge)
  | Sub(fe,ge)  -> Sub(D fe, D ge)
  | Mul(fe,ge)  -> Add(Mul(D fe, ge), Mul(fe, D ge))
  | Div(fe,ge)  -> Div(Sub(Mul(D fe,ge), Mul(fe,D ge)),
                       Mul(ge,ge))
  | Sin fe      -> Mul(Cos fe, D fe)
  | Cos fe      -> Mul(Const -1.0, Mul(Sin fe, D fe))
  | Log fe      -> Div(D fe, fe)
  | Exp fe      -> Mul(Exp fe, D fe);;
val D : Fexpr -> Fexpr
```

Table 6.2 *Differentiation function*

The following examples illustrate the use of the function:

```
D(Sin(Mul(X, X)));;
val it : Fexpr =
  Mul (Cos (Mul (X,X)),
        Add (Mul (Const 1.0,X),Mul (X,Const 1.0)))

D(Mul(Const 3.0, Exp X));;
val it : Fexpr =
  Add (Mul (Const 0.0,Exp X),
        Mul (Const 3.0,Mul (Exp X,Const 1.0)))
```

Note, that these examples show results which can be reduced. For example, the above value of D(Mul(Const 3.0, Exp X)) could be reduced to Mul(Const 3.0, Exp X) if a product with a zero factor was reduced to zero, and if adding zero or multiplying by one was absorbed. It is an interesting, non-trivial, task to declare a function that reduces expressions to a particular, simple form.

Conversion to textual representation

The following function: toString: Fexpr -> string, will produce a textual representation of a function expression:

```
let rec toString = function
    | Const x        -> string x
    | X              -> "x"
    | Add(fe1,fe2)   -> "(" + (toString fe1) + ")"
                        + " + " + "(" + (toString fe2) + ")"
    | Sub(fe1,fe2)   -> "(" + (toString fe1) + ")"
                        + " - " + "(" + (toString fe2) + ")"
    | Mul(fe1,fe2)   -> "(" + (toString fe1) + ")"
                        + " * " + "(" + (toString fe2) + ")"
    | Div(fe1,fe2)   -> "(" + (toString fe1) + ")"
                        + " / " + "(" + (toString fe2) + ")"
    | Sin fe         -> "sin(" + (toString fe) + ")"
    | Cos fe         -> "cos(" + (toString fe) + ")"
    | Log fe         -> "log(" + (toString fe) + ")"
    | Exp fe         -> "exp(" + (toString fe) + ")";;
val toString : Fexpr -> string

toString(Mul(Cos(Mul(X, X)),
             Add(Mul(Const 1.0, X), Mul(X, Const 1.0)))));;
val it : string =
  "(cos((x) * (x))) * (((1) * (x)) + ((x) * (1)))"

toString(Add(Mul(X, Mul(X, X)) , Mul(X, X)));;
val it : string = "((x) * ((x) * (x))) + ((x) * (x))"
```

The function `toString` puts brackets around every operand of an operator and every argument of a function. It is possible to declare a better `toString` function that avoids unnecessary brackets. See Exercise 6.3.

6.3 Binary trees. Parameterized types

The constructors in a type declaration may have polymorphic types containing type variables. These type variables are *parameters* of the type, and written in angle brackets <...> just following the type constructor in the declaration.

An example of a type declaration with parameters is the type `BinTree<'a,'b>` of *binary trees* with leaves containing elements of type ′ a and nodes containing elements of type ′ b:

```
type BinTree<'a,'b> =
    | Leaf of 'a
    | Node of BinTree<'a,'b> * 'b * BinTree<'a,'b>;;
```

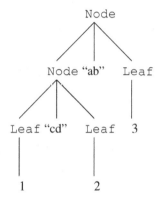

Figure 6.7 A tree t_1 of type `BinTree<int,string>`

The tree t_1 in Figure 6.7 corresponds to the value

```
let t1 = Node(Node(Leaf 1,"cd",Leaf 2),"ab",Leaf 3);;
```

of type `BinTree<int,string>`. The top node with element `"ab"` is called the *root* of the tree t_1 (trees are drawn upside-down in computer science with the root at the top and the leaves at the bottom). The trees t_2 and t_3 in Figure 6.8 corresponding to the values

```
let t2 = Node(Leaf 1,"cd",Leaf 2);;
let t3 = Leaf 3;;
```

are called the *left sub-tree* and *the right sub-tree* of t_1.

The type `BinTree` is *polymorphic* and allows polymorphic values like:

```
Node(Node(Leaf [],[],Leaf []),[],Leaf []);;
```

of type `BinTree<'a list,'b list>`.

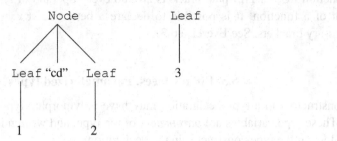

Figure 6.8 Left and right sub-tree t_2 and t_3 of the tree t_1

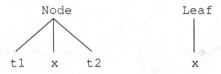

Figure 6.9 Trees for patterns `Node(t1,x,t2)` and `Leaf x`

The constructors `Node` and `Leaf` can be used in *patterns* like

```
Leaf x
Node(t1,x,t2)
```

corresponding to the pattern trees in Figure 6.9. Using this we may, for example, declare a function `depth` computing the depth of a binary tree:

```
let rec depth = function
    | Leaf _         -> 0
    | Node(t1,_,t2) -> 1 + max (depth t1) (depth t2);;
val depth : BinTree<'a,'b> -> int

depth t1;;
val it : int = 2
```

Figure 6.10 Simplified drawing of the tree `t1` in Figure 6.7

In the following we will often use simplified drawings of trees where the constructors have been left out and replaced by the value attached to the node. Such a simplified drawing of the tree `t1` in Figure 6.7 is shown in Figure 6.10.

6.4 Traversal of binary trees. Search trees

A *traversal* of a binary tree is a function *visiting the nodes* of the tree in a certain order. We may hence assume that the leafs do not carry any information corresponding to a simplified `BinTree` type:

```
type BinTree<'a> = | Leaf
                   | Node of BinTree<'a> * 'a * BinTree<'a>;;
```

A traversal of a tree of this type is then described by a function of type:

```
BinTree<'a> -> 'a list
```

We consider three kinds of traversals:

Pre-order traversal: First visit the root node, then traverse the left sub-tree in pre-order and finally traverse the right sub-tree in pre-order.

In-order traversal: First traverse the left sub-tree in in-order, then visit the root node and finally traverse the right sub-tree in in-order.

Post-order traversal: First traverse the left sub-tree in post-order, then traverse the right sub-tree in post-order and finally visit the root node.

The declarations look as follows:

```
let rec preOrder = function
    | Leaf          -> []
    | Node(tl,x,tr) -> x :: (preOrder tl) @ (preOrder tr);;
val preOrder : BinTree<'a> -> 'a list

let rec inOrder = function
    | Leaf          -> []
    | Node(tl,x,tr) -> (inOrder tl) @ [x] @ (inOrder tr);;
val inOrder : BinTree<'a> -> 'a list

let rec postOrder = function
    | Leaf          -> []
    | Node(tl,x,tr) -> (postOrder tl) @ (postOrder tr) @ [x];;
val postOrder : BinTree<'a> -> 'a list
```

We define values `t3` and `t4` of type `BinTree<int>` by:

```
let t3 = Node(Node(Leaf, -3, Leaf), 0, Node(Leaf, 2, Leaf));;
let t4 = Node(t3, 5, Node(Leaf, 7, Leaf));;
```

Figure 6.11 Trees corresponding to values `t3` and `t4`

Simplified drawings of the corresponding trees without constructors are shown in Figure 6.11. We will use such simplified drawings in the following.

Applying the traversal functions to t4 we get:

```
preOrder t4;;
val it : int list = [5; 0; -3; 2; 7]

inOrder t4;;
val it : int list = [-3; 0; 2; 5; 7]

postOrder t4;;
val it : int list = [-3; 2; 0; 7; 5]
```

The reader should compare these lists with the figure and the oral descriptions of the traversal functions.

Traversal of binary trees can more generally be described by `fold` and `foldBack` functions defined such that the following holds:

```
preFold f e t      = List.fold f e (preOrder t)
preFoldBack f t e = List.foldBack f (preOrder t) e
```

and similar for in-order and post-order traversals. These functions should be declared to accumulate the values in the nodes while traversing the tree – without actually building the list. We show one of the declarations:

```
let rec postFoldBack f t e =
    match t with
    | Leaf              -> e
    | Node(tl,x,tr) ->
            let ex = f x e
            let er = postFoldBack f tr ex
            postFoldBack f tl er;;
val postFoldBack : ('a -> 'b -> 'b) -> BinTree<'a> -> 'b -> 'b

postFoldBack (fun x xs -> x::xs) t4 [];;
val it : int list = [-3; 2; 0; 7; 5]
```

The other declarations are left as exercises.

The type system of F# allows a great variety of tree types and there is no standard `Tree` library with a standard `tree` type. Functions like `inOrder` or `inFold` are hence defined individually according to need in each program using a tree type.

There are also imperative tree traversal functions where an imperative function is called whenever an element in the tree is visited, see Section 8.9.

Search trees

We restrict the type variable `'a` in our `BinTree` type to types with an ordering:

```
type BinTree<'a when 'a : comparison> =
      | Leaf
      | Node of BinTree<'a> * 'a * BinTree<'a>;;
```

A value of type `BinTree<'a>` is then called a *search tree* if it satisfies the following condition:

Every node $\text{Node}(t_{\text{left}}, a, t_{\text{right}})$ satisfies:
  $a' < a$ for every value a' occurring in t_{left} and
  $a'' > a$ for every value a'' occurring in t_{right}.

This condition is called the *search tree invariant*. The trees t3 and t4 defined above and shown in Figure 6.11 satisfy this invariant and are hence search trees.

A search tree can be used to represent a *finite set* $\{a_0, a_1, \ldots, a_{n-1}\}$. This representation is particularly efficient when the tree is balanced (see discussion on Page 136).

A function `add` for adding a value to a search tree can be defined as follows:

```
let rec add x t =
    match t with
    | Leaf                        -> Node(Leaf,x,Leaf)
    | Node(tl,a,tr) when x<a -> Node(add x tl,a,tr)
    | Node(tl,a,tr) when x>a -> Node(tl,a,add x tr)
    | _                           -> t;;
val add: 'a -> BinTree<'a> -> BinTree<'a> when 'a: comparison
```

It builds a single-node tree when adding a value x to an empty tree. When adding to a non-empty tree with root a the value is added to the left sub-tree if x < a and to the right sub-tree if x > a. The tree is left unchanged if x = a because the value x is then already member of the represented set.

Adding the value 4 to the search tree t4

```
let t5 = add 4 t4;;
val t5 : BinTree<int> =
  Node
    (Node(Node(Leaf,-3,Leaf),0,Node(Leaf,2,Node(Leaf,4,Leaf))),
     5,Node(Leaf,7,Leaf))
```

gives the tree in Figure 6.12.

Figure 6.12 Search trees corresponding to the value t5

It follows by an inductive argument that an *in-order traversal* of a *search tree* will visit the elements in *ascending order* because the elements in the left sub-tree are smaller than the root element while the elements in the right sub-tree are larger – and this applies inductively to any sub-tree. We get for instance:

```
inOrder t5;;
val it : int list = [-3; 0; 2; 4; 5; 7]
```

An in-order traversal of a search tree will hence give a list where the elements in the nodes occur in ascending order.

A function `contains` for testing set membership can be declared by:

```
let rec contains x = function
    | Leaf                          -> false
    | Node(tl,a,_) when x<a -> contains x tl
    | Node(_,a,tr) when x>a -> contains x tr
    | _                             -> true;;
val contains : 'a -> BinTree<'a> -> bool when 'a : comparison

contains 4 t5;;
val it : bool = true
```

It uses the search tree property in only testing the left sub-tree if x < the root node value and only the right sub-tree if x > the root node value. The number of comparisons made when evaluating a function value: `contains` x t is hence *less or equal* to the *depth* of the tree t. It follows that the tree t5 in Figure 6.12 is not an optimal representation of the set, because the set can be represented by the tree of depth 2 in Figure 6.13. The tree t5 was created by the above `add` function, and it would hence require a more sophisticated `add` function to get the "balanced" tree in Figure 6.13 instead.

Figure 6.13 Search tree of depth 2 representing same set as t5

The number of nodes in a balanced tree with depth k is approximately 2^k and the depth of a balanced tree with n nodes is hence approximately $\log_2 n$. The Set and Map collections in the F# library use balanced search trees to get efficient implementations. A function like `Set.contains` will hence require circa $\log_2 n$ comparisons when used on a set with n elements. Searching a value (e.g., using `List.exists`) in a list of length n may require up to n comparisons. That makes a big difference for large n (e.g., $\log_2 n \approx 20$ when $n = 1000000$).

6.5 Expression trees

Tree representation of expressions is a common technique in compiler technology. This section gives a bit of the flavour of this technique. The subject is related to the function expression trees presented in Section 6.2.

We consider integer expressions of the form:

integer constant
identifier
– expression
expression + expression
expression – expression
*expression * expression*
let *identifier = expression* in *expression*
(*expression*)

They are represented by expression trees of the following type:

```
type ExprTree = | Const of int
                | Ident of string
                | Minus of ExprTree
                | Sum   of ExprTree * ExprTree
                | Diff  of ExprTree * ExprTree
                | Prod  of ExprTree * ExprTree
                | Let of string * ExprTree * ExprTree;;
```

such that, for example, the expression:

```
a * (-3 + (let x = 5 in x + a))
```

is represented by the value:

```
let et =
    Prod(Ident "a",
         Sum(Minus (Const 3),
             Let("x", Const 5, Sum(Ident "x", Ident "a"))));;
```

An expression is evaluated in an *environment* containing *bindings* of identifiers to values. An environment is represented by a value *env* of type map<string,int> containing entries with identifier and corresponding value. A let tree

$$Let\,(str, t_1, t_2)$$

is evaluated as follows in an environment *env*:

1. Evaluate t_1 to value v_1
2. Evaluate t_2 in the environment *env* extended with the binding of *str* to *v*.

An evaluation function

```
eval: ExprTree -> map<string,int> -> int
```

can now be defined recursively by dividing into cases according to the structure of the tree:

```
let rec eval t env =
    match t with
    | Const n       -> n
    | Ident s       -> Map.find s env
    | Minus t       -> - (eval t env)
    | Sum(t1,t2)    -> eval t1 env + eval t2 env
    | Diff(t1,t2)   -> eval t1 env - eval t2 env
    | Prod(t1,t2)   -> eval t1 env * eval t2 env
    | Let(s,t1,t2)  -> let v1   = eval t1 env
                       let env1 = Map.add s v1 env
                       eval t2 env1;;
val eval : ExprTree -> Map<string,int> -> int
```

We may, for example, evaluate the above representation et of an expression in the environment env where the identifier "a" is bound to the value -7:

```
let env = Map.add "a" -7 Map.empty;;
```

```
eval et env;;
val it : int = 35
```

6.6 Trees with a variable number of sub-trees. Mutual recursion

Trees with a variable number of sub-trees are obtained by using a type where each node contains a (possibly empty) list of sub-trees. An example is the type:

```
type ListTree<'a> = Node of 'a * (ListTree<'a> list);;
```

Values of ListTree type represent trees where:

Node(x, [])	represents a leaf tree containing the value x
Node(x, $[t_0; \ldots; t_{n-1}]$)	represents a tree with value x in the root and with n sub-trees represented by the values $t_0, \ldots, t_{n-1}$

Such a tree is shown in Figure 6.14. It is represented by the value t1 where

```
let t7 = Node(7,[]);;     let t6 = Node(6,[]);;
let t5 = Node(5,[]);;     let t3 = Node(3,[]);;
let t2 = Node(2,[t5]);;   let t4 = Node(4,[t6; t7]);;
let t1 = Node(1,[t2; t3; t4]);;
```

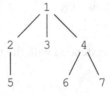

Figure 6.14 Tree represented by the value t1

Traversal of list trees

We consider two kinds of traversal of list-trees: depth-first and breadth-first traversal. These traversals correspond to the following order of the elements of the tree in Figure 6.14:

Depth-first: 1, 2, 5, 3, 4, 6, 7
Breadth-first: 1, 2, 3, 4, 5, 6, 7

In both cases we define a function to generate the list of nodes as well as `fold` and `foldBack` functions. The declarations involve functions on *lists* because the sub-trees of a node are organized as a list.

In the depth-first order we first visit the root node and then the nodes in each element of the list of immediate sub-trees: The function `depthFirst` generating a list of elements is declared using the library function `List.collect` (cf. Table 5.1) to apply `depthFirst` to each sub-tree in the list and afterwards collect the obtained lists into one list:

```
let rec depthFirst (Node(x,ts)) =
    x :: (List.collect depthFirst ts);;
val depthFirst : ListTree<'a> -> 'a list
```

The function `depthFirstFold f` is declared using `List.fold` to apply the function to each tree in the list of sub-trees and to transfer the accumulated value to the call on the next sub-tree:

```
let rec depthFirstFold f e (Node(x,ts)) =
    List.fold (depthFirstFold f) (f e x) ts;;
val depthFirstFold: ('a->'b->'a) -> 'a -> ListTree<'b> -> 'a

depthFirstFold (fun a x -> x::a) [] t1;;
val it : int list = [7; 6; 4; 3; 5; 2; 1]
```

The reader should appreciate this short and elegant combination of library functions.

The declaration of `depthFirstFoldBack` is left as an exercise to the reader (cf. Exercise 6.12).

In the breadth-first order we should first visit the root and then the roots of the immediate sub-trees and so on. This view of the problem does, unfortunately, not lead to any useful recursion because the remaining part becomes organized in an inconvenient list of lists of sub-trees.

A nice recursive pattern is instead obtained by constantly keeping track of the list `rest` of sub-trees where the nodes still remain to be visited. Using this idea on the tree in Figure 6.14 we get:

Visit	rest
1	`[t2; t3; t4]`
2	`[t3; t4; t5]`
3	`[t4; t5]`
4	`[t5; t6; t7]`
...	...

Each step in this scheme will do the following:

1. Remove the head element t of the list rest.
2. Get a new rest list by appending the list of immediate sub-trees of t.
3. Visit the root of t.

The traversal finishes when the list rest becomes empty.

This pattern is used in the following declarations where the argument of the auxiliary function breadthFirstList is a list corresponding to the rest list of sub-trees:

```
let rec breadthFirstList = function
  | []                       -> []
  | (Node(x,ts)) :: rest ->
        x :: breadthFirstList(rest@ts);;
val breadthFirstList : ListTree<'a> list -> 'a list

let breadthFirst t = breadthFirstList [t];;
val breadthFirst : ListTree<'a> -> 'a list

breadthFirst t1;;
val it : int list = [1; 2; 3; 4; 5; 6; 7]
```

The declaration of breadthFirstFoldBack follows the same pattern:

```
let rec breadthFirstFoldBackList f ts e =
    match ts with
    | []      -> e
    | (Node(x,ts))::rest ->
            f x (breadthFirstFoldBackList f (rest@ts) e);;
val breadthFirstFoldBackList :
  ('a -> 'b -> 'b) -> ListTree<'a> list -> 'b -> 'b

let breadthFirstFoldBack f t e =
                breadthFirstFoldBackList f [t] e;;
val breadthFirstFoldBack :
  ('a -> 'b -> 'b) -> ListTree<'a> -> 'b -> 'b

breadthFirstFoldBack (fun x a -> x::a) t1 [];;
val it : int list = [1; 2; 3; 4; 5; 6; 7]
```

The declaration of breadthFirstFold is left as an exercise to the reader (cf. Exercise 6.12).

There are also imperative versions of these tree traversals where an imperative function is called whenever a node is visited, see Section 8.9 for depth-first traversal and Section 8.13 for breadth-first traversal. The breadth-first traversal uses an imperative queue.

Example of list trees: File system

A file system is a list of named files and named directories where each directory contains another file system. Figure 6.15 shows a directory named d_1 with its associated file system.

The directory d_1 contains two files a_1 and a_4 and two directories d_2 and d_3. The directory d_2 contains a file a_2 and a directory d_3, and so on. Note that the same name may occur in different directories. This structure is an example of a tree with variable number of sub-trees.

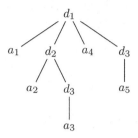

Figure 6.15 Directory with file system

Discarding the contents of files we represent a file system and its contents by two declarations:

```
type FileSys = Element list
and Element  = | File of string
               | Dir of string * FileSys;;
```

The first declaration refers to a type `Element` which is declared in the second declaration. This "forward" reference to the type `Element` is allowed by the F# system because `Element` is declared in the second declaration using the keyword `and`. These two declarations constitute an example of *mutually recursive* type declarations, as the type `Element` occurs in the declaration of `FileSys` and the type `FileSys` occurs in the declaration of `Element`.

The directory shown in Figure 6.15 is represented by the value:

```
let d1 =
  Dir("d1",[File "a1";
            Dir("d2", [File "a2"; Dir("d3", [File "a3"])]);
            File "a4";
            Dir("d3", [File "a5"])
           ]);;
```

The declarations below yield functions `namesFileSys` and `namesElement` extracting a list of names of all files (including files in subdirectories) for file systems and elements, respectively:

```
let rec namesFileSys = function
    | []     -> []
    | e::es -> (namesElement e) @ (namesFileSys es)
and namesElement = function
    | File s    -> [s]
    | Dir(s,fs) -> s :: (namesFileSys fs);;
val namesFileSys : Element list -> string list
val namesElement : Element -> string list
```

The above function declarations are *mutually recursive* as the identifier namesElement occurs in the declaration of namesFileSys while the identifier namesFileSys occurs in the declaration of namesElement. Mutually recursive functions are declared using the keyword and to combine the individual function declarations.

The names of file and directories in the directory d1 may now be extracted:

```
namesElement d1;;
val it : string list = ["d1"; "a1"; "d2"; "a2";
                        "d3"; "a3"; "a4"; "d3"; "a5"]
```

6.7 Electrical circuits

We consider electrical circuits built from *components* by *serial* or *parallel* composition. We represent a circuit by a value of the following type:

```
type Circuit<'a> = | Comp of 'a
                   | Ser  of Circuit<'a> * Circuit<'a>
                   | Par  of Circuit<'a> * Circuit<'a>;;
```

In Figure 6.16 we show a circuit containing three components with attached values 0.25, 1.0, and 1.5 together with the tree representing the circuit:

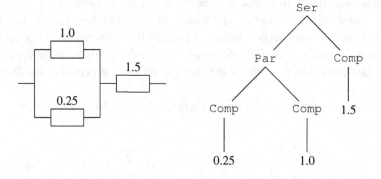

Figure 6.16 Circuit and corresponding tree

In F# the value is written Ser(Par(Comp 0.25, Comp 1.0), Comp 1.5):

```
let cmp = Ser(Par(Comp 0.25, Comp 1.0), Comp 1.5);;
val cmp : Circuit<float>
        = Ser(Par(Comp 0.25,Comp 1.0),Comp 1.5)
```

Using this representation of circuits we can define a function count for computing the number of components in a circuit:

```
let rec count = function
    | Comp _      -> 1
    | Ser(c1,c2) -> count c1 + count c2
    | Par(c1,c2) -> count c1 + count c2;;
val count : Circuit<'a> -> int
```

For example:

```
count cmp;;
val it : int = 3
```

We consider now circuits consisting of resistances where the attached values are the resistances of the individual components. Suppose c_1 and c_2 are two circuits with resistances r_1 and r_2, respectively. The resistance of a serial combination of c_1 and c_2 is $r_1 + r_2$, and the resistance of a parallel combination of c_1 and c_2 is given by the formula:

$$\frac{1}{1/r_1 + 1/r_2}$$

Thus, a function `resistance` computing the resistance of a circuit can be declared by:

```
let rec resistance = function
    | Comp r      -> r
    | Ser(c1,c2) -> resistance c1 + resistance c2
    | Par(c1,c2) ->
          1.0 / (1.0/resistance c1 + 1.0/resistance c2);;
val resistance : Circuit<float> -> float
```

For example:

```
resistance cmp;;
val it : float = 1.7
```

Tree recursion

The functions `count` and `resistance` on circuits can be expressed using a generic higher-order function `circRec` for traversing circuits. This function must be parameterized with three functions c, s and p, where

c :	`'a -> 'b`	The value for a single component.
s :	`'b -> 'b -> 'b`	The combined value for two circuits connected in series.
p :	`'b -> 'b -> 'b`	The combined value for two circuits connected in parallel.

Note that s and p have the type `'b -> 'b -> 'b` because they operate on the values for two circuits. Thus, a general higher-order recursion function for circuits will have the type:

```
('a -> 'b) * ('b -> 'b -> 'b) * ('b -> 'b -> 'b)
    -> Circuit<'a> -> 'b
```

and the function is declared by:

```
let rec circRec (c,s,p) = function
    | Comp x      -> c x
    | Ser(c1,c2) ->
          s (circRec (c,s,p) c1) (circRec (c,s,p) c2)
    | Par(c1,c2) ->
          p (circRec (c,s,p) c1) (circRec (c,s,p) c2);;
```

The function `circRec` can, for example, be used to compute the number of components in a circuit by use of the following functions *c*, *s*, and *p*:

c   is   fun _ -> 1   Each component counts for 1.
s   is   (+)   The count for a serial composition is the sum of the counts.
p   is   (+)   The count for a parallel composition is the sum of the counts.

```
let count circ = circRec((fun _ -> 1), (+), (+)) circ : int;;
val count : Circuit<'a> -> int
```

The type `int` is required to resolve the overloaded plus operators.

```
count(Ser(Par(Comp 0.25, Comp 1.0), Comp 1.5));;
val it : int = 3
```

Suppose again that the value attached to every component in a circuit is the resistance of the component. Then the function `circRec` can be used to compute the resistance of a circuit by use of the following functions *c*, *s*, and *p*:

c   is   fun r -> r
           The attached value is the resistance.

s   is   (+)
           The resistance of a serial composition is the sum of the resistances.

p   is   fun r1 r2 -> 1.0/(1.0/r1+1.0/r2)
           The resistance of a parallel composition is computed by this formula.

Using these functions for *c*, *s* and *p* we get:

```
let resistance =
    circRec(
        (fun r -> r),
        (+),
        (fun r1 r2 -> 1.0/(1.0/r1 + 1.0/r2)));;
val resistance : (Circuit<float> -> float)

resistance(Ser(Par(Comp 0.25, Comp 1.0), Comp 1.5));;
val it : float = 1.7
```

Summary

We have introduced the notion of finite trees and motivated this concept through a variety of examples. In F# a recursive type declaration is used to represent a set of values which are trees. The constructors of the type correspond to the rules for building trees, and patterns containing constructors are used when declaring functions on trees. We have also introduced the notions of parameterized types, and mutually recursive type and function declarations.

Exercises

6.1 Declare a function *red* of type `Fexpr -> Fexpr` to reduce expressions generated from the differentiation program in Section 6.2. For example, sub-expressions of form `Const 1.0 * e` can be reduced to *e*. (A solution is satisfactory if the expression becomes "nicer". It is difficult to design a reduce function so that all trivial sub-expressions are eliminated.)

6.2 Postfix form is a particular representation of arithmetic expressions where each operator is preceded by its operand(s), for example:

$(x + 7.0)$ has postfix form $x\ 7.0\ +$

$(x + 7.0) * (x - 5.0)$ has postfix form $x\ 7.0\ +\ x\ 5.0\ -\ *$

Declare an F# function with type `Fexpr -> string` computing the textual, postfix form of expression trees from Section 6.2.

6.3 Make a refined version of the `toString` function on Page 130 using the following conventions: A subtrahend, factor or dividend must be in brackets if it is an addition or subtraction. A divisor must be in brackets if it is an addition, subtraction, multiplication or division. The argument of a function must be in brackets unless it is a constant or the variable x. (Hint: use a set of mutually recursive declarations.)

6.4 Consider binary trees of type `BinTree<'a,'b>` as defined in Section 6.3. Declare functions

1. `leafVals: BinTree<'a,'b> -> Set<'a>` such that `leafVals` *t* is the set of values occurring the leaves of *t*,
2. `nodeVals: BinTree<'a,'b> -> Set<'b>` such that `nodeVals` *t* is the set of values occurring the nodes of *t*, and
3. `vals: BinTree<'a,'b> -> Set<'a>*Set<'b>` such that `vals` $t = (ls, ns)$, where *ls* is the set of values occurring the leaves of *l* and *ns* is the set of values occurring the nodes of *t*

6.5 An ancestor tree contains the name of a person and of some of the ancestors of this person. We define the type `AncTree` by:

```
type AncTree = | Unspec
               | Info of AncTree * string * AncTree;;
```

The left sub-tree is the ancestor tree of the farther while the right sub-tree is the ancestor tree of the mother. Write a value of type `ancTree` with at least 5 nodes and make a drawing of the corresponding tree.

Declare functions `maleAnc` and `femaleAnc` to compute the list of names of male and female ancestors of a person in an ancestor tree.

6.6 Consider search trees of type `BinTree<'a>` as defined in Section 6.4. Declare an F# function that can delete an element in such a tree. Hint: Make use of an auxiliary function that deletes the smallest element in a non-empty search tree (and returns that value).

6.7 1. Define a type to represent formulas in propositional logic. A proposition is either an atom given by its name which is a string, or a composite proposition built from atoms using the operators for negation ($\neg$), conjunction ($\wedge$), and disjunction ($\vee$).

2. A proposition is in *negation normal form* if the negation operator only appears as applied directly to atoms. Write an F# function transforming a proposition into an equivalent proposition in negation normal form, using the de Morgan laws:

$$\neg(p \wedge q) \quad \Leftrightarrow \quad (\neg p) \vee (\neg q)$$
$$\neg(p \vee q) \quad \Leftrightarrow \quad (\neg p) \wedge (\neg q)$$

and the law: $\neg(\neg p) \Leftrightarrow p$.

3. A *literal* is an atom or its negation. A proposition is in *conjunctive normal form* if it is a conjunction of propositions, where each conjunct (i.e., proposition in the conjunction) is a disjunction of literals. Write an F# function that transforms a proposition into an equivalent proposition in conjunctive normal form, using the above result and the laws:

$$p \vee (q \wedge r) \quad \Leftrightarrow \quad (p \vee q) \wedge (p \vee r)$$
$$(p \wedge q) \vee r \quad \Leftrightarrow \quad (p \vee r) \wedge (q \vee r)$$

4. A proposition is a *tautology* if it has truth value *true* for any assignment of truth values to the atoms. A disjunction of literals is a tautology exactly when it contains the atom as well as the negated atom for some name occurring in the disjunction. A conjunction is a tautology precisely when each conjunct is a tautology. Write a tautology checker in F#, that is, an F# function which determines whether a proposition is a tautology or not.

6.8   We consider a simple calculator with instructions for addition, subtraction, multiplication and division of floats, and the functions: sin, cos, log and exp.

The *instruction set* of the calculator is modelled by the following F# type:

```
type Instruction = | ADD | SUB | MULT | DIV | SIN
                   | COS | LOG | EXP  | PUSH of float
```

The calculator is a *stack machine*, where a *stack* is a list of floats.

The *execution* of an instruction maps a stack to a new stack:

The execution of ADD with stack $\boxed{a \ b \ c \ \cdots}$ yields a new stack: $\boxed{(b+a) \ c \ \cdots}$, where the top two elements a and b on the stack have been replaced by the single element $(b+a)$. Similarly with regard to the instructions, SUB, MULT and DIV, which all work on the *top* two elements of the stack.

The execution of one of the instructions SIN, COS, LOG and EXP applies the corresponding function to the top element of the stack. For example, the execution of LOG with stack $\boxed{a \ b \ c \ \cdots}$ yields the new stack: $\boxed{\log(a) \ b \ c \ \cdots}$.

The execution of PUSH r with the stack $\boxed{a \ b \ c \ \cdots}$ *pushes* r on top of the stack, that is, the new stack is: $\boxed{r \ a \ b \ c \ \cdots}$.

1. Declare a type Stack for representing the stack, and declare an F# function to interpret the execution of a single instruction:

```
intpInstr: Stack -> Instruction -> Stack
```

2. A *program* for the calculator is a list of instructions $[i_1, i_2, \ldots, i_n]$. A program is *executed* by executing the instructions $i_1, i_2, \ldots, i_n$ one after the other, in that order, starting with an empty stack. The result of the execution is the top value of the stack when all instructions have been executed.

Declare an F# function to interpret the execution of a program:

```
intpProg: Instruction list -> float
```

3. Declare an F# function

```
trans: Fexpr * float -> Instruction list
```

where `Fexpr` is the type for expression trees declared in Section 6.2. The value of the expression $trans(fe, x)$ is a program *prg* such that `intpProg`(*prg*) gives the float value of *fe* when X has the value x. Hint: The instruction list can be obtained from the postfix form of the expression. (See Exercise 6.2.)

6.9 A company consists of departments with sub-departments, which again can have sub-departments, and so on. (The company can also be considered as a department.)

1. Assume that each department has a name and a (possibly empty) list of sub-departments. Declare an F# type `Department`.
2. Extend this type so that each department has its own gross income.
3. Declare a function to extract a list of pairs (*department name, gross income*), for all departments.
4. Declare a function to extract the total income for a given department by adding up its gross income, including the income of its sub-departments.
5. Declare a function to extract a list of pairs (*department name, total income*) for all departments.
6. Declare a function `format` of type `Department -> string`, which can be used to get a textual form of a department such that names of sub-departments will occur suitably indented (e.g., with four spaces) on separate lines. (Use `printf` to print out the result. Do not use `printf` in the declaration of `format`.)

6.10 Consider expression trees of type `ExprTree` declared in Section 6.5. Extend the type with an if-then-else expression of the form: `if` b `then` e_1 `else` e_2, where b is a boolean expression and e_1 and e_2 are expressions. An example could be:

```
if a*3>b+c && a>0 then c+d else e
```

Furthermore, extend the declaration of the `eval` function accordingly. Hint: make use of a mutually recursive type and function declarations.

6.11 Write the steps of the evaluation of the expression:

```
depthFirstFold (fun a x -> x::a) [] t1
```

See Page 139.

6.12 Declare the functions `depthFirstFold` and `breadthFirstFoldBack` on list trees, cf. Section 6.6.

7

Modules

Throughout the book we have used programs from the F# core library and from the .NET library, and we have seen that programs from these libraries are reused in many different applications. In this chapter we show how the user can make own libraries by means of modules consisting of signature and implementation files. The implementation file contains the declarations of the entities in the library while the signature file specifies the user's interface to the library.

Overloaded operators are defined by adding augmentations to type definitions. Type augmentations can also be used to customize the equality and comparison operators and the string conversion function. Libraries with polymorphic types are obtained by using signatures containing type variables.

These features of the module system are illustrated by small examples: plane geometric vectors and queues of values with arbitrary type. The last part of the chapter illustrates the module system by a larger example of piecewise linear plane curves. The curve library is used to describe the recursively defined family of Hilbert curves, and these curves are shown in a window using the .NET library. The theme of an exercise is a picture library used to describe families of recursively defined pictures like Escher's fishes.

7.1 Abstractions

A key concept in designing a good program library is *abstraction*: the library must provide a service where a user can get a general understanding of *what* a library function is doing without being forced to learn details about *how* this function is implemented. The interface to any standard library, like, for example, the Set library, is based on useful abstractions, in this case the (mathematical) concept of a set. Based on a general understanding of this concept you may use the Set library while still being able to focus your main attention on other aspects of your program.

Modules are the technical means of dividing a programming problem into smaller parts, but this process must be guided by useful abstractions. Creation of useful abstractions is the basis for obtaining a successful modular program design.

Abstractions are described on the *semantical* level by:

- Description of a collection of entities to be *represented* by an F# type.
- Description of specific values and computations to be *implemented* by F# values and functions.

The above example of the `Set` library comes with a natural language explanation of the concept of sets and of operations on sets plus certain special sets like the empty set and singleton sets (cf. Section 5.2). Throughout the book we follow this style in describing the semantics, as seen from a user, of the library in two parts:

- A general, narrative description of the conceptual framework.

- A precise, but short description of the *intended working* of each type, value and function.

Parts of this description may be included as comments in the signature file.

Abstractions are described on the *syntactical* level by *specifications*. The main forms are:

```
type TypeName ...
val Name : type
```

They are part of an F# program and found in the *signature* file of a module. They specify entities to be *represented* and *implemented* in the library.

A type specification without type expression

```
type TypeName
```

hides the structure of the type from the user and this structure is then only found in the implementation of the library. The user's access to the library is restricted to use values and functions according to the specifications in the signature and the user cannot look into details of the representation of values of this type or make such values "by hand." This feature of the interface to a library is called *data hiding*. It gives the means for protecting the integrity of representations of values such that, for example, invariants are not violated.

7.2 Signature and implementation

An F# *module* consists of F# source files that are compiled together to make a *library*. This library can then later be used by other programs. The first file in the compilation is a *signature* file containing *specifications* of the user's interface to the resulting program library while the other consists of F# declarations to define the *implementation* of this interface. Signature and implementation files are text files edited by the programmer while the library file is produced by the F# compiler when signature and implementation are compiled together.

The compilation of a pair of signature and implementation requires that the implementation *matches* the signature: each *specification* in the signature should be *implemented* by a corresponding *declaration* in the implementation file. A declaration in the implementation may have a more general type than specified in the signature but the type is then specialized to the type in the signature. Declarations of entities that do not appear in the signature are *local* to the implementation and not visible to a user of the library.

Example: vectors in the plane

Consider the example of vectors in the plane in Section 3.3. We want to make a vector library with hidden `Vector` type. Besides the functions in the earlier version of this example we have to provide a function `make` to make values of type `Vector` and a function `coord` to inspect a value of this type because the user would otherwise not be able to make or inspect any such value.

The signature should hence contain a specification of a (hidden) type `Vector` without type expression:

```
type Vector
```

together with specifications of the functions. This gives the following signature of a module with *module name* `Vector`:

```
module Vector                                   // Vector signature
type Vector
val ( ~-. )  : Vector -> Vector               // Vector sign change
val ( +. )   : Vector -> Vector -> Vector     // Vector sum
val ( -. )   : Vector -> Vector -> Vector     // Vector difference
val ( *. )   : float  -> Vector -> Vector     // Product wth number
val ( &. )   : Vector -> Vector -> float       // Dot product
val norm     : Vector -> float                 // Length of vector
val make     : float * float -> Vector         // Make vector
val coord    : Vector -> float * float         // Get coordinates
```

The implementation must contain a definition of the type `Vector` and declarations of all values specified in the signature. The type `Vector` specified as hidden in the signature must be a tagged type or a record type, so we have to add a tag, say `V`, in the type definition:

```
module Vector                        // Vector implementation
type Vector = V of float * float
let (~-.)  (V(x,y))              = V(-x,-y)
let (+.)   (V(x1,y1)) (V(x2,y2)) = V(x1+x2,y1+y2)
let (-.)   v1         v2         = v1 +. -. v2
let ( *.) a           (V(x1,y1)) = V(a*x1,a*y1)
let (&.)   (V(x1,y1)) (V(x2,y2)) = x1*x2 + y1*y2
let norm   (V(x1,y1))            = sqrt(x1*x1+y1*y1)
let make   (x,y)                 = V(x,y)
let coord (V(x,y))               = (x,y)
```

The resulting library can be used as follows:

```
open Vector;;
let a = make(1.0,-2.0);;
val a : Vector

let b = make(3.0,4.0);;
val b : Vector
```

```
let c = 2.0 *. a -. b;;
val c : Vector

coord c;;
val it : float * float = (-1.0, -8.0)

let d = c &. a;;
val d : float = 15.0

let e = norm b;;
val e : float = 5.0
```

Note that the response from the system displays only the type name and no value when an expression of type Vector is entered: the structure of the type is hidden from the user.

Remark: The above method of defining infix operators in a library is *not recommended*. One should instead use the syntax described in Section 7.3. The reason is that the operators in this example are only available in a program using the library when the library has been *opened*, in our case by "open Vector". One would normally prefer *not* to open the library in order to limit the "pollution of the namespace". Entities in the library are then accessed using composite names like Vector.make, and the operators will then only be available in the inconvenient prefix form like Vector.(+.) and the elegance of the infix operators is not available. It is even worse if we, for instance, declare an operator + on vectors using the above syntax. This declaration will then override the existing declaration of + when the module is opened, and the + operator on numbers will no longer be available.

The module-declaration in signature and implementation can use a *composite* module name, for example:

```
module MyLibrary.Vector
```

A program may then access the library in any of the following ways:

```
open MyLibrary.Vector;;
let a = make(1.0,-2.0);;
```

or

```
open MyLibrary;;
let a = Vector.make(1.0,-2.0);;
```

or

```
let a = Mylibrary.Vector.make(1.0,-2.0);;
```

Files and compilation

The F# module system uses the file types fsi, fs and dll as follows:

FileName.fsi	F# signature file	Text file edited by programmer
FileName.fs	F# implementation file	Text file edited by programmer
FileName.dll	Library file	Binary output file from F# compiler

The *separate compilation* of a module is supported by any of the development platforms for F#. Using the batch compiler `fsc` (cf. Section 1.10) the compilation of a library with signature file *SignatureName*.`fsi` and implementation file *LibraryName*.`fs` is made by the command:

    fsc -a Signature.fsi Library.fs

This compilation produces a library file:

    Library.dll

The library gets the same file name as the implementation file – with a different file type – while the signature can have a different file name. These file names should not be confused with the module name introduced by the `module`-declarations in signature and implementation files as `Vector` in the above example.

Compilation of a program using the library *Library*.`dll` is made by a command like:

    fsc ... -r Library.dll ...

Compilation of library and program should use the *same version* of F# and .NET.

A library *Library*.`dll` may be used as follows from an interactive environment:

1. Move the library file *Library*.`dll` to a special directory, for example:
   `c:\Documents and Settings\FsharpBook\lib`
2. Refer to the library from the interactive environment using an `#r` directive:
   `#r @"c:\Documents and Settings\FsharpBook\lib\Library.dll";;`

7.3 Type augmentation. Operators in modules

A *type augmentation* adds declarations to the definition of a tagged type or a record type and it allows declaration of (overloaded) operators. The type augmentation uses an OO-flavoured syntax. This is illustrated in the signature and implementation files in Tables 7.1 and 7.2. The operators +, − and ∗ on numbers are overloaded to denote also operations on values of type `Vector` and the operator ∗ is even overloaded to denote two different operations on vectors. Resolving the overloading is made using the types of the operands, so the two versions of the operator ∗ could not have identical operand types.

```
module Vector
[<Sealed>]
type Vector =
    static member ( ~- ) : Vector -> Vector
    static member ( + )  : Vector * Vector -> Vector
    static member ( - )  : Vector * Vector -> Vector
    static member ( * )  : float  * Vector -> Vector
    static member ( * )  : Vector * Vector -> float
val make : float * float -> Vector
val coord: Vector -> float * float
val norm : Vector -> float
```

Table 7.1 *Signature file with type augmentation*

```
module Vector
type Vector =
     | V of float * float
     static member (~-)  (V(x,y))                = V(-x,-y)
     static member (+)   (V(x1,y1),V(x2,y2))     = V(x1+x2,y1+y2)
     static member (-)   (V(x1,y1),V(x2,y2))     = V(x1-x2,y1-y2)
     static member (*)   (a, V(x,y))             = V(a*x,a*y)
     static member (*)   (V(x1,y1),V(x2,y2))     = x1*x2 + y1*y2
let make(x,y)       = V(x,y)
let coord(V(x,y))   = (x,y)
let norm(V(x,y))    = sqrt(x*x + y*y)
```

Table 7.2 *Implementation file with type augmentation*

The member declarations cannot be intermixed with let declarations (but local let declarations are, of course, allowed inside the expressions in the declarations).

The functions make, coord and norm are specified and implemented as usual F# functions – the OO-features should only be used to obtain an effect (here: operators) that cannot be obtained using normal F# style.

Note that the implementation file in Table 7.2 compiles without signature file if the module declaration is commented out. This is often convenient during the implementation and test of a module. Furthermore, the output from the interactive F# compiler in such a compilation can be useful in getting details in the signature correct.

Note the following:

- The *attribute* [<Sealed>] is mandatory when a type augmentation is used. It protects the library against unintentional use in the OO-world.
- The heading "|" in the type and the declarations in the augmentation must be at the same indentation level.
- The "member" specification and declaration of an infix operator (e.g. +) corresponds to a type of form $type_1 * type_2 \rightarrow type_3$, while the earlier val specification and let declaration (of e.g. (+.)) on Page 151 use a higher-order type of form $type_1 \rightarrow type_2 \rightarrow type_3$. The indicated type is required to get the overloading. The resulting prefix function (like e.g. (+)) will, nevertheless, get the usual higher-order type.
- The operators +, – and * are available on vectors without opening the library. The operators can still be used on numbers.
- The functions make, coord and norm could have been declared as "static members" using the OO notation. The usual F# form is more succinct and should be used whenever possible.

The following are examples of use of the Vector library specified in Table 7.1:

```
let a = Vector.make(1.0,-2.0);;
val a : Vector.Vector

let b = Vector.make(3.0,4.0);;
val b : Vector.Vector
```

```
let c = 2.0 * a - b;;
val c : Vector.Vector

Vector.coord c;;
val it : float * float = (-1.0, -8.0)

let d = c * a;;
val d : float = 15.0

let e = Vector.norm b;;
val e : float = 5.0

let g = (+) a b;;
val g : Vector.Vector

Vector.coord g;;
val it : float * float = (4.0, 2.0)
```

7.4 Type extension

The implementation in Table 7.2 can instead be made using a *type extension*;

```
type ... with ...
```

as shown in Table 7.3. This implementation compiles with the signature in Table 7.1 and has the same effect as the implementation in Table 7.2, but it offers the possibility of inserting usual function declarations between the type definition and the member declarations like make and coord in Table 7.3. Such functions can be used in the member declarations and that may sometime allow simplifications. This possibility is used later in the example of plane curves in Section 7.9.

```
module Vector
type Vector = V of float * float
let make(x,y)     = V(x,y)
let coord(V(x,y)) = (x,y)
type Vector with
     static member (~-) (V(x,y))             = V(-x,-y)
     static member (+) (V(x1,y1),V(x2,y2)) = V(x1+x2,y1+y2)
     static member (-) (V(x1,y1),V(x2,y2)) = V(x1-x2,y1-y2)
     static member (*) (a, V(x,y))           = V(a*x,a*y)
     static member (*) (V(x1,y1),V(x2,y2)) = x1*x2 + y1*y2
let norm(V(x,y))  = sqrt(x*x + y*y)
```

Table 7.3 *Implementation module with type extension*

7.5 Classes and objects

There are full features for Object-oriented (OO) programming in F#, but this is not a major theme of this book. We just give a brief introduction to cover the topics that are needed when using the .NET library in an F# program and when making computational expressions as described in a later chapter. The OO-features in F# are only used on a larger scale when implementing applications that can be used from programs made in another .NET language.

A *class* definition looks syntactically like an augmented type definition where the type expression has been removed and replaced by declarations of *constructor* functions. A class in F# determines a type and a value of such a type is called an *object*. An object is obtained by calling a constructor of the class. The call of a constructor is often preceded by the keyword new. We illustrate classes and objects by an OO-version of our vector example:

```
type ObjVector(X: float, Y: float) =
    member v.x = X
    member v.y = Y
    member v.coord() = (v.x, v.y)
    member v.norm() = sqrt(v.x * v.x + v.y * v.y)
    static member (~-) (v: ObjVector) = ObjVector(- v.x,- v.y)
    static member (+)  (v1: ObjVector, v2:ObjVector)
        = ObjVector(v1.x + v2.x, v1.y + v2.y)
    static member (-)  (v1: ObjVector, v2:ObjVector)
        = ObjVector(v1.x - v2.x, v1.y - v2.y)
    static member (*) (a,v:ObjVector) = ObjVector(a*v.x,a*v.y)
    static member (*)  (v1: ObjVector, v2:ObjVector)
        = v1.x * v2.x + v1.y * v2.y
```

The constructor ObjVector initializes the members x and y using the parameter values X and Y. The following show some uses of the class:

```
let a = ObjVector(1.0,-2.0);;
val a : ObjVector

let b = ObjVector(Y = 4.0, X = 3.0);;    // Named arguments
val b : ObjVector

b.coord();;
val it : float * float = (3.0, 4.0)

let c = 2.0 * a - b;;
val c : ObjVector

c.coord();;
val it : float * float = (-1.0, -8.0)

b.x;;
val it : float = 3.0
```

```
let d = c * a;;
val d : float = 15.0

let e = b.norm();;
val e : float = 5.0

let g = (+) a b;;
val g : ObjVector

g.coord();;
val it : float * float = (4.0,2.0)
```

The above examples

```
let b = ObjVector (Y=4.0, X=3.0);;
```

illustrates the use of *named arguments* where arguments in a function call are identified by name instead of position in the argument list. Named arguments can make call of functions from the .NET library more readable as the meaning of each argument is visible from the context, while the meaning of an argument can otherwise only be found by studying the documentation of the function in question.

The example of plane curves uses a similar feature called *optional property setting* (cf. Section 7.9).

Note that members coord, norm and x are written as a suffix to the values c and b. They are in the OO-world considered as belonging to the values c and b. Using fun-expressions they determine functions

```
fun v -> v.coord()
fun v -> v.norm()
fun v -> v.x
```

where, for example:

$$(\texttt{fun v -> v.coord()}) \; c = c.coord()$$

Using OO-style constructs is daily life for the F# programmer as the .NET library is 100 percent OO, and the OO-features of F# give a quite streamlined access to this library. An object member is used as argument of a higher-order function by packaging it into a fun-expression as shown above.

7.6 Parameterized modules. Type variables in signatures

A module in F# can be *parameterized* by type variables and may thereby implement polymorphic types, values and functions. This is illustrated by the example of a *queue*: A queue is a row of values of the same type. The put function inserts a new value at the rear end of the queue while the get function gets the front element. An exception should be raised if get is attempted on an empty queue. This idea is specified in the signature in Table 7.4.

The implementation uses an interesting data representation due to L.C. Paulson (cf. [10], Chapter 7) where a queue is represented by two lists, a `front` list containing the first queue elements in the order of insertion and a `rear` list containing the remaining queue elements in the reverse order of insertion. The representation of a queue containing values 1, 2, 3 may hence look as follows:

```
front   [1]
rear    [3; 2]
```

Using `put` to insert a value, say 4, will simply "cons" the value onto the `rear` list:

```
front   [1]
rear    [4; 3; 2]
```

while `get` removes the heading element 1 from the `front` list:

```
front   []
rear    [4; 3; 2]
```

A call of `get` in this situation with empty `front` list will *reverse* the `rear` list to get the list [2; 3; 4] with the queue elements in the order of insertion. This list is then used as `front` list while the `rear` list becomes empty.

```
front   [3; 4]           (the front element 2 has been removed by get)
rear    []
```

The implementation module in Table 7.5 uses this idea and represents a `Queue` value as a record `{front:'a list; rear:'a list}` containing the two lists. Note that the representation of a queue is not *unique* because *different* pairs of front and rear lists may represent the *same* queue.

```
module Queue
type Queue<'a>
val empty : Queue<'a>
val put   : 'a -> Queue<'a> -> Queue<'a>
val get   : Queue<'a> -> 'a * Queue<'a>
exception EmptyQueue
```

Table 7.4 *Signature of parameterized* Queue *module*

```
module Queue
exception EmptyQueue
type Queue<'a> = {front: 'a list; rear: 'a list}
let empty = {front = []; rear = []}
let put y {front = xs; rear = ys} = {front = xs; rear = y::ys}
let rec get = function
            | {front = x::xs; rear = ys} ->
                (x,{front = xs; rear = ys})
            | {front = []; rear = []} -> raise EmptyQueue
            | {front = []; rear = ys} ->
                get {front = List.rev ys; rear = []}
```

Table 7.5 *Implementation of parameterized* Queue *module*

The Queue library can be used as follows:

```
let q0 = Queue.empty: Queue.Queue<int>;;
val q0 : Queue.Queue<int>

let q1 = Queue.put 1 q0;;
val q1 : Queue.Queue<int>

let q2 = Queue.put 2 q1;;
val q2 : Queue.Queue<int>

let (x,q3) = Queue.get q2;;
val x : int = 1
val q3 : Queue.Queue<int>

let q4 = Queue.put 4 q3;;
val q4 : Queue.Queue<int>

let (x2,q5) = Queue.get q4;;
val x2 : int = 2
val q5 : Queue.Queue<int>

let (x3,q6) = Queue.get q5;;
val x3 : int = 4
val q6 : Queue.Queue<int>
```

7.7 Customizing equality, hashing and the string function

The F# compiler will automatically generate a default equality operator for the above type Queue<′a> whenever the type variable ′a is instantiated with an equality type. This default equality operator is, however, *not* the wanted operator because it distinguishes values that we want to consider equal. We may for instance get a queue containing the single integer 2 in two ways: as the above queue value q3 where the integers 1 and 2 are put into the empty queue q0 followed by a get to remove the integer 1, or as the below queue value qnew where we just put the integer 2 into the empty queue q0. These two values are considered different by the default equality operator:

```
let qnew = Queue.put 2 q0 ;;
val qnew : Queue.Queue<int>
qnew = q3;;
val it : bool = false
```

The reason is that the queues qnew and q3 are *represented* by *different* values of type Queue:

| The value of | qnew | is represented by | {front = []; rear = [2]} |
| The value of | q3 | is represented by | {front = [2]; rear = []} |

and the default equality operator is based on *structural* equality of the representing values. Hence, qnew and q3 are considered different by this operator.

```
module Queue
exception EmptyQueue
[<CustomEquality;NoComparison>]
type Queue<'a when 'a : equality> =
    {front: 'a list; rear: 'a list}
    member q.list() = q.front @ (List.rev q.rear)
    override q1.Equals qobj =
        match qobj with
        | :? Queue<'a> as q2 -> q1.list() = q2.list()
        | _ -> false
    override q.GetHashCode() = hash (q.list())
    override q.ToString() = string (q.list())
```

Declarations of empty, put and get are as in Table 7.5.
In signature: `type Queue<'a when 'a : equality>`

Table 7.6 *Type definition with augmentation for equality, hashing and* `string`

It is possible to *override* the default equality operator using a type augmentation as shown in Table 7.6. The signature in Table 7.4 needs an equality constraint on the type variable `'a` of queue elements as the `Equals` function uses equality for `'a list` values:

```
type Queue<'a when 'a : equality>
```

The signature can otherwise be used unchanged.

The `Equals` function contains the clause:

```
:? Queue<'a> as q2 ->...
```

It expresses a match on *type*. The value of `qobj` matches the pattern if the type of `qobj` matches the type `Queue<'a>` in the pattern, that is, if the type of `qobj` is an instance of this type. The identifier `q2` is then bound to the value of `qobj`.

Note the following:

- The customized equality compares single lists containing all queue elements. This list `q.list()` is obtained from the used representation `{front=xs; rear=ys}` of a queue as the `front` list `q.front` with the reversed of the `rear` list `q.rear` appended.
- The overriding cannot be given in a separate type extension. There are hence no possibility of declaring a local function to be used in the `member`-declarations. The frequently used expression `q.front @ (List.rev q.rear)` is therefore defined as a `member` function `q.list()`.
- The compiler gives a warning if the hash function is not customized because values considered equal should have same hash code. This condition becomes critical if the imperative collections `HashSet` or `Directory` (cf. Section 8.11) are used with elements of type `Queue`.
- Overriding `ToString` gives a reasonable conversion of a queue to a string by using `string` on `q.list()`.

Applying the new `Queue` module with customized comparison and `string` function to the example in Section 7.6 with declarations of q0,q1,...,q6 and s we now get:

```
qnew = q3;;
val it : bool = true

string q2;;
val it : string = "[1; 2]"
```

7.8 Customizing ordering and indexing

Using a suitable type augmentation one may also customize the *ordering:* $q_1 < q_2$ and *indexing: q.[n]* on values of a defined type. The corresponding type augmentation in the queue example is shown in Table 7.7.

The ordering is declared by overriding the `CompareTo` method in the `IComparable` interface. The implemented comparison uses `compare` on the lists of the queue elements in insertion order. The signature must tell that this interface is used:

```
interface System.IComparable
```

The indexing is expressed by the `get` part of an `Item` member function. The implementation uses list indexing in the list of queue elements in insertion order. The signature must contain the corresponding specification:

```
member Item : int -> 'a with get
```

```
[<Sealed>]
type Queue<'a when 'a : comparison> =
    interface System.IComparable
    member Item : int -> 'a with get
```

Signature of Queue with ordering and indexing: type part

```
[<CustomEquality;CustomComparison>]
type Queue<'a when 'a : comparison> =
    {front: 'a list; rear: 'a list}
    member q.list() = q.front @ (List.rev q.rear)
    interface System.IComparable with
      member q1.CompareTo qobj =
        match qobj with
        | :? Queue<'a> as q2 -> compare (q1.list()) (q2.list())
        | _ ->
          invalidArg "qobj"
                     "cannot compare values of different types"
    member q.Item
      with get n = (q.list()).[n]
```

Implementation of Queue with ordering and indexing

Note: Equality and hashing as in Table 7.6 are also needed

Table 7.7 *Type augmentation for ordering and indexing in queue module*

The following illustrates uses of ordering and indexing:

```
let q0 = Queue.empty;;
let q1 = Queue.put 1 q0;;
let q2 = Queue.put 2 q1;;

q2 > q1 ;;
val it : bool = true

q2.[1] ;;
val it : int = 2
```

7.9 Example: Piecewise linear plane curves

In this example we consider piecewise linear curves in the plane following an idea due to Fokkinga (cf. [4]). Such a curve consists of a point P_0 and a (possible empty) sequence of line segments P_0P_1, P_1P_2, ..., $P_{n-2}P_{n-1}$ where $P_0, P_1, \ldots, P_{n-1}$ are points in the plane. The point P_0 is called the *start point* of the curve while P_{n-1} is called the *end point*. We use usual rectangular, Cartesian coordinates in the plane, so points and vectors in the plane correspond to coordinates that are pairs of `float` numbers.

We want represent a curve by a F# value and to implement the operations on curves shown in Table 7.8. A corresponding signature is shown in Table 7.9. Note that the user of the library can understand and use the functions while thinking purely in geometrical terms, so we have obtained the wanted abstraction.

Syntax	Function
$point(x, y)$	The curve consisting of the single point with coordinates (x, y)
$c_1 + c_2$	The curve consisting of the curve c_1, the segment from the end point of c_1 to the start point of c_2 and the curve c_2.
$a * c$	The curve obtained from c by multiplication with factor a from the start point of c
$c \mid\hat{} \ a$	The curve obtained by rotating c the angle a (in degrees) around its start point
$c \dashrightarrow (x, y)$	The curve obtained from c by the parallel translation in the plane moving the start point of c to the point with coordinates (x, y)
$c >< a$	The curve obtained from c by horizontal reflection in the vertical line with equation $x = a$
$verticRefl\ c\ b$	The curve obtained from c by vertical reflection in the horizontal line with equation $y = b$
$boundingBox\ c$	The pair $((x_{min}, y_{min}), (x_{max}, y_{max}))$ of coordinates of lower left and upper right corner of the bounding box of the curve c
$width\ c$	The width of the bounding box of c
$height\ c$	The height of the bounding box of c
$toList\ c$	The list $[(x_0, y_0);\ (x_1, y_1);\ldots(x_{n-1}, y_{n-1})]$ of coordinates of the curve points $P_0, P_1; \ldots; P_{n-1}$

Table 7.8 *Operations on curves*

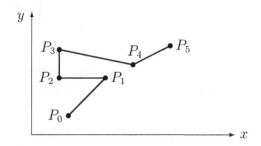

Use of the infix operators | ^ for the rotate function is overloaded to also allow integer angle values. The infix operators allow `Curve` expressions to be written using a minimum of parentheses.

```
module Curve
[<Sealed>]
type Curve =
     static member ( + ) : Curve * Curve -> Curve
     static member ( * ) : float * Curve -> Curve
     static member ( |^) : Curve * float -> Curve
     static member ( |^) : Curve * int   -> Curve
     static member (-->) : Curve * (float * float) -> Curve
     static member (><)  : Curve * float -> Curve
val point       : float * float -> Curve
val verticRefl  : Curve -> float -> Curve
val boundingBox : Curve -> (float * float) * (float * float)
val width       : Curve -> float
val height      : Curve -> float
val toList      : Curve -> (float * float) list
```

Table 7.9 *Signature of* `Curve` *library*

We present an application of the `Curve` library before presenting its implementation.

Example: Hilbert curves

The Hilbert curves $h_0, h_1, h_2, \dots$ form a system of curves, where h_0 consists of the point with coordinates $(0, 0)$ while each curve h_{n+1} is obtained by joining four curves c_1, c_2, c_3, c_4 obtained from h_n by transformations composed of reflections, rotations and translations. The Hilbert curves h_0, h_1, h_2 and h_3 are shown in Figure 7.1. All Hilbert curves start in the origin and the connecting segments (dotted lines in the figure) are of length 1.

We want to declare a function

```
hilbert: Curve.Curve -> Curve.Curve
```

such that

$$h_{n+1} = \text{hilbert } h_n \quad \text{for } n = 0, 1, 2, \dots$$

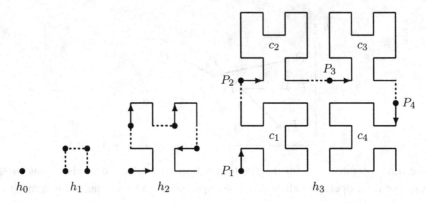

Figure 7.1 Hilbert curves

Studying Figure 7.1 we note that c_2 and c_3 can be obtained from h_n by parallel translations while c_1 and c_4 must be obtained from a mirror image of h_n. The following figure shows the curve c_0 obtained by horizontal reflection of h_n in the vertical line through the start point $(0.0, 0.0)$ and the curves obtained from c_0 by rotations through $-90°$ and $90°$:

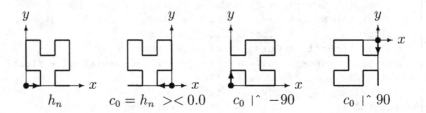

Using the width and height of h_n:

```
w = Curve.width hₙ
h = Curve.height hₙ
```

we can express the coordinates of the start points P_1, P_2, P_3, P_4 of c_1, c_2, c_3, c_4:

```
P₁ : (0.0,  0.0)
P₂ : (0.0,  w + 1.0)
P₃ : (h + 1.0,  w + 1.0)
P₄ : (h + h + 1.0,  w)
```

Note that the height and width of c_1 and c_4 are the width and height, respectively, of h_n. The height of h_n is actually equal to its width.

These considerations leads to the wanted declaration:

```
let h0 = Curve.point (0.0,0.0);;
val h0 : Curve.Curve
```

```
let hilbert hn =
    let w  = Curve.width hn
    let h  = Curve.height hn
    let c0 = hn >< 0.0
    let c1 = c0 |^ -90
    let c2 = hn --> (0.0, w + 1.0)
    let c3 = hn --> (h + 1.0, w + 1.0)
    let c4 = (c0 |^ 90) --> (h + h + 1.0, w)
    c1 + c2 + c3 + c4;;
val hilbert : Curve.Curve -> Curve.Curve
```

Note that the programming of the `hilbert` function has been done using geometric concepts only. We do not need any knowledge about the implementation of the `Curve` library.

Displaying curves

We want to make a function to display a curve in a window using the .NET library. Before getting to the programming we have to make some geometric considerations.

The display is made in a *panel* belonging to a window. The panel uses Cartesian coordinates where the y-axis points *downwards* and the upper left corner of the panel has panel coordinates $(0, 0)$. The situation is depicted in Figure 7.2. The thick box is the panel with width `pw` and height `ph`. The picture shows that a curve point with coordinates (x, y) has panel coordinates:

$$\begin{aligned} x_{panel} &= x \\ y_{panel} &= ph - y \end{aligned} \quad (*)$$

The program uses two libraries:

`System.Windows.Forms` containing facilities to set up a *window* with scroll-bars and underlying *panel* to contain the drawing

`System.Drawing` containing facilities to *draw* the curve in the panel

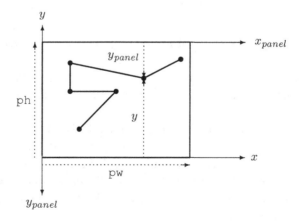

Figure 7.2 Panel coordinates

```
open System.Drawing
open System.Windows.Forms
Application.EnableVisualStyles();;

let winSize = Size(450,300);; // Initial window size in pixels

let display(title: string,(c: Curve.Curve,pw: int,ph: int)) =
    let f(x,y) = Point(int(round x), ph - int(round y))
    let clst = Curve.toList c
    let Ptlst = List.map f clst
    let pArr = Array.ofList Ptlst

    let pen = new Pen(Color.Black)
    let draw(g:Graphics) = g.DrawLines(pen,pArr)

    let panel = new Panel(Dock=DockStyle.Fill)
    panel.Paint.Add(fun e -> draw(e.Graphics))

    let win = new Form(Text=title,Size=winSize,AutoScroll=true,
                       AutoScrollMinSize=Size(pw,ph))
    win.Controls.Add(panel)
    win.Show();;
val display : string * (Curve.Curve * int * int) -> unit
```

Table 7.10 *The* display *function*

The function display declared in Table 7.10 has two parameters: the title to be written on top of the window and a triple comprising the Curve to be displayed plus width pw and height ph of the panel. The function consists of five parts:

1. The function f converts a set of coordinates (x, y) to a Point object containing the corresponding panel coordinates. The panel coordinates are integers and the conversion from float to int consists of a round followed by an int conversion. The formula $(*)$ on Page 165 is used in converting to panel coordinates.
   The list clst of coordinates of points on the curve is extracted and the function f is applied to each element to get the corresponding list Ptlst of Point objects. Finally the corresponding array pArr of Point objects is made. It is ready to be used by the Graphics member function DrawLines.
2. A Pen object pen is created and a function draw drawing the curve on a Graphics object is declared. It calls DrawLines using pen and the array pArr of curve point coordinates.
3. The Panel object is created and configured to fill all of the window (DockStyle). The draw function is added to the panel's collection of Paint objects
4. The window (Form) is created using the specified title. The size is set and scrolling is enabled. The value of AutoScrollMinSize is set to allow the window to scroll to any part of the panel, and scrolling is activated. Finally, the panel is added to the collection of Controls of the window.
5. The window is shown (win.Show()).

A window is a live object that handles a number of events. The actual window has only events corresponding to manipulation of the window like: resizing of window, use of scrollbars, window comes in to foreground. The part of the panel inside the window is then redrawn using the function in the `Paint` collection of the panel. The parameter `e` is actually an `Event` object.

Some of the above calls of constructors use *optional property setting* like the argument `Dock=DockStyle.Fill` in the argument list of constructor `Panel`. This constructor has actually no `Dock` argument. The specified value `DockStyle.Fill` is instead used as initial value of the `Dock` property of the created `Panel` object.

A curve requires some adjustment before the `display` function can be used: the curve must be suitable scaled to get a proper size of the details of the curve, and the curve must be moved away from the boundary of the panel as boundary points are invisible. This job is done by the function `adjust`. It multiplies the curve `c` by the factor `a` and makes a parallel translation of the curve to leave a blank band of 10 pixels in the panel around the curve:

```
let adjust(c:Curve.Curve, a: float) =
    let c1 = a * c --> (10.0, 10.0)
    let (_,(maxX,maxY)) = Curve.boundingBox c1
    let pw = int(round maxX) + 20
    let ph = int(round maxY) + 20
    (c1,pw,ph);;
```

The value of `adjust` can be used directly as second parameter in the `display` function.

Displaying Hilbert Curves

The `display` function can be used to display Hilbert curves (using the above declarations of value `h0` and function `hilbert`):

```
let h1 = hilbert h0;;
let h2 = hilbert h1;;
let h3 = hilbert h2;;
let h4 = hilbert h3;;
```

```
let h5 = hilbert h4;;
let h6 = hilbert h5;;
display("Hilbert Curve 6", adjust(h6, 10.0));;
```

The displayed curve has been scaled by a factor 10.0 to get a reasonable drawing.

Implementation of the Curve *library*

The F# implementation of the Curve library is given in Tables 7.11 and 7.12.

A curve is represented by a value of tagged type

```
C of (float * float) * ((float * float) list)
```

containing the coordinates of the start point of the curve plus the (possibly empty) list of coordinates of the remaining points. Any value of this type represents a curve (there is no invariant) and the functions can hence be implemented without any error case where an exception should be raised.

```
module Curve
type Curve =  C of (float*float) * ((float*float) list)

let map  f (C(p0,ps)) = C(f p0,List.map f ps)
let mapP g (C(p0,ps)) = C(p0,List.map (g p0) ps)

type Curve with
  static member(+) (c1:Curve, c2:Curve) =
    match (c1,c2) with
    | (C(p1,ps1),C(p2,ps2)) -> C(p1,ps1@(p2::ps2))
  static member (*) (a: float, c: Curve) =
    let multA  (x0,y0) (x,y) =
      (x0 + a * (x - x0), y0 + a * (y - y0))
    mapP multA c
  static member (|^) (c:Curve, ang: float) =
    let piFact = System.Math.PI / 180.0
    let cs = cos (piFact * ang)
    let sn = sin (piFact * ang)
    let rot (x0,y0) (x,y) =
      let (dx,dy) = (x - x0,y - y0)
      (x0 + cs * dx - sn * dy, y0 + sn * dx + cs * dy)
    mapP rot c
  static member (|^) (c:Curve, ang: int) = c |^ (float ang)
  static member (-->) (c: Curve, (x1,y1): float*float) =
    match c with
    | C((x0,y0),_) -> map (fun (x,y) -> (x-x0+x1, y-y0+y1)) c
  static member (><) (c:Curve, a: float) =
    map (fun (x,y) -> (2.0 * a - x, y)) c
```

Table 7.11 *First part of the implementation of* Curve *library*

```
let point (p: float*float) = C (p,[])
let verticRefl (c:Curve) (b:float) =
    map (fun (x,y) -> (x, 2.0*b - y)) c
let boundingBox (C((x0,y0),ps)) =
    let minmax ((minX,minY),(maxX,maxY)) ((x,y):float*float) =
        ((min minX x, min minY y),(max maxX x, max maxY y))
    List.fold minmax ((x0,y0),(x0,y0)) ps
let width (c:Curve)  = let ((minX,_),(maxX,_)) = boundingBox c
                       maxX - minX
let height (c:Curve) = let ((_,minY),(_,maxY)) = boundingBox c
                       maxY - minY
let toList (C(p,ps)) = p :: ps
```

Table 7.12 *Last part of the implementation of* Curve *library*

A simplification is obtained by introducing two higher-order local functions. The first function map applies a function f to the coordinates of each curve point including the start point. It is used in declaring functions like parallel translation --> and reflection >< where the same transformation is applied to all curve points.

The second function mapP leaves the start point p0 unchanged and applies a partially evaluated function g p0 to the coordinates of the remaining curve points. It is used in declaring functions like multiplication * or rotation |^.

The combined curve c1+c2 is obtained as the start point of c1 together with the list of remaining points of c1 with all points of c2 appended.

The multiplication with factor a from the point $P_0 : (x_0, y_0)$ maps a point $P : (x, y)$ to the point $P' : (x', y')$ where $\overrightarrow{P_0 P'} = a\, \overrightarrow{P_0 P}$, that is;

$$(x' - x_0, y' - y_0) = (a\, (x - x_0),\ a\, (y - y_0))$$

and the function multA is declared accordingly.

The declaration of rot is based on the fact that the rotation with angle v around P_0 maps a point P in to the point P' where $\overrightarrow{P_0 P'}$ is obtained from $\overrightarrow{P_0, P}$ by a rotation with angle v.

The function minmax extends a (bounding) box with lower left corner $(minX, minY)$ and upper right corner $(maxX, maxY)$ to contain also the point (x, y). The bounding box of the curve is then obtained starting with the one-point box containing the start point and folding the minmax function over the remaining points of the curve.

Summary

We have introduced the notions of module, signature and implementation – concepts that are needed when a programmer makes his own libraries. Moreover, we have introduced the notion of type augmentation and shown how it can be used to declare overloaded operators and to customize the equality and comparison operations and the string conversion.

Exercises

7.1   Make an implementation file of the vector example in this section using a record type:
```
type Vector = {x: float; y: float}
```
while using the same signature file.

7.2   Make signature and implementation files for a library of complex numbers with overloaded arithmetic operators (cf. Exercise 3.3).

7.3   Make signature and implementation files for a library of multi-sets of integers represented by weakly ascending lists (cf. Exercise 4.11).

7.4   Make signature and implementation files for a library of polynomials with integer coefficients (cf. Exercise 4.22).

7.5   Customize the `string` function in the library of polynomials in Exercise 7.4.

7.6   Make an indexing in the library of multi-sets of integers in Exercise 7.3 such that the value of `s.[n]` is the number of occurences of n in the multi-set s.

7.7   Make an indexing in the library of polynomials in Exercise 7.4 such that $p.$ `[n]` is the coffecient to x^n in the polynomium p.

7.8   The Sierpinski curves $s_0, s_1, s_2, \ldots$ are a system of curves, where the curve s_{n+1} is obtained by joining four curves which are obtained from the curve s_n by transformations composed of reflections, rotations and translations.

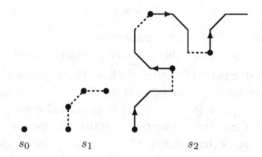

s_0 s_1 s_2

The figure shows the Sierpinski curves s_0, s_1 and s_2 and how each of the curves s_1 and s_2 is obtained by joining four curves. All vertical and horizontally segments in a Sierpinski curve have length 1 and all curves $s_0, s_1, \ldots$ start in the origin. Use the `Curve` library to declare the function `sierpinski` that computes the curve s_{n+1} from the curve s_n for any $n = 0, 1, \ldots$. Use this function to display the curve s_4 in a window.

7.9   The Peano curves $p_0, p_1, p_2, \ldots$ are a system of curves, where the curve p_{n+1} is obtained by joining 9 curves which are obtained from the curve p_n by transformations composed of reflections, rotations and translations.

The figure shows the Peano curves p_0, p_1 og p_2 and how each of the curves p_1 and p_2 is obtained by joining 9 curves. All Peano curves start in the origin and the joining segments (thin lines in

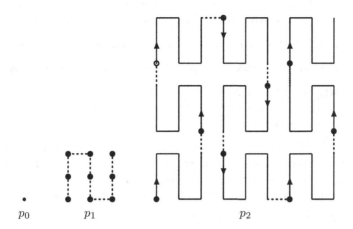

p_0 p_1 p_2

the Figure) are of length 1. Use the `Curve` library to declare the function `peano` that computes the curve p_{n+1} from the curve p_n for any $n = 0, 1, \ldots$ (in getting from p_n to p_{n+1} it may be convenient to group the 9 curves into 3 groups each consisting of 3 curves and first build the curve for each of these 3 groups). Use the `peano` function to make a program display the curve p_4 in a window.

7.10   Add a minus operator of type `Curve -> Curve` to the `Curve` library. It should compute the reversed curve, that is, $- c$ should contain the same point as c but taken in the opposite order.

7.11   Make a library for manipulation of pictures (following ideas due to Henderson, cf. [6]). A picture is a set of segments together with a rectangular, upright bounding box in the plane. The bounding box is not shown when drawing a picture but it is used when defining operations on pictures. We use usual rectangular, Cartesian coordinates in the plane, so points in the plane are represented by coordinates which are pairs (x, y) of float numbers. The point with coordinates `(0.0,0.0)` is called the *origin* of the plane. A picture is normally placed in the coordinate system such that the bounding box is situated in the lower left corner of the first quadrant.

If c is a float number with $c > 0.0$ then a picture can be scaled by factor c by mapping each point (x, y) to the point $(c \star x, c \star y)$. The scaled picture will have width $c \star a$ and height $c \star b$ where a and b are width and height of the original picture. Scaling is used in some of the below operations in order to adjust the width or the height of a picture.

The library should contain the following functions on pictures:

Grid: Computes a picture directly from width and height of the bounding box and the coordinates of the pairs of end-points of the segments in the picture. The function should be declared such that all the numbers in the input are integers (the function must convert to float numbers as used in the value representing a picture).

Rotate: Computes the picture p' obtained from the picture p by first rotating $90°$ in the positive (counter-clockwise) direction around the origin and then translating the resulting picture to the right to get its lower left-hand corner into the origin. The height of p' will be the width of p and the width of p' will be the height of p.

Flip: Computes the picture obtained from a picture by horizontal reflection around the vertical line through the middle of the bounding box.

Beside: Computes the picture obtained from two pictures p_1 and p_2 by uniting p_1 with a version of p_2 that has been placed to the right of p_1 and scaled to the same height.

Above: Computes the picture obtained from two pictures p_1 and p_2 by uniting p_2 with a version of p_1 that has been placed on top of p_2 and scaled to the same width.

Row: Computes the picture obtained by placing n copies of a picture p beside each other.

Column: Computes the picture obtained by placing n copies of a picture p on top of each other.

Coordinates: Computes the pair $((width, height), segmentList)$ where *width* and *height* are width and height of a picture while *segmentList* is a list of coordinate pairs $((x, y), (x', y'))$ of end-points of the segments in the picture.

You should chose your own names of the functions and use operators whenever appropriate. Furthermore, you should implement a function to display a picture in a window. (Hint: DrawLine $(Pen, Point_1, Point_2)$ draws a segment.)

The library should be used to construct pictures of persons and Escher's fishes – as described in the following.

Persons

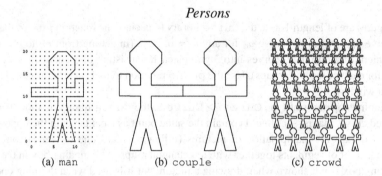

(a) man (b) couple (c) crowd

Figure 7.3 The man picture and derived pictures

The starting point is the picture man shown in Figure 7.3. It has width 14 and heigh 20. Using the functions on pictures you should now make programs to construct the pictures couple and crowd shown in Figure 7.3.

Escher's fishes

The starting point of Escher's fishes is the four (16×16) pictures p, q, r, and s shown in Figure 7.4. By combining these four pictures we get the picture t in Figure 7.5, while the picture a is obtained by combining suitably rotated copies of q. Finally the picture b1 is obtained by combining two suitably rotated copies of t.

The Escher fish pictures e0, e1 and e2 are now obtained by combining the pictures in Figure 7.5 as shown in Figure 7.6. The pictures b2, b3 and b4 are obtained from b1 by successive rotations. The transition from an Escher picture to the next adds a border around the picture consisting of a picture a in each corner, a row of b1's at the top, a column of b2's at the left, a row of b3's at the bottom, and a column of b4's at the right. In this border there will be one b1 on top of an a and two b1's on top of a b1, one b2 to the left of an a and two b2's to the left of a b2, etc.

You should make a program to generate the Escher fish pictures e0, e1 and e2.

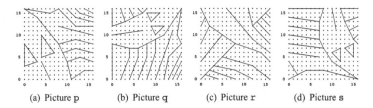

(a) Picture p   (b) Picture q   (c) Picture r   (d) Picture s

Figure 7.4 Basic fish pictures

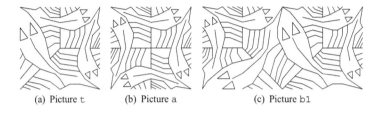

(a) Picture t   (b) Picture a   (c) Picture b1

Figure 7.5 Escher fish building blocks

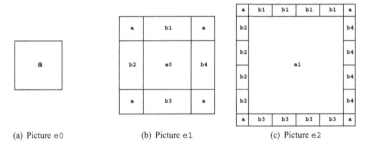

(a) Picture e0   (b) Picture e1   (c) Picture e2

Figure 7.6 Building Escher fish pictures

8

Imperative features

Imperative features are language constructs to express commands using and modifying the state of mutable objects. The working of these features are explained using a new component, the *store*, beside the environment. A store consists of a set of locations containing values, together with operators to access and change the store. We explain why the restriction on polymorphically typed expressions is needed because of the imperative features. The F# concept of a mutable record field gives the means of assigning values to object members. The `while` loop is introduced and we study its relationship with iterative functions. The F# and .NET libraries offer imperative collections: arrays, imperative sets and imperative maps.

8.1 Locations

A (mutable) *location* is a part of the computer memory where the F# program may store different values at different points in time. A location is obtained by executing a `let mutable` declaration, for example:

```
let mutable x = 1;;
val mutable x : int = 1
```

The keyword `mutable` requests F# to create a *location*, and the answer tells that x is bound to a location of *type* `int`, currently containing the value 1. The situation obtained is illustrated as follows:

$$x \mapsto loc_1 \qquad loc_1: 1$$

Locations may be of any type:

```
let mutable y = (3,(5,8));;
val mutable y : int * (int * int) = (3, (5, 8))

let mutable z = [1;2;3];;
val mutable z : int list = [1; 2; 3]

let mutable w = Some (3,(5,8));;
val mutable w : (int * (int * int)) option
            = Some (3, (5, 8))

let mutable f = sin ;;
val mutable f : (float -> float)
```

After these declarations we have the following situation:

Environment	Store
$x \mapsto loc_1$	loc_1: 1
$y \mapsto loc_2$	loc_2: (3,(5,8))
$z \mapsto loc_3$	loc_3: [1;2;3]
$w \mapsto loc_4$	loc_4: Some (3,(5,8))
$f \mapsto loc_5$	loc_5: "the sine function"

A set of locations with contents is called a *store*.

The F# concept of location should be interpreted in an "abstract" sense: An F# location of basic type (like `int`) corresponds to a physical memory location in the computer containing the stored value. An F# location of, for example, a `list` type corresponds on the other hand to a physical memory location containing a link to the list that is stored elsewhere in memory. This difference in management of physical memory is, however, not visible from the F# program.

We shall study the memory management of the system in Chapter 9.

8.2 Operators on locations

There are two operations on a location:

Operator	Symbol	Usage	Legend
Assign	<-	exp_1 <- exp_2	Assign value to location
ContentsOf		exp	Contents of location

An assignment expression exp_1 <- exp_2 is evaluated as follows:

1. Evaluate exp_1 to get a location *loc*.
2. Evaluate exp_2 to get a value v.
3. Store the value v in the location *loc*.
4. Deliver the value () of type `unit` as the result.

We may, for example, assign the value 7 to x:

```
x <- 7;;
val it : unit = ()
```

The evaluation proceeds as follows:

	x <- 7	$x \mapsto loc_1$	loc_1: 1
$\rightsquigarrow$	loc_1 <- 7	$x \mapsto loc_1$	loc_1: 1
$\rightsquigarrow$	()	$x \mapsto loc_1$	loc_1: 7

This evaluation has a *side effect*: the content of the location loc_1 is changed. It is called a side-effect because it is not visible in the result which is just the uninteresting value () of type `unit`. Note that the binding of x is *unaffected* by the assignment: x remains bound to the same location.

We may do more complex assignments:

```
f <- cos;;
val it : unit = ()

y <- (-2, (3,1));;
val it : unit = ()
```

but the value assigned to a location must have the same type as the location, so the following attempt fails:

```
x <- (2,3);;
  x <- (2,3);;
  ------^^^
...: error FS0001: This expression was expected to
have type
      int
but here has type
    'a * 'b
```

A contentsOf expression *exp* is evaluated as follows:

1. Evaluate *exp* to get a location *loc*.
2. Deliver the contents v of the location *loc* as the result.

The contentsOf operator has no visible operator symbol and the operator is automatically inserted by the F# compiler according to the following *coercion rule*:

> A contentsOf operator is automatically inserted by the F# compiler whenever a location occurs in a context where a value is required. The right-hand side of a let-declaration is such a context.

Assume that we have the binding of x and corresponding location loc_1 as above:

$$x \mapsto loc_1 \qquad loc_1 : 7$$

The evaluation of the expression x <- x + 1 will then proceed as follows:

$$
\begin{array}{llll}
& x <- x + 1 & x \mapsto loc_1 & loc_1 : 7 \\
\rightsquigarrow & loc_1 <- loc_1 + 1 & x \mapsto loc_1 & loc_1 : 7 \\
\rightsquigarrow & loc_1 <- \text{contentsOf}(loc_1) + 1 & x \mapsto loc_1 & loc_1 : 7 \\
\rightsquigarrow & loc_1 <- 7 + 1 & x \mapsto loc_1 & loc_1 : 7 \\
\rightsquigarrow & loc_1 <- 8 & x \mapsto loc_1 & loc_1 : 7 \\
\rightsquigarrow & () & x \mapsto loc_1 & loc_1 : 8 \\
\end{array}
$$

The contentsOf operator is inserted by the coercion rule because the plus operator requires a value as operand.

The coercion rule also apply when making a declaration:

```
let t = x;;
val t : int = 8
```

where the right-hand side x would otherwise evaluate to a location. The identifier t is hence bound to the value 8:

$$x \mapsto loc_1 \qquad loc_1: 8$$
$$t \mapsto 8$$

An assignment to x will have no effect on t as there is no connection between the value stored in the location loc_1 and the value bound to t:

```
x <- 17;;
val it : unit = ()

t ;;
val it : int = 8
```

The coercion rule also apply if we enter the identifier x as an expression to be evaluated by F# because this is interpreted as a declaration let it = x of the identifier it:

```
x;;
val it : int = 17
```

Hence, a location is *not* a value but an expression may evaluate to a location when, for example, used as the left-hand side of an assignment.

Locations cannot occur as components in tuples or tagged values, as elements in lists or as values of functions. The situation for records is different as described in Section 8.5.

A remark on the mutable declaration

The "mutable" keyword in the declaration let mutable x = 1 describes a property of the entity to be bound to the identifier x and *not* a property of x. A syntax like

```
let x = mutable 1    // NOT legal F#
```

might hence have been more appropriate as the declaration creates a *mutable location* to be bound to the identifier x. The actual F# syntax has the advantage that the coercion rule automatically applies when the right-hand side evaluates to a location like in the above example let t = x where x is bound to a *location* but t becomes bound to a *value*.

8.3 Default values

A mutable declaration requires an *initial value* to be stored in the location. This value is obtained by evaluating the expression on the right-hand side of the declaration. It is sometimes awkward or even impossible for the programmer to make a proper initial value at the time of declaration. One may then use the *default value* of the type in question:

```
Unchecked.defaultof<type>
```

on the right-hand side of the declaration. Such a value is available for any type. It may serve as a placeholder in the location until replaced by a proper value. Default values should be used only for this purpose.

8.4 Sequential composition

The semicolon symbol ";" denotes the *sequential composition* operator (while the double semicolon ";;" is a terminator symbol). This operator combines two *expressions* exp_1 and exp_2 to form a new *expression*:

$$exp_1 \; ; \; exp_2$$

The expression $exp_1 \; ; \; exp_2$ is evaluated as follows:

1. Evaluate exp_1 and discard the result.
2. Evaluate exp_2 and supply the result as the result of evaluating $exp_1 \; ; \; exp_2$.

Hence, if exp_2 has type τ then $exp_1 \; ; \; exp_2$ has type τ as well.

The F# compiler issues a warning if exp_1 is of type different from unit as the result of the evaluation might be of some use. This warning is avoided by using the ignore function:

$$\text{ignore}\,(exp_1) \; ; \; exp_2 \qquad \text{or} \qquad exp_1 \,|> \text{ignore} \; ; \; exp_2$$

where ignore $a = ()$ for any value a.

We may combine two assignments using sequential composition:

```
let mutable x = 5;;
let mutable y = 7;;
x <- y + 1 ; y <- x + 2;;
(x,y);;
val it : int * int = (8 ,10)
```

Note that the second assignment uses the new value stored in the location denoted by x.

The operator ";" may be omitted if the expressions are written on separate lines, that is,

$$exp_1$$
$$exp_2$$

means $(exp_1) \; ; \; exp_2$.

8.5 Mutable record fields

A mutable record field is obtained by prefixing the label in the *record type declaration* by the keyword mutable, for example:

```
type intRec  = { mutable count : int };;
```

Executing a declaration of a value of this type

```
let r1 = { count = 0 };;
val r1 : intRec = {count = 0;}
```

creates the following entities:

1. A value (record) of type intRec,
2. a location containing the value 0 (due to keyword mutable in the record type),
3. a local binding inside the record of the record label count to the location, and
4. a binding of the identifier r1 to the record.

So the following is added to environment and store:

Environment	Store
r1 $\mapsto$ { count $\mapsto loc_2$ }	loc_2: 0

One may assign a value to the count field in r1:

```
r1.count <- 5;;
val it : unit = ()
```

This assignment changes the contents of the associated location:

Environment	Store
r1 $\mapsto$ { count $\mapsto loc_2$ }	loc_2: 5

One may declare a function incrementing the counter value of an intRec record and delivering the new counter value as the result:

```
let incr (x: intRec) =
    x.count <- x.count + 1
    x.count;;
val incr : intRec -> int

incr r1;;
val it : int = 6

incr r1;;
val it : int = 7
```

We may even declare a function returning a closure with an internal counter:

```
let makeCounter() =
    let counter = { count = 0 }
    fun () -> incr counter;;
val makeCounter : unit -> (unit -> int)
```

```
let clock = makeCounter();;
val clock : (unit -> int)

clock();;
val it : int = 1

clock();;
val it : int = 2
```

Equality of records with mutable fields is defined as for records without such fields. Consider the declarations:

```
let x = { count = 0 };;
val x : intRec = {count = 0;}
let y = { count = 0 };;
val x : intRec = {count = 0;}
let z = y;;
val z : intRec = {count = 0;}
```

The values bound to x, y and z are considered equal:

```
x = y;;
val it : bool = true
y = z;;
val it : bool = true
```

An assignment to the count field in the record bound to y has interesting consequences:

```
y.count <- 1;;
val it : unit = ()
x = y;;
val it : bool = false
y = z;;
val it : bool = true
z;;
val it : intRec = {count = 1;}
```

The assignment to the count field of y has hence not only changed y but also z. Environment and store give the explanation: the declarations create the following environment and store (prior to the assignment of y.count) where x=y and y=z:

Environment	Store
$x \mapsto \{ \text{count} \mapsto loc_3 \}$	loc_3: 0
$y \mapsto \{ \text{count} \mapsto loc_4 \}$	loc_4: 0
$z \mapsto \{ \text{count} \mapsto loc_4 \}$	

The assignment changes the store but leaves the environment unchanged:

Environment	Store
$x \mapsto \{ \text{count} \mapsto loc_3 \}$	loc_3: 0
$y \mapsto \{ \text{count} \mapsto loc_4 \}$	loc_4: 1
$z \mapsto \{ \text{count} \mapsto loc_4 \}$	

The crucial point is that the records bound to y and z *share* the location loc_4. One says that z is an *alias* of y. Sharing and aliasing can have unexpected and unpleasant effects in imperative programming. These phenomena do not exist in pure functional programming where a value is immutable – not to be changed.

It should be remembered that a record is a *value* in F# – assignment to a record is not possible. If required, one may declare a location containing a record:

```
let mutable t = x;;
val mutable t : intRec = {count = 0;}
```

This gives the following environment and store:

Environment	Store
$x \mapsto \{\text{count} \mapsto loc_3\}$	loc_3: 0
$y \mapsto \{\text{count} \mapsto loc_4\}$	loc_4: 1
$z \mapsto \{\text{count} \mapsto loc_4\}$	
$t \mapsto loc_5$	loc_5: $\{\text{count} \mapsto loc_3\}$

and one may, for example, assign the value of y to t:

```
t <- y;;
val it : unit = ()
t;;
val it : intRec = {count = 1;}
```

This assignment changes the contents of loc_5 to the value $\{\text{count} \mapsto loc_4\}$.

The above examples illustrate some of the (pleasant and unpleasant) features of records with mutable fields. The real importance is, however, their key role in handling objects from F#. An assignable member of an object appears in F# as a mutable record field that can be assigned using the <- operator, for example:

```
open System.Globalization;;
open System.Threading;;
Thread.CurrentThread.CurrentCulture <- CultureInfo "en-US";;
```

modifying the value of the CurrentCulture member of the CurrentThread object.

8.6 References

The F# compiler does *not* accept use of locally declared mutables in locally declared functions.[1] The above clock example could hence not be made without using records.

The ref type provides a shorthand for a record type containing a single mutable field, and the ref function provides a shorthand for a value of this type. They appear[2] as defined as follows:

```
type 'a ref  = { mutable contents: 'a }
let ref v    = { contents = v }
```

[1] The restriction is related to the memory management where problems might arise if a function was allowed to return a closure using a locally defined mutable.

[2] The symbol ! cannot be used as a *user-defined* prefix operator.

```
let (~!) r   = r.contents
let (:=) r v = r.contents <- v
```

The declaration

```
let x = ref [1; 2];;
val x : int list ref = {contents = [1;2];}
```

will hence give the following extension of environment and store:

Environment	Store
x ↦ { contents ↦ *loc* }	*loc*: [1;2]

with a location *loc* of type int list containing the value [1;2], and a binding of x to the record {contents ↦ *loc*}.

The operators ! and := work as follows:

```
!x;;
val it : int list = [1; 2]]
x := [3;4];;
val it : unit = ()
!x;;
val it : int list = [3; 4]
```

The makeCounter example in the previous section can be made using references:

```
let incr r = (r := !r + 1 ; !r);;
let makeCounter() =
    let counter = ref 0
    fun () -> incr counter;;
```

8.7 While loops

If b denotes an expression of type bool and e denotes an expression of any type, then

$$\text{while } b \text{ do } e$$

will be an expression of type unit. This expression is evaluated as follows:

1. Evaluate the expression b.
2. If the result is true, then evaluate the expression e and repeat the evaluation of the expression while b do e. If the result is false, then terminate the evaluation of while b do e and return the result () of type unit.

These rules are expressed in the following *evaluation steps* for a while loop:

$$\begin{array}{lll} \text{while } b \text{ do } e & \rightsquigarrow & e \text{ ; while } b \text{ do } e \quad \text{if } b \text{ evaluates to true} \\ \text{while } b \text{ do } e & \rightsquigarrow & () \qquad\qquad\qquad\quad \text{if } b \text{ evaluates to false} \end{array}$$

where we have used the sequential composition operator ";" (cf. Section 8.4).

A while loop is only useful when evaluated in a context where some identifiers are bound to mutables. The expression e should contain assignment to some of these mutables and b should comprises tests of some of their values.

The `while` loop:

$$\text{while } b \text{ do } e$$

has the same evaluation steps as the expression:

$$\text{wh ()}$$

where the function wh is declared by:

```
let rec wh() = if b then (e ; wh()) else ();;
```

The evaluation of wh() will evaluate the expression e repeatedly until b becomes false and that is exactly what is done by the evaluation of the `while` loop (we assume that the identifier wh does not occur in b or e). Thus, any `while` loop can be expressed by a recursive function declaration.

It should be noted that the F# compiler generates essentially the same binary code for the while-loop and the function wh (the recursive call wh() is compiled to a branch instruction). There is hence *no* performance advantage in using the loop instead of the recursive declaration. See also Section 9.5, especially the examples on Page 211.

8.8 Imperative functions on lists and other collections

The F# library contains functions `iter` and `iteri` on lists:

```
List.iter:   ('a -> unit) -> 'a list -> unit
List.iteri:  (int -> 'a -> unit) -> 'a list -> unit
```

These functions are used to *iterate* the effect of an imperative function over the elements of a list. Let

$$\text{lst} = [v_0;\ v_1;\ \ldots;\ v_{n-1}]$$

be a list with elements of type 'a and let

$$f: \text{'a -> unit}$$

be an imperative function. The evaluation of the expression

```
List.iter f lst
```

will then successively apply the function f to the elements $v_0, v_1, \ldots, v_{n-1}$ of the list. The result (of type `unit`) of the evaluation is of no interest and the interesting part of the evaluation is the side-effect. The following is a (not very interesting) application of `List.iter`:

```
let mutable sum = 0;;
let f x = sum <- sum + x;;
List.iter f [1; 2; -3; 5];;
val it : unit = ()
sum;;
val it : int = 5
```

The function `iteri` includes the index k of the element v_k in the computations. Let `f` be a function of type

```
f: int -> 'a -> unit
```

The evaluation of the expression

```
List.iteri f lst
```

will then successively evaluate the function calls:

$$f\ 0\ v_0, \quad f\ 1\ v_1, \quad \ldots, \quad f\ (n-1)\ v_{n-1}$$

The interesting part of the evaluation is again the side-effect. The following is another (not very interesting) application of `List.iteri`:

```
let mutable t = 0;;
let f k x = t <- t + k * x;;
List.iteri f [1; 2; -3; 5];;
t;;
val it : int = 11
```

The evaluation of `List.iteri f [1; 2; -3; 5]` accumulates the value:

```
0 + 0 * 1 + 1 * 2 + 2 * (-3) + 3 * 5 = 11
```

in the variable `t`.

The functions `iter` and `iteri` on other collections like `Seq`, `Set` and `Map` work in a similar way.

We refer to Exercise 9.14 for an analysis of the run time of the function `List.iter` and `Set.iter`.

8.9 Imperative tree traversal

The tree traversal functions introduced in Section 6.3 and Section 6.6 have imperative counterparts where an imperative function is called whenever an element in a tree is visited. Such functions are useful in many applications and give for instance a convenient way of producing output while traversing a tree. In solving a programming problem you will often make problem-specific imperative traversal functions corresponding to a problem-specific tree type. The declarations in this section and in Section 8.13 could then serve as models for such declarations.

The imperative traversal functions on a binary tree are obtained directly from the definition of the traversal in Section 6.3 using the same `binTree<'a>` type:

```
let rec preIter f = function
    | Leaf           -> ()
    | Node(tl,x,tr) -> f x ; preIter f tl ; preIter f tr;;
val preIter : ('a -> unit) -> BinTree<'a> -> unit
```

```
let rec inIter f = function
    | Leaf              -> ()
    | Node(tl,x,tr) -> inIter f tl ; f x ; inIter f tr;;
val inIter : ('a -> unit) -> BinTree<'a> -> unit
```

and similar for postIter. Applying, for example, preIter to the tree t4 in Section 6.3 gives:

```
preIter (fun x -> printf " %d" x) t4;;
  5 0 -3 2 7
```

We may in a similar way define a function for imperative depth-first traversal of list trees as described in Section 6.6:

```
let rec depthFirstIter f (Node(x,ts)) =
    f x ; List.iter (depthFirstIter f) ts;;
val depthFirstIter : ('a -> unit) -> ListTree<'a> -> unit
```

Applying this function to the tree t1 in Section 6.6 we get:

```
depthFirstIter (fun x -> printf " %d" x) t1;;
  1 2 5 3 4 6 7
```

The breadthFirstIter function is declared in Section 8.13.

8.10 Arrays

The addresses in the *physical* memory of the computer are integers. Consider a sequence of n equally sized contiguous memory locations $loc_0, loc_1, \ldots, loc_{n-1}$ as shown in Figure 8.1.

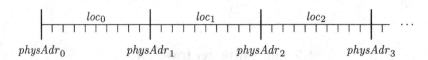

Figure 8.1 Memory layout of an array

The physical address $physAdr_k$ of the k'th location loc_k can in this situation be computed by the formula:

$$physAdr_k = physAdr_0 + k \cdot s$$

where s denotes the size of one location. The machine code computation of $physAdr_k$ requires hence only two arithmetic operations.

This addressing scheme is used to implement arrays. An *array* of length n consists of n locations $loc_0, loc_1, \ldots, loc_{n-1}$ of the same type. The numbers $0, 1, \ldots, n-1$ are called the *indices* of the elements. The type of the array is written

$$\tau\,[\,]$$

where τ is the type of the elements.

Arrays have the advantage over lists that any array location can be accessed and modified in a constant (short) time, that is, in a small number of computations which is independent of the size of the array. On the other hand, an array is a mutable object — the old value is lost when a location is modified. Furthermore, an array cannot be extended by more elements in a simple way as the adjacent physical memory (after the last element in the array) might be occupied for other use. A selection of operations on arrays is shown in Table 8.1.

An array can be entered using the "[| ... |]" notation, for example:

```
let a = [|4;5;6;7|];;
val a : int [] = [|4; 5; 6; 7|]

let b = [|'a' .. 'f'|];;
val b : char [] = [|'a'; 'b'; 'c'; 'd'; 'e'; 'f'|]
```

Individual array locations are assigned using indexing:

```
b.[2] <- 'z';;
val it : unit = ()
b;;
val it : char [] = [|'a'; 'b'; 'z'; 'd'; 'e'; 'f'|]
```

Name	Type	Function
.[ ]	$'a$ [] $*$ int $\to$ $'a$ "location"	$arr.[k]$ is loc_k. May raise IndexOutOfRangeException
Array.length	$'a$ [] $\to$ int	Length n of array
Array.ofList	$'a$ list $\to$ $'a$ []	Array.ofList $[x_0;...]$ is new array of values $x_0,...$
Array.toList	$'a$ [] $\to$ $'a$ list	Array.toList arr is list $[val_0;...;val_{n-1}]$
Array.ofSeq	seq<$'a$> $\to$ $'a$ []	Array init'ed to seq elem's
Array.toSeq	$'a$ [] $\to$ seq<$'a$>	Seq of array val's
Array.map	$'a \to 'b$ $\to$ $'a$ [] $\to$ $'b$ []	Array.map f arr is new array of f val_0, f $val_1,...$
Array.mapi	int $\to 'a \to 'b$ $\to$ $'a$ [] $\to$ $'b$ []	Array.mapi f arr is new array of f 0 val_0, f 1 $val_1,...$
Array.iter	$'a \to$ unit $\to$ $'a$ [] $\to$ unit	Array.iter f arr is the effect of f $val_0; f$ $val_1; ...$
Array.iteri	int $\to 'a \to$ unit $\to$ $'a$ [] $\to$ unit	Array.iteri f arr is the effect of f 0 $val_0; f$ 1 $val_1; ...$
Array.fold	$'b \to 'a \to 'b$ $\to$ $'b \to 'a$ [] $\to 'b$	Array.fold f b arr is f $(...(f$ b $val_0)...)$ val_{n-1}
Array.foldBack	$'a \to 'b \to 'b$ $\to$ $'a$ [] $\to 'b \to 'b$	Array.foldBack f arr b is f val_0 $(...(f$ val_{n-1} $b)...)$

Metasymbol *arr* denotes an array of locations $loc_0, ..., loc_{n-1}$ containing the values $val_0, ..., val_{n-1}$

Table 8.1 *Operations on arrays*

Example: Histogram

Arrays are very convenient when counting frequencies and making a histogram. The following small program reeds a text file given by its directory path and count the frequency of each character ′A′ to ′Z′ (not distinguishing small and capital letters) and prints the resulting histogram. The reader may consult Section 10.3 about the used text I/O functions and Section 10.7 about printf formats.

```
open System;;
open System.IO;;

let Acode = int 'A'

let histogram path =
    let charCount    = [| for n in 'A'..'Z' -> 0 |]
    let file = File.OpenText path
    while (not file.EndOfStream) do
        let ch = char( file.Read() )
        if (Char.IsLetter ch) then
            let n = int (Char.ToUpper ch)   - Acode
            charCount.[n] <- charCount.[n] + 1
        else ()
    file.Close()
    let printOne n c = printf "%c:  %4d\n" (char(n + Acode)) c
    Array.iteri printOne charCount;;
```

Calling the function histogram on the path of the source file histogram.fsx will, for example, give the output:

```
A:      20
B:       0
C:      22
...
X:       1
Y:       3
Z:       1
```

where we have only shown some of the lines.

8.11 Imperative set and map

The .NET library System.Collections.Generic contains classes implementing imperative sets and maps:

Set	Map	Data representation
SortedSet<'a>	SortedDictionary<'a,'b>	Search tree
HashSet<'a>	Dictionary<'a,'b>	Hash-key table

The classes SortedSet<'a> and SortedDictionary<'a,'b> are imperative versions of set<'a> and map<'a,'b> where the member functions modify the collection in a "destructive" update without retaining the old value. They should only be used in algorithms using and maintaining a single "current" collection without ever referring to "old" values.

The `HashSet<'a>` and `Dictionary<'a,'b>` are implemented using hash-key technique: The basic data structure is an array (say of length N) where an element a (entry (a, b)) is stored in the array location with index:

$$index(a) = \text{hash}(a) \ \% \ \text{N}$$

where `hash` is the hash function of the equality type `'a`. This is a rather efficient scheme, but it runs into problems when multiple elements (entries) have the same index and hence should be stored in the same array location. This *collision* problem is solved by storing the colliding elements (entries) in a linked structure that can be accessed via the index value. The `HashSet<'a>` and `Dictionary<'a,'b>` collections have the following characteristics:

- The operations are very efficient.
- They are strictly imperative with destructive updating.
- They do not offer a traversal of the elements (entries) in sorted order.

A selections of operations on the imperative set and map classes are shown in Tables 8.2 and 8.3.

Indexing in a `Directory` by a key can be used to update a value by assignment:

map.[*key*] <- *newValue*

and this construction may also be used to add a new entry to the directory.

Name	Type	Function
`SortedSet`<*type*>	unit -> *Set<type>*	Create an empty SortedSet
`HashSet`<*type*>	unit -> *Set<type>*	Creates an empty HashSet
hashSet.`Count`	int	No. of elements in *hashSet*
set.`Add`	*type* -> unit	Add element to *set*
set.`Contains`	*type* -> bool	Value contained in *set*?
set.`Remove`	*type* -> bool	Remove value from *set*, `false`: value not inset
set.`UnionWith`	*Set<type>* -> unit	Add elements in other set
set.`IntersectWith`	*Set<type>* -> unit	Remove elements of other set
set.`IsProperSubsetOf`	*Set<type>* -> bool	Is proper subset of set ?
set.`IsSubsetOf`	*Set<type>* -> bool	Is subset of set ?
set.`Overlaps`	*Set<type>* -> bool	Overlaps set ?

Metasymbols: *Set<type>* denotes `SortedSet`<*type*> or `HashSet`<*type*>
set and *hashSet* denote values of types *Set<type>* and `HashSet`<*type*>
Table 8.2 *A selection of operations on* `SortedSet` *and* `HashSet`

Imperative features

Name	Type	Function
`SortedDictionary<`*kTyp*`,`*vTyp*`>`		Creates empty Sorted
	`unit ->` *Map<kTyp, vTyp>*	Dictionary
`Dictionary<`*kTyp*`,`*vTyp*`>`	`unit ->` *Map<kTyp, vTyp>*	Creates empty Dictionary
dir`.Count`	`int`	No of elements in *map*
map`.Add`	*kTyp* `*` *vTyp* `-> unit`	Add entry to *map*
map`.ContainsKey`	*kTyp* `-> bool`	*map* contains key ?
map`.ContainsValue`	*vTyp* `-> bool`	*map* contains value ?
map`.Remove`	*kTyp* `-> bool`	Remove an entry from *map*
		`false`: entry not found
map`.TryGetValue`	*kTyp* `-> bool *` *vTyp*	Search entry by key
dir`.[ ]`	*kTyp* `->` *vTyp* "`mutable`"	Value location for key

Metasymbols: *Map<kTyp, vTyp>* denotes `SortedDictionary<`*kTyp*`,`*vTyp*`>`
or `Dictionary<`*kTyp*`,`*vTyp*`>`, *map* denotes a value of type *Map<kTyp, vTyp>*
while *dir* denotes a value of type `Dictionary<`*kTyp*`,`*vTyp*`>`

Table 8.3 *A selection of operations on* `SortedDictionary` *and* `Dictionary`

8.12 Functions on collections. Enumerator functions

Operations on collections should preferably be done using standard library functions, but this is not always feasible. This section presents means for defining functions on collections in a way that resembles the definition of functions on lists using list patterns as described in Chapter 4.

Enumerator functions

The `System.Collections.Generic` library contains imperative features for element-wise traversal of any of the collections – including the F# collections `list`, `set`, `map`, etc. The `enumerator` function of the book (to be declared on Page 193) makes these features available in a functional setting. Applying `enumerator` to a collection yields a function:

$$\text{enumerator}(collection): \text{unit} \rightarrow elementType \text{ option}$$

where *elementType* is determined as follows:

collection	elementType
NonMapOrDictionaryCollection<`'a`*>*	`'a`
MapOrDictionaryCollection<`'a`*,*`'b`*>*	`KeyValuePair<`'a`,`'b`>`

An element *entry* of type `KeyValuePair<`'a`,`'b`>` corresponds to an entry in the map or dictionary, and it has components:

    entry`.Key`   of type `'a`
    entry`.Value`   of type `'b`

Applying `enumerator` to a set creates an imperative *enumerator function* where successive calls yield the elements in the set:

```
let f = enumerator (Set.ofList [3 ; 1; 5]);;
val f : (unit -> int option)
```

```
f();;
val it : int option = Some 1

f();;
val it : int option = Some 3

f();;
val it : int option = Some 5

f();;
val it : int option = None
```

Applying the function `enumerator` to a dictionary creates a similar enumerator function but the entries are obtained as values of the corresponding `KeyValuePair` type:

```
let d = SortedDictionary<string,int>();;
d.Add("cd",3) ; d.Add("ab",5);;
let g = enumerator d;;
val g : (unit -> KeyValuePair<string,int> option)
g();;
val it : KeyValuePair<string,int> option =
    Some [ab, 5] {Key = "ab"; Value = 5;}
g();;
val it : KeyValuePair<string,int> option =
    Some [cd, 3] {Key = "cd"; Value = 3;}
g();;
val it : KeyValuePair<string,int> option = None
```

The elements in a `set<'a>` or `SortedSet<'a>` collection are traversed in the order given by the ordering in the type `'a` while the elements in a `HashSet<'a>` collection are traversed in some order depending on the hashing function and the order in which elements were added. The entries in a `map<'a,'b>` or `SortedDictionary<'a,'b>` collection are traversed in the order given by the ordering in the type `'a` while the elements in a `Dictionary<'a,'b>` collection are traversed in some order depending on hashing function and the creation of the collection.

The enumerator may, for example, be used to define the `tryFind` function on sets:

```
let tryFind p (s: Set<'a>) =
    let f = enumerator s
    let rec tFnd () =
        match f() with
        | None    -> None
        | Some x ->
            if (p x) then Some x else tFnd()
    tFnd();;
val tryFind : ('a -> bool) -> Set<'a> -> 'a option
                            when 'a : comparison
```

```
let s = Set.ofList [1;3;4;5];;
val s : Set<int> = set [1; 3; 4; 5]

tryFind (fun n -> n%2 = 0) s;;
val it : int option = Some 4
```

We refer to Exercise 9.13 for an analysis of the run time of this function and the version declared on Page 109 .

Declaring the enumerator *function*

The declarations of the enumerator function is based on the concept of an *enumerator object* for a collection. An enumerator object is a mutable data structure that is able to describe a traversal of the collection by pointing to each element one after the other. The implementation of the enumerator object depends on the data representation of the associated collection but all enumerator objects are of the same polymorphic type IEnumerator<'c>. This polymorphism has been obtained by letting any enumerator implement the *interface*:

```
type IEnumerator<'c> =
    abstract Current : 'c
    abstract MoveNext : unit -> bool;;
```

for some type 'c. An enumerator object *enum* points to the element *enum*.Current and it is forwarded to the next element by evaluating *enum*.MoveNext(). An initial call of MoveNext is required to get a fresh enumerator to point to the first element, and the value of MoveNext becomes false when the enumerator gets beyond the last element in the collection.

Each collection has its own GetEnumerator member to create an enumerator object. This object gets the following type:

Collection	Enumerator object
NonMapOrDictionaryCollection<'a>	IEnumerator<'a>
MapOrDictionaryCollection<'a,'b>	IEnumerator<KeyValuePair<'a,'b>>

The implementation is made such that the GetEnumerator member for any specific collection can be considered an instance of a polymorphic GetEnumerator member working on any collection. This polymorphism has been obtained by letting each collection implement the interface:

```
type IEnumerable<'c> =
    abstract GetEnumerator : unit -> IEnumerator<'c>
```

Any collection is hence construed as an object of type IEnumerable<'c> where 'c is the type parameter of the enumerator object as described above.

The enumerator function refers to the collection using the IEnumerable type and may hence be applied to any collection. It creates a reference e to an enumerator object and this reference is then used inside a local function f that is returned as the result. A reference is required because of the restriction on the use of mutable in closures:

```
open System.Collections.Generic;;

let enumerator (m: IEnumerable<'c>) =
    let e = ref (m.GetEnumerator())
    let f () =
        match (!e).MoveNext() with
        | false -> None
        | _     -> Some ((!e).Current)
    f;;
val enumerator : IEnumerable<'c> -> (unit -> 'c option)
```

Enumerators versus list patterns

The elegant and efficient use of list patterns as described in Chapter 4 depends on the fact that the tail of a list is represented directly by a sub-component of the data structure representing the list. Matching a list with the pattern x::xs is hence a very fast operation, and the same applies to matching with other list patterns.

The situation is different for set and map collections. Consider, for example, a set s represented by a balanced search tree. Finding the first (least) element x of s is a very fast operation, but the remaining part of the search tree consists of two separate trees and is *not* represented by a sub-tree of the search tree. The time for computing Set.remove x s is in fact proportional to the depth of the search tree and hence proportional to the logarithm of the number of elements in the set. The computation time for making a complete recursion over a set with successive computations Set.remove x s of trees representing sub-sets is hence proportional to $n \log n$ where n is the number of elements in the set.

The enumerator function of a set (or map) represented by a search tree is based on the idea of in-order traversal of the tree. The enumerator uses an imperative data structure to represent a stage in this traversal, where a specific element (entry) is reached. Each call of the enumerator function steps this data structure forward to the next element (entry) by a small modification with constant computation time. The computation time for making a complete recursion over a search-tree based set (or map) using the enumerator function is hence proportional to the number of elements in the set (entries in the map), and the time performance equals the time performance of pattern-matching for lists.

The enumerator functions for the hash-key based HashSet and Dictionary collections work in a different way because we have a different data representation using an array as described in Section 8.11. The traversal scans forward through the array (and through each linked structure of colliding elements). The time used by a complete recursion over a hashed collection using the enumerator function is hence proportional to the number of elements (entries) in the set (map), and this corresponds to the time used by a complete recursion over a list using pattern-matching.

8.13 Imperative queue

The `System.Collections.Generic` library contains an imperative queue implementation in the form of a `Queue<'a>` class with members:

$$q.\text{Enqueue: 'a -> unit}$$
$$q.\text{Dequeue: unit -> 'a}$$
$$q.\text{Count: int}$$

The queue is implemented using an array where the front queue element is stored in an
array location with index *frontIndex* while the rest of the queue is stored in the succeeding
locations with a wraparound to the beginning of the array if the queue extends beyond the
end of the array.

frontIndex

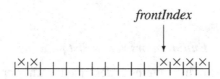

The `Dequeue` operation returns the array element with index *frontIndex* and advances *front-
Index* to the next array position (with a possible wraparound) while the `Enqueue` operation
stores the enqueued value in the first free array location. An `Enqueue` operation with a
filled array causes an *array replacement* where a new, larger array is reserved and all queue
elements are moved to the new array upon which the old array is abandoned.

A queue can be used to make the following elegant and interesting implementation of the
breadth-first traversal of list trees in Section 6.6.

```
type ListTree<'a> = Node of 'a * (ListTree<'a> list);;

let breadthFirstIter f ltr =
    let remains = Queue<ListTree<'a>>()
    remains.Enqueue ltr
    while (remains.Count <> 0) do
        let (Node (x,tl)) = remains.Dequeue()
        List.iter (remains.Enqueue) tl
        f x;;
val breadthFirstIter : ('a -> unit) -> listTree<'a> -> unit
```

The idea is to let the *queue* `remains` contain those list trees where the nodes remain to be
visited, initially the tree `ltr`. A list tree `Node (x,tl)` is dequeued, the elements of the
list `tl` of sub-trees are enqueued one-by-one using `List.iter` – and the root node `x` is
visited. This procedure is repeated until the queue becomes empty.

8.14 Restrictions on polymorphic expressions

The purpose of the restriction on polymorphic expressions in Section 4.5 is to ensure that the use of mutables is type safe. The problem is illustrated by the following hypothetical example:

```
let mutable a = [];;   // NOT allowed !!
val mutable a = []

let f x = a <- (x :: a);;
val f : 'a -> unit

f(1);;
it : unit = ()
f("ab");;
it : unit = ()
a;;
it : ? list = ["ab"; 1]  *** Oops! type error !
```

The point is that F# would be forced to infer a type of f prior to any use of the function. This would result in the type 'a -> unit because apparently values of any type can be cons'ed onto the *empty* list. Hence each of the applications f(1) and f("ab") would type check because int as well as string are instances of the polymorphic type 'a. The type check would hence fail to discover the illegal expression "ab"::[1] emerging during the evaluation of f("ab").

The declaration

```
let mutable a = [];;
```

is construed as binding a to the value of the polymorphic expression "mutable []" and this expression is *not* considered a value expression. The declaration is hence rejected by the restriction on the use of polymorphic expressions.

Summary

The chapter provides a semantical framework, the *store*, for understanding the imperative features of F# that operate on and modify the state of mutable objects. A store consists of a set of locations containing values, together with operators to access and change the store. The main imperative constructs of F# is introduced together with extracts of .NET libraries for imperative collections, including arrays, sets and maps. We explain why the restriction on polymorphically typed expressions is needed because of the imperative features.

Exercises

8.1   Make a drawing of the environment and store obtained by the following declarations and assignments:

```
let mutable x = 1;;
let mutable y = (x,2);;
let z = y;;
x <- 7;;
```

8.2   The sequence of declarations:

```
let mutable a = []
let f x = a <- (x :: a)
f(1);;
```

are accepted by F#. Explain why.

8.3   Make a drawing of the environment and store obtained by the following declarations and assignments:

```
type t1 = { mutable a : int };;
type t2 = { mutable b : int ; c : t1 };;
let x = { a = 1 };;
let y = { b = x.a ; c = x };;
x.a <- 3;;
```

8.4   Declare `null` to denote the default value of the record type:

```
type t = { mutable link : t ; data : int };;
```

Declare some other values of type `t` and use assignment to build chains and circles of values of type `t`. Declare a function to insert an element in the front of a chain of values of type `t`.

8.5   Give a declaration of the `gcd` function using a `while` loop instead of recursion (cf. Section 1.8).

8.6   Declare a function for computing Fibonacci numbers F_n (see Exercise 1.5) using a `while` loop. Hint: introduce variables to contain the two previously computed Fibonacci numbers.

8.7   Use a `HashSet` traversal `for` loop to declare a function

      `HashSetFold: ('b -> 'a -> 'b) -> 'b -> HashSet<'a> -> 'b`

such that

      $f\ b\ set = f\ (\ldots (f\ (f\ b\ a_0)\ a_1)\ldots)\ a_{n-1}$

where $a_0, \ldots, a_{n-1}$ are the elements of the `HashSet` *set*.

8.8   Declare a `DictionaryFold` function. The type should correspond to the type of `Map.fold`.

8.9   Make declarations of `breadthFirst` and `breadthFirstFold` for list trees using an imperative queue.

Hint: unfold the while-loop in the declaration of `breadthFirstIter` to a local recursive function and use argument and value of this function to build the result.

9

Efficiency

The efficiency of a program is measured in terms of its memory requirements and its running time. In this chapter we shall introduce the concepts *stack* and *heap* because a basic understanding of these concepts is necessary in order to understand the memory management of the system, including the *garbage collection*.

Furthermore, we shall study techniques that in many cases can be used to improve the efficiency of a given function, where the idea is to search for a more general function, whose declaration has a certain form called *iterative* or *tail recursive*. Two techniques for deriving tail-recursive functions will be presented: One is based on using *accumulating parameters* and the other is based on the concept of a *continuation*, that represents the rest of the computation. The continuation-based technique is generally applicable. The technique using accumulating parameters applies in certain cases only, but when applicable it usually gives the best results. We give examples showing the usefulness of these programming techniques.

We relate the notion of iterative function to `while` loops and provide examples showing that tail-recursive programs are in fact running faster than the corresponding programs using while loops.

The techniques for deriving tail-recursive functions are useful programming techniques that often can be used to obtain performance gains. The techniques do not replace a conscious choice of good algorithms and data structures. For a systematic study of efficient algorithms, we refer to textbooks on "Algorithms and Data Structures."

9.1 Resource measures

The performance of an algorithm given by a function declaration in F# is expressed by figures for the resources used in the *evaluation* of a function value:

- *Use of computer memory:* The *maximum size* of computer memory needed to represent *expressions* and *bindings* during the evaluation.
- *Computation time:* The *number* of individual *computation steps*.

The important issue is to estimate how these figures depend on the "size'" of the argument for "large" arguments, for example, number of digits of integer argument, length of list argument, depth (i.e. number of levels) of tree argument, etc. These performance figures are essentially language independent, so implementations of the same algorithm in another programming language will show a similar behaviour.

Efficiency in performance is not the only important issue in programming. Correctness and readability are often more important because the program should be understandable to the readers (including the programmer herself). The choice of function declaration should therefore be based on a trade-off between performance and readability (that is, simplicity), using the simplest declaration for any particular function in a program – unless, there is a risk that it becomes a performance bottleneck for the overall program.

9.2 Memory management

The memory used by an F# program is spilt into a *stack* and a *heap*, where primitive values, such as numbers and truth values are allocated on the stack, while composite values such as lists and trees, closures and (most) objects are allocated on the heap. A basic understanding of the stack and the heap is necessary to understand the memory resources required by a program.

Consider the following declaration at the outermost level:

```
let xs = [5;6;7];;
val xs : int list = [5; 6; 7]

let ys = 3::4::xs;;
val ys : int list = [3; 4; 5; 6; 7]

let zs = xs @ ys;;
val zs : int list = [5; 6; 7; 3; 4; 5; 6; 7]

let n = 27;;
val n : int = 27
```

The stack and the heap corresponding to these declarations are shown in Figure 9.1.

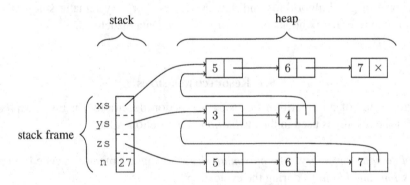

Figure 9.1 Memory: Stack and Heap for top-level declarations

The stack contains an entry for each binding. The entry for the integer n contains the integer value 27, while the entries for the lists xs, ys and zs contain links (i.e. memory pointers) pointing at the implementations of these lists. A list $[x_0; \ldots; x_{n-1}]$ is implemented by a linked data structure, where each list element x_i is implemented by a *cons cell* containing the value x_i and a link to the cons cell implementing the next element in the list:

- The entry for xs in the stack contains a link to the cons cell for its first element 5 in the heap.

- The entry for ys in the stack contains a link to the cons cell for its first element 3. This cons cell contains a link to the cons cell for the next element 4 and that cons cell contains in turn a link to the first cons cell of xs.

- The entry for zs in the stack contains a link to the first cons cell of a copy of the linked list for xs (the first argument of @ in xs @ ys). The last cons cell of that copied linked list contains a link to the start of the linked list for ys.

Since a list is a functional (immutable) data structure, we have that:

1. The linked lists for ys is not copied when building a linked list for y::ys.

2. Fresh cons cells are made for the elements of xs when building a linked list for xs @ ys, as the last cons cell in the new linked list for xs must refer to the first cons cell of the linked list for ys. The running time of @ is, therefore, linear in the length of its first argument. This running time is in agreement with the declaration of append in Section 4.4 and with the linked-list based implementation used by the built-in append function.

These two properties will be exploited later in this section.

Basic operations on Stack and Heap

The consecutive piece of stack memory corresponding to bindings at the same level is called a *stack frame*. During the evaluation of an expression a new stack frame is added whenever new bindings arise, for example, due to local declarations and expressions or because a function is called. This is illustrated using the following declarations:

```
let zs = let xs = [1;2]
         let ys = [3;4]
         xs@ys;;
```

The evaluation of the outermost declaration will start with an empty heap and a stack frame sf_0 containing a (so far undefined) entry for zs:

Pushing a stack frame

The start of the evaluation of the local declarations will *push* an new stack frame on top of sf_0. This stack frame has entries for the locally declared variables xs and ys and some extra entries including one for the *result* of the local expression $xs @ ys$:

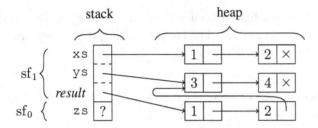

Notice that a copy of the list xs is made in the heap during the evaluation of $xs @ ys$.

Popping a stack frame

When the result of the local expression $xs @ ys$ has been computed, the stack frame sf_1 is *popped*, that is, removed from the stack, and the reference to the first cons cell of $xs @ ys$ is copied to the stack entry for zs:

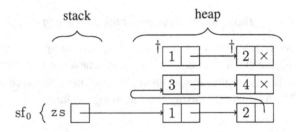

The resulting heap after the evaluation of the declaration for zs contains two cons cells marked with '†'. These cells are obsolete because they cannot be reached from any binding, and they are therefore later removed from the heap by the *garbage collector* that manages the heap behind the scene.

The management of the stack follows the evaluation of declarations and function calls in a simple manner, and the used part of the stack is always a consecutive sequence of the relevant stack frames. We illustrate this by a simple example. Consider the following declarations:

```
let rec f n =
    match n with
    | 0 -> 0
    | n -> f(n-1) + n;;

let x = f 3;;
```

The first part of the evaluation of f 3 makes repeated bindings of n corresponding to the recursive function calls:

$$
\begin{aligned}
& \text{f } 3 \\
\rightsquigarrow\ & (\text{f } n,\ [n \mapsto 3]) \\
\rightsquigarrow\ & (\text{f }(n-1) + n,\ [n \mapsto 3]) \\
\rightsquigarrow\ & \text{f } 2 + (n,\ [n \mapsto 3]) \\
\rightsquigarrow\ & (\text{f } n,\ [n \mapsto 2]) + (n,\ [n \mapsto 3]) \\
& \ldots \\
\rightsquigarrow\ & (\text{f } n,\ [n \mapsto 0]) + (n,\ [n \mapsto 1]) + (n,\ [n \mapsto 2]) + (n,\ [n \mapsto 3])
\end{aligned}
$$

These bindings are implemented by four stack frames $sf_1, \ldots, sf_4$ pushed on top of the initial stack frame sf_0 corresponding to f and x. Each of the stack frames $sf_1, \ldots, sf_4$ corresponds to an uncompleted evaluation of a function call:

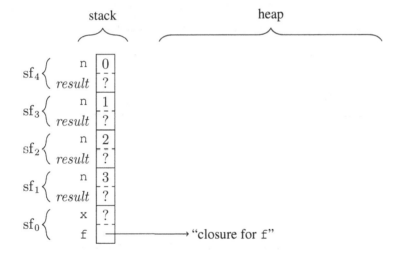

The next evaluation step marks the completion of the "innermost" functions call f 0

$$
\begin{aligned}
& (\text{f } n,\ [n \mapsto 0]) + (n,\ [n \mapsto 1]) + (n,\ [n \mapsto 2]) + (n,\ [n \mapsto 3]) \\
\rightsquigarrow\ & 0 + (n,\ [n \mapsto 1]) + (n,\ [n \mapsto 2]) + (n,\ [n \mapsto 3])
\end{aligned}
$$

and the binding $n \mapsto 0$ is hence no longer needed. The implementation releases the memory used to implement this binding by popping the frame sf_4 off the stack:

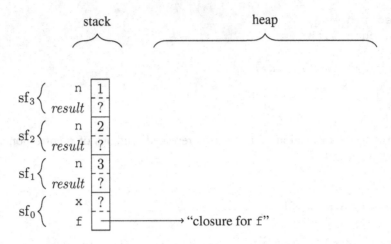

When the evaluation terminates the stack frames sf_3, sf_2 and sf_1 are all popped and the initial stack frame sf_0 contains a binding of x to 6.

The stack management using the push and pop operations is very simple because the stack is maintained as a contiguous sequence of the relevant stack frames. The stack memory will hence never be fragmented.

Garbage and garbage collection

We shall now study garbage collection closer using the declarations:

```
let xs = [1;2];;

let rec g = function
    | 0 -> xs
    | n -> let ys = n::g(n-1)
           List.rev ys;;
val g : int -> int list

g 2;;
val it : int list = [1; 1; 2; 2]
```

Application of this function will produce garbage due to the local declaration of a list and due to the use of List.rev. The stack and the heap upon the termination of g 2 is shown in Figure 9.2. The stack contains just one stack frame corresponding to the top-level declarations.

The heap contains five cons cells marked with '†', that are obsolete because they cannot be reached from any binding, and they are removed from the heap by the garbage collector. It is left for Exercise 9.1 to produced this stack and heap for an evaluation of g 2. The amount of garbage produced using g grows with the size of the argument, and it is easy to measure how much garbage the system has to collect.

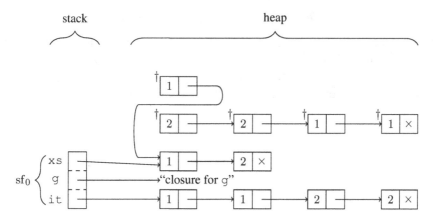

Figure 9.2 Memory: Stack and Heap upon termination of evaluation of g 2

Measuring running time and garbage collection

The directive #time, that works as a toggle, can be used in the interactive F# environment to extract information about running time and garbage collection of an operation:

```
#time;;

--> Timing now on

g 10000;;
Real: 00:00:01.315, CPU: 00:00:01.326,
GC gen0: 356, gen1: 24, gen2: 0
val it : int list = [9999; 9997; 9995; 9993; 9991; 9989; 9987;...]
```

The measurement includes two times: The *Real time* is the clock time elapsed during the execution of the operation, in this case 1.315 second. The *CPU time* is the total time spent by the operation on all CPUs (or cores) on your computer. If you are not exploiting the parallelism of multiple cores, then these two times should approximately be the same.

The garbage collector manages the heap as partitioned into three groups or *generations*: gen0, gen1 and gen2, according to their age. The objects in gen0 are the youngest while the objects in gen2 are the oldest. The typical situation is that objects die young, that is, garbage typically occurs among young objects, and the garbage collector is designed for that situation. During the above evaluation of g 10000, the garbage collector reclaimed (collected) 356 objects among the youngest ones from group gen0 and 24 objects from gen1.

The limits of the stack and the heap

The stack and heap sizes are resources that we must be aware of. The following examples illustrate maximal stack and heap sizes and shows that the maximal heap size is order of magnitudes larger than the maximal stack size.

Consider first the following function that can generate a list:

```
let rec bigList n = if n=0 then [] else 1::bigList(n-1);;
val bigList : int -> int list

bigList 120000;;
val it : int list = [1; 1; 1; 1; 1; 1; 1; 1; 1; 1; 1;...]

bigList 130000;;
Process is terminated due to StackOverflowException.
```

A call bigList *n* will generate *n* consecutive stack frames each with a binding of n and the examples show that 120000 such stack frames are manageable while 130000 are not.

Another declaration of a function that can generate the same lists as the above one is given below. This function can generate lists that are about 100 times longer than those generated above, and when memory problems arise it is because the heap is exhausted:

```
let rec bigListA n xs = if n=0 then xs
                        else bigListA (n-1) (1::xs);;
val bigListA : int -> int list -> int list

let xsVeryBig = bigListA 12000000 [];;
val xsVeryBig : int list = [1; 1; 1; 1; 1; 1; 1; 1; 1;...]

let xsTooBig = bigListA 13000000 [];;
System.OutOfMemoryException:
    Exception of type 'System.OutOfMemoryException' was thrown.
    at FSI_0002.bigListA(Int32 n, FSharpList`1 xs)
    at <StartupCode$FSI_0014>.$FSI_0014.main@()
Stopped due to error
```

In the next sections we study techniques that can be used to minimize the memory usage.

9.3 Two problems

In this section we reconsider the declarations of the factorial function fact (Page 6) and the reverse function for lists naiveRev (Page 80). We shall see that evaluation of a function value for fact uses more computer memory than necessary, and that the evaluation of a function value for naiveRev requires more evaluation steps than necessary. More efficient implementations for these functions are given in the next section.

The factorial function

The factorial function has previously been declared by:

```
let rec fact = function
    | 0 -> 1
    | n -> n * fact(n-1);;
val fact : int -> int
```

We have seen that the evaluation of the expression `fact` (N) proceeds through a number of evaluation steps building an expression with a size proportional to the argument N upon which the expression is evaluated:

$$
\begin{aligned}
&\texttt{fact}(N) \\
\rightsquigarrow\ & (\texttt{n * fact(n-1)}\ ,\ [\texttt{n} \mapsto N]) \\
\rightsquigarrow\ & N * \texttt{fact}(N-1) \\
\rightsquigarrow\ & N * (\texttt{n * fact(n-1)}\ ,\ [\texttt{n} \mapsto N-1]) \\
\rightsquigarrow\ & N * ((N-1) * \texttt{fact}(N-2)) \\
&\vdots \\
\rightsquigarrow\ & N * ((N-1) * ((N-2) * (\cdots (4 * (3 * (2 * 1))) \cdots))) \\
\rightsquigarrow\ & N * ((N-1) * ((N-2) * (\cdots (4 * (3 * 2)) \cdots))) \\
&\vdots \\
\rightsquigarrow\ & N!
\end{aligned}
$$

The maximal size of the memory needed during this evaluation is proportional to N, because the F# system must remember (in the heap) all N factors of the expression: $N*((N-1)*((N-2)*(\cdots(4*(3*(2*1)))\cdots)))$ during the evaluation. Furthermore, during the evaluation the stack will grow until it has $N+1$ stack frame corresponding to the nested calls of `fact`.

The reverse function

The naive declaration for the reverse function is as follows:

```
let rec naiveRev = function
    | []    -> []
    | x::xs -> naiveRev xs @ [x];;
val naiveRev : 'a list -> 'a list
```

A part of the evaluation of the expression `naiveRev` $[x_1, x_2, \ldots, x_n]$ is:

$$
\begin{aligned}
&\texttt{naiveRev } [x_1, x_2, \ldots, x_n] \\
\rightsquigarrow\ & \texttt{naiveRev } [x_2, \ldots, x_n] \texttt{@} [x_1] \\
\rightsquigarrow\ & (\texttt{naiveRev } [x_3, \ldots, x_n] \texttt{@} [x_2]) \texttt{@} [x_1] \\
&\vdots \\
\rightsquigarrow\ & ((\cdots (([\ ] \texttt{@} [x_n]) \texttt{@} [x_{n-1}]) \texttt{@} \cdots \texttt{@} [x_2]) \texttt{@} [x_1])
\end{aligned}
$$

There are $n + 1$ evaluation steps above and heap space of size proportional to n is required by the F# system to represent the last expression. These figures are to be expected for reversing a list of size n.

However, the further evaluation

$$((\cdots(([\,]\,@\,[x_n])@\,[x_{n-1}])@\cdots@\,[x_2])@\,[x_1]) \rightsquigarrow [x_n, x_{n-1}, \ldots, x_2, x_1]$$

requires a number of evaluation steps that is proportional to n^2.

To see this, observe first that $m + 1$ evaluation steps are needed to evaluate the expression $[y_1, \ldots, y_m]\,@zs$ as $y_1 :: (y_2 :: \ldots :: (y_m :: zs)\ldots)$.

Thus,

$$
\begin{array}{ll}
[\,]\,@\,[x_n] \rightsquigarrow [x_n] & \text{requires 1 step} \\
[x_n]\,@\,[x_{n-1}] \rightsquigarrow [x_n, x_{n-1}] & \text{requires 2 steps} \\
\qquad\qquad\vdots & \\
[x_n, x_{n-1}, \ldots, x_2]\,@\,[x_1] \rightsquigarrow [x_n, x_{n-1}, \ldots, x_2, x_1] & \text{requires } n \text{ steps}
\end{array}
$$

Hence, the evaluation of $((\cdots(([\,]\,@\,[x_n])@\,[x_{n-1}])@\cdots@\,[x_2])@\,[x_1])$ requires

$$1 + 2 + \cdots n = \frac{n(n+1)}{2}$$

steps, which is proportional to n^2.

9.4 Solutions using accumulating parameters

In this section we will show how to obtain much improved implementations of the above functions by considering more general functions, where the argument has been extended by an extra component ("m" and "ys"):

$$
\begin{array}{lll}
\texttt{factA}\,(n, m) & = & n! \cdot m, \text{ for } n \geq 0 \\
\texttt{revA}\,([x_1, \ldots, x_n], ys) & = & [x_n, \ldots, x_1]\,@ys
\end{array}
$$

Note, that $n! = \texttt{factA}\,(n, 1)$ and $\texttt{rev}\,[x_1, \ldots, x_n] = \texttt{revA}\,([x_1, \ldots, x_n], [\,])$. So good implementations for the above functions will provide good implementations for the factorial and the reverse functions also.

The factorial function

The function $\texttt{factA}$ is declared by:

```
let rec factA = function
    | (0,m) -> m
    | (n,m) -> factA(n-1,n*m);;
val factA : int * int -> int
```

Consider the following evaluation:

$$
\begin{aligned}
&\texttt{factA(5,1)} \\
\rightsquigarrow\ &\left(\texttt{factA(n,m)},\ [n \mapsto 5, m \mapsto 1]\right) \\
\rightsquigarrow\ &\left(\texttt{factA(n-1,n*m)},\ [n \mapsto 5, m \mapsto 1]\right) \\
\rightsquigarrow\ &\texttt{factA(4,5)} \\
\rightsquigarrow\ &\left(\texttt{factA(n,m)},\ [n \mapsto 4, m \mapsto 5]\right) \\
\rightsquigarrow\ &\left(\texttt{factA(n-1,n*m)},\ [n \mapsto 4, m \mapsto 5]\right) \\
\rightsquigarrow\ &\texttt{factA(3,20)} \\
\rightsquigarrow\ &\ldots \\
\rightsquigarrow\ &\texttt{factA(0,120)} \\
\rightsquigarrow\ &\left(m,\ [m \mapsto 120]\right) \\
\rightsquigarrow\ &120
\end{aligned}
$$

This evaluation of `factA(5,1)` has the properties we are looking for:

1. It does not build large expressions.
2. The number of steps needed to evaluate $\texttt{factA}(n, m)$ is proportional to n.

The argument pattern m in the above declaration is called an *accumulating parameter*, since the result is gradually built in this parameter during the evaluation.

The main part of the above evaluation of `factA(5,1)` is the gradual evaluation of arguments in the recursive calls of the function:

$$(5, 1),\ (4, 5),\ (3, 20),\ (2, 60),\ (1, 120),\ (0, 120)$$

Each of these values is obtained from the previous one by applying the function:

```
fun (n,m) -> (n-1, n*m)
```

so the evaluation of the arguments can be viewed as repeated (or iterated) applications of this function.

The use of `factA` gives a clear improvement to the use of `fact`. Consider the following example measuring the time of 1000000 computations of 16! using these two function:

```
let xs16 = List.init 1000000 (fun i -> 16);;
val xs16 : int list = [16; 16; 16; 16; 16; 16; 16; 16; ...]

#time;;

for i in xs16 do let _ = fact i in ();;
Real: 00:00:00.051, CPU: 00:00:00.046,
GC gen0: 0, gen1: 0, gen2: 0
val it : unit = ()

for i in xs16 do let _ = factA(i,1) in ();;
Real: 00:00:00.024, CPU: 00:00:00.031,
GC gen0: 0, gen1: 0, gen2: 0
val it : unit = ()
```

The performance gain of using factA is actually much better than the factor 2 indicated by the above examples becomes the run time of the for construct alone is about 12 ms:

```
for i in xs16 do let _ = () in ();;
Real: 00:00:00.012, CPU: 00:00:00.015,
GC gen0: 0, gen1: 0, gen2: 0
val it : unit = ()
```

The reverse function

The function revA is declared by:

```
let rec revA = function
    | ([], ys)      -> ys
    | (x::xs, ys) -> revA(xs, x::ys);;
```

Consider the following evaluation (where the bindings are omitted):

$$
\begin{aligned}
& \text{revA}([1,2,3],[]) \\
\rightsquigarrow\ & \text{revA}([2,3],1::[]) \\
\rightsquigarrow\ & \text{revA}([2,3],[1]) \\
\rightsquigarrow\ & \text{revA}([3],2::[1]) \\
\rightsquigarrow\ & \text{revA}([3],[2,1]) \\
\rightsquigarrow\ & \text{revA}([],3::[2,1]) \\
\rightsquigarrow\ & \text{revA}([],[3,2,1]) \\
\rightsquigarrow\ & [3,2,1]
\end{aligned}
$$

This evaluation of revA([1,2,3],[]) again has the properties we are looking for:

1. It does not build large expressions.
2. The number of steps needed to evaluate $\text{revA}(xs, ys)$ is proportional to the length of *xs*.

It makes a big difference for lists with large length n whether the number of evaluation steps is proportional to n or to n^2.

The argument pattern ys in the above declaration is the accumulating parameter in this example since the result list is gradually built in this parameter during the evaluation.

Note, that each argument in the recursive calls of revA is obtained from the argument in the previous call by applying the function:

```
fun (x::xs, ys) -> (xs, x::ys)
```

The use of revA gives a dramatically improvement to the use of naiveRev. Consider the following example measuring the time used for reversing the list of elements from 1 to 20000:

```
let xs20000 = [1 .. 20000];;

naiveRev xs20000;;
Real: 00:00:07.624, CPU: 00:00:07.597,
GC gen0: 825, gen1: 253, gen2: 0
val it : int list = [20000; 19999; 19998; 19997; 19996;...]
```

```
revA(xs20000,[]);;
Real: 00:00:00.001, CPU: 00:00:00.000,
GC gen0: 0, gen1: 0, gen2: 0
val it : int list = [20000; 19999; 19998; 19997; 19996; ...]
```

The naive version takes 7.624 seconds while the iterative version takes just 1 ms. One way to consider the transition from the naive version to the iterative version is that the use of append (@) has been reduced to a use of cons (::) and this has a dramatic effect of the garbage collection. No object is reclaimed by the garbage collector when revA is used, whereas 825+253 obsolete objects were reclaimed using the naive version and this extra memory management takes time.

Returning to the list-generating functions on Page 204, the function bigListA is a more general function than bigList, where the argument xs is the accumulating parameter.

9.5 Iterative function declarations

The above declarations for factA, revA and bigListA have a certain form that we will study in this section.

A declaration of a function $g : \tau \rightarrow \tau'$ is said to be an *iteration of a function* $f : \tau \rightarrow \tau$ if it is an instance of the *schema*:

```
let rec g z = if p z then g(f z) else h z;;
```

for suitable predicate $p : \tau \rightarrow$ bool and function $h : \tau \rightarrow \tau'$.

A function declaration following the above schema is called an *iterative* declaration. It is *tail-recursive* in the sense that every recursive call of the function is a *tail call*, that is, the last operation that is evaluated in the body of the declaration. For convenience we only study tail-recursive declarations of the above form in this subsection.

The function factA

The function factA is an iterative function because it can be declared as:

```
let rec factA(n,m) = if n<>0 then factA(n-1,n*m) else m;;
```

which is an instance of the above schema with:

```
let f(n,m) = (n-1, n*m)

let p(n,m) = n<>0

let h(n,m) = m;;
```

The function revA

The function revA is also an iterative function:

```
let rec revA(xs,ys) =
    if (not (List.isEmpty xs))
    then revA(List.tail xs, (List.head xs)::ys)
    else ys;;
```

which is an instance of the above schema with:

```
let f(xs,ys) = (List.tail xs, (List.head xs)::ys)

let p(xs,ys) = not (List.isEmpty xs)

let h(xs,ys) = ys
```

When a declaration of a function in an obvious way can be transformed into the above form, we will call it an iterative function without further argument.

The fold *function on lists*

The fold function on lists as declared in Section 5.1:

```
let rec fold f e = function
    | x::xs -> fold f (f e x) xs
    | []    -> e  ;;
```

is an iterative function. The declaration can be written as:

```
let rec fold f e xs =
    if not (List.isEmpty xs)
    then fold f (f e (List.head xs)) (List.tail xs)
    else e;;
```

which is an instance of the above schema. The above function revA is actually an application of this iterative function:

```
let revA(xs,ys) = fold (fun e x -> x::e) ys xs;;
```

Evaluation of iterative functions

The evaluation for an arbitrary iterative function:

```
let rec g z = if p z then g(f z) else h z;;
```

proceeds in the same manner as the evaluations of factA and revA:

We define the n'th *iteration* $f^n x$, for $n \geq 0$, of a function $f : \tau -> \tau$ as follows:

$$\begin{aligned} f^0 x &= x \\ f^{k+1} x &= f(f^k x), \text{ for } k \geq 0 \end{aligned}$$

Thus,

$$f^0 x = x, \quad f^1 x = fx, \quad \ldots, \quad f^n x = \underbrace{f(f(\cdots f\, x \cdots))}_{n}$$

Suppose that

$$
\begin{aligned}
p(f^i x) &\rightsquigarrow \texttt{true} \quad &\text{for all } i : 0 \le i < n, \text{ and} \\
p(f^n x) &\rightsquigarrow \texttt{false}
\end{aligned}
$$

Then, the evaluation of the expression $g\, x$ proceeds as follows:

$$
\begin{aligned}
&g\, x \\
\rightsquigarrow\ &(\texttt{if } p\, z \texttt{ then } g(f\ z) \texttt{ else } h\ z\,, [z \mapsto x]) \\
\rightsquigarrow\ &(g(f\ z), [z \mapsto x]) \\
\rightsquigarrow\ &g(f^1 x) \\
\rightsquigarrow\ &(\texttt{if } p\, z \texttt{ then } g(f\ z) \texttt{ else } h\ z\,, [z \mapsto f^1 x]) \\
\rightsquigarrow\ &(g(f\ z), [z \mapsto f^1 x]) \\
\rightsquigarrow\ &g(f^2 x) \\
\rightsquigarrow\ &\ldots \\
\rightsquigarrow\ &(\texttt{if } p\, z \texttt{ then } g(f\ z) \texttt{ else } h\ z\,, [z \mapsto f^n x]) \\
\rightsquigarrow\ &(h\ z, [z \mapsto f^n x]) \\
\rightsquigarrow\ &h(f^n x)
\end{aligned}
$$

This evaluation has three desirable properties:

1. It does not build large expressions, as the argument $f\ z$ of $g(f\ z)$ is evaluated at each step due to the eager evaluation strategy of F#,
2. there are n recursive calls of g, and
3. there is only one environment used at each stage of this evaluation.

The first property implies that heap allocation of long expressions with pending operations can be avoided, the second property implies a linear unfolding of the recursive function g, and the last property implies that just one stack frame is needed during an evaluation of $g\, x$ (ignoring stack frames needed due to calls of other functions).

Since `bigListA` is a tail-recursive function, the stack will not grow during the evaluation of `bigListA` nxs and the heap is hence the limiting memory resource when using this function as we learned in connection with the examples on Page 204.

Iterations as loops

We observed in Section 8.7 that every while loop can be expressed as an iteration. It is also the case that every iterative function g:

```
let rec g z = if p z then g(f z) else h z;;
```

can be expressed as a while loop:

```
let rec g z =
    let zi = ref z
    while p !zi do zi := f !zi
    h(!zi);;
```

Using this translation scheme for the iterative version `factA` of the factorial function, we arrive at the declaration:

```
let factW n =
    let ni = ref n
    let r  = ref 1
    while !ni>0 do
        r := !r * !ni ; ni := !ni-1
    !r;;
```

where it is taken into account that the argument z in the translation scheme in this case is a pair `(n,r)`.

There is no efficiency gain in transforming an iteration to a while-loop. Consider for example 1000000 computations of 16! using `factA(16,1)` and `factW 16`:

```
#time;;

for i in 1 .. 1000000 do let _ = factA(16,1) in ();;
Real: 00:00:00.024, CPU: 00:00:00.031,
GC gen0: 0, gen1: 0, gen2: 0
val it : unit = ()

for i in 1 .. 1000000 do let _ = factW 16 in ();;
Real: 00:00:00.048, CPU: 00:00:00.046,
GC gen0: 9, gen1: 0, gen2: 0
val it : unit = ()
```

which shows that the tail-recursive function actually is faster than the imperative while-loop based version.

9.6 Tail recursion obtained using continuations

A tail-recursive version of a function can in some cases be obtained by introducing an accumulating parameter as we have seen in the above examples, but this technique is insufficient in the general case. However, there is a general technique that can transform an arbitrary declaration of a recursive function $f : \tau_1 \text{->} \tau_2$ into a tail-recursive one. The technique adds an extra argument c that is a function. At present we assume that each branch in the recursive declaration of f contains at most one recursive call of f. The tail recursive version fC of f is then of type $\tau_1 \text{->} (\tau_2 \text{->} \tau_2) \text{->} \tau_2$ with parameters v and c of types $v : \tau_1$ and $c : \tau_2 \text{->} \tau_2$.

The evaluation of a function value $f(v)$ comprises recursive calls of f with arguments $v_0, v_1, \ldots, v_n$ where $v_0 = v$ and where v_n corresponds to a base case in the declaration of f. The corresponding evaluation of fC:

$$fC\ v_0\ c_0 \rightsquigarrow fC\ v_1\ c_1 \rightsquigarrow \ldots \rightsquigarrow fC\ v_n\ c_n \rightsquigarrow c_n(f\ v_n) \rightsquigarrow \ldots$$

contains functions $c_0, c_1, \ldots, c_n$ with the crucial property:

$$c_k(f\ v_k) = f(v) \quad \text{for} \quad k = 0, 1, \ldots, n$$

This property expresses that the function c_k contains the *rest* of the computation once you have computed $f(v_k)$. It is therefore called a *continuation*. The evaluation of *f*C starts with $c_0 = $ id where id is the pre-defined identity function satisfying id $a =$ `a for any a. The effects of the recursive calls of f are gradually accumulated in the continuations c_k during the evaluation of *f*C v id, and the evaluation ends by applying the continuation c_n to the value $f(v_n)$ in a base case.

The notion of a continuation has a much wider scope than achieving tail-recursive functions (the focus in this chapter) and we refer to [12] for an in-depth study of this concept.

Consider, for example, the simple declaration of bigList from Section 9.2:

```
let rec bigList n = if n=0 then [] else 1::bigList(n-1);;
val bigList : int -> int list
```

that was used to illustrate the stack limit problems due to the fact that it is not a tail-recursive function. The continuation-based version bigListC n c has a extra argument

```
c: int list -> int list
```

that is a continuation. The declaration of bigListC is:

```
let rec bigListC n c =
    if n=0 then c []
    else bigListC (n-1) (fun res -> c(1::res));;
val bigListC : int -> (int list -> 'a) -> 'a
```

The base case of bigListC is obtained from the the base case of bigList by feeding that result into the continuation c. For the recursive case, let res denote the value of the recursive call of bigList(n-1). The rest of the computation of bigList n is then 1::res. Hence, the continuation of bigListC(n-1) is

```
fun res -> c(1::res)
```

because c is the continuation of bigListC n.

The function is called using the pre-defined identity function id as continuation:

```
bigListC 3 id;;
val it : int list = [1; 1; 1]
```

The important observations are:

- bigListC is a tail-recursive function, and
- the calls of c are tail calls in the base case of bigListC as well as in the continuation:
  fun res -> c(1::res).

The stack will hence neither grow due to the evaluation of recursive calls of bigListC nor due to calls of the continuations that have been built in the heap.

Consider the examples:

```
bigListA 12000000 [];;
Real: 00:00:01.142, CPU: 00:00:01.138,
GC gen0: 34, gen1: 22, gen2: 0
val it : int list = [1; 1; 1; 1; 1; 1; 1; 1; 1; 1; 1; 1; 1; 1;...]
```

```
bigListC 12000000 id;;
Real: 00:00:05.742, CPU: 00:00:05.538,
GC gen0: 60, gen1: 48, gen2: 3
val it : int list = [1; 1; 1; 1; 1; 1; 1; 1; 1; 1; 1; 1; 1; 1;...]

bigListC 16000000 id;;
Real: 00:00:08.586, CPU: 00:00:08.314,
GC gen0: 80, gen1: 60, gen2: 3
val it : int list = [1; 1; 1; 1; 1; 1; 1; 1; 1; 1; 1; 1; 1; 1;...]

bigListC 17000000 id;;
System.OutOfMemoryException: Exception of type
'System.OutOfMemoryException' was thrown. Stopped due to error
```

These examples show:

1. The version using an accumulating parameter is much faster (about five times) than that using continuations.
2. The version using continuations can handle about 30% longer lists.

The run-time disadvantage of a continuation-based declaration is even more clear with an iterative function like factA where no data structure is required to be built in the heap, when compared to bigListC. See Exercise 9.6.

More general recursions

We shall now study the use of continuations in a more general setting with several recursive calls of the function. This situation occurs, for example, in connection with binary trees.

Consider a function count, that counts the number of nodes in binary tree on the basis of the type BinTree<'a> defined in Section 6.4:

```
type BinTree<'a> = | Leaf
                   | Node of BinTree<'a> * 'a * BinTree<'a>;;

let rec count = function
    | Leaf            -> 0
    | Node(tl,n,tr) -> count tl + count tr + 1;;
```

A counting function: countA: int -> BinTree<'a> -> int using an accumulating parameter will not be tail-recursive due to the expression containing recursive calls on the left as well as the right sub-trees of a node (try, for example, Exercise 9.8). A tail-recursive version can, however, be developed for a continuation-based version:

```
countC: BinTree<'a> -> (int -> 'b) -> 'b
```

The base case countC Leaf c returns c 0. The continuation of countC tl in the case: countC (Node(n,tl,tr)) c is the function that takes the result vl for the left subtree and calls countC tr. The continuation of countC tr must take the result vr for the right subtree and feed vl+vr+1 into the continuation c:

```
let rec countC t c =
  match t with
  | Leaf           -> c 0
  | Node(tl,n,tr) ->
      countC tl (fun vl -> countC tr (fun vr -> c(vl+vr+1)));;
val countC : BinTree<'a> -> (int -> 'b) -> 'b

countC (Node(Node(Leaf,1,Leaf),2,Node(Leaf,3,Leaf))) id;;
val it : int = 3
```

Note that both calls of countC are tail calls, and so are the calls of the continuation c, and the stack will therefore not grow due to the evaluation of countC and the associated continuations.

The comparison of count and countC shows similar figures as the comparison of bigList and bigListC: The continuation-based version can handle much larger trees since the stack space will not be exhausted (try Exercise 9.11); but it is about 4 times slower than count when counting a balanced tree with 20000000 nodes:

```
let rec genTree xs =
    match xs with
    | [| |]    -> Leaf
    | [| x |] -> Node(Leaf,x,Leaf)
    | _       -> let m = xs.Length / 2
                 let xsl = xs.[0..m-1]
                 let xm  = xs.[m]
                 let xsr = xs.[m+1 ..]
                 Node(genTree xsl, xm, genTree xsr);;
val genTree : 'a [] -> BinTree<'a>

let t n = genTree [| 1..n |];;

let t20000000 = t 20000000;;

count t20000000;;
Real: 00:00:00.453, CPU: 00:00:00.889,
                    GC gen0: 0, gen1: 0, gen2: 0
val it : int = 20000000

countC t20000000  id;;
Real: 00:00:01.733, CPU: 00:00:01.716,
GC gen0: 305, gen1: 1, gen2: 0
val it : int = 20000000
```

It is possible to replace one of the continuations in the recursive case of the declaration of countC by a simple accumulator and arrive at a tail-recursive function with the type

```
countAC : BinTree<'a> -> int -> (int -> 'b) -> 'b
```

such that count t = countAC t 0 id. The declaration and analysis of this function is left for Exercise 9.9.

Summary

We have introduced the concepts stack and heap that are needed in order to get a basic understanding of the memory management in the system.

Furthermore, we have introduced the concept of tail-recursive functions and two techniques for deriving a tail-recursive version of a given function, where one is based on accumulating parameters and the other on the notion of a continuation. The stack will not grow during the evaluation of tail-recursive functions (ignoring the calls of other recursive functions), and using these techniques will in many typical cases give good performance gains.

A transformation from tail-recursive functions to loops was shown, together with experiments showing that the tail-recursive functions run faster than the corresponding imperative while-loop based versions.

Exercises

9.1   Consider the function g declared on Page 202 and the stack and heap after the evaluation of g 2 shown in Figure 9.2. Reproduce this resulting stack and heap by a systematic application of push and pop operations on the stack, and heap allocations that follow the step by step evaluation of g 2.

9.2   Show that the gcd function on Page 16 is iterative.

9.3   Declare an iterative solution to exercise 1.6.

9.4   Give iterative declarations of the list function List.length.

9.5   Express the function List.fold in terms of an iterative function itfold iterating a function of type $'a\ list * 'b -> 'a\ list * 'b$.

9.6   Declare a continuation-based version of the factorial function and compare the run time with the results in Section 9.4.

9.7   Develop the following three versions of functions computing Fibonacci numbers F_n (see Exercise 1.5):

1. A version fibA: int -> int -> int -> int with two accumulating parameters n_1 and n_2, where fibA $n\ n_1\ n_2 = F_n$, when $n_1 = F_{n-1}$ and $n_2 = F_{n-2}$. Hint: consider suitable definitions of F_{-1} and F_{-2}.

2. A continuation-based version fibC: int -> (int -> int) -> int that is based on the definition of F_n given in Exercise 1.5.

Compare these two functions using the directive #time, and compare this with the while-loop based solution of Exercise 8.6.

9.8   Develop a version of the counting function for binary trees

```
countA: int -> BinTree<'a> -> int
```

that makes use of an accumulating parameter. Observe that this function is not tail recursive.

9.9   Declare a tail-recursive functions with the type

```
countAC : BinTree<'a> -> int -> (int -> 'b) -> 'b
```

such that count t = countAC t 0 id. The intuition with countAC $t\ a\ c$ is that a is the number of nodes being counted so far and c is the continuation.

9.10 Consider the following list-generating function:

```
let rec bigListK n k =
    if n=0 then k []
    else bigListK (n-1) (fun res -> 1::k(res));;
```

The call `bigListK 130000 id` causes a stack overflow. Analyze this problem.

9.11 Declare tail-recursive functions `leftTree` and `rightTree`. By use of `leftTree` it should be possible to generate a big unbalanced tree to the left containing $n + 1$ values in the nodes so that n is the value in the root, $n - 1$ is the value in the root of the left subtree, and so on. All subtree to the right are leaves. Similarly, using `rightTree` it should be possible to generate a big unbalanced tree to the right.

1. Use these functions to show the stack limit when using `count` and `countA` from Exercise 9.8.
2. Use these functions to test the performance of `countC` and `countAC` from Exercise 9.9.

9.12 Develop a continuation-based version of the function `preOrder` from Section 6.4, and compare the performance of the two functions.

9.13 Compare the run times of the two versions of the function `tryFind` that are declared on Page 109 and on Page 191.

9.14 Comparison of the efficiency of iteration functions for list and sets.

In this exercise you should declare functions

iter*CollM*: (′a -> unit) -> *Coll*<′a> -> unit

so that iter*CollM* f col performs $f\, v_0$; $f\, v_1$; ...; $f\, v_n$ when col has $v_0, v_1, \ldots, v_n$ as the elements, and M is the method of traversal that can be based on a tail-recursive function or using an enumerator.

1. Declare a tail-recursive function to iterate a function over the elements of a list.
2. Declare a enumerator-based version. See Page 192.
3. Declare a tail-recursive version that iterate over the elements of a set on the basis of the recursion scheme that repeatedly removes the minimal elements from the set. (See e.g. the declaration of `tryFind` on Page 109.)
4. Compare the run times of the above iteration functions and the library functions `List.iter` and `Set.iter`. Use, for example, sets and lists containing the integers from 0 to 10000000 and the function `ignore`.

10

Text processing programs

Processing text files containing structured data is a common problem in programming – you may just think of analysing any kind of textual data generated by electronic equipment or retrieved data from the web.

In this chapter we show how such programs can be made in a systematic and elegant way using F# and the .NET library. Data are extracted from text files using functions from the `RegularExpressions` library. The data processing of the extracted data is done with a systematic use of F# collections types `list<'a>`, `Map<'a,'b>` and `Set<'a>`. Easy access from F# programs to the extensive text processing features of the .NET library is given in a special `TextProcessing` library that can be copied from the home page of the book. The chapter centers on a real-world example illustrating the techniques.

Time performance of programs is always a problem, even with todays very fast computers. Poor performance of text processing programs is often caused by operations on very long strings. The method in this chapter uses three strategies to avoid using very long strings:

1. Text input is in most cases read and processed in small pieces (one or a few lines).

2. Text is generated and written in small pieces.

3. Large amounts of internal program data are stored in many small pieces in F# collections like `list`, `set` or `map`.

The main focus is on methods for handling textual data both as input and output, but we also illustrate other topics: how to save binary data on the disk to be restored later by another program, and how to read and analyse source files of web-pages. The techniques are illustrated using an example: the generation of a web-page containing a keyword index of the F# and .NET library documentation.

10.1 Keyword index example: Problem statement

Our running example is the generation of a keyword index for the F# and .NET library documentation. The result of this programming effort should be a web-page containing an alphabetically sorted list of keywords, such as the one shown in Figure 10.1. Whenever a user viewing this web-page makes a double click on a keyword, for example, `observer`, a corresponding web-page in the library documentation should automatically be selected by the internet browser.

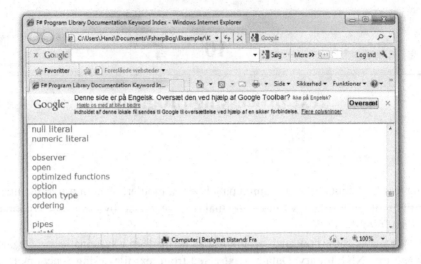

Figure 10.1 A browser's view of `index.html`

```
. . .
"Control.Observable Module (F#)" observer event~observer
"Control.WebExtensions Module (F#)" async~web~operation
"Microsoft.FSharp.Core Namespace (F#)"
"Core.ExtraTopLevelOperators Module (F#)" top~level~operators
"Core.LanguagePrimitives Module (F#)" language~primitives
"Core.NumericLiterals Module (F#)" numeric~literal
. . .
```

Table 10.1 *An extract from* `keywords.txt`

The source data to generate the keyword index are found in the `keyword.txt` file that is edited manually by the programmer generating the index (cf. Table 10.1). Each line in this file contains the *title* of a library documentation web-page together with the *keywords* that should refer to this particular web-page. Space characters inside keywords are written using a tilde character such that spaces can be used to separate keywords. The line:

```
"Control.Observable Module (F#)" observer event~observer
```

contains the keywords:

```
        observer   and   event observer
```

(the second containing a space character) with links to the library documentation web-page with title:

```
Control.Observable Module (F#)
```

The programs generating the keyword index from these (and other) data are described in Section 10.8.

10.2 Capturing data using regular expressions

A basic problem in processing textual data is to *capture* the relevant information. In the keyword program we may, for example, input a text line containing a title and two keywords:

```
"Control.Observable Module (F#)" observer event˜observer
```

and we want to capture the value

```
("Control.Observable Module (F#)",
        ["observer"; "event observer"])
```

of type `string * (string list)` containing the title and the list of keywords.

This section presents a systematic technique of constructing functions performing such captures. Using the technique involves three steps

1. An (informal) understanding of the *syntactical structure* of the input.
2. Formalizing this understanding using *regular expressions*.
3. Constructing the function capturing the data.

The difficult part is describing the syntactical structure in terms of regular expressions.

Informal syntactical structure of strings

The syntactic structure of an input line in the keyword index example is illustrated in the following picture using the above line as an example:

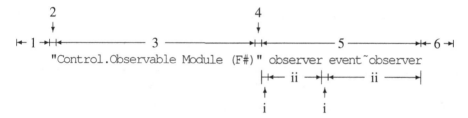

We want to capture the parts labelled (3) and (ii) in the figure.

This syntactical structure of an input line can be described by stating that the line should consists of the following parts:

1. Zero or more blank characters.
2. A quote character.
3. One or more non-quote characters (title to be captured).
4. A quote character.
5. Zero or more occurrences of a sequence of.

   i. One or more blank characters.
   ii. One or more non-blank characters (keyword to be captured).

6. Zero or more blank characters.

Construct	Legend
char	Matched by the character *char*. Character *char* must be different from `. $ ^ { [(	)] } * + ?`
`\`*specialChar*	Matched by *specialChar* in above list (e.g. `$` matches `\$`)
`\`*ddd*	Matched by character with octal value *ddd*
`\S`	Matched by any non-blank character
`\s`	Matched by any blank character
`\w`	Matched by any letter or digit
`\d`	Matched by any decimal digit
`[`*charSet*`]`	Matched by any character in *charSet*
`[^`*charSet*`]`	Matched by any character not in *charSet*
regExpr$_1$ regExpr$_2$	Matched by the concatenation of a string matching *regExpr$_1$* and a string matching *regExpr$_2$*
regExpr `*`	Matched by the concatenation of zero or more strings each matching *regExpr*
regExpr `+`	Matched by the concatenation of one or more strings each matching *regExpr*
regExpr `?`	Matched by the empty string or a string matching *regExpr*
regExpr$_1$ `|` *regExpr$_2$*	Matched by a string matching *regExpr$_1$* or *regExpr$_2$*
`(?:` *regExpr*`)`	Weird notation for usual bracketing of an expression
`(` *regExpr* `)`	Capturing group
`\G`	The matching must start at the beginning of the string or the specified sub-string (`\G` is not matched to any character)
`$`	The matching must terminate at end of string (`$` is not matched to any character)

charSet = Sequence of chars, char matches and char ranges: *char$_1$–char$_2$*
The documentation of the `System.Text.RegularExpressions` library contains a link to a regular expression manual.
The F# Power Pack uses another syntax for regular expressions.

Table 10.2 *Selected parts of regular expression syntax*

Regular expressions

Regular expressions formalize the above informal ideas. A regular expression works as a *pattern* for *strings*. Some strings will *match* a regular expression, others will not. We will pay special attention to two kinds of elements in the above informal description:

1. Classes of characters like "a quote character," "a non-blank character."
2. Constructs like "sequence of," "one or more," "zero or more."

They are formalized in the regular expression notation as:

1. Single character expressions matched by single characters.
2. Operators for building composite expressions.

Selected parts of the regular expression notation in the .NET library is described in Table 10.2. The upper part of this table contains single character expressions:

- The regular expression `\S` is matched, for example, by the character P,
- the regular expression `\d` is matched, for example by the character 5, and
- the regular expression `\042` is just matched by the character ".

The single character expressions [...] and [^...] are matched by any single character in a set of characters:

- The expression [ab] is matched by any single character among a, b or *space*, and
- the expression [^cd] is matched by any single character except c and d.

Brackets are used in any algebraic notation whenever an operator is applied to a composite expression like in the expression $(a + b)^2$. In regular expressions we need a further kind of brackets to mark the parts corresponding to data to be captured. There are hence two kinds of brackets in regular expressions:

1. *Usual* brackets to enclose a sub-expression when used as operand of an operator.
2. *Capturing* brackets enclosing sub-expressions describing data to be captured.

The designers of the notation have for some mysterious reason decided to use the normal parentheses (...) as capturing brackets while the strange notation (?:...) is used to denote usual brackets. You just have to accept that the weird symbol (?: is the way of writing a usual left bracket in this notation.

Using the notation in Table 10.2 we get the wanted formalization of our description of the syntactical structure of lines in the keyword file in form of the regular expression:

```
\G\s*\042([^\042]+)\042(?:\s+([^\s]+))*\s*$
```

The details in this regular expression can be explained using a picture similar to the previous picture explaining the structure of the string:

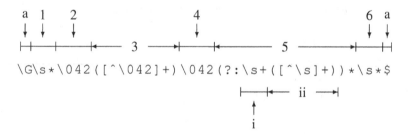

The first and last symbols \G and $ labelled (a) are *anchors* used to restrain the matching to all of a string. They are not matched to any characters. The other parts work as follows:

		Expression	Matched by
1		\s*	Zero or more blank characters
2		\042	A quote character
3		([^\042]+)	Capturing group of one or more non-quote characters
4		\042	A quote character
5		(?:...)*	Zero or more occurrences of:
	i	\s+	One or more blank characters
	ii	([^\s]+)	Capturing group of one or more non-blank chars
6		\s*	Zero or more blank characters

Name	Type	Legend
Regex	string -> Regex	Creates regex object for regular expression
regex.Match	string -> Match	Searches a match to regular expression in string
match.Length	int	Length of matched string
match.Success	bool	Result of matching
regex.Replace	string * string -> string	*regex*.Replace (*string*$_1$, *string*$_2$) replaces each match of *regex* in *string*$_1$ by *string*$_2$

Table 10.3 *The* Regex *class with* Match *and* Replace *functions*

String matching and data capturing

The System.Text.RegularExpressions library contains the types and functions for the .NET regular expressions. A regular expression as the above string is imbedded in a Regex object using the Regex constructor (cf. Table 10.3):

```
open System.Text.RegularExpressions;;
let reg =
    Regex @"\G\s*\042([^\042]+)\042(?:\s+([^\s]+))*\s*$";;
```

We use verbatim string constants @"..." (cf. Section 2.3) to suppress any conversion of escape sequences because we want to keep all backslash characters unchanged in the string. The expression:

regex.Match *string*

evaluates to an object *match* expressing the outcome of matching the string with the regular expression. A true value of *match*.Success signals a successful matching. The matching will in general try any sub-string of the string but it can be restrained using anchors \G and $ as in the above regular expression where matching only applies to the full string.

The matching of a string to a regular expression determines a mapping from the characters of the string to the single-character expressions of the regular expression. In our example we get the mapping shown in the following picture:

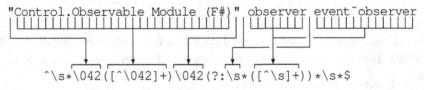

The *capturing groups* in the regular expression are numbered 1, 2, ... according to the order of the opening brackets. In our case we have two capturing groups ([^\042]+) and ([^\s]+). The first is not in the scope of any operator and will hence capture exactly once while the second is in the scope of a * operator and may hence capture zero or more times. The picture shows that the second capturing group will capture twice in this case.

The functions captureSimple and captureList in the TextProcessing library of the book (cf. Table 10.4) give a convenient way of extracting the captured data from the Match object. The matching and data capture will then proceed as follows:

```
captureSingle : Match -> int -> string
   captureSingle m n  returns the first captured string of group n
   of the Match m. Raises an exception if no such captured data.
captureList : Match -> int -> string list
   captureList m n  returns the list of captured strings of group n
   of the Match m. Raises an exception if the match was unsuccessful.
captureCount : Match -> int -> int
   captureCount m n  returns the number of captures of group n
captureCountList : Match -> int list
   captureCountList m = [cnt₀; cnt₁;...; cntₖ] where cntₙ is the
   number of captures of group n (and cnt₀ is some integer).
```

Table 10.4 *Functions from the* TextProcessing *library of the book. See also Appendix B*

```
open TextProcessing;;
let m = reg.Match
   "\"Control.Observable Module (F#)\" observer event~observer";;

m.Success;;
val it : bool = true

captureSingle m 1;;
val it : string = "Control.Observable Module (F#)"

captureList m 2;;
val it : string list = ["observer"; "event~observer"]
```

Conversion of captured data

The data captured as described above are strings. In case of a string of digits (possibly with decimal point) you usually want a *conversion* to values of other types like int or float. Such conversions can be made using the conversion functions named by the type name like int or float. Another example of conversion is the capture of a textual representation of a date-time. Such a string may be converted to a DateTime value using the DateTime.Parse function.

Our example contains a captured title in its final form while the captured keywords need some conversion as any tilde character in the captured string should be replaced by a space character. This conversion is done using the Replace function (cf. Table 10.3) in the Regex library:

```
let tildeReg = Regex @"~";;
let tildeReplace str = tildeReg.Replace(str," ");;
val tildeReplace : string -> string

tildeReplace "event~observer";;
val it : string = "event observer"
```

Nested data

The Match object and function are less elegant in case of nested data like:

```
John 35 2 Sophie 27 Richard 17 89 3
```

where we want to capture the data in a form using nested lists:

```
[("John", [35; 2]); ("Sophie", [27]);
                  ("Richard", [17; 89; 3])]
```

The nested syntactic structure is faithfully described in the regular expression

```
let regNest =
    Regex @"\G(\s*([a-zA-Z]+)(?:\s+(\d+))*)*\s*$";;
```

with anchors \G and $ enclosing

(...)*	Zero or more occurences of capturing group of
\s*	Zero or more spaces
([a-zA-z]+)	Capturing group of one or more letters
(?:...)*	Zero or more occurences of:
\s+	One or more spaces
(\d+)	Capturing groups of one or more digits
\s*	Zero or more spaces

The data groups captured by Match:

```
group 1:   " John 35 2"," Sophie 27"," Richard 17 89 3"
group 2:   "John","Sophie","Richard"
group 3:   "35","2","27","17","89","3"
```

can, however, not be used directly to get the above nested list structure – the data captured by group 3 do not reflect the nesting.

A systematic method to capture such data using grammars and parsers is presented in Section 12.10. At present we show two ad hoc ideas to capture the nested data:

- Capture in two steps.
- Using successive calls of Match.

Capture in two steps

The two steps are:

1. An "outer" data capture of a list of *person data* strings. In the example it should capture the list ["John 35 2"; " Sophie 27"; " Richard 17 89 3"] of strings.
2. An "inner" capture of data from each person data string. It should, for example, capture the value ("John", [35; 2]) when applied to the string "John 35 2".

The outer data capture uses the regular expression

```
let regOuter = Regex @"\G(\s*[a-zA-Z]+(?:\s+\d+)*)*\s*$";;
```

obtained from the above expression regNest by leaving out the two innermost capturing groups. It captures a list of person data strings:

```
let m = regOuter.Match
            " John 35 2 Sophie 27 Richard 17 89 3 ";;
captureList m 1;;
val it : string list =
        [" John 35 2"; " Sophie 27"; " Richard 17 89 3"]
```

The inner data capture uses the regular expression:

```
let regPerson1 =
    Regex @"\G\s*([a-zA-Z]+)(?:\s+(\d+))*\s*$";;
```

It captures the person name as a letter string and each integer value as a digit string. The digit strings need further conversions to the corresponding int values. This is done using the List.map function to apply the conversion function int to each digit string:

```
let extractPersonData subStr =
  let m = regPerson1.Match subStr
  (captureSingle m 1, List.map int (captureList m 2));;
val extractPersonData : string -> string * int list
```

Combining these ideas we get the following function:

```
let getData1 str =
  let m = regOuter.Match str
  match (m.Success) with
  | false -> None
  | _     ->
      Some (List.map extractPersonData (captureList m 1));;
val getData1 : string -> (string * int list) list option

getData1 " John 35 2 Sophie 27 Richard 17 89 3 ";;
val it : (string * int list) list option =
  Some [("John", [35; 2]);
        ("Sophie", [27]); ("Richard", [17; 89; 3])]
```

Using successive calls of Match

The capture is made using successive matches where each match captures from a sub-string containing the data of one person, for example:

sub-string	" John 35 2 "	capturing	("John", [35; 2])
sub-string	"Sophie 27 "	capturing	("Sophie", [27])
sub-string	"Richard 17 89 3 "	capturing	("Richard", [17;89;3])

We use the version of Match with a parameter specifying the start position of the sub-string to be matched:

regex.Match (*string*, *pos*)

combined with the regular expression:

```
let regPerson2 =
    Regex @"\G\s*([a-zA-Z]+)(?:\s+(\d+))*\s*";;
```

obtained from the regular expression regPerson1 by removing the trailing anchor $.

Each of the person data sub-strings will then match this regular expression when matching from the *start position* of the sub-string, for instance when matching from the position (=11) of the character "S" in "Sophie":

```
let m =
   regPerson2.Match
      (" John 35 2 Sophie 27 Richard 17 89 3 ", 11);;
captureSingle m 1;;
val it : string = "Sophie"
captureList m 2;;
val it : string list = ["27"]
m.Length ;;
val it : int = 10
```

The length of the captured sub-string is given by m.Length and the new position:

$$newPosition = startPosition + \text{m.Length}$$

is the position of the first character "R" in the next person data sub-string.

These are combined in the function personDataList that tries to extract a list of person data from the string str starting at position pos and terminating at position top:

```
let rec personDataList str pos top =
   if pos >= top then Some []
   else let m = regPerson2.Match(str,pos)
        match m.Success with
        | false -> None
        | true  -> let data = (captureSingle m 1,
                                List.map int (captureList m 2))
                   let newPos = pos + m.Length
                   match (personDataList str newPos top) with
                   | None      -> None
                   | Some lst -> Some (data :: lst);;
val personDataList : string -> int -> int
                     -> (string * int list) list option
```

The function returns an empty list "Some []" if pos $\geq$ top. Otherwise, a match with the regular expression regPerson2 is tried. A negative result "None" is returned if the match is unsuccessful. Otherwise the data are captured and the new position calculated. The result now depends on the outcome of a recursive call using the new position: A negative result is propagated – otherwise a positive result is obtained by "cons'ing" the captured person data onto the list found in the recursive call.

When applying personDataList to a string we start at position 0 with top position equal to the length of the string:

```
let getData2 (s: string) = personDataList s 0 s.Length;;
getData2 " John 35 2 Sophie 27 Richard 17 89 3 ";;
val it : (string * int list) list option =
   Some [("John", [35; 2]); ("Sophie", [27]);
         ("Richard", [17; 89; 3])]
```

Several syntactic forms

Use of lines of different syntactic form is frequent: The textual data from a piece of electronic equipment may for instance have the form:

Heading line
Measurement Line
    . . .
Measurement Line
Heading Line
Measurement Line
    . . .

where each heading line initiates a new series of measurements. In this situation one may use one regular expression *regExpr*$_1$ to describe the syntax of a header line and another expression *regExpr*$_2$ to describe the syntax of a measurement line. The program analyzing an input line can then use the results *match*. Success (cf. Table 10.3) of matching the line against *regExpr*$_1$ or *regExpr*$_2$ to get a division into cases.

10.3 Text I/O

Reading and writing text files is done using `File.OpenText` to create a `StreamReader` or using `File.CreateText` to create a `StreamWriter` as described in Table 10.5. These readers and writers are instances of the `TextReader` and `TextWriter` classes that also comprise the `StringReader` and `StringWriter` classes to read and write strings in memory using the same I/O functions (an example of using a `StringReader` is found in Section 10.9. The reader may consult [9] for further details).

The I/O functions insert and remove new-line characters in a proper way. An input line obtained by calling `ReadLine` contains *no* newline character while each call of `WriteLine` adds a new-line at the end of the line. The division into lines inside a text file is hence determined by the successive calls of `WriteLine` plus possible new line characters occurring in the strings written to the file. This structure is retrieved when reading the file line-by-line using successive calls of `ReadLine`.

Name	Type	Legend
`File.OpenText`	`string -> StreamReader`	`File.OpenText` (*path*) creates a `StreamReader` to file given by *path*
reader.`ReadLine`	`unit -> string`	Inputs a line from *reader*
reader.`EndOfStream`	`bool`	Indicates no more data in *reader*
reader.`Close`	`unit -> unit`	Closes reading from input medium
`File.CreateText`	`string -> StreamWriter`	`File.CreateText` (*path*) creates a `StreamWriter` for writing on a new file as specified by *path*
writer.`WriteLine`	`string -> unit`	Outputs string and newline to *writer*
writer.`Write`	`string -> unit`	Outputs string to *writer*
writer.`Flush`	`unit -> unit`	Flushes buffer of *writer*
writer.`Close`	`unit -> unit`	Closes writing to output medium

Table 10.5 *Selected* `System.IO` *library functions*

A `StreamWriter` has an internal *data buffer*. Part of a string sent to the writer may be temporarily stored in the buffer for later writing to the output medium. A call of `Flush` ensures that the buffer contents is written to the medium.

It is often possible to process an input text on a line-by-line basis. The program will then input one or more lines, do some computations, input the next lines, etc. This pattern of computation is captured in the functions of the `TextProcessing` library of the book described in Table 10.6. Signature and implementation files are given in Appendix B.

A typical application of `fileFold` is to build a collection using a function f that captures data from a single input line (as described in Section 10.2) and adds the data to the collection. A typical application of `fileIter` is to generate a side effect for each input line such as output of some data or updating of an imperative data structure. The applications of `fileXfold` and `fileXiter` are similar, but involve several lines of the file.

`fileFold: ('a -> string -> 'a) -> 'a -> string -> 'a`
  `fileFold f e path = f (... (f (f e lin`$_0$`) lin`$_1$`) ...) lin`$_{n-1}$` where`
  $lin_0, lin_1, \ldots, lin_{n-1}$ are the lines in the file given by *path*

`fileIter: (string -> unit) -> string -> unit`
  `fileIter` *g path* will apply *g* successively to each line in the file given by *path*

`fileXfold: ('a -> StreamReader -> 'a) -> 'a -> string -> 'a`
  `fileXfold` *f e path* creates a `StreamReader` *rdr* to read from the file given by
  path and makes successive calls *f e rdr* with accumulating parameter *e* until end
  of the file. Reading from the file is done by *f* using the *rdr* parameter.

`fileXiter: (StreamReader -> unit) -> string -> unit`
  `fileXiter` *g e path* creates a `StreamReader` *rdr* to read from the file given by
  path and makes successive calls *f rdr* until end of the file. Reading from the file
  is done by *f* using the *rdr* parameter.

Table 10.6 *File functions of the* `TextProcessing` *library of the book. See also Appendix B*

10.4 File handling. Save and restore values in files

The `File` class of the `System.IO` library contains a large collection of functions to handle files. A few of these functions are described in Table 10.7.

The `Exists` function is useful in a program if you want to ensure that an existing file is not unintentionally overwritten because of errors in the parameters of the program call. The `Replace` function is used in maintaining a file discipline with a current version and a backup version.

The `saveValue` function in the `TextProcessing` library of the book (cf. Table 10.8) can be used to store a value from a program in a disk file. Another program may then later restore the value from the disk file using the `restoreValue` function.

```
File.Delete: string -> unit
    File.Delete path deletes the file given by path (if possible).
File.Exists: string -> bool
    File.Exists path = true if a file as specified by path exists and false otherwise.
File.Move: string * string -> unit
    File.Move (oldPath, newPath) moves file given by oldPath to newPath (if possible).
File.Replace: string * string * string -> unit
    File.Replace (tempPath, currPath, backupPath) deletes the file given by backupPath,
    renames the file given by currPath to backupPath and renames the file given by
    tempPath to currPath.
```

Table 10.7 *Some file handling function from the* System.IO *library*

```
saveValue: 'a -> string -> unit
    saveValue value path saves the value val in a disk file as specified by path
restoreValue: string -> 'a
    restoreValue path restores a value that has previously been saved in the file
    given by path. Explicit typing of the restored value is required as the data saved
    in the file do not comprise the F# type of the saved value.
```

Table 10.8 *Save/restore functions from the books* TextProcessing *library. See also Appendix B*

The following examples show how to save two values on the disk:

```
open TextProcessing;;
let v1 = Map.ofList [("a", [1..3]); ("b", [4..10])];;
val v1 : Map<string,int list> =
  map [("a", [1; 2; 3]); ("b", [4; 5; 6; 7; 8; 9; 10])]

saveValue v1 "v1.bin";;
val it : unit = ()

let v2 = [(fun x-> x+3); (fun x -> 2*x*x)];;
val v2 : (int -> int) list = [<fun:v2@20>; <fun:v2@20-1>]

saveValue v2 "v2.bin";;
val it : unit = ()
```

These values are restored as follows:

```
let value1:Map<string,int list> = restoreValue "v1.bin";;
val value1 : Map<string,int list> =
  map [("a", [1; 2; 3]); ("b", [4; 5; 6; 7; 8; 9; 10])]

let [f;g]: (int->int) list = restoreValue "v2.bin";;
val g : (int -> int)
val f : (int -> int)

f 7;;
val it : int = 10

g 2;;
val it : int = 8
```

Note that arbitrary values, including functions, can be saved on the disk and retrieved again and that the type annotations are necessary when restoring the values, because the F# system otherwise would have no information about the types of retrieved values. Furthermore, we have omitted the warning concerning the incomplete pattern [f; g] in the last example.

10.5 Reserving, using and disposing resources

A function like `File.OpenText` *reserves other resources* beside allocating a piece of memory for the stream reader object: The disk file is *reserved* for input to avoid any output to the file while it is being used for input. This reservation must be *released* when the program has ceased reading the file.

The release of such resources reserved by functions in the .NET and F# libraries can be managed in a uniform way by using a `use`-binding instead of a `let`-binding when reserving the resources, that is:

```
use reader = File.OpenText path
```

instead of

```
let reader = File.OpenText path
```

The keyword `use` indicates to the system that the binding of *reader* comprises resources that should be released once the program is no longer using the object bound to *reader*. The system will in this case release these resources when the binding of the identifier *reader* cannot be accessed any longer from the program. One usually places the `use` declaration inside a function such that the object is automatically released on return from the function.

This mechanism is implemented in the library functions by letting all objects that own resources implement the `IDisposable` interface. This interface contains a `Dispose` operation that is called when the object is released. Declaring `use`-bindings can only be done for such objects.

10.6 Culture-dependent information. String orderings

The .NET library `System.Globalization` offers facilities to handle culture-dependent information like:

- Alphabet with national characters. Ordering of strings, keyboard layout.
- Number printing layout (period or comma). Currency and amounts.
- Date-time format including names of months and days of the week.

Culture-dependent information is collected in a `CultureInfo` object. Such an object is created using the `Name` of the culture, for example

```
open System.Globalization;;
let SpanishArgentina = CultureInfo "es-AR";;
```

The complete collection of the (more than 350) supported cultures is found in the sequence

```
CultureInfo.GetCultures(CultureTypes.AllCultures)
```

and you can get a complete (and long) list of `Name` and `DisplayName` by calling the printing function:

```
let printCultures () =
  Seq.iter
    (fun (a:CultureInfo) ->
        printf "%-12s %s\n" a.Name a.DisplayName)
    (CultureInfo.GetCultures(CultureTypes.AllCultures));;
```

The (mutable) `cultureInfo` object:

```
System.Threading.Thread.CurrentThread.CurrentCulture
```

is used by default in culture-dependent formatting (cf. Section 10.7). The `Name` field:

```
System.Threading.Thread.CurrentThread.CurrentCulture.Name
```

gives the name of the current culture.

Culture-dependent string orderings

The .NET library comprises culture-dependent string orderings. The `orderString` type in the `TextProcessing` library of the book gives a convenient access to these orderings from an F# program (cf. Table 10.9).

Applying the function

```
orderString: string -> string -> orderString
```

to a culture name:

```
let f = orderString cultureName
```

yields a function:

```
f : string -> orderString
```

to create `orderString` values with specified culture,

```
orderString: string -> (string -> orderString)
  orderString cultureName
    is a function to create orderString values with given culture.
string: orderString -> string
  string orderString  is the character string contained in orderString.
orderCulture: orderString -> string
  orderCulture orderString  is the culture name of the used string ordering.
```

Table 10.9 *The* `orderString` *type in the books* `TextProcessing` *library. See also Appendix B*

for example:

```
open System.Globalization;;
open TextProcessing;;

let svString = orderString "sv-SE";;
val svString : (string -> orderString)

let dkString = orderString "da-DK";;
val dkString : (string -> orderString)

let enString = orderString "en-US";;
val enString : (string -> orderString)
```

The comparison operators compare, <, <=, > and >= are customized on orderString values to the string ordering determined by the culture. We may, for example, observe that the alphabetic order of the national letters ø and å is different in Sweden and Denmark:

```
svString "ø" < svString "å";;
val it : bool = false

dkString "ø" < dkString "å";;
val it : bool = true
```

Comparing orderString values with different culture raises an exception:

```
dkString "a" < svString "b";;
... Exception of type 'TextProcessing+StringOrderingMismatch' ...
```

The string function gives the string imbedded in an orderString value, while the function orderCulture gives the culture:

```
let str = svString "abc";;
string str;;
val it : string = "abc"
orderCulture str;;
val it : string = "sv-SE"
```

It is easy to define an "en-US" sorting of lists of strings:

```
let enListSort lst =
    List.map string (List.sort (List.map enString lst));;
val enListSort : string list -> string list
```

This function uses List.map to apply enString to each string in a list of strings. The resulting list of orderString values is then sorted using List.sort. Finally, the strings are recovered by applying string to each element in the sorted list using List.map.

The "en-US" ordering has interesting properties: Alphabetic order of characters overrules upper/lower case. For example:

```
enListSort ["Ab" ; "ab" ; "AC" ; "ad" ] ;;
val it : string list = ["ab"; "Ab"; "AC"; "ad"]
```

Special characters and digits precede letters:

```
enListSort ["a"; "B"; "3"; "7"; "+"; ";"] ;;
val it : string list = [";"; "+"; "3"; "7"; "a"; "B"]
```

The string ordering corresponds to the order of the entries in a dictionary. This is almost the lexicographical order (ignoring case) – but not quite, for example:

```
enListSort ["multicore";"multi-core";"multic";"multi-"];;
val it : string list
        = ["multi-"; "multic"; "multicore"; "multi-core"]
```

The string "multicore" precedes "multi-core" because the minus character in this context is considered a hyphen in a hyphenated word, while the string "multi-" precedes "multic" because the minus character in this context is considered a minus sign, and this character precedes the letter "c".

Note the convenient use of a sorting function. One may also obtain textual output sorted according to culture by using values of orderString type as keys in set or map collections: the fold and iter functions will then traverse the elements of such a collection using the described ordering. The same applies to the enumerator functions of SortedSet and SortedDictionary collections (cf. Section 8.12).

The ordering of orderString values is defined using the String.Compare function:

$$\text{String.Compare}(string_1, string_2, cultureInfo)$$

The user may consult the documentation of this function in [9] for further information about the culture-dependent orderings.

10.7 Conversion to textual form. Date and time

The F# and .NET libraries offer two ways of converting data in a program to textual form: the sprintf function with related functions and the String.Format function with related functions. The latter is the most advanced, comprising culture-dependent conversion of date or time using a CultureInfo object.

The sprintf *function*

The sprintf function and its fellow functions are called as follows:

sprintf *printfFormatString* v_0 ... v_{n-1}
printf *printfFormatString* v_0 ... v_{n-1}
fprintf *writer printfFormatString* v_0 ... v_{n-1}
eprintf *printfFormatString* v_0 ... v_{n-1}

where *printfFormatString* is a string constant containing a text intermixed with *format placeholders* $fph_0, fph_1, \ldots, fph_{n-1}$ specifying the formatting of the corresponding arguments. The resulting string is obtained from the format string by replacing each format placeholder by result of formatting the corresponding argument.

b	Format boolean value as `true` or `false`
s	String
d, i	Format any basic integer type value as decimal number possibly with sign
u	Format any basic integer type value as unsigned decimal number
e, E	Format floating point value with mantissa and exponent
f, F	Format floating point value in decimal notation
o	Format value using conversion function `string`

Table 10.10 *Some possible format types in a format placeholder*

0	Put zeroes instead of blanks in from of number
–	Left-justify result (within specified width)
+	Use + sign on positive numbers

Table 10.11 *Some possible flags in a format placeholder*

The function `sprintf` delivers the formatted string as the result, while the other functions writes this string on some output media:

```
printf              writes on Console.Out.
fprintf writer      writes on StreamWriter writer
eprintf             writes on Console.Error.
```

A format placeholder has the general form :

%{*flags*}{*width*}{ .*precision*}*formatType*

where {...} means that this part is optional. Frequently used format types and flags are shown in Table 10.10 and Table 10.11.

The integers *width* and *precision* are used in formatting numbers, where *width* specifies the total number of printing positions while *precision* specifies the number of decimals:

```
sprintf "%bhood" (1=2);;
val it : string = "falsehood"
sprintf "%-6d" 67;;
val it : string = "67      "
sprintf "%+8e" 653.27;;
val it : string = "+6.532700e+002"
sprintf "a%+7.2fb" 35.62849;;
val it : string = "a +35.63b"
```

Further information in the documentation of the F# Core Printf Module in [9].

Date and time

A *point of time* is uniquely determined by its universal time (UTC) value (defined by the number of 100 ns ticks since New Year midnight year 1 A.C. at Greenwich). A point in time corresponds to different date-time values at different locations depending on *time zone* and local rules for *daylight saving time*. A standard computer configuration keeps track of local time and UTC time. They are available at any time as the present values of the variables:

```
open System;;
let localNow = DateTime.Now;;      // local time
let UtcNow  = DateTime.UtcNow;; // Utc time
```

It is in general not possible to convert an arbitrary date-time object to universal time.

The `System.TimeZoneInfo` class contains a large array of `TimeZoneInfo` objects

```
let zones = TimeZoneInfo.GetSystemTimeZones()
```

A `TimeZoneInfo` object can be used to convert between local standard time and universal time, but the conversion does not cater for daylight saving time. Further information can be found in

Conversion to textual form using `String.Format`

The function (static member) `Format` of the `String` class in the `System` library has a large number of overloads, in particular:

$$\text{String.Format}\,(\textit{formatString, values})$$
$$\text{String.Format}\,(\textit{cultureInfo , formatString, values})$$

where

cultureInfo	A `CultureInfo` object.
formatString	String constant consisting of *fixed texts* intermixed with *format items*.
values	One or several expressions $e_0, e_1, \ldots, e_{n-1}$ separated by comma.

where

fixed text	String not containing any brace characters { or }.
format item	has one of the forms:
	{ *index* }
	{ *index* : *format* }
	{ *index* , *alignment* }
	{ *index* , *alignment* : *format* }

where

index	$k = 0, 1, \ldots$ identifies the argument v_k to be formatted.
alignment	Number of printing positions including heading spaces.
format	One-letter *format code* optionally followed by precision.

C or c	Currency with national currency symbol
D or d	Decimal notation
E or e	Exponential notation
F or f	Fixed point notation
N or n	Number
X or x	Hexadecimal

Table 10.12 *Selected Numeric Format Codes*

d	Short date
D	Long date
t	Short time
T	Long time
F	Long date and long time
g	Short date and short time
M or m	Month and day
Y or y	Year and month

Table 10.13 *Selected Date-time Format Codes*

Precision is an integer between 0 and 99 specifying the number of decimals. There are two kinds of formats: numeric formats as shown in Table 10.12 and date-time formats as shown in Table 10.13. (Further information can be found in the .NET documentation web-pages for Numeric Format Strings and Date Time Format Strings.)

Some examples:

```
open System ;;
String.Format("{,7:F2}",35.2) ;;
val it : string = "  35,20"
let dk = CultureInfo "da-DK" ;;
let en = CultureInfo "en-US" ;;
let ru = CultureInfo "ru-RU" ;;
let now = DateTime.Now ;;
String.Format(dk, "{1:d}...{0:c}", 45, now) ;;
val it : string = "17-10-2011...kr 45,00"
String.Format(ru,"{0:d}",now) ;;
val it : string = "17.10.2011"
String.Format(en,"{0:d}",now) ;;
val it : string = "10/17/2011"
String.Format(en,"{0:F}",now) ;;
val it : string = "Monday, October 17, 2011 2:57:50 PM"
let ar = CultureInfo "es-AR" ;;
String.Format(ar,"{0:F}",now) ;;
val it : string = "lunes, 17 de octubre de 2011 02:57:50 p.m."
```

10.8 Keyword index example: The IndexGen program

We shall now return to the keyword index problem described in Section 10.1. A solution to this problem will be described using the concepts introduced previously in this chapter. We will just describe the main ingredients in the following. The complete program for the solution appears in Appendix A.2. A system diagram for the program generating the keyword web-page, called −IndexGen− is shown in Figure 10.2.

The program reads a keyword file keywords.txt and a binary file webCat.bin and produces a keyword index web-page index.html. An extract from keywords.txt is given in Table 10.1. This file is organized into lines where each line contains a title and a list of keywords, like the line containing the title Control.Observable Module (F#) and two keywords: observer and event observer.

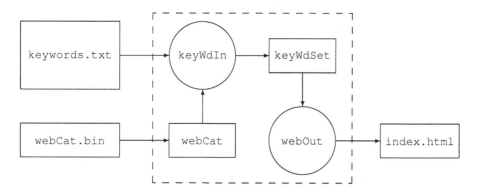

Figure 10.2 System diagram for `IndexGen` program

The box `webCat` in the system diagram (see Figure 10.2) is a map from titles to uri's:

```
webCat: Map<string,string>
```

Such a map is called a *webCat map* in the following, and could contain the entry with:

```
key:    "Control.Observable Module (F#)"
value:  "http://msdn.microsoft.com/en-us/library/ee370313"
```

The file `webCat.bin` is a binary file for a webCat map and we shall see in Section 10.9 how this file to a large extend can be generated automatically.

The set `keyWdSet` in the system diagram (see Figure 10.2) has the type:

```
keyWdSet: Set<orderString*string>
```

An element in this set is called a *webEntry* and consists of a pair of keyword and associated uri, where the keyword is encoded in an `orderString` value. The set could include the following two elements:

```
("observer",
        "http://msdn.microsoft.com/en-us/library/ee370313")
("event observer",
        "http://msdn.microsoft.com/en-us/library/ee370313")
```

A set like `keyWdSet` is called a *webEntry set* in the following.

The set `keyWdSet` is generated from the files: `keyword.txt` and `webCat.bin` by the function: `keyWdIn`. The `index.html` file is generated by the `webOut` function on the basis of `keyWdSet`. Table 10.14 gives a short extract of the generated web-page and Figure 10.1 shows how the `index.html` file is shown in a browser. Clicking on the keyword `observer` in the browser will show the web-page with uri:

```
http://msdn.microsoft.com/en-us/library/ee370313
```

that is, the web-page containing the documentation of `observer`.

```
...
<a href="http://msdn.microsoft.com/en-us/library/ee353608">
null literal</a><br />
<a href="http://msdn.microsoft.com/en-us/library/ee353820">
numeric literal</a><br />
<br />
<a href="http://msdn.microsoft.com/en-us/library/ee370313">
observer</a><br />
<a href="http://msdn.microsoft.com/en-us/library/ee353721">
open</a><br />
<a href="http://msdn.microsoft.com/en-us/library/ee340450">
...
```

Table 10.14 *An extract of* `index.html`

Data Capture

We now show how to capture the text in our keyword index file (see Section 10.1) to allow *comment lines* in the keyword file. We will allow two types of *comment* lines, a blank line and a line starting with two slash characters.

These two syntactic patterns are described by the regular expression comReg containing the "or" operator |. Note that the sub-expression \G// for comment lines is without trailing anchor "$". A string will hence match this pattern just if the two first characters in the string are slash characters.

```
let comReg = Regex @"(?:\G\s*$)|(?:\G//)";;
```

A normal line with keyword data matches the regular expression:

```
let reg =
    Regex @"\G\s*\042([^\042]+)\042(?:\s+([^\s]+))*\s*$";;
```

The getData function should return a result of type:

```
type resType = | KeywData of string * string list
               | Comment
               | SyntError of string;;
```

and the replacement of tilde characters by spaces is made by the function tildeReplace:

```
let tildeReg = Regex @"~";;
let tildeReplace str = tildeReg.Replace(str," ");;
```

These ideas and the techniques from Section 10.2 are combined in the function getData:

```
let getData str =
    let m = reg.Match str
    if m.Success
    then KeywData(captureSingle m 1,
                  List.map tildeReplace (captureList m 2))
    else let m = comReg.Match str
         if m.Success then Comment
         else SyntError str;;
val getData : string -> resType
```

The function `keyWdIn`

This part uses the techniques in Section 10.6 to create a webEntry set, where the keywords are ordered using a cultural dependent ordering.

The declarations of `keyWdIn` is as follows:

```
let enString = orderString "en-US";;
val enString : (string -> orderString)

let keyWdIn() =
  let webCat = restoreValue "webCat.bin"
  let handleLine (keywSet: Set<orderString*string>) str =
    match getData str with
    | Comment           -> keywSet
    | SyntError str   -> failwith ("SyntaxError: " + str)
    | KeywData (title,keywL) ->
      let uri = Map.find title webCat
      let addKeywd kws kw = Set.add (enString kw, uri) kws
      List.fold addKeywd keywSet keywL
  let keyWdSet = Set.empty<orderString*string>
  fileFold handleLine keyWdSet "keywords.txt";;
val keyWdIn : unit -> Set<orderString * string>
```

The idea is to build a webEntry set by folding a function `handleLine` over all the lines of the `keywords.txt` file. The function `handleLine` translates the title in a line to the corresponding uri using the webCat map (that has earlier been input from the `webCat.bin` file). This uri is then paired with each keyword in the line and these pairs are inserted in the webEntry set.

The function `webOut`

The function

```
webOut: Set<orderString * string> -> unit
```

that generate the file `index.html` on the basis of a webEntry set is given in Table 10.15. The file `index.html` is encoded in the HTML (Hyper Text Mark-up Language) format. The `preamble` contains the HTML string that sets up the web-page while the `postamble` contains the HTML-tags that must appear at the end of the file. Please consult Appendix A.1 for a brief introduction to HTML, and Appendix A.2 for the complete source code.

The file `index.html` is opened and the pre-amble is written on the file. A function `outAct` to output a single keyword line is declared, and the keywords with uri's in the webEntry set `keyWdSet` are written on the file using `Set.fold`. The post-amble is written and the file is closed.

The local `outAct` function

```
outAct: char -> (orderString * string) -> char
```

outputs one keyword with uri from `keyWdSet` to the web-page. An *extra empty line* is inserted whenever the first character of the keyword is a letter different from the previous

```
let preamble =  "<!DOCTYPE ......  /p>";;
let postamble = "</body></html>" ;;

let webOut(keyWdSet) =
  use webPage = File.CreateText "index.html"
  let outAct oldChar (orderKwd: orderString,uri: string) =
    let keyword = string orderKwd
    let newChar = keyword.[0]
    if Char.ToLower newChar <> Char.ToLower oldChar
        && Char.IsLetter newChar
    then webPage.WriteLine "<br />"
    else ()
    webPage.Write "<a href="
    webPage.Write uri
    webPage.WriteLine "">"
    webPage.Write (HttpUtility.HtmlEncode keyword)
    webPage.WriteLine "</a><br />"
    newChar

  webPage.WriteLine preamble
  Set.fold outAct 'a' keyWdSet |> ignore
  webPage.WriteLine postamble
  webPage.Close()
```

Table 10.15 *The* webOut *function*

first character. The argument of the function is, therefore, the *first character* of the *previous keyword* and the value of the function is the first character of the just treated keyword.

The keyword is extracted from the orderString value. It becomes a displayed text in the web-page and must hence be encoded in HTML encoding. This is done using the HttpUtility function HtmlEncode from the System.Web library. The uri becomes an attribute and should hence *not* be encoded.

10.9 Keyword index example: Analysis of a web-source

This function addresses the problem of creating a suitable webCat map. A major challenge is that the library documentation is spread over a huge number of different web-pages.

The documentation web-pages that are used in the keyword index have the property that they are *organized in two trees*. Any web-page of interest can be reached by following links starting from one of the root pages:

- F# Core Library Reference
- .NET Framework Class Library

These root pages have the following uri's:

- http://msdn.microsoft.com/en-us/library/ee353567.aspx
- http://msdn.microsoft.com/en-us/library/gg145045.aspx

Scanning the HTML source of the web-page of the F# Core Library Reference we may for instance find the following link to another documentation web-page:

```
<a data-tochassubtree="true"
href="/en-us/library/ee370255"
id="ee340636_VS.100_en-us"
title="System.Collections Namespace (F#)">
System.Collections Namespace (F#)</a>
```

This can be used to find the new title `System.Collections Namespace (F#)` with associated path `/en-us/library/ee370255`. The path is relative to the current web-page but it can be converted to an absolute uri.

Using an XML reader

Analysis of the HTML-source of a web-page can be made using an XML reader, provided that the web-page conforms to the XML-syntax. This is, fortunately, the case for the F# and .NET documentation pages. The *complete* HTML-source of the web-page with given `uri` is read in *one* operation and made available as a string (named `doc`). A `stringReader` is created, and an `XMLReader` is then created to be used in the analysis of the HTML-source:

```
let baseUri = Uri uri
let webCl = new WebClient()
let doc = webCl.DownloadString baseUri
use docRd  = new StringReader(doc)
let settings = XmlReaderSettings(DtdProcessing
                                 = DtdProcessing.Ignore)
use reader = XmlReader.Create(docRd,settings)
```

The `ignore` setting of `DtdProcessing` is required for some security reasons. The XML reader is a mutable data structure pointing at any time to an XML *node* in the HTML-source. Successive calls of *reader*.`Read()` will step the reader through the nodes. Properties of the current node are found as the current values of members of the *reader* object, where we will use the following properties of the current node:

reader.`NodeType`:	`XmlNodeType`
reader.`Name`:	`string`
reader.`Value`:	`string`
reader.`GetAttribute`:	`string -> string`
reader.`Depth`:	`int`

We use the following values of `XmlNodeType`:

`XmlNodeType.Element`	HTML element as given by *reader*.`Name`
`XmlNodeType.EndElement`	HTML end element as given by *reader*.`Name`
`XmlNodeType.Text`	Text to be displayed as given by *reader*.`Value`

The library documentation

The data capture from a Microsoft library documentation page uses a specific property that is common for these pages, namely the *navigation menu* shown in the left column of the page. It contains *buttons* like the following:

> ...
> Visual F#
> F# Core Library Reference
> **Microsoft.FSharp Collections Namespace**
> Collections.Array Module (F#)
> Collections.Array2D Module (F#)
> ...

The button shown in orange (here in **bold**) points to the current page. It is indented one level. The interesting part (for us) are the buttons just below pointing to the next level of documentation. The start of this sub-menu of the navigation menu is indicated in the web-source by a `div` start element with `class` attribute `toclevel2 children`:

```
<div ... class="toclevel2 children" ...>
```

while the end of the sub-menu is indicated by a matching `div` end element `</div>` at the same level (that is, with the same `Depth`).

A button is given by

```
<a ... href="path" ... >text</a>
```

as described in Appendix A.1.

These observations are captured in the function `nextInfo` in Table 10.16 that steps an `XmlReader` forward to the next "node of interest".

The possible values returned by `nextInfo` indicate:

`StartInfo` d	Found the start `div` element of the sub-menu at depth d.
`EndDiv` d	Found an end `div` element at depth d.
`RefInfo` (*text*, *path*)	Found a button `<a ...href="path"...>text</a>`.
`EndOfFile`	The `XmlReader` has reached the end of the file.

The function `nextInfo` shown in Table 10.16 is the essential ingredient in constructing the function `getWebRefs`

```
val getWEBrefs : string -> (string * string) list
```

that takes a uri as argument and reads through the corresponding web-page source and extracts the list of pairs (*title*, *uri*) corresponding to buttons in the above described sub-menu of the navigation menu. The complete program is found in Appendix A.3. The reader may pay special attention to the following:

- The use of the `HttpUtility.HtmlDecode` function.
- The use of an `Uri` object to convert a *path* in a link to the corresponding absolute *uri*.

```
type infoType =
    | StartInfo of int | EndDiv of int
    | RefInfo of string * string | EndOfFile;;

let rec nextInfo(r:XmlReader) =
    if not (r.Read()) then EndOfFile
    else match r.NodeType with
        | XmlNodeType.Element ->
          match r.Name with
          | "div" when (r.GetAttribute "class"
                            = "toclevel2 children")
                -> StartInfo (r.Depth)
          | "a" -> let path = r.GetAttribute "href"
                   ignore(r.Read())
                   RefInfo(r.Value,path)
          | _ -> nextInfo r
        | XmlNodeType.EndElement when r.Name = "div"
                -> EndDiv (r.Depth)
        | _     -> nextInfo r;;
val nextInfo: XmlReader -> infoType
```

Table 10.16 *The* nextInfo *function*

10.10 Keyword index example: Putting it all together

The keyword index is generated using the text files:

- webCat0.txt
- keywords.txt

and the programs:

- NextLevelRefs
- MakeWebCat
- IndexGen

The text file webCat0.txt is shown in Table 10.17. It contains two pairs of lines with the title and uri of the two root documentation pages. The text file keywords.txt contains titles of documentation web-pages with associated keywords and an extract of the file is shown in Table 10.1.

The keyword index is generates in three steps:

1. Generate the text files webCat1.txt and webCat2.txt using NextLevelRefs.
2. Generate the binary file webCat.bin using MakeWebCat.
3. Generate the text file index.html using IndexGen.

```
F# Core Library Reference
http://msdn.microsoft.com/en-us/library/ee353567.aspx
.NET Framework Class Library
http://msdn.microsoft.com/en-us/library/gg145045.aspx
```

Table 10.17 *The file* webCat0.txt

Generating webCat1.txt *and* webCat2.txt

This step uses the program NextLevelRefs (as shown in Appendix A.3). It operates on *webCat* text files that consists of consecutive pairs of lines containing title and uri for documentation web-pages (like webCat0.txt). The program is called with such a file as input. It applies the function getWebRefs to each uri in the input file and produces a webCat output file containing all titles and uri's found in this way.

The program is called twice: first with input file webCat0.txt to create the new webCat file webCat1.txt containing all titles with uri's one level down in the library documentation trees and then with input file webCat1.txt to create the new webCat file webCat2.txt containing all titles with uri's two levels down in the library documentation trees.

Using a free-standing NextLevelRefs program (cf. Section 1.10 and Section 7.2) one makes two calls in a command prompt (assuming that the webCat files and the program are placed in the same directory):

```
NextLevelRefs webCat0.txt webCat1.txt
NextLevelRefs webCat1.txt webCat2.txt
```

Using the file NextLevelRefs.fsx in an interactive environment one makes two calls of the main function:

```
main [| "webCat0.txt"; "webCat1.txt" |];;
val it : int = 0
main [| "webCat1.txt"; "webCat2.txt" |];;
val it : int = 0
```

where the webCat files are placed in a directory defined by the interactive environment. The keyword index is designed to contain references to documentation web-pages two levels down in the trees, so the files webCat0.txt, webCat1.txt and webCat2.txt contain all the information needed to build the webCat - but in textual form.

An extract of the file webCat1.txt is shown in Table 10.18. The files webCat1.txt and webCat2.txt has the same structure as webCat0.txt containing pairs of lines with title and associated uri of documentation web-pages:

```
...
Microsoft.FSharp.Collections Namespace (F#)
http://msdn.microsoft.com/en-us/library/ee353413
Microsoft.FSharp.Control Namespace (F#)
http://msdn.microsoft.com/en-us/library/ee340440
Microsoft.FSharp.Core Namespace (F#)
http://msdn.microsoft.com/en-us/library/ee353649
...
```

Table 10.18 *Extract of the file* `webCat1.txt`

```
open System.IO;;
open TextProcessing;;

let addOneRef (e: Map<string,string>) (rd: StreamReader) =
  Map.add (rd.ReadLine()) (rd.ReadLine()) e;;

let addRefsInFile (e: Map<string,string>) path =
  fileXfold addOneRef e path;;

[<EntryPoint>]
let main (args: string[]) =
  let webCat = Array.fold
                 addRefsInFile
               Map.empty
               args
  saveValue webCat "webCat.bin"
  0;;
```

Table 10.19 *The file* `MakeWebCat.fsx`

Generating `webCat.bin`

This is done using the `MakeWebCat` program shown in Table 10.19. A free-standing version of this program is called as follows in a command window:

```
MakeWebCat webCat0.txt webCat1.txt webCat2.txt
```

The program inputs the title-uri pairs in each of the specified webCat input files and collects the corresponding webCat entries in the `webCat` map. This map is then saved in the file `webCat.bin` using the `saveValue` function in the books `TextProcessing` library.

Using the file `MakeWebCat.fsx` in an interactive environment one should make the following call of the `main` function:

```
main [| "webCat0.txt";  "webCat1.txt";  "webCat2.txt" |];;
val it : int = 0
```

Generating the `index.html` *file*

The stage is now set for calling the `IndexGen` program described in Section 10.8. A free-standing `IndexGen` program is called:

```
IndexGen
```

from a command window, assuming that the `webCat.bin` and `keywords.txt` are placed in the same directory as the program. The program restores the `webCat` map from the binary file `webCat.bin` and reads the text file `keywords.txt`. The data are captured as described in Section 10.8 and each keyword is combined with the uri found by searching the corresponding title in the `webCat` map. Upon that the `index.html` file is produced by the `webOut` function.

Using the file `IndexGen` in an interactive environment one makes the following call of its `main` function

```
main [||];;
val it : int = 0
```

Summary

In this chapter we have studied a part of the text processing facilities available in F# and the .NET library, including

- regular expressions,
- textual input and output from and to files,
- save and retrieval of F# values on and from files,
- culture-dependant ordering of strings,
- retrieval of web-information, and
- processing XML files.

These text-processing facilities are generally applicable, and we have illustrated their expressive power in the construction of a program that can generate a web-page containing a keyword index of the F# and .NET library documentation.

Exercises

10.1 The term "word" is used in this exercise to denote a string not containing blank characters. The blank characters of a string do hence divide the string into words. Make a program `WordCount` that is called with two parameters:

    `WordCount` *inputFile outputFile*

The program should read the input file and produce an output file where each line contains a word found in the input file together with the number of occurrences, for example, "peter 3". The words should appears in alphabetic order and the program should not distinguish between small and capital letters.

10.2 The HTML elements `<pre>`...`</pre>` encloses a *pre-formatted* part of the web-page. This part is displayed exactly as written, including spaces and line breaks, but each line should, of course, be encoded in HTML encoding. Parts of this text can be copied using copy-paste when the page is displayed using a web-browser. Make a program with program call

    `examplePage` *fileName*`.txt`

that inputs the contents of the text file *fileName*`.txt` and produces a web-page *fileName*`.html` containing the contents of this file as preformatted text.

10.3 This exercise is a continuation of Exercise 10.1.

  1. We do not consider the hyphen character "−" a proper character in a word. Make a function to capture the list of words in a string while removing any hyphen character.

  2. Make a function of type `string -> (string list) * (string option)` removing hyphen characters like the previous one, but treating the last word in the line in a special way: we get the result

    $([word_0; \ldots; word_{n-1}], \text{None})$

  if the last word in the string does not end with a hyphen character, and

    $([word_0; \ldots; word_{n-2}], \text{Some } word_{n-1})$

  if the last word terminates with a hyphen character.

Make a new version of the `WordCount` program in Exercise 10.1 that in general ignores hyphen characters but handles words that are divided from a text line to the next by means of a hyphen character.

10.4 A position on Earth is given by geographic longitude and latitude written in the form:

    `14°27'35.03" E 55°13'47" N`

containing degrees, minutes (1/60 degrees) and seconds (1/60 minutes) where the letters E or W denote positive or negative sign on a longitude while N or S denote positive or negative sign on an latitude. The seconds (here: 35.03) may have a decimal point followed by decimals or it may just be an integer. The unit symbols (° and ' and ") are assumed to consist of one or several non-digit and non-letter characters. Make a program to capture a position from a string as a value of type `float*float`.

10.5 Make alternative versions of the programs `IndexGen` and `WebCatGen` in the keyword index problem, where `WebCat` and `KeyWdSet` are represented using the imperative collections `Dictionary` and `SortedSet` (see Section 8.11). The programs should use `iter` functions to build these imperative collections. The files `keywords.txt`, `webCat0.txt`, `webCat1.txt` and `webCat2.txt` can be found on the web-page of the book.

11

Sequences

A *sequence* is a possibly infinite, ordered collection of elements $\mathtt{seq}\,[e_0; e_1; \ldots]$. The elements of a sequence are computed on demand only, as it would make no sense to actually compute an infinite sequence. Thus, at any stage in a computation, just a finite portion of the sequence has been computed.

The notion of a sequence provides a useful abstraction in a variety of applications where you are dealing with elements that should be processed one after the other. Sequences are supported by the collection library of F# and many of the library functions on lists presented in Chapter 5 have similar sequence variants. Furthermore, sequences can be defined in F# using *sequence expressions*, defining a process for generating the elements.

The type `seq<'a>` is a synonym for the .NET type `IEnumerable<'a>` and any .NET framework type that implements this interface can be used as a sequence. One consequence of this is, for the F# language, that lists and arrays (that are specializations of sequences) can be used as sequence arguments for the functions in the `Seq` library. Another consequence is that results from the *Language-Integrated Query* or *LINQ* component of the .NET framework can be viewed as F# sequences. LINQ gives query support for different kinds of sources like SQL databases and XML repositories. We shall exploit this in connection with a database for a simple product-register application, where we shall introduce the concept *type provider* that makes it possible to work with values from external data sources (like SQL databases) in a type safe manner, and the concept of *query expressions* that gives support for expressing queries on SQL databases in F#.

Sequence expressions and query expressions are special kinds of computation expressions (also called workflows), a concept of F# that will be addressed in Chapter 12.

11.1 The sequence concept in F#

A finite sequence can be formed like a list using the "sequence builder" *seq* (see also Section 11.7):

```
seq [10; 7; -25];;
val it : seq<int> = [10; 7; -25]
```

and we obtain a value of type `seq<int>`. This simple example works just like a list.

251

To study the special features of sequences, we will consider infinite sequences. An infinite sequence can be obtained by using the library function:

```
Seq.initInfinite: (int -> 'a) -> seq<'a>
```

The value of `Seq.initInfinite` f, denotes the infinite sequence:

$$\text{seq}\,[f(0); f(1); f(2); \ldots]$$

where the elements are computed on demand.

The sequence of natural numbers $0, 1, 2, \ldots$ is obtained as follows:

```
let nat = Seq.initInfinite (fun i -> i);;
val nat : seq<int>
```

and the i'th element in the sequence `nat`, when numbering starts with 0, is obtained using the function `Seq.nth: int -> seq<'a> -> 'a`. For example:

```
Seq.nth 5 nat;;
val it : int = 5
```

So far just the fifth element of `nat` is computed – this is the only element demanded.

To study the consequences of such *on demand* computation we modify the example so that the number is printed whenever it is demanded, using the `printfn` function (Section 10.7). Evaluation of the expression `printfn "%d" i` has the side-effect that the integer i is printed on the console, for example:

```
printfn "%d" 10;;
10
val it : unit = ()
```

The natural number sequence with print of demanded elements is declared as follows:

```
let idWithPrint i = printfn "%d" i
                    i;;
val idWithPrint : int -> int

let natWithPrint = Seq.initInfinite idWithPrint;;
val natWithPrint : seq<int>
```

The function `idWithPrint` is the identity function on integers that has the side-effect of printing the returned value, for example:

```
idWithPrint 5;;
5
val it : int = 5
```

Extracting the third and fifth elements of `natWithPrint` will print just those elements:

```
Seq.nth 3 natWithPrint;;
3
val it : int = 3
```

```
Seq.nth 5 natWithPrint;;
5
val it : int = 5
```

In particular, the elements 0, 1, 2, and 4 are not computed at all.

Extracting the third element again will result in a reprint of that element:

```
Seq.nth 5 natWithPrint;;
5
val it : int = 5
```

Thus the n'th element of a sequence is recomputed each time it is demanded. If elements are needed once only or if the re-computation is cheap or giving a desired side-effect, then this is fine.

Cached sequences

A *cached sequence* can be used if a re-computation of elements (such as 5 above) is undesirable. A cached sequence remembers the initial portion of the sequence that has already been computed. This initial portion, also called a *prefix*, comprises the elements $e_0, \ldots, e_n$, when e_n is the demanded element with the highest index n.

We will illustrate this notion of cached sequence using the previous example. A cached sequence of natural numbers is obtained using the library function

```
Seq.cache: seq<'a> -> seq<'a>
```

and it is used as follows:

```
let natWithPrintCached = Seq.cache natWithPrint;;
val natWithPrintCached : seq<int>
```

Demanding the third element of this sequence will lead to a computation of the prefix $0, 1, 2, 3$ as we can see from the output from the system:

```
Seq.nth 3 natWithPrintCached;;
0
1
2
3
val it : int = 3
```

Demanding the fifth element will extend the prefix to $0, 1, 2, 3, 4, 5$ but just two elements are computed and hence printed:

```
Seq.nth 5 natWithPrintCached;;
4
5
val it : int = 5
```

and there is no re-computation of cached elements:

```
Seq.nth 5 natWithPrintCached;;
val it : int = 5
```

Operation
Meaning
empty: seq<'a>, where
empty denotes the empty sequence
init: int -> (int -> 'a) -> seq<'a>, where
init $n\ f$ = seq$[f(0);\ldots;f(n-1)]$
initInfinite: (int -> 'a) -> seq<'a>, where
initInfinite f = seq $[f(0);f(1);\ldots]$
nth: int -> seq<'a> -> 'a, where
nth $i\ s = e_{i-1}$
cache: seq<'a> -> seq<'a>, where
cache sq gives a cached sequence
append: seq<'a> -> seq<'a> -> seq<'a>, where
append $sq_1\ sq_2$ appends two sequences
skip: int -> seq<'a> -> seq<'a>, where
skip $i\ s$ = seq$[e_i;e_{i+1};\ldots]$
ofList: 'a list -> seq<'a>, where
ofList $[a_0;\ldots;a_{n-1}]$ = seq$[a_0;\ldots;a_{n-1}]$
toList: seq<'a> -> 'a list, where
toList seq $s = [a_0;\ldots;a_{n-1}]$ – just defined for finite sequences
take: int -> seq<'a> -> seq<'a>, where
take $n\ s$ = seq $[e_0;\ldots;e_{n-1}]$ – undefined when s has fewer than n elements
map: ('a -> 'b) -> seq<'a> -> seq<'>, where
map $f\ s$ = seq$[f(e_0);f(e_1);\ldots]$
filter: ('a -> bool) -> seq<'a> -> seq<'a>, where
filter $p\ s = s'$ where s' is obtained from s by deletion of elements $e_i :\ p(e_i) = $ false
collect: ('a -> seq<'c>) -> seq<'a> -> seq<'c>, where
collect $f\ s$ is obtained by concatenation of the sequences $f\ e_i$ for $i = 1,2,3\ldots$

In this table s is a possibly infinite sequence $s = $ seq$[e_0;e_1;\ldots]$.

Table 11.1 *Selected functions from the sequence library* Seq

11.2 Some operations on sequences

The Seq library contains a rich collection of functions. Some of those are described in Table 11.1. In the remaining part of this chapter we illustrate the use of these functions.

Creating sequences

The empty sequence is denoted Seq.empty. A one element sequence, that is, a *singleton* sequence, is created using Seq.singleton, and a finite sequence can be generated from a list using Seq.ofList. For example:

```
Seq.empty;;
val it : seq<'a> = seq []

Seq.singleton "abc";;
val it : seq<string> = seq ["abc"]
```

```
Seq.ofList [(true,"a"); (false,"b"); (false,"ab")];;
val it : seq<bool * string>
       = [(true, "a"); (false, "b"); (false, "ab")]
```

The function `Seq.init` is used to generate a finite sequence. The value of `Seq.init` $n\,f$ is the sequence

$$\text{seq}\,[f(0); f(1); f(2); \ldots; f(n-1)]$$

having n elements. For example:

```
Seq.init 3 (fun i -> 2*i);;
val it : seq<int> = seq [0; 2; 4]
```

Appending sequences

The operation `Seq.append` appending sequences works for finite sequences like @ on lists, except for the "on demand" property:

```
let s1 = Seq.append (seq [1;2;3;4]) (seq [5;6]);;
val s1 : seq<int>

Seq.toList s1;;
val it : int list = [1; 2; 3; 4; 5; 6]
```

where the computation of the elements of `s1` is delayed until they are demanded by the conversion of the sequence to a list using `Seq.toList`.

If s denotes an infinite sequence, then `Seq.append` $s\,s'$ is equal to s for any sequence s'. For example:

```
let s2 = Seq.append nat s1;;
val s2 : seq<int>

Seq.nth 1000 s2;;
val it : int = 1000
```

If $s = \text{seq}\,[e_0; \ldots; e_{n-1}]$ and $s' = \text{seq}\,[e'_0; e'_1; \ldots]$, then

$$s'' = \text{Seq.append}\ s\ s' = \text{seq}\,[e_0; \ldots; e_{n-1}; e'_0; e'_1; \ldots]$$

that is, s'' is the sequence, where

$$\text{Seq.nth}\ i\ s'' = \begin{cases} e_i & \text{for } 0 \leq i < n \\ e'_{i-n} & \text{for } n \geq i, \text{provided that } s' \text{ has at least } i - n \text{ elements} \end{cases}$$

For example:

```
let s3 = Seq.append s1 nat;;
(Seq.nth 2 s3 = Seq.nth 2 s1)
&& (Seq.nth 10 s3 = Seq.nth (10-6) nat);;
val it : bool = true
```

since `s1` has six elements.

There is no function in the `Seq` library that directly corresponds to the function for cons'ing an element x to a list xs, that is, $x : : xs$. But a cons function for sequence is easily defined using `Seq.singleton` and `Seq.append`:

```
let cons x sq = Seq.append (Seq.singleton x) sq;;
val cons : 'a -> seq<'a> -> seq<'a>
```

```
cons 5 (seq [6; 7; 8]);;
val it : seq<int> = seq [5; 6; 7; 8]
```

11.3 Delays, recursion and side-effects

The functions above yield sequences that are lazy, that is, elements of the resulting sequence are not computed unless they are needed. The same is not necessarily true when sequences are defined by recursive functions. This is illustrated by the following *failing attempt* to declare a function that generates the sequence of integers starting from i:

```
let rec from i = cons i (from(i+1));;
val from : int -> seq<int>
```

Applying this function to any integer i yields a non-terminating evaluation:

$$\begin{aligned} &\texttt{from}\, i \\ \rightsquigarrow\quad &\texttt{cons}\, i\, \big(\underline{\texttt{from}\, (i+1)}\big) \\ \rightsquigarrow\quad &\texttt{cons}\, i\, \big(\underline{\texttt{cons}\, (i+1)\, \big(\texttt{from}\, (i+2)\big)}\big) \\ \rightsquigarrow\quad &\ldots \end{aligned}$$

The problem is that the arguments to `cons` are evaluated before the application of `cons` can create a "lazy" sequence using `Seq.append`. This is caused by the eager evaluation strategy of F#, and it results in an infinite recursive unfolding of `from`.

This problem can be avoided as described below by using the function

```
Seq.delay: (unit -> seq<'a>) -> seq<'a>
```

that suspends the computation of a sequence. We first motivate this function:

Suppose that e is an expression of type `seq<'a>`. The closure `fun () -> e` is then a value of type `unit -> seq<'a>` and this value can be viewed as a *lazy* representation of the value of e. A sequence generated by `seq` is for instance not lazy:

```
seq [idWithPrint 1];;
1
val it : seq<int> = [1]
```

but "packing" this expression into a closure

```
let sf = fun () -> seq [idWithPrint 1];;
val sf : unit -> seq<int>
```

gives a representation of the sequence where the element remain unevaluated. The element is evaluated when the function is applied:

```
sf();;
1
val it : seq<int> = [1]
```

The function `Seq.delay` converts a closure like `sf` into a lazy sequence:

```
let s1 = Seq.delay sf;;
val s1 : seq<int>

Seq.nth 0 s1;;
1
val it : int = 1
```

There are two ways of using `Seq.delay` to modify the above recursive declaration of `from` in order to avoid the problem with non-terminating evaluations. Either the recursive call of `from` can be delayed:

```
let rec from1 i = cons i (Seq.delay (fun () -> from1(i+1)));;
val from1 : int -> seq<int>
```

or the computation of the function value can be delayed:

```
let rec from2 i = Seq.delay (fun () -> cons i (from2(i+1)));;
val from2 : int -> seq<int>
```

Both of these functions can be used to generate lazy sequences:

```
let nat10 = from1 10;;
val nat10 : seq<int>

let nat15 = from2 15;;
val nat15 : seq<int>

Seq.nth 5 nat10;;
val it : int = 15

Scq.nth 5 nat15;;
val it : int = 20
```

There is a difference between these results of turning `from` into a function that generates lazy sequences. This difference becomes visible in the presence of the side-effect of printing the computed numbers using the `idWithPrint` function:

```
let rec fromWithPrint1 i =
    cons (idWithPrint i)
        (Seq.delay (fun () -> fromWithPrint1(i+1)));;
val fromWithPrint1 : int -> seq<int>

let rec fromWithPrint2 i =
    Seq.delay (fun () -> cons (idWithPrint i)
                              (fromWithPrint2(i+1)));;
val fromWithPrint2 : int -> seq<int>
```

The first element of a sequence created by using `fromWithPrint1` is eagerly computed when the sequence is created

```
let nat10a = fromWithPrint1 10;;
10
val nat10a : seq<int>
```

since the argument `idWithPrint i` to `cons` is computed, due to the eager evaluation strategy of F#, before `cons` can create a lazy sequence. Therefore, 10 is printed out when the above declaration of `nat10a` is elaborated and not later when an element of the sequence is demanded:

```
Seq.nth 3 nat10a;;
11
12
13
val it : int = 13
```

On the other hand, no element of a sequence created by `fromWithPrint2` is created at declaration time, since the value of that function is delayed, and all side-effects show up when elements are demanded:

```
let nat10b = fromWithPrint2 10;;
val nat10b : seq<int>

Seq.nth 3 nat10b;;
10
11
12
13
val it : int = 13
```

11.4 Example: Sieve of Eratosthenes

The Greek mathematician Eratosthenes (194 – 176 BC) invented a process, called the sieve of Eratosthenes, for generating the sequence of prime numbers. The process starts with the sequence of natural numbers that are greater than 1. The process is described as follows:

1. Select the head element p of the current sequence as the next prime number.
2. Remove multiples of p from the current sequence, yielding a new sequence.
3. Repeat the process from 1. with the new sequence.

Suppose a is the head element of the sequence at the start of some iteration of the process. No number between 2 and $a - 1$ divides a since since multiples of those numbers have been removed from the sequence by step 2. in the process.

The first three iterations of the process can be illustrated as follows:

First	:	2	3	4	5	6	7	8	9	10	11	12	13	14	15	16	17	...
Second	:		3		5		7		9		11		13		15		17	...
Third	:				5		7				11		13				17	...

The function that removes all multiples of a number from a sequence is called `sift`, and it is declared using the `filter` function for sequences:

```
let sift a sq = Seq.filter (fun n -> n % a <> 0) sq;;
val sift : int -> seq<int> -> seq<int>
```

The above iterations are exemplified in F# as follows:

```
Seq.initInfinite (fun i -> i+2);;
val it : seq<int> = seq [2; 3; 4; 5; ...]

sift 2 it;;
val it : seq<int> = seq [3; 5; 7; 9; ...]

sift 3 it;;
val it : seq<int> = seq [5; 7; 11; 13; ...]
```

The "Sieve of Erastothenes", corresponding to the process above, is obtained by a recursive application of `sieve` to the sequence $\text{seq}\,[2; 3; 4; 5; \ldots]$:

```
let rec sieve sq =
    Seq.delay (fun () ->
                   let p = Seq.nth 0 sq
                   cons p (sieve(sift p (Seq.skip 1 sq))));;
val sieve : seq<int> -> seq<int>

let primes = sieve (Seq.initInfinite (fun n -> n+2));;
val primes : seq<int>
```

The head and tail of a sequence are extracted in the above declaration by the functions `Seq.nth 0` and `Seq.skip 1`, respectively. See also Table 11.2.

The function that finds the n'th prime number is declared as follows:

```
let nthPrime n = Seq.nth n primes;;
val nthPrime : int -> int
```

The 5'th and 100'th prime numbers are fast to compute (remember that numbering starts at 0); but it requires some seconds to compute the 700'th prime number:

```
nthPrime 5;;
val it : int = 13

nthPrime 100;;
val it : int = 547

nthPrime 700;;
val it : int = 5281
```

A re-computation of the 700'th prime number takes the same time as before, and a computations of the 705'th prime number would take approximately the same time. A use of a cached prime number sequence will improve on that:

```
let primesCached = Seq.cache primes;;


let nthPrime1 n = Seq.nth n primesCached;;
val nthPrime1 : int -> int
```

Computing the 700'th prime number takes the same time as before; but a subsequent computation of the 705'th is fast since that computation is based on a prefix containing the first 700 prime numbers.

An alternative to the above declaration of `primesCached` is to let the sieve function return a cached sequence:

```
let rec sieve sq =
    Seq.cache
        (Seq.delay (fun () ->
                    let p = Seq.nth 0 sq
                    cons p (sieve(sift p (Seq.skip 1 sq)))))));;
```

11.5 Limits of sequences: Newton-Raphson approximations

The Newton-Raphson method for computing the square root of a number is based on the fact that $\sqrt{a}$, for $a \geq 0$, is the limit of a sequence:

$$\text{seq}\,[x_0; x_1; x_2; \ldots]$$

where $x_0 > 0$ and

$$x_{i+1} = (a/x_i + x_i)/2 \tag{11.1}$$

for any $i \geq 0$.

It is easy to generate such infinite sequences using F# and to use the elements to approximate the square root of a number a within a given tolerance.

The computation of the next element in the sequence on the basis of a and the current element x follows from (11.1):

```
let next a x = (a/x + x)/2.0;;
val next : float -> float -> float
```

This function should be iterated over a sequence and to this end two auxiliary functions are defined:

```
let rec iter f x = function
                  | 0 -> x
                  | n -> iter f (f x) (n-1);;
val iter : ('a -> 'a) -> 'a -> int -> 'a


let iterate f x = Seq.initInfinite (fun i -> iter f x i);;
val iterate : ('a -> 'a) -> 'a -> seq<'a>
```

where `iter` makes an n-fold application of a function:

$$\texttt{iter } f \; x \; n = f(f(f(\cdots f(x) \cdots))) = f^n(x)$$

and `iterate` gives a sequence on the basis of the iteration of a function:

$$\texttt{iterate } f \; x = \texttt{seq}\,[x; f(x); f(f(x)); f(f(f(x))); \ldots]$$

The "Newton-Raphson" sequence for $\sqrt{2}$ that starts at 1.0 is:

```
iterate (next 2.0) 1.0;;
val it : seq<float> = seq [1.0;1.5;1.416666667;1.414215686;...]
```

The following function traverses trough a sequence *sq* using an enumerator (see Section 8.12) and returns the first element where the distance to the next is within a given tolerance *eps*:

```
let rec inTolerance (eps:float) sq =
    let f = enumerator sq
    let nextVal() = Option.get(f())
    let rec loop a = let b = nextVal()
                     if abs(a-b) > eps then loop b else a
    loop(nextVal());;
```

The sequence argument `sq` is assumed to be infinite and the enumerator f will always return some value, which is exploited by the function `nextVal`. The square roots of a can be computed according to Newton-Raphson's method within tolerance 10^{-6}.

```
let sRoot a = inTolerance 1E-6 (iterate (next a) 1.0);;
val sRoot : float -> float

sRoot 2.0;;
val it : float = 1.414213562
```

This example illustrates the expressiveness of infinite sequences, but the above programs can definitely be improved, in particular when considering efficiency issues. See, for example, Exercise 11.5 and Exercise 11.6. But notice that none of these sequence-based solutions is as efficient as a solution that just remembers the last computed approximation and terminates when the next approximation is within the given tolerance.

11.6 Sequence expressions

A *sequence expression* is a special kind of computational expression (cf. Chapter 12) that allows a step-by-step generation of sequences.

The corresponding general form of expressions to generate sequences is

$$seq \{ seqexp \}$$

where *seqexp* is a sequence expression.

Suppose that we aim at generating a sequence of type `seq<'a>`. Then the following sequence expressions are fundamental for the generation:

- The sequence expression `yield` x, with $x : $ `'a`, adds the element x to the sequence.
- The sequence expression `yield!` sq, with $sq : $ `seq<'a>`, adds the sequence sq to the sequence.

The following examples show three ways of generating the integer sequence $seq[1, 2; 3]$ using `yield` and `yield!` constructs:

```
let s123a = seq {yield 1
                 yield 2
                 yield 3 };;
```

```
let s123b = seq {yield 1
                 yield! seq [2; 3] };;
```

```
let s123c = seq {yield! seq [1; 2]
                 yield 3              };;
```

These examples all show a *combination* of sequence expressions of the form:

$$seqexp_1$$
$$seqexp_2$$

The meaning of this combination is the sequence obtained by appending the sequence denoted by $seqexp_1$ with the sequence denoted by $seqexp_2$.

Expressions denoting sequences may in general be obtained using functions from the `Seq` library; but sequence expressions have the advantage that the generated sequences by construction are lazy, but not cached, and elements are therefore generated by demand only. Hence an explicit use of `Seq.delay` can be avoided when using sequence expressions.

This implicit delaying of a sequence is exploited in the following declaration of the function `from` from Section 11.2:

```
let rec from i = seq {yield i
                      yield! from (i+1)};;
val from : int -> seq<int>

let s10 = from 10;;
val s10 : seq<int>

Seq.nth 5 s10;;
val it : int = 15
```

Construct	Legend
yield *exp*	generate element
yield! *exp*	generate sequence
seqexp$_1$ *seqexp*$_2$	combination of two sequences by appending them
let *pat* = *exp* *seqexp*	local declaration
for *pat* in *exp* do *seqexp*	iteration
if *exp* then *seqexp*	filter
if *exp* then *seqexp* else *seqexp*	conditional

Table 11.2 *Constructs for sequence expressions*

A summary of constructs used in sequence expressions is given in Table 11.2.

Example: Sieve of Eratosthenes

The Sieve of Eratosthenes can also be formulated using sequence expressions.

The function sift *a sq* makes a filtering of the elements of the sequence *sq* by removing multiples of *a*. This is expressed using an iteration over *sq* and a filter:

```
let sift a sq = seq {for n in sq do
                        if  n % a <> 0 then
                            yield n            };;
val sift : int -> seq<int> -> seq<int>
```

The use of sequence expressions gives, in this case, a more "verbose" alternative to the succinct formulation using Seq.filter in Section 11.4.

The use of sequence expressions in the declaration of sieve *sq* is attractive since the explicit delay of the recursive call can be avoided and the combination sequence expressions is a brief alternative to using Seq.append:

```
let rec sieve sq =
    seq {let p = Seq.nth 0 sq
         yield p
         yield! sieve(sift p (Seq.skip 1 sq)) };;
val sieve : seq<int> -> seq<int>
```

The remaining parts of the example are unchanged, for example:

```
let primes = sieve(Seq.initInfinite (fun n -> n+2));;
val primes : seq<int>

let nthPrime n = Seq.nth n primes;;
val nthPrime : int -> int
```

Example: Search in a directory

We shall now use sequences in connection with the search for certain files in a directory. Although there is a finite number of files to be considered, it is natural to exploit the laziness of sequences since a search typically succeeds before the whole directory structure is exhausted.

The function `allFiles` declared below gives a sequence of all files in a directory, including those in subdirectories. The sequence of files and directories are extracted using the functions `Directory.GetFiles` and `Directory.GetDirectories` from the library `System.IO`:

```
open System.IO;;

let rec allFiles dir = seq {
  yield! Directory.GetFiles dir
  yield! Seq.collect allFiles (Directory.GetDirectories dir) };;
val allFiles : string -> seq<string>
```

The function

```
Seq.collect: ('a -> seq<'c>) -> seq<'a> -> seq<'c>
```

combines the map and concatenate functionality. The value of `Seq.collect` $f\,sq$ is obtained (lazily) by applying f to each element e_i of the sequence sq. The result is obtained by concatenation of all the sequences $f(e_i)$, for $i = 0, 1, 2, \ldots$.

Hence the expression

```
Seq.collect allFiles (Directory.GetDirectories dir)
```

recursively extracts all files in sub-directories of `dir` and concatenates the results.

The sequence of all files in the directory `C:\mrh\Forskning\Cambridge\`, for example, can be extracted as follows:

```
// set current directory
Directory.SetCurrentDirectory @"C:\mrh\Forskning\Cambridge\";;

let files = allFiles ".";;
val files : seq<string>

Seq.nth 100 files;;
val it : string = ".\BOOK\Satisfiability.fs"
```

A composite file name like `.\BOOK\Satisfiability.fs` can be split into three parts: a path `.\BOOK\`, a file name `Satisfiability` and an extension `fs`. These three parts can be extracted from a composite file name using regular expressions (see Page 222):

- The path matches a sequence of characters ending with a backslash "\", that is, it matches the regular expression "\S*\\".
- The file name matches a non-empty sequence of characters not containing backslash "\", that is, it matches the regular expression "[^\\]+".

Suppose that `reExts` is a regular expression matching certain file extensions. Then the following regular expression (where the string is obtained by joining several strings) matches composite file names having one of these file extensions:

```
Regex (@"\G(\S*\\)([^\\]+)\." + "(" + reExts + ")"+ "$")
         ‾‾‾‾‾‾  ‾‾‾‾‾‾‾‾          ‾‾‾‾‾‾‾‾‾‾‾‾‾‾‾‾‾‾‾‾‾‾
          path    file name              extension
```

Note that the extension is the suffix of the composite file name that starts just after the last period (`.`). The regular expression has three capturing groups (enclosed in normal brackets (and)) so that the path, the name and the extension can be extracted from a matched composite file name. The function `captureSingle` from the `TextProcessing` library (cf. Table 10.4) is used to extract captured strings in the following declaration of `searchFiles` *files exts* that gives those files in the sequence *files* that have an extension in the list *exts*:

```
open System.Text.RegularExpressions;;

let rec searchFiles files exts =
    let reExts =
        List.foldBack (fun ext re -> ext+"|"+re) exts ""
    let re = Regex (@"\G(\S*\\)([^\\]+)\.(" + reExts + ")$")
    seq {for fn in files do
            let m = re.Match fn
            if m.Success
            then let path = TextProcessing.captureSingle m 1
                 let name = TextProcessing.captureSingle m 2
                 let ext  = TextProcessing.captureSingle m 3
                 yield (path, name, ext)          };;
val searchFiles : seq<string> -> string list
                    -> seq<string * string * string>
```

The search for F# files (with extensions `fs` or `fsi`) is initiated as follows:

```
let funFiles =
    Seq.cache (searchFiles (allFiles ".") ["fs";"fsi"]);;
val funFiles : seq<string * string * string>
```

In this case a cached sequence is chosen so that a search can exploit the already computed part of the sequence from previous searches:

```
Seq.nth 6 funFiles;;
val it : string * string * string = (".\BOOK\","Curve","fsi")

Seq.nth 11 funFiles;;
val it : string * string * string
       = (".\BOOK\", "Satisfiability", "fs")
```

11.7 Specializations of sequences

The type seq<'a> is a synonym for the .NET type IEnumerable<'a> and any .NET framework type that implements this interface can be used as a sequence. Since lists and arrays are specializations of sequences they can be used as sequence arguments for the functions in the Seq library.

Specialization of Seq-*library functions*

Using the function Seq.append

```
Seq.append: seq<'a> -> seq<'a> -> seq<'a>
```

a sequence can, for example, be formed by appending two lists:

```
let sq1 = Seq.append [1; 2; 3] [4; 5; 6];;
val sq1 : seq<int>
```

by appending two arrays (see Section 8.10)

```
let sq2 = Seq.append [|1; 2; 3|] [|4; 5; 6|];;
val sq2 : seq<int>
```

and by appending a list and an array:

```
let sq3 = Seq.append [1; 2; 3] [|4; 5; 6|];;
val sq3 : seq<int>
```

Similarly, the range *rng* in a for-construct: for *i* in *rng* do *seqexp* can be a sequence. This is exploited in the following example where the range is the first eleven natural numbers:

```
let squares = seq {for i in 0..10 do yield i*i };;
val squares : seq<int>
```

Range expressions

In a construction of a sequence constant, like

```
seq [1; 2; 3; 4];;
val it : seq<int> = [1; 2; 3; 4]
```

the sequence builder seq is actually a built-in function on sequences:

```
seq;;
val it : (seq<'a> -> seq<'a>) = <fun:clo@16-2>
```

and when applying seq to the list in the above example, we are just exploiting that lists are specializations of sequences.

Hence the range expressions [*b* .. *e*] and [*b* .. *s* .. *e*] for lists described in Section 4.2 can, in a natural manner, be used to generate finite sequences:

```
let evenUpTo n = seq [0..2.. n];;
val evenUpTo : int -> seq<int>
```

Sequences constructed using this function will not be lazy:

```
let e20 = evenUpTo 20;;
val e20 : seq<int> = [0; 2; 4; 6; 8; 10; 12; 14; 16; 18; 20]
```

The answer from the system shows that the sequences constructed in this way will not be lazy, as the answer shows all eleven elements. The reason is that the construct [0..2.. n] eagerly will construct a list.

11.8 Type providers and databases

The *Language-Integrated Query* or *LINQ* component of the .NET framework gives query support for different kinds of sources like SQL databases and XML documents. We shall now exploit that LINQ queries for SQL databases return values of type IEnumerable<T>, and hence the result of these queries can be viewed as F# sequences.

An obstacle in doing so is that the type system of an SQL database is different from that of F#. To overcome this obstacle a *type provider* for SQL is used. An F# type provider for SQL makes it possible to work directly with the tables of the database in a type safe manner. There are type providers for other external sources than SQL databases, and it is possible to make user-defined type providers; but we will just illustrate the use of a type provider for SQL in connection with a database for a simple *product-register* application.

A database for a Product Register

Suppose for the moment that the product register is a database ProductRegister containing the two tables shown in Figure 11.1.

Part:

PartId	PartName	IsBasic
0	"Part0"	1
1	"Part1"	1
2	"Part2"	0
3	"Part3"	0

PartsList:

PartsListId	PartId	Quantity
2	0	5
2	1	4
3	1	3
3	2	4

- The SQL-types of the attributes are:

    PartId, PartsListId, Quantity: int, PartName: varchar(50) and IsBasic: bit

- The table Part has PartId as key.
- The table PartsList has (PartsListId, PartId) as composite key.

Figure 11.1 A Product Register Database with two tables: Part and PartsList

The table Part stores information about four parts named: "Part0", ... ,"Part3", where "Part0" and "Part1" are basic parts (with empty parts lists) since their IsBasic attribute is 1 (the SQL representation of true), while "Part2" and "Part3" are composite parts since their IsBasic attribute is 0 (representing false). The PartId attribute of the Part table is a unique identifier, that is, a *key*, for the description of a part.

The table PartsList contains the parts lists for all the composite parts. The attribute pair (PartsListId, PartId) is a composite key. A row (pid, id, q) in this table, therefore, describes that exactly q pieces of the part identified by id is required in the parts list of the composite part identified by pid. For example, the parts list for "Part 3" comprises 3 pieces of "Part 1" and 4 pieces of "Part 2".

Starting on Page 274 it is shown how this database can be created and updated. But before that we address the issue of making queries to this database from F#.

F# Type Providers for SQL

A *type provider* is a component that automatically generates types and functions for external data sources like SQL databases and Web services. Below we shall use a built-in SQL type provider for F#. In order to access and use this type provider, the following assemblies should be referenced: FSharp.Data.TypeProviders.dll, System.Data.dll and System.Data.Linq.dll, and namespaces should be opened (see Figure 11.2 for the complete code) prior to the execution of the following declarations:

```
type schema =
    SqlDataConnection<"Data Source=IMM-NBMRH\SQLEXPRESS;
                       InitialCatalog=ProductRegister;
                       Integrated Security=True">;;
type schema

let db = schema.GetDataContext();;
val db:
    schema.ServiceTypes.SimpleDataContextTypes.ProductRegister
```

The SQL type provider: SqlDataConnection has a *connection string* as argument. This connection string has three parts: A definition of the *data source*, in this case an SQL

```
#if INTERACTIVE
#r "FSharp.Data.TypeProviders.dll"
#r "System.Data.dll"
#r "System.Data.Linq.dll"
#endif

open System
open Microsoft.FSharp.Data.TypeProviders
open System.Data.Linq.SqlClient
open System.Linq

type schema =
    SqlDataConnection<"Data Source=IMM-NBMRH\SQLEXPRESS;
                       Initial Catalog=ProductRegister;
                       Integrated Security=True">;;

let db = schema.GetDataContext();;
```

Figure 11.2 Creating a type provider for the ProductRegister database

server, the *initial catalog*, in this case the database name, and the *integrated security*, which in this case is true, meaning that the .NET credentials of the current user will be used for authentication.

The type `schema` contains all the generated types that represent the database and `db` is an object containing the database tables. The two database tables can be accessed as follows:

```
let partTable = db.Part;;
val partTable : Data.Linq.Table<schema.ServiceTypes.Part>

let partsListTable = db.PartsList;;
val partsListTable:
    Data.Linq.Table<schema.ServiceTypes.PartsList>
```

The answers from the F# system do not reveal the F# values of these two tables.

They are in fact lazy sequences. For example:

```
partTable;;
val it : Data.Linq.Table<schema.ServiceTypes.Part> =
  seq [Part {IsBasic = true; PartId = 0; PartName = "Part0";};
       Part {IsBasic = true; PartId = 1; PartName = "Part1";};
       Part {IsBasic = false; PartId = 2;PartName = "Part2";};
       Part {IsBasic = false; PartId = 3;PartName = "Part3";}]
```

where all the elements are shown in this case just because the interactive environment always prints a short prefix of a lazy sequence. The elements of this sequence are objects belonging to a class `Part` that has the attributes of the table as public fields:

```
let r = Seq.nth 2 partTable;;
val r : schema.ServiceTypes.Part

r.PartId;;
val it : int = 2

r.PartName;;
val it : string = "Part2"

r.IsBasic;;
val it : bool = false
```

Note that the SQL types `bit` and `varchar(50)` are translated to the F# types `bool` and `string`, respectively, by the type provider.

The list of F# elements of the `PartsList` table is obtained as follows:

```
Seq.toList partsListTable;;
val it : schema.ServiceTypes.PartsList list =
  [PartsList {PartId = 0; PartsListId = 2; Quantity = 5;};
   PartsList {PartId = 1; PartsListId = 2; Quantity = 4;};
   PartsList {PartId = 1; PartsListId = 3; Quantity = 3;};
   PartsList {PartId = 2; PartsListId = 3; Quantity = 4;}]
```

Database queries can be expressed using the functions from the sequence library since the tables in the database can be accessed like sequences when using the above type provider. The names of all composite parts can, for example, be extracted as follows:

```
Seq.fold
  (fun ns (r:schema.ServiceTypes.Part)
          -> if r.IsBasic then ns else r.PartName::ns)
  []
  partTable;;
val it : string list = ["Part3"; "Part2"]
```

Query expressions

We shall now introduce *query expressions* as means for extracting information from the database. A query expression is a computation expression (just like sequence expressions) and it occurs in expressions of the form:

```
query { queryexp }
```

The construct `select` v adds the element v to the answer to the query just like `yield` v adds an element to a sequence:

```
query {select (1, "a") };;
val it : IQueryable<int * string> = seq [(1, "a")]
```

The value of this query expression has type `IQueryable<int * string>`. The type `IQueryable<T>` is a specialization of `IEnumerable<T>` and, therefore, values of type `IQueryable<T>` can be treated as sequences.

There is a rich collection of query-expression constructs that translates to SQL queries. We will now introduce a small part these constructs by illustrating how the following operations of relational algebra can be expressed: projection, selection and join.

Projection

A *projection* operation extracts certain columns of a table and such a projection can be expressed using an *iteration*.

For example, a query for the projection of the `Part` table with respect to `PartName` and `IsBasic` is declared as follows:

```
let q1 = query {for part in db.Part do
                select (part.PartName, part.IsBasic) };;

q1;;
val it : IQueryable<string * bool> =
  seq [("Part0", true); ("Part1", true);
       ("Part2", false); ("Part3", false)]
```

Selection

A *selection* operation extracts certain rows of a table and such a selection can be expressed using an iteration together with a *where*-clause and a selection.

For example, the query selecting the composite parts from the `Part` table is declared by:

```
let q2 =
  query {for part in db.Part do
          where (not part.IsBasic)
          select (part.PartId, part.PartName, part.IsBasic)};;

q2;;
val it : IQueryable<int * string * bool> =
  seq [(2, "Part2", false); (3, "Part3", false)]
```

Join

A *join* operation combines the rows of two tables A and B. There are many different kinds of such combinations that are supported by SQL and query expressions. We shall here just consider what is called an *equi*-join, where a row $a \in A$ is combined with a row $b \in B$ only if $a.L_A = b.L_B$, where L_A is a given attribute of A and L_B is a given attribute of B.

By an equi-join of `PartsList` and `Part` tables with `PartsListId` of `PartsList` equal to `PartId` of `Part` we can extract tuples from `PartsList` where identifiers for parts list are replaced by their names:

```
let q3 = query {for pl in db.PartsList do
                join part in db.Part on
                    (pl.PartsListId = part.PartId)
                select(part.PartName, pl.PartId, pl.Quantity)
                };;
q3;;
val it : IQueryable<string * int * int> =
  seq [("Part2", 0, 5); ("Part2", 1, 4);
       ("Part3", 1, 3); ("Part3", 2, 4)]
```

Hence "`Part2`" is a composite part consisting of 5 pieces of the part with `PartId` equal to 0 and 4 pieces of the part with `PartId` equal to 1. By the use of nested joins we can make a query where these identifiers also are replaced by their names. The result of q4 cannot be used in a join since the elements have a tuple type and not a record type. We therefore introduce a record type:

```
type partListElement =
    {PartName:string; PartId:int; Quantity:int}
```

In the following nested join, the local query qa is the variant of q3 that gives elements of type `partListElement`:

```
let q4 =
   query {let qa = query {for pl in db.PartsList do
                          join part in db.Part on
                               (pl.PartsListId = part.PartId)
                          select {PartName = part.PartName;
                                  PartId = pl.PartId;
                                  Quantity = pl.Quantity} }
          for pl in qa do
          join part in db.Part on
             (pl.PartId = part.PartId)
          select (pl.PartName, part.PartName, pl.Quantity) };;
q4;;
val it : IQueryable<string * string * int> =
   seq
     [("Part2", "Part0", 5); ("Part2", "Part1", 4);
      ("Part3", "Part1", 3); ("Part3", "Part2", 4)]
```

Aggregate operations

In SQL there are so-called aggregate operations that depend on a whole table or all the values in a column of a table, such as counting the number of elements in a table or finding the average of the elements in a column. There are also query-expression constructs for these functions, for example, count that counts the number of elements selected so far, exactlyOne that returns the single element selected, and raises an exception if no element or more than one element have been selected, and contains v that checks whether v is among the so far selected elements.

The following function counts the number of rows in Part. Since we shall use consecutive numbers $0, 1, \ldots, n - 1$ as identifiers for existing parts, the number of rows n is the next identifier that can be used as a key. This function is therefore named nextID:

```
let nextId() = query {for part in db.Part do
                      count };;
val nextId : unit -> int
```

The function getDesc extracts the description of a given identifier

```
let getDesc id =
    query {for part in db.Part do
           where (part.PartId=id)
           select (part.PartName,part.IsBasic)
           exactlyOne                          };;
val getDesc : int -> string * bool
```

where the description consists of the name and truth values of the Name and IsBasic attributes. For example:

```
nextId();;
val it : int = 4

getDesc 3;;
val it : string * bool = ("Part3", false)
```

```
getDesc 4;;
System.InvalidOperationException: Sequence contains no elements
```

The predicate `containsPartId` checks whether a given identifier is in the `Part` table:

```
let containsPartId id = query {for part in db.Part do
                                select part.PartId
                                contains id };;
val containsPartId : int -> bool

containsPartId 3;;
val it : bool = true
containsPartId 4;;
val it : bool = false
```

Example: Parts Break Down

We shall now consider the problem of computing a parts list containing all the basic parts needed to produce a given part. By a parts list we shall now understand a list of pairs: $[(id_1, k_1), \ldots, (id_n, k_n)]$ where id_i is the identifier of a part and k_i is the quantity needed of that part.

The following function extracts the parts list for a given part:

```
let getPartsList id =
    query {for pl in db.PartsList do
           where (pl.PartsListId = id)
           select (pl.PartId,pl.Quantity) };;
val getPartsList : int -> IQueryable<int * int>

getPartsList 3;;
val it : IQueryable<int * int> = seq [(1, 3); (2, 4)]
```

We shall need functions for adding a pair (id, k) to given parts list, for merging two parts lists and for multiplying all quantities in a parts list by a constant. These functions are "usual" auxiliary list functions:

```
let rec add pl (id,q) =
    match pl with
    | []                         -> [(id,q)]
    | (id1,q1)::pl1 when id=id1 -> (id,q+q1)::pl1
    | idq::pl1                    -> idq :: add pl1 (id,q);;
val add : ('a * int) list -> 'a * int -> ('a * int) list
            when 'a : equality

let mergePartsList pl1 pl2 = List.fold add pl1 pl2;;
val mergePartsList :
  ('a * int) list -> ('a * int) list -> ('a * int) list
  when 'a : equality

let mult k pl = List.map (fun (id,q) -> (id,k*q)) pl;;
val mult : int -> ('a * int) list -> ('a * int) list
```

The following function `partBreakDown` that computes a parts list containing all basic parts needed for producing a given part is declared in mutual recursion with the function `partsListBreakDown` that computes a parts list containing all basic parts needed for producing a given parts list. These functions access the database to extract the description and the parts list of a given part using `getDesc` and `getPartsList`.

```
let rec partBreakDown id =
    match getDesc id with
    | (_,true)   -> [(id,1)]
    | _          ->
        partsListBreakDown(Seq.toList(getPartsList id))
and partsListBreakDown = function
    | (id,q)::pl -> let pl1 = mult q (partBreakDown id)
                    let pl2 = partsListBreakDown pl
                    mergePartsList pl1 pl2
    | []         -> [];;
val partBreakDown : int -> (int * int) list
val partsListBreakDown : (int * int) list -> (int * int) list

partBreakDown 3;;
val it : (int * int) list = [(1, 19); (0, 20)]

partBreakDown 1;;
val it : (int * int) list = [(1, 1)]
```

Creating a database

Executing the F# program in Figure 11.3 will setup the `ProductRegister` database with empty `Part` and `PartList` tables.

Updating a database

The type `scheme` contains service types and constructors for elements of the tables in the database. For example

```
new schema.ServiceTypes.Part(PartId=id, PartName=s, IsBasic=b)
```

generates a new part object that can belong to the `Part` table.

Table objects like `db.Part` and `db.PartsList` have members `InsertOnSubmit` and `InsertAllOnSubmit` that you can give a single row and a collection of rows, respectively, to be inserted in the tables. These insertions are effectuated only when the function `SubmitChanges` from the LINQ `DataContext` type has been applied.

Consider for example the following function that inserts a basic part into the `Part` table given its part name:

```
open System.Configuration
open System.Data
open System.Data.SqlClient

let connString = @"Data Source=IMM-NBMRH\SQLEXPRESS;
                   Initial Catalog=ProductRegister;
                   Integrated Security=True";;
let conn = new SqlConnection(connString)

conn.Open();;

let execNonQuery conn s =
    let comm = new SqlCommand(s, conn, CommandTimeout = 10)
    comm.ExecuteNonQuery() |> ignore;;

execNonQuery conn "CREATE TABLE Part (
    PartId int NOT NULL,
    PartName varchar(50) NOT NULL,
    IsBasic bit NOT NULL,
    PRIMARY KEY (PartId))";;

execNonQuery conn "CREATE TABLE PartsList (
    PartsListId int NOT NULL,
    PartId int NOT NULL,
    Quantity int NOT NULL,
    PRIMARY KEY (PartsListId, PartId))";;
```

Figure 11.3 F# program creating the tables of `ProductRegister`

```
let addBasic s =
    let id = nextId()
    let part = new schema.ServiceTypes.Part(PartId = id,
                                            PartName = s,
                                            IsBasic = true)
    db.Part.InsertOnSubmit(part)
    db.DataContext.SubmitChanges()
    Some id;;
val addBasic : string -> int option
```

The function generates a key for the part and this key is returned by the function.

The insertion of a composite part into the database is based on its name s and its parts list: $[(id_1, k_1), \ldots (id_n, k_n)]$. Such an insertion is only meaningful when the identifiers id_i, for $1 \leq i \leq n$, are already defined in the `Part` table and when all the quantities k_i, for $1 \leq i \leq n$, are positive integers. This well-formedness constraint is checked by the following function:

```
let isWellFormed pl =
    List.forall (fun (id,k) -> containsPartId id && k>0) pl;;
val isWellFormed : (int * int) list -> bool
```

If this well-formedness constraint is satisfied, then the following function inserts a new composite part into the `Part` table and its parts list into the `PartsList` table:

```
let addComposite s pl =
  if isWellFormed pl
  then
    let id = nextId()
    let part =
      new schema.ServiceTypes.Part(PartId=id,
                                   PartName=s,
                                   IsBasic = false)
    let partslist =
      List.map
        (fun (pid,k) ->
           new schema.ServiceTypes.PartsList(PartsListId=id,
                                             PartId=pid,
                                             Quantity=k))
          pl
    db.Part.InsertOnSubmit(part)
    db.PartsList.InsertAllOnSubmit(partslist)
    db.DataContext.SubmitChanges()
    Some id
  else None;;
val addComposite : string -> (int * int) list -> int option
```

The tables in Figure 11.1 are generated from an initial `ProductRegister` database with two empty tables by evaluation of the following declarations:

```
let id0 = Option.get (addBasic "Part0");;
val id0 : int = 0

let id1 = Option.get (addBasic "Part1");;
val id1 : int = 1

let id2 =
    Option.get (addComposite "Part2" [(id0,5);(id1,4)]);;
val id2 : int = 2

let id3 =
    Option.get (addComposite "Part3" [(id1,3);(id2,4)]);;
val id3 : int = 3
```

Summary

This chapter has introduced the notion of sequence, which is an ordered, possibly infinite, collection of elements where the computation of elements is on demand only. Sequences are convenient to use in applications where you are dealing with elements that are processed one after they other. Functions from the sequence part of the collection library of F# have been introduced together with cached sequences that prevents a recomputation of already computed sequence elements. Furthermore, sequences can be defined in F# using sequence expressions defining a step-by-step process for generating the elements.

The type `seq<'a>` is a synonym for the .NET type `IEnumerable<'a>` and any .NET framework type that implements this interface can be used as a sequence. This has been studied in connection with the *Language-Integrated Query* or *LINQ* component of the .NET framework. LINQ gives query support for different kinds of data sources like SQL databases and XML repositories. We have used LINQ in connection with a database for a simple product-register application, where an F# type provider made it possible to work with values from the external data sources (an SQL databases in this case) in a type safe manner. The concept of query expressions was introduced since it gives powerful support for expressing queries on SQL databases in F#.

Exercises

11.1 Make a declaration for the sequence of odd numbers.

11.2 Make a declaration for the sequence of numbers $1, 1, 2, 6, \ldots, n!, \ldots$.

11.3 Make a declaration for the sequence of $\texttt{seq}\,[1; 1; 2; 6; \ldots; n!; \ldots]$, where the $i + 1$'st element is generated from the $i'th$ element by multiplication with $i + 1$.

11.4 Declare a function that, for given i and n, selects the sublist $[a_i; a_{i+1}; \ldots; a_{i+n-1}]$ of a sequence $\texttt{seq}\,[a_0; a_1; \ldots]$.

11.5 The declaration of the function $\texttt{iterate}\ f$ on Page 260 has the drawback that $f^n\,x$ is computed when the $n'th$ element is demanded. Give an alternative declaration of this function using the property that the $n + 1$'st element of the sequence can be computed from the n'th element by an application of f.

11.6 Have a look at the `unfold` function from the Seq library. Make a declaration of the `sRoot` function from Section 11.5 using `Seq.unfold`. That declaration should be based on the idea that the sequence generation is stopped when the desired tolerance is reached. Measure the possible performance gains.

11.7 The exponential functions can be approximated using the Taylor's series:

$$e^x = \frac{1}{0!} + \frac{x^1}{1!} + \cdots + \frac{x^k}{k!} + \cdots \tag{11.2}$$

1. Declare a function that for a given x can generate the sequence of summands in (11.2). Hint: Notice that the next summand can be generated from the previous one.

2. Declare a function that accumulates the elements of a sequence of floats. I.e. given a sequence $\texttt{seq}\,[x_0; x_1; x_2; \ldots]$ it generates the sequence $\texttt{seq}\,[x_0; x_0 + x_1; x_0 + x_1 + x_2; \ldots]$.

3. Declare a function to generate the sequence of approximations for the function e^x on the basis of (11.2).

4. Declare a function to approximate e^x within a given tolerance.

11.8   The Madhava-Leibniz series (also called Gregory-Leibniz series) for π is:

$$\pi = 4 \sum_{n=0}^{\infty} \frac{(-1)^n}{2n+1}$$

Use this series to approximate π. (Note that there are other series for π, which converge much faster than the above one.)

11.9   Declare a sequence denoting the following enumeration of the integers:

$$0, -1, 1, -2, 2, -3, 3, \ldots$$

11.10 Use the functions in the Seq library to declare a function cartesian *sqx sqy* that gives a sequence containing all pairs (x, y) where x is a member of *sqx* and y is a member of *sqy*. Make an alternative declaration using sequence expressions.

11.11 Solve Exercise 11.3 using sequence expressions.

11.12 Solve Exercise 11.7 using sequence expressions.

11.13 Solve Exercise 11.8 using sequence expressions.

11.14 Solve Exercise 11.9 using sequence expressions.

11.15 Give a database-based solution to the cash-register example introduced in Section 4.6.

11.16 Give a database-based solution to Exercise 4.23.

12

Computation expressions

A *computation expression* of F# provides the means to express a specific kind of computations in a way where low-level details are hidden and only visible through the use of special syntactic constructs like `yield`, `let!`, `return`, etc. These constructs are not part of the normal F# syntax and are only allowed inside computation expressions. Each kind of computation expression is defined by a *computation builder object* that contains the meaning of the special constructs.

A computation expression *ce* belonging to the builder object *comp* appears in the F# program in a construct of the form:

> *comp { ce }*

This construct is an expression that evaluates to a value called a *computation*.

We have already seen examples of computation expressions in the form of sequence expressions with builder object `seq` (cf. Table 11.2) and query expressions with builder object `query` (cf. Section 11.8). The sequence computation expressions allow us to define computations on sequences without having to bother about the laziness and other implementation details, and the query expressions allow you to make database queries. In Chapter 13 we introduce asynchronous computation expressions with builder object `async` where you can define asynchronous computations without having to bother about low-level details in the current state of the system. The `seq`, `query` and `async` computation expressions are parts of F#.

This chapter describes the internals of computation expressions and how you may define your own builder objects. This allow you to define new kinds of computations with special state, flow of control and data management. The implementation of these special features is in the builder object only, and the low-level implementation details are therefore invisible at the computation-expression level.

The chapter explains and illustrates the machinery of computation expressions using a number of examples of builder objects. The builder object `mySeq` explains the use and meaning of the `yield` and `for` constructs using sequence expressions, while the `maybe` builder object explains the use and meaning of the `let!` and `return` constructs by using them to handle error cases in the evaluation of expressions represented by trees. This is followed by a description of some fundamental properties of the `For`, `Yield`, `Bind` and `Return` builder object methods that correspond to laws in the theory of monads – the mathematical foundation of computation expressions. The chapter ends with a presentation of monadic parsers. They provide a general method to construct programs capturing data from strings with a complex syntactic structure.

12.1 The agenda when defining your own computations

Defining a new kind of computation expressions comprises three parts:

- Defining the computation type *comp*<' a>.
- Defining the computation builder class *CompBuilderClass*.
- Declaring the computation builder object *comp*.

This may look as follows:

```
type comp<'a> = ...
...
type CompBuilderClass() =
    t.Bind(c: comp<'a>, f: 'a->comp<'b>): comp<'b> = ...
    t.Return(x: 'a): comp<'a> = ...
    ...
let comp = CompBuilderClass()
```

The members *comp*.Bind and *comp*.Return provide the meaning of let! and return and those constructs are therefore allowed in the computation expression *ce* in connection with expressions of the form *comp*{ *ce*}. An overview of the technical setting is given in Section 12.4, where Table 12.2 presents the main syntactical constructs and their translations to composition of members from the associated builder object, while Table 12.3 gives the usual types of the members.

The same name (meta symbol *comp*) is usually used for the type of computations as well as for the builder object (an exception is the computation type Async<' a> with builder object async). This double use of the name causes no conflict as the type and the builder object are used in different contexts

By a *computation* we shall understand a value of type *comp*<' a> for some type ' a. The pragmatics behind the development of new kinds of computations is that they are like recipes in a cook book. A computation encapsulates pieces of programs but these pieces are only executed if the computation is *started*. In the same way, a recipe is usually an operational description of how to cook a dish; but the actual cooking is postponed until the recipe is started (used) by a cook.

Evaluating a computation expression, for example:

```
let c = comp { ... }
```

is like editing a recipe. The special syntactic constructs in Table 12.2 build combined computations in the same way as the *pour* "operator" builds a combined recipe in: "cook the vegetables, make a béchamel sauce and *pour* the sauce on the vegetables."

Each kind of computation expression has it own means for starting computations, for instance:

seq<' a>: Operations starting computations are, for example, indexing *sq*. [*n*] that gives a value of type ' a and the function Seq.toList that gives a value of type ' a list.

Async<' a>: An example is the function Async.Start starting the computation where the execution in the normal case will cause some side-effects and eventually terminate with a result of type ' a.

12.2 Introducing computation expressions using sequence expressions

In the introduction of sequence expressions in Section 11.6 it was shown that such expressions are more convenient to use in certain cases than the functions of the Seq-library. In this section we shall introduce the basic notions of computation expressions by showing how user-defined sequence expressions can be implemented.

Consider the sequence expression:

```
seq {for i in seq [1 .. 3] do
        for ch in seq ['a' .. 'd'] do
           yield (i,ch) };;
```

that expresses the sequence of pairs: (1,'a'), (1,'b'), ..., (3,'d'). This sequence expression can be considered a *recipe* to get this sequence since the *evaluation* of the declaration:

```
let pairRecipe = seq {for i in seq [1 .. 3] do
                         for ch in seq ['a' .. 'd'] do
                            yield (i,ch) };;
val pairRecipe : seq<int * char>
```

will not cause any pair to be computed. Instead pairRecipe is bound to a *computation* (or a recipe) that can be *started* (or cooked) at a later stage, for example, when the last element is requested:

```
Seq.nth 11 pairRecipe;;
val it : int * char = (3, 'd')
```

We will now show how the outer for-construct above

```
for i in seq {1 .. 3} do ce(i)
```

can be expressed using functions from the Seq library, and the obtained insight will be used in the next section to implement our own computation expressions for sequences.

We denote the computation seq { *ce*(i) } corresponding to the body *ce*(i) by f i:

```
let f i = seq {for ch in seq ['a' .. 'd'] do
                  yield (i,ch) };;
val f : 'a -> seq<'a * char>
```

and we get:

```
f 1;;
val it : seq<int*char> = seq [(1,'a');(1,'b');(1,'c');(1,'d')]
f 2;;
val it : seq<int*char> = seq [(2,'a');(2,'b');(2,'c');(2,'d')]
f 3;;
val it : seq<int*char> = seq [(3,'a');(3,'b');(3,'c');(3,'d')]
```

The sequence (1,'a'), (1,'b'), ..., (3,'d') of pairs denoted by pairRecipe is hence obtained by appending the three sequences f 1, f 2 and f 3, and we get:

```
seq [(1,'a'); ... ;(3,'d')] = Seq.collect f (seq [1 .. 3])
```

where we have used the definition of Seq.collect in Table 11.1 on Page 254.

The meaning of the actual `for` construct can hence be expressed using `Seq.Collect`:

```
seq { for i in seq [1 .. 3] do ce(i) }
= Seq.collect f (seq [1 .. 3])
```

where:

```
f = fun i -> seq { ce(i) }
```

12.3 The basic functions: `For` and `Yield`

A new kind of computation expressions can be declared in F# through the declaration of a *builder* class, that implements a suitable selection of functions (cf. Section 12.1). We illustrate this concepts by defining a builder class for sequences. This builder class contains member functions that can perform operations on values of a parameterized type, that here is named `mySeq<'a>`:

```
type mySeq<'a> = seq<'a>;;
```

To be able to make a computation expression corresponding to the `pairRecipe` example, the builder class must provide implementations for the two functions:

```
For:    mySeq<'a> * ('a-> mySeq<'b>) -> mySeq<'b>
Yield:   'a -> mySeq<'a>
```

where `For` defines the meaning of the `for` construct and `Yield` defines the meaning of the `yield` construct, in the sense of the translations shown in Table 12.1.

Construct: C	Translation: $T(C)$
`for` x `in` e `do` *ce*	`For(`e`, fun` x `->` $T(ce)$`)`
`yield` e	`Yield(`e`)`

Table 12.1 *Translations for* `for` *and* `yield`

It was shown above that the `for` construct can be expressed using `Seq.collect`. Furthermore, the function `Yield`, with the type `'a -> mySeq<'a>` "lifts" an element to a sequence and, therefore, `Yield` a returns the singleton sequence just containing a. Hence, we arrive at the definitions:

$$\text{For}(sq, f) = \texttt{Seq.collect}\ f\ sq \tag{12.1}$$

$$\text{Yield}(a) = \texttt{Seq.singleton}\ a \tag{12.2}$$

The machinery is illustrated in Figure 12.1 on the `pairRecipe` example, where an ellipse represents a sequence and a dashed box represent a sequence obtained by concatenating the contained sequences. The figure illustrates the meaning of the `for` construct, where f is applied to each element of $i \in sq$. Each application $f(i)$ contribute with a part of the resulting sequence where the result is obtained by concatenation of the sequences:

$$f(1), f(2), f(3)$$

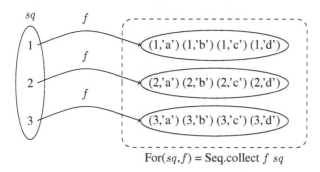

$$\text{For}(sq, f) = \text{Seq.collect } f \ sq$$

Figure 12.1 An example illustrating the definition of `For`(sq,f)

The declaration of a builder class is based directly on (12.1) and (12.2):

```
type MySeqClass() =
    member bld.Yield a: mySeq<'a> = Seq.singleton a
    member bld.For(sq:mySeq<'a>, f:'a -> mySeq<'b>):mySeq<'b>
            = Seq.collect f sq;;
```

and the builder object is obtained as follows:

```
let mySeq = MySeqClass();;
```

We can now make our own computation expressions (limited to the `for` and `yield` constructs), for example, to declare a function that makes the *Cartesian* product of two sequences *sqx* and *sqy* by constructing a sequence containing all pairs (x, y) where x is a member of *sqx* and y is a member of *sqy*:

```
let cartesian sqx sqy = mySeq {for x in sqx do
                                  for y in sqy do
                                    yield (x,y) };;
val cartesian : mySeq<'a> -> mySeq<'b> -> mySeq<'a * 'b>
```

A declaration based on recursive functions or on the functions in the `Seq` library would not have a comparable simplicity. Try, for example, Exercise 11.10.

Using the translation in Table 12.1, this declaration is, behind the scene, translated to:

```
let cartesian sqx sqy =
    mySeq.For(sqx,
              fun x -> mySeq.For(sqy,
                                 fun y -> mySeq.Yield (x,y)));;
```

We shall not go into further details here concerning how `mySeq` can be extended to capture more facilities of sequence expressions. Sequence expressions are handled in F# by a direct translation to composition of functions from the `Seq`-library and not by the use of a builder class. Further information can be found in the on-line documentation of F#.

Construct: C	**Translation**: $T(C)$
do! e ce	comp.Bind(e, fun () -> $T(ce)$)
if e then ce	if e then $T(ce)$ else comp.Zero()
for pat in e do ce	comp.For(e, fun pat -> $T(ce)$)
let! $pat = e$ ce	comp.Bind(e, fun pat -> $T(ce)$)
return e	comp.Return(e)
return! e	comp.ReturnFrom(e)
try ce finally e	comp.TryFinally (comp.Delay(fun () -> $T(ce)$), fun () -> e)
use $pat = e$ ce	comp.Using(e, fun pat -> $T(ce)$)
while e do ce	comp.While (fun () -> e, comp.Delay(fun () -> $T(ce)$))
yield e	comp.Yield(e)
yield! e	comp.YieldFrom(e)
ce_1 ; ce_2	comp.Combine($T(ce_1)$, comp.Delay(fun () -> $T(ce_2)$))

Table 12.2 *Translation of selected syntactic forms inside* comp{...}

12.4 The technical setting when defining your own computations

Defining a builder class *CompBuilderClass* for a type *comp<'a>* of computations is like defining a (rather simple) programming language. The syntactical constructs, like for and yield, that are possible in expressions *comp* { *ce* } are given in advance; but the meaning of the wanted constructs must be provided in the class *CompBuilderClass* of the builder object *comp*. The meaning of an expression *ce* is given by a translation $T(ce)$, as described in Table 12.1, to a composition of the member functions of the builder object *comp*.

A selection of possible syntactical constructs for computation expressions are enumerated in Table 12.2. Meta symbols are used in this table as follows:

- *ce*, *ce₁* and *ce₂* denote computation expressions occurring inside the brackets in an expression *comp* { ... }.
- *e* denotes an expression. That expression may have the form *comp'* { *ce'* } and may be subject to further translations using the builder object *comp'*.
- *pat* denotes a pattern.

Usual types of the member functions are given in Table 12.3. The builder class *Comp-BuilderClass* must contain declarations of member functions such that the translation gives a correctly typed expression; but there are rather few restrictions beside that. One restriction is that the builder class *CompBuilderClass* must contain either the members For and Yield or the members Bind and Return (or all four member functions). These operations are the fundamental ones and we shall study their properties in Section 12.9.

We shall not do any attempt to cover all these constructs, but subsequent sections will describe Bind, Return, ReturnFrom, Zero and Delay.

The meaning of an expression *comp* { *ce* } is defined by a translation as follows:

$$comp\ \{ce\} = \begin{cases} comp.\text{Delay}(\text{fun}() \rightarrow T(ce)) & \text{if Delay is defined} \\ T(ce) & \text{otherwise} \end{cases}$$

Member	Type(s)	Used in
Bind	$comp<'a> * ('a -> comp<'b>)$ $-> comp<'b>$	defining `let!` and `do!`
Combine	$comp<'a> * comp<'a> -> comp<'a>$ $comp<unit> * comp<'a>$ $-> comp<'a>$	sequencing in computation expressions
Delay	$(unit -> comp<'a>) -> comp<'a>$	controlling side-effects
For	$seq<'b> * ('b -> comp<'a>)$ $-> comp<'a>$ $seq<'b> * ('b -> comp<'a>)$ $-> seq<'a>$	defining `for...do`
Return	$'a -> comp<'a>$	defining `return`
ReturnFrom	$comp<'a> -> comp<'a>$	defining `return!`
TryFinally	$comp<'a> * (unit -> unit)$ $-> comp<'a>$	defining `try...finally`
Using	$'b * ('b -> comp<'a>) -> comp<'a>$ when $'a :> IDisposable$	defining use-bindings
While	$(unit -> bool) * comp<'a>$ $-> comp<'a>$	defining `while...do`
Yield	$<'a> -> comp<'a>$	defining `yield`
YieldFrom	$comp<'a> -> comp<'a>$	defining `yield!`
Zero	$unit -> comp<'a>$	empty `else`-branches

Table 12.3 *Usual types for members of a builder object comp*

Hence, the member function `Delay` provides an possibility to impose a delay from the very start of a computation expression. We shall have a closer look at this in Section 12.8.

12.5 Example: Expression evaluation with error handling

Consider the following type for expressions that are generated from integer constants and variables, using operators for addition and integer division:

```
type Expr = | Num of int | Var of string
            | Add of Expr*Expr | Div of Expr*Expr;;
```

An expression evaluates to a value in a given environment *env* : `Map<string,int>` that associates values with variables. Errors may, however, occur due to a division by zero or in the case that the environment does not give any value to a variable.

To avoid evaluations terminating by an exception we declare a function of type:

```
I: expr -> Map<string,int> -> option<int>
```

where

$$\text{I } e \text{ } env = \begin{cases} \text{None} & \text{in case of errors, and} \\ \text{Some } v & \text{otherwise, where } v \text{ is the result of evaluating } e \text{ in } env. \end{cases}$$

The function can be declared as follows:

```
let I e env =
    let rec eval = function
        | Num i        -> Some i
        | Var x        -> Map.tryFind x env
        | Add(e1,e2) -> match (eval e1, eval e2) with
                            | (Some v1, Some v2) -> Some(v1+v2)
                            | _                  -> None
        | Div(e1,e2) -> match (eval e1, eval e2) with
                            | (_ , Some 0)       -> None
                            | (Some v1, Some v2) -> Some(v1/v2)
                            | _                  -> None
    eval e;;
```

Unfortunately, about half of this declaration addresses the manipulation of option values in a rather un-elegant manner. The declaration of I is dominated by the error-handling and the actual applications of the operators are almost put aside in a corner. We want to construct a maybe<'a> computation expression with an associated builder class MaybeClass that takes care of the Some/None distinguishing cases of the error handling.

12.6 The basic functions: Bind, Return, ReturnFrom **and** Zero

We first present a simple version of the type maybe<'a> to introduce the main concepts behind the members of the builder class. This first version will not allow delaying and activation of computations, but these concepts are included in subsequent versions of the builder class. A value of the type maybe<'a> is like a container possibly containing a value and the type is declared as follows:

```
type maybe<'a> = option<'a>;;
```

where the value None denotes an error situation – the container is empty – and Some v denotes that the container contains the value v.

It is not necessary to introduce maybe<'a> as a synonym for option<'a>; but in doing so we are following the convention introduced in Section 12.1 that the type and the builder object should have the same name.

We shall use expressions maybe{ *ce* } where the constructs let!, return, return! and if...then...(no else clause) are used in the computational expression *ce*. To do so the builder class MaybeClass must contain declarations for the members:

```
Bind       :   maybe<'a> * ('a-> maybe<'b>) -> maybe<'b>
Return     :   'a -> maybe<'a>
ReturnFrom:    maybe<'a> -> maybe<'a>
Zero       :   unit -> maybe<'a>
```

where Bind defines the meaning of the let! construct, Return the meaning of the return construct, ReturnFrom the meaning of the return! construct, and Zero defines the meaning of the if-then construct in the sense of the translations shown in Table 12.4.

Construct: C	**Translation**: $T(C)$
`let! ` $x = e$ *ce*	`Bind(`e, `fun ` x `-> ` $T(ce)$`)`
`return ` e	`Return(`e`)`
`return! ` e	`ReturnFrom(`e`)`
`if ` e ` then ` *ce*	`if ` e ` then ` $T(ce)$ ` else Zero()`

Table 12.4 *Translations for* `let!`, `return`, `return!` *and* `if-then`

The operational readings of these constructs are as follows:

- The construct `let!` $x = m$ in *ce* reads:

  - Bind x to the value in the container m (if this value exists) and
  - use this binding in *ce*.

  This construct is analogous to the `for` construct in the previous section.
- The construct `return` e reads: put e in a container.

  This construct is analogous to the `yield` construct in the previous section.
- The construct `return!` e reads: here is the container e.

  Note that e must be a container.
- The value `Zero()` is used in the case of an empty `else` clause.

With this intuition and the fact that `let!` $x = m$ in *ce* is translated to $\text{Bind}(T(m), f)$ where $f = \text{fun } x \rightarrow T(ce)$, we arrive at the declaration:

```
type MaybeClass() =
    member bld.Bind(m:maybe<'a>, f:'a->maybe<'b>):maybe<'b> =
        match m with | None    -> None
                     | Some a -> f a
    member bld.Return a:maybe<'a> = Some a
    member bld.ReturnFrom m:maybe<'a> = m
    member bld.Zero():maybe<'a> = None;;
let maybe = MaybeClass();;
```

By use of expressions `maybe{ce}` the handling of error situations is managed by the `Bind` function and not in the handling of dyadic operators and divisions:

```
let I e env =
    let rec eval = function
        | Num i      -> maybe {return i}
        | Var x      -> maybe {return! Map.tryFind x env}
        | Add(e1,e2) -> maybe {let! v1 = eval e1
                               let! v2 = eval e2
                               return v1+v2}
        | Div(e1,e2) -> maybe {let! v2 = eval e2
                               if v2<>0 then
                                   let! v1 = eval e1
                                   return v1/v2}
    eval e;;
val I : expr -> Map<string,int> -> maybe<int>
```

Observe that the tags None and Some are absent from this program and that the declarations focus just on the computation of the value of an expression.

For example:

```
let e1 = Add(Div(Num 1, Num 0), Num 2);;
let e2 = Add(Add(Var "x", Var "y"), Num 2);;

let env = Map.ofList [("x",1);("y",2)];;

let v1 = I e1 env;;
val v1 : maybe<int> = None

let v2 = I e2 env;;
val v2 : maybe<int> = Some 5
```

The examples show that the maybe computation expressions eagerly evaluate e1 and e2 to values of type maybe<int>. Hence the computation expressions for this simple version of the class MaybeClass are not real recipes, they actually correspond to cooked dishes. This deficiency is repaired in the next section.

12.7 Controlling the computations: Delay and Start

The evaluation of an expression *e* can be *delayed* by "packing" it into a closure:

```
fun () -> e
```

as we already have seen in Section 11.3. For example:

```
let c1 = fun () -> 1+2;;
val c1 : unit -> int
```

The addition operation is *started* by a function application:

```
c1();;
val it : int = 3
```

We use another definition of the type maybe<'a>:

```
type maybe<'a> = unit -> option<'a>;;
```

in order to be able to control the delay and activation of maybe computation expressions. A value of this type is a recipe in the shape of a closure, and the delaying of computations is "hard coded" into the type. Such recipes must be started explicitly when the value of the computation is asked for. The following functions for delay and start will be used:

```
let delay v = fun () -> v;;
val delay : 'a -> unit -> 'a

let start m = m();;
val start : (unit -> 'a) -> 'a
```

The builder class MaybeClass is revised to get another meaning of the let! construct. The new definition of Bind captures that the construct

```
let! x = m in ce
```

matches the following operational reading:

1. Start the computation m.
2. Bind x to the value a of this computation if it terminates properly with a in the container.
3. Use this binding in the recipe ce.

Notice that the let ! construct translates to $\text{Bind}(m, f)$ where f is fun x -> T(ce).
These considerations lead to the first revised version of the builder class:

```
type MaybeClass() =
    member bld.Bind(m:maybe<'a>, f:'a->maybe<'b>):maybe<'b> =
            match start m with
                    | None    -> delay None
                    | Some a -> f a
    member bld.Return a:maybe<'a> = delay(Some a)
    member bld.ReturnFrom v:maybe<'a> = delay v
    member bld.Zero():maybe<'a> = delay None;;

let maybe = MaybeClass();;
```

The declaration for Bind matches the operational reading of the let ! construct. Delays of the option-values are needed to lift these values to the type maybe.

Notice that the declaration of T e env can be based on this revised maybe builder without any change. Doing so gives controlled computations in the sense of recipes:

```
let v1 = I e1 env;;
val v1 : maybe<int>

let v2 = I e2 env;;
val v2 : maybe<int>
```

The recipes v1 and v2 must be started to get values computed:

```
start v1;;
val it : int option = None

start v2;;
val it : int option = Some 5
```

Since an expression like maybe { let ! x = m ... } translates to Bind(m, ...) the computation m will actually be started (check the declaration of Bind) and the values v1 and v2 contain in this sense partly cooked ingredients. This can be observed if side effects are introduced into, for example, in the clause where addition is treated:

```
...
| Add(e1,e2) ->
    maybe {let! v1 = eval e1
           let! v2 = eval e2
           return (printfn "v1: %i   v2: %i" v1 v2 ; v1+v2)}
...
```

The result of executing the following declarations with this version of `maybe`:

```
let v2 = I e2 env;;
v1: 1   v2: 2
v1: 3   v2: 2
val v2 : maybe<int>

start v2;;
val it : int option = Some 5
```

shows that the computation is started and active until the outermost `return` or `return!` statement is reached.

12.8 The basic function: `Delay`

The builder class `CompBuilderClass` of a type `comp<'a>` with builder object `comp` may contain a member:

```
Delay: (unit -> comp<'a>) -> comp<'a>
```

The translation of an expression `comp{ce}` will then use this delay function in the translation of a computation expression *ce*:

$$\text{comp } \{ \, ce \, \} \qquad \text{translates to} \qquad \text{comp.Delay(fun () -> } T(ce))$$

This gives a possibility to enforce a delay from the very start of a computation expression: We add the following declaration of `Delay` to the `MaybeClass` declaration in the previous section:

```
type MaybeClass() =
    ... As above from Bind to Zero ...
    member bld.Delay f:maybe<'a> = fun () -> start (f());;
```

The effect of this can be observed using the above "side-effect example," where the printing of the two lines with values to be added move from the declaration of `v2` to its activation:

```
let v2 = I e2 env;;
val v2 : maybe<'a>

start v2;;
v1: 1  v2: 2
v1: 3  v2: 2
val it : int option = Some 5
```

Hence, with the introduction of the `Delay` member in the class declaration, the expressions of the form `maybe{ce}` will denote genuine recipes. These recipes are expressed in an operational manner by describing *how* to cook the dish; but the actual cooking is delayed until the recipe is started.

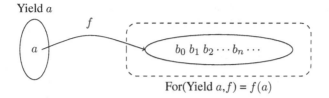

$$\text{For}(\text{Yield } a, f) = f(a)$$

Figure 12.2 An illustration of the law: For(Yield a,f) = $f(a)$

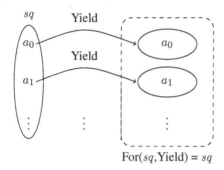

$$\text{For}(sq, \text{Yield}) = sq$$

Figure 12.3 An illustration of the law: For(sq, Yield) = sq

12.9 The fundamental properties of For and Yield, Bind and Return

When declaring builder classes like `MySeqClass` and `MaybeClass` the only restriction imposed on `For` and `Yield` and `Bind` and `Return` is that they should have the correct types. But there are some laws that meaningful implementations should obey. These laws originate from the theory of *monads* for functional programming, a theory that provides the mathematical foundation for computation expressions.

The intuition behind these laws will be presented using the builder class for `mySeq<' a>` as example, where values of this type are considered as *containers* for values of type `' a` and computation expressions are recipes for filling containers. But the laws are not biased towards the `mySeq` computation expression builder.

The laws for For and Yield

The first law expresses that Yield is a kind of left unit for For:

$$\text{For}(\text{Yield } a, f) = f(a) \tag{12.3}$$

Hence binding f to the element of the container yielded by a is the same as applying f to a. This is illustrated in Figure 12.2.

The second law expresses that Yield is a right unit for For:

$$\text{For}(sq, \text{Yield}) = sq \tag{12.4}$$

Hence yielding the elements of a container sq equals that container. This is illustrated in Figure 12.3.

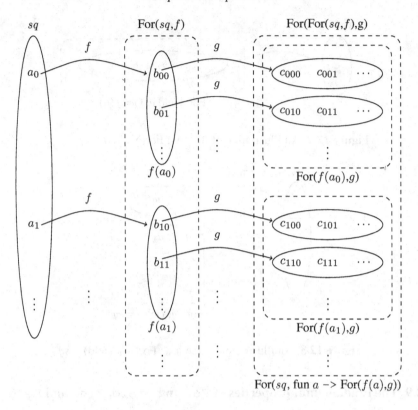

$$\text{For}(sq, \text{ fun } a \rightarrow \text{For}(f(a),g))$$

Figure 12.4 The law: $\text{For}(\text{For}(sq,f),g) = \text{For}(sq, \text{ fun } a \rightarrow \text{For}(f(a),g))$

The last law expresses a kind of associativity of `For`:

$$\text{For}(\text{For}(sq, f), g) = \text{For}(sq, \text{fun } a \rightarrow \text{For}(f(a), g)) \qquad (12.5)$$

This law is explained in terms of the `for` construct. Observe first that the computation expression `for` a `in` sq `do` $f(a)$ translates as follows:

$$T(\text{for } a \text{ in } sq \text{ do } f(a)) = \text{For}(sq, \text{fun } a \rightarrow f(a)) = \text{For}(sq, f)$$

Using this technique we arrive at the following alternative formulation of the law:

for b in (for a in sq do $f(a)$) do		for a in sq do
$g(b)$	is equivalent to	for b in $f(a)$ do
		$g(b)$

The law expresses two ways of filling a container. The left-hand-side way is by filling it using $g(b)$ where b is in the container obtained from `for` a `in` sq `do` $f(a)$). The right-hand-side way is by filling it using $g(b_{ij})$ where b_{ij} is in the container obtained from $f(a_i)$, where a_i is in the container sq. This is illustrated in Figure 12.4.

The laws for `Bind` *and* `Return`

We shall now have a closer look at the resemblance between `Bind` and `Return` and `For` and `Yield`, respectively. Actually the types for `For` and `Yield` may be considered special cases of the type of `Bind` and `Return`, and it is possible to define computation expressions for sequences that make use of `let!` and `return` rather than `for` and `yield`.

To illustrate this, consider the following (not recommendable) declarations:

```
type myStrangeSeq<'a> = seq<'a>;;

type MyStrangeSeqClass() =
    member bld.Return a: myStrangeSeq<'a> =
        Seq.singleton a
    member bld.Bind(sqs, f):myStrangeSeq<'b> =
        Seq.collect f sqs;;

let myStrangeSeq = MyStrangeSeqClass();;
```

The `pairRecipe` example can now be given in the following way:

```
let pairRecipe = myStrangeSeq {let! i = seq {1..3}
                               let! ch = seq {'a'..'d'}
                               return (i,ch)};;
val pairRecipe : myStrangeSeq<int * char>

Seq.toList pairRecipe;;
val it : (int * char) list =
  [(1, 'a'); (1, 'b'); (1, 'c'); (1, 'd');
   (2, 'a'); (2, 'b'); (2, 'c'); (2, 'd');
   (3, 'a'); (3, 'b'); (3, 'c'); (3, 'd')]
```

Therefore, the fundamental laws `Bind` and `Return` are the same as those for `For` and `Yield`:

$$\text{Bind}(\text{Return } a, f) = f(a) \tag{12.6}$$

$$\text{Bind}(m, \text{Return}) = m \tag{12.7}$$

$$\text{Bind}(\text{Bind}(m, f), g) = \text{Bind}(m, \text{fun } a \rightarrow \text{Bind}(f(a), g)) \tag{12.8}$$

It is left as an exercise to justify that these properties hold for the `maybe` example.

12.10 Monadic parsers

This section is a continuation of Section 10.2 where regular expressions were used in capturing data from text lines. Functions using match on regular expressions with capturing groups give an efficient capture of data with a simple structure. The capability of such functions is, however, limited and we had, for example, to use ad hoc tricks in Section 10.2 to capture data with a nested list structure. Data with a *recursive structure* appearing, for example, in representing *expressions* to be input by the program cannot be handled in this way.

Techniques to construct *parsers* to solve such a problem are well-known in compiler technology (as described, for example, in [2]). In this section we use a technique known as monadic parsing that has been developed by the "Haskell community" (cf. [15, 14, 7]). It gives a simple construction of parsers that is well-suited for small-scaled parsing – and it gives an interesting example of computation expressions. Large-scaled parsing used for instance in compilers is made using a parser generator (cf. [12, 13]). The following presentation of monadic parsers in F# is based on the Haskell implementation described in [7].

The first step in constructing a parser is to make a *grammar* describing the structure of the input data. This comprises making regular expressions to describe the *tokens*, i.e. the smallest pieces of information: names, numbers, operators and delimiters to be captured by *token parsers* constructed from the regular expressions. The combination of the token parsers to get a parser is then based directly on the grammar. We define a number of *parser combinators* to be used in this construction. The definition of the parser will usually consist of a set of mutually recursive declarations.

We use two examples to illustrate the technique: the simple example of person data from Section 10.2 and the more complicated example of algebraic expressions. In the first example we may, for example, get an input line of the form:

```
John 35 2 Sophie 27 Richard 17 89 3
```

and the captured value should then be:

```
[("John", [35;2]); ("Sophie", [27]); ("Richard", [17;89;3])]
```

of type

```
(string * (int list)) list
```

In the second example we have algebraic expressions like the string:

```
-a1 + 2 * (a2 - 3)
```

We want to capture this string as the value:

```
Add (Neg (Var "a1"), Mul (Num 2, Sub (Var "a2", Num 3)))
```

of type

```
type Expr = | Num of int | Var of string
            | Neg of Expr | Add of Expr * Expr
            | Sub of Expr * Expr | Mul of Expr * Expr;;
```

The captured value corresponds to the expression tree in Figure 12.5. This example has a number of interesting features beside the recursion: two levels of operator precedence (multiplication and addition operators), a precedence level with two operators (+ and –), and use of the same operator symbol (–) with two different meanings as prefix and infix operator.

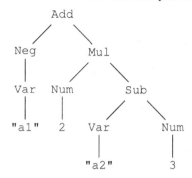

Figure 12.5 Expression tree for expression `-a1 + 2 * (a2 - 3)`

Grammars

In the first example we have two tokens `name` and `number` with regular expressions:

```
open System.Text.RegularExpressions;;
let nameReg   = Regex @"\G\s*([a-zA-Z][a-zA-Z0-9]*)";;
let numberReg = Regex @"\G\s*([0-9]+)";;
```

where the tokens `name` and `number` denote the set of strings matching the corresponding regular expressions `nameReg` and `numberReg`.

We shall capture structured data through rules described by *context-free grammars*. For the person data, the rules should capture strings with the wanted syntax:

- A personData string consists of a series of zero or more person strings.
- A person string consists of a `name` followed by a series of zero or more `number`s.

The corresponding context-free grammar looks as follows:

$$
\begin{array}{lcl}
\text{personData} & ::= & \text{personList} \\
\text{personList} & ::= & \Lambda \mid \text{person personList} \\
\text{person} & ::= & \texttt{name} \text{ numberList} \\
\text{numberList} & ::= & \Lambda \mid \texttt{number} \text{ numberList}
\end{array}
$$

This grammar has the following components:

- Four *non-terminal symbols*: personData, personList, person and numberList.
- Two *tokens*: `name` and `number`.
- Four *rules*. Each rule has a non-terminal at the left-hand side and a *definition* at the right-hand side. A definition may have one or more *choices* separated by | and each choice consists of a possibly empty sequence of tokens and non-terminal symbols. The Greek letter Λ is used to denote the empty sequence in grammars.

In order to be able to distinguish tokens from non-terminal symbols in a grammar, we write a token in teletype font (like in `name` and `number`) while a non-terminal symbol is written in roman font (like in person and numberList).

Each non-terminal symbol denotes a *syntax class* that is the set of all strings that can be generated from that non-terminal symbol. A string is generated from a non-terminal symbol by a *derivation* that repeatedly replaces a non-terminal symbol by a choice in its definition or a token by a matching string. The derivation terminates when there are no more non-terminals or tokens to be substituted.

For example, the string `Peter 5 John` belongs to the syntax class personData due to the derivation:

$$
\begin{aligned}
& \text{personData} \\
\Rightarrow\ & \text{personList} \\
\Rightarrow\ & \text{person personList} \\
\Rightarrow\ & \text{name numberList personList} \\
\Rightarrow\ & \text{"Peter" numberList personList} \\
\Rightarrow\ & \text{"Peter" number numberList personList} \\
\Rightarrow\ & \text{"Peter 5" numberList personList} \\
\Rightarrow\ & \text{"Peter 5" } \Lambda \text{ personList} \\
\Rightarrow\ & \text{"Peter 5" person personList} \\
\Rightarrow\ & \text{"Peter 5" name numberList personList} \\
\Rightarrow\ & \text{"Peter 5 John" numberList personList} \\
\Rightarrow\ & \text{"Peter 5 John" } \Lambda \text{ personList} \\
\Rightarrow\ & \text{"Peter 5 John" } \Lambda \\
\Rightarrow\ & \text{"Peter 5 John"}
\end{aligned}
$$

While a derivation generates a string from a non-terminal symbol, we are interested in the parsing of a string, that is, the creation of a derivation on the basis of a given string. The technique for monadic parsing to be presented will make this derivation on the basis of recursive definitions following the structure of the grammar, and for this approach to be well-defined the grammar must satisfy that there is no derivation of the form:

$$ N \Rightarrow \cdots \Rightarrow Nw $$

where N is a non-terminal symbol and w is a sequence of tokens, non-terminal symbols and strings. In particular, there should be no *left-recursive rule* of the form:

$$ N \ ::= \ N\, w $$

in the grammar. See Exercises 12.3 and 12.4.

We shall use grammars written in EBNF notation (extended Backus Naur form) allowing, for example, use of the repetition operator $*$ that was introduced in connection with regular expressions (cf. Section 10.2). Using the EBNF notation the above grammar gets a more compact form:

$$
\begin{aligned}
\text{personData} \quad &::= \quad \text{person} * \\
\text{person} \quad &::= \quad \text{name number} *
\end{aligned}
$$

In the second example with expressions we have tokens num, var, addOp, mulOp, sign, leftPar, rightPar, and eos where eos denotes end of string. The corresponding regular expressions are as follows:

```
let numReg        = Regex @"\G\s*((?:\053|-|)\s*[0-9]+)";;
let varReg        = Regex @"\G\s*([a-zA-z][a-zA-Z0-9]*)";;
let plusMinReg    = Regex @"\G\s*(\053|\055)";;
let addOpReg      = plusMinReg;;
let signReg       = plusMinReg;;
let mulOpReg      = Regex @"\G\s*(\052)";;
let leftParReg    = Regex @"\G\s*(\050)";;
let rightParReg   = Regex @"\G\s*(\051)";;
let eosReg        = Regex @"\G(\s*)$";;
```

The cautious reader will observe that the `addOp` and `sign` tokens have the same regular expressions. We will comment on this in the subsection on token parsers.

We choose syntax classes expr, term and factor to express the composite forms in expressions and we get at the following grammar for expressions, where the rule for factor has a number of different choices:

expr	::=	term (addOp term)*
term	::=	factor (mulOp factor)*
factor	::=	num | var | sign factor | leftPar expr rightPar

Building a grammar of this kind requires careful considerations of the following syntactic issues:

- Precedence levels of operators.
- Left or right association of operators.

The example with expressions has two levels of precedence of operators:

1. Multiplication operator `*`.
2. Addition operators `+` and `-`.

while all operators associate to the left. The precedence rules of operators are captured in the grammar:

- A factor can be used as a term.
- A term cannot be used as a factor – it has to be viewed as an expression and then enclosed in parentheses in order to get a factor.

The associations of the operators are capture in the structure of the constructs expressing repetitions, and the rule for term would, for example, have been:

$$\text{term} \quad ::= \quad (\text{factor mulOp})* \text{ factor}$$

if the multiplication operator should associate to the right.

The original grammars (in the Algol 60 report) used *left recursion* in the grammar of expressions, like in the following:

expr	::=	term | expr addOp term
term	::=	factor | term mulOp factor
factor	::=	num | var | sign factor | leftPar expr rightPar

The left recursion appears in the rule where expr can be expanded to expr addOp term and similar for term. This grammar has the (theoretical) advantage that the steps in the derivation of an expression correspond to the steps in building the expression tree. Such grammars can, however, *not* be used in our method because the corresponding parser will enter an infinite loop. See Exercise 12.4.

Parsers

Each character in the input string is identified by its *position* that is an non-negative integer. A *parser* with *result type* ' a scans the string searching for matches starting a specified *start position pos*. A *match* is a pair (a, pos') of a *captured value* a of type ' a and the *end position pos'* where a succeeding parsing may take over. The parser is hence "consuming" the characters from position *pos* up to (but not including) the end position *pos'* in producing the result a. The collection of all possible matches starting at a specified position can hence be represented by a list:

$$[(a_0, pos_0); \ (a_1, pos_1); \ \ldots; \ (a_{n-1}, pos_{n-1})]$$

This corresponds to the following type of a parser with result type ' a:

```
type parser<'a> = string -> int -> ('a * int) list;;
```

Note that we allow several possible matches. This is not a complication – it is actually a key feature in monadic parsers. An empty list indicates that the parser has failed to find any matches. Suppose, for example, that we have a parser expr for algebraic expressions. Parsing the input string "-a1 + 2 * (a2 - 3)" from position 0, using the expression expr "-a1 + 2 * (a2 - 3)" 0, should then give a list with three matches:

```
[(Neg (Var "a1"), 3);
 (Add (Neg (Var "a1"),Num 2), 7);
 (Add (Neg (Var "a1"),Mul (Num 2,Sub (Var "a2",Num 3))),18)]
```

Position 3 is just after "-a1", position 7 is just after "2" while position 18 is at the end of the string.

Token parsers

Tokens are parsed using *token parsers*. We consider two kinds of token parsers:

1. A token parser with captured data (normally to be converted).
2. A token parser without relevant captured data.

A token parser of the first kind is made using the token function. The regular expression reg must contain a capturing group. The function conv converts the captured data:

```
open TextProcessing;;

let token (reg: Regex) (conv: string -> 'a) : parser<'a> =
    fun str pos ->
        let ma = reg.Match(str,pos)
```

```
          match ma.Success with
            | false -> []
            | _      ->
                let pos2 = pos + ma.Length
                [( conv(captureSingle ma 1), pos2)];;
```
val token : (Regex -> (string->'a) -> parser<'a>) = <fun:...>

Token parsers without captured data are made using the emptyToken function. The regular expression need not contain any capturing group and there are no conversion function. The parser captures the dummy value () of type unit and its function is solely to recognize and "consume" the data matching the regular expression:

```
let emptyToken (reg: Regex) : parser<unit> =
    fun str pos ->
        let ma = reg.Match(str,pos)
        match ma.Success with
        | false -> []
        | _      -> let pos2 = pos + ma.Length
                    [( (), pos2)];;
```
val emptyToken : (Regex -> parser<unit>) = <fun:clo...>

Note that the function captureSingle from the TextProcessing library (cf. Table 10.4 and Appendix B) is used in the above declarations.

Token parsers in the examples

We declare token parsers name and number in the first example using the corresponding regular expressions:

```
let name   = token nameReg id;;
let number = token numberReg int;;
```

The conversion function is the pre-defined identity function id for the name token parser because the captured string should be used literally "as is". The number token parser uses the conversion function int to convert the captured string of digits to an integer. The token parsers num, var, sign, addOp, mulOp, leftPar and rightPar in the second example should give values that can be used directly in building the expression tree (like the tree shown in Figure 12.5). The token parser addOp should hence capture a "value" that can be used to join two sub-trees, for example:

```
fun x y -> Add(x,y)
```

of type:

```
Expr -> Expr -> Expr
```

when parsing the character '+'. The addOp token parser will hence be of type:

```
parser<Expr->Expr->Expr>
```

These token parsers use the following conversion functions:

```
let numFct (str: string) = Num (int str);;
let varFct = Var;;
let addOpFct = function
    | "+" -> fun x y -> Add(x,y)
    |  _  -> fun x y -> Sub(x,y);;
let mulOpFct _ = fun x y -> Mul(x,y);;
let signFct = function
    | "+" ->  id
    |  _  ->  fun x -> Neg x;;
```

and their declarations are as follows:

```
let num      = token numReg numFct;;
let var      = token varReg varFct;;
let addOp    = token addOpReg addOpFct;;
let mulOp    = token mulOpReg mulOpFct;;
let sign     = token signReg signFct;;
let leftPar  = emptyToken leftParReg;;
let rightPar = emptyToken rightParReg;;
let eos      = emptyToken eosReg;;
```

The cautious reader will observe that the token parsers addOp and sign parse the *same* strings – with *different* captures. This works in monadic parsing because the parsing is strictly *top-down*: The expr parser (to be constructed later) acts according to the context and calls the addOp token parser when an addition operator may occur – and the sign token parser when a sign change operator may occur.

Computation expressions for building parsers

The computation expressions aim at simplifying the construction of a parser by hiding all the technicalities concerning the character positions in the input string. The key point in defining the parser computation expressions is to define the Bind member in the builder class that provides the meaning to the computation expression:

```
let! a = p
ce(a)
```

where p:parser<'a> is a parser giving parses of type 'a and the computation expression $ce(a)$ has type parser<'b>. The construct is translated to $Bind(p, f)$, where f is fun a -> $T(ce(a))$ using the translation T described in Section 12.4.

The operational reading of this construct is:

1. Start the parser p,
2. bind a to a result a of the parser p, and
3. use this binding in the computation expression $ce(a)$.

The parser p is activated by a function application p str pos, where str is the input string and pos is a position. This resembles the activation of a maybe value on Page 288. This activation of p gives a list of pairs $[(a_0, pos_0), \ldots, (a_n, pos_n)]$, where a_i is a captured value

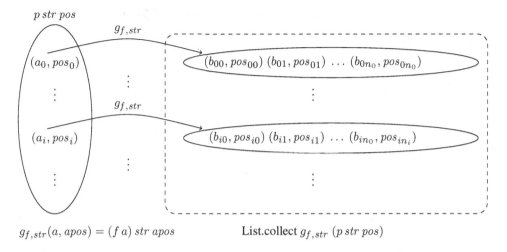

$$g_{f,str}(a, apos) = (f\ a)\ str\ apos \qquad\qquad \text{List.collect } g_{f,str}\ (p\ str\ pos)$$

Figure 12.6 Illustrating `Bind(p,f)` = fun *str pos* -> `collect` $g_{f,str}$ (*p str pos*)

for the part of the input string that starts at position *pos* and ends at $pos_i - 1$. Application of *f* to a_i yields a parser that must be activated to the input string *str* and the start position pos_i for that parser. This resembles the definition of the `for` construct for sequences, see Figure 12.1. This complete process is illustrated in Figure 12.6. Notice that the `Bind` function takes care of all the data management concerning the positions.

These ideas lead to the following computation expression class and builder object:

```
type ParserClass() =
  member t.Bind(p: parser<'a>, f: 'a->parser<'b>):parser<'b> =
    fun str pos ->
      List.collect (fun (a,apos) -> f a str apos) (p str pos)
  member bld.Zero() = (fun _ _ -> []): parser<'a>
  member bld.Return a = (fun str pos -> [(a,pos)]): parser<'a>
  member bld.ReturnFrom (p: parser<'a>) = p;;

let parser = ParserClass();;
```

The zero result `bld.Zero()` is the parser without any matches.

The "constant" parser (corresponding to the right-hand side of `bld.Return`):

```
parser { return a }
```

"captures" the value a without consuming any characters, that is, it gives the value a at the end position of the previously used parser.

When a string cannot be parsed the final result is the empty list; but no informative error report is handled by the builder class. In Exercise 12.8 you are asked make new builder class for parsers that takes care of a simple error handling.

Sequencing of parsers. Parsers for fixed forms

Assume that we have n parsers

$$p_1 : \text{parser}<'a_1>$$
$$p_2 : \text{parser}<'a_2>$$
$$\cdots$$
$$p_n : \text{parser}<'a_n>$$

and a function:

$$F: \ 'a_1 \ * \ 'a_2 \ * \ \cdots \ * \ 'a_n \ -> \ 'b$$

for some types $'a_1, 'a_2, \ldots, 'a_n, 'b$.

Any match of the *sequenced parser* starting from position *pos* is then obtained by getting a sequence of contiguous matches (starting from position *pos*):

$$(a_1, pos_1), \ (a_2, pos_2), \ldots, (a_n, pos_n)$$

of the parser $p_1, p_2, \ldots, p_n$ and applying the function F to the captured values to get a match of the sequenced parser (starting from position *pos*):

$$(\ F(a_1, a_2, \ldots, a_n), \ pos_n \ )$$

Using computation expression the sequenced parser can be written:

$$\text{parser} \ \{ \ \text{let!} \ a_1 \ = \ p_1$$
$$\text{let!} \ a_2 \ = \ p_2$$
$$\cdots$$
$$\text{let!} \ a_n \ = \ p_n$$
$$\text{return} \ F(a_1, a_2, \ldots, a_n) \ \}$$

The `return` expression is inserted at a place where activation of the parsers $p_1, p_2, \ldots, p_n$ have already consumed all relevant characters and where it only remains to return the value $F(a_1, a_2, \ldots, a_n)$ without consuming any further characters.

Sequencing of parsers is used when building parsers for *fixed forms* (containing no part that is repeated an unspecified number of times). The simplest examples are parsers built using the `pairOf` combinator:

```
let pairOf p1 p2 = parser {let! x1 = p1
                           let! x2 = p2
                           return (x1,x2)};;
val pairOf : (parser<'a> -> parser<'b> -> parser<'a*'b>) = ...
```

We may, for instance, combine the `name` and `number` token parsers using `pairOf`:

```
let nameNumber = pairOf name number;;
val nameNumber : parser<string * int>

nameNumber " abc 473 " 0;;
val it : ((string * int) * int) list = [(("abc", 473), 8)]
```

In building a parser in the first example we will use the `pairOf` parser combinator to combine parsers of a name and of a list of numbers.

One may define a `tripleOf` combinator in a similar way, but it is not of much use as most grammars require specially built parsers for their sequencing constructs. In the expression example we have, for instance, the form of an *expression enclosed in parentheses*. A simplified version of this is a form with a variable enclosed in parentheses like:

```
( abc)
```

A parser for this form can be obtained by sequencing the token parsers `leftPar`, `var` and `rightPar`:

```
let varInPars = parser {let! _ = leftPar
                        let! x = var
                        let! _ = rightPar
                        return x };;
val varInPars : parser<expr>

varInPars "( abc) " 0;;
val it : (expr * int) list = [(Var "abc", 6)]
```

The recursive declaration of the `expr` parser given later in this section comprises a sequencing of the parsers `leftPar`, `expr` and `rightPar`.

The choice combinator

The choice combinator `<|>` defines the choice parser:

```
p1 <|> p2
```

for two parsers of same type:

```
p1; parser<'a>
p2: parser<'a>
```

The set of matches of `p1 <|> p2` is simply the *union* of the set of matches of `p1` and the set of matches of `p2`.

This is captured in the following declaration where the lists of matches of `p2` is appended to the list of matches of `p1`:

```
let (<|>) (p1: parser<'a>) (p2: parser<'a>) =
    (fun str pos -> (p1 str pos) @ (p2 str pos)): parser<'a>;;
val ( <|> ) : parser<'a> -> parser<'a> -> parser<'a>
```

We may for instance make a parser capturing a variable or a number:

```
let numOrVar = num <|> var;;
val numOrVar : parser<expr>

numOrVar "ab 35" 0;;
val it : (expr * int) list = [(Var "ab", 2)]
numOrVar "ab 35" 2;;
val it : (expr * int) list = [(Num 35, 5)]
```

Repetitive constructs. Combinators `listOf,` `infixL` ***and*** `infixR`

The `listOf` combinator is used when parsing lists where the parser p captures a single list element:

```
let rec listOf p = parser {return []}
                       <|> parser {let! x  = p
                                   let! xs = listOf p
                                   return x::xs};;
val listOf : parser<'a> -> parser<'a list>
```

The parser `listOf p` will either return an empty list:

```
parser {return []}
```

or parse one list element:

```
let! x  = p
```

and put this element in front of the remaining list and return the result:

```
let! xs = listOf p
return x::xs
```

The parser `listOf number` will for instance parse lists of numbers:

```
(listOf number) " 3 5 7 " 0;;
val it : (int list * int) list =
  [([], 0); ([3], 2); ([3; 5], 4); ([3; 5; 7], 6)]
```

The `infixL` combinator is used when building a parser for a syntactic form where an arbitrary number of operands are intermixed with infix operators that are on the same precedence level and associates to the left.

As an example we consider strings like

```
a - b + 5
```

where numbers or variables are intermixed with addition operators (+ or −). A parser for this form can be obtained using the below defined `infixL` operator:

```
let psL = numOrVar |> infixL addOp numOrVar;;
val psL : parser<expr>

psL "a - b + 5" 0;;
val it : (expr * int) list =
  [(Var "a", 1); (Sub (Var "a",Var "b"), 5);
   (Add (Sub (Var "a",Var "b"),Num 5), 9)]
```

The three matches in the result correspond to the strings:

String	Captured value
"a"	`Var "a"`
"a - b"	`Sub(Var "a", Var "b")`
"a - b + 5"	`Add(Sub(Var "a", Var "b"), Num 5)`

Note that the last expression tree:

```
Add(Sub(Var "a", Var "b"), Num 5)
```

of the full string "a − b + 5" reflects the *left association* of the operators: *first* we subtract b from a and *afterwards* we add 5 to the result.

The `infixL` combinator is defined in a slightly more general setting with two *operand parsers* p and q:

```
p : parser<'a>
q : parser<'b>
```

and an *operator parser* op:

```
op: parser<'a -> 'b -> 'a>
```

corresponding to strings with one operand *astr* matching p, n operators $op_1, \ldots, op_n$ matching op, and n operands $bstr_1, \ldots, bstr_n$ matching q:

$$astr \quad op_1 \quad bstr_1 \quad op_2 \quad bstr_2 \quad \ldots \quad bstr_{n-1} \quad op_n \quad bstr_n$$

The parser p |> `infixL` op q should have $n + 1$ matches on this string corresponding to a sequence of matches of p, op and q:

String	Capture		Captures of p |> `infixL` op q
astr	p	captures a	a
op_1	op	captures f_1	
$bstr_1$	q	captures b_1	$a_1 = f_1\, a\, b_1$
op_2	op	captures f_2	
$bstr_2$	q	captures b_2	$a_2 = f_2\, a_1\, b_2$
		...	
op_n	op	captures f_n	
$bstr_n$	q	captures b_n	$a_n = f_n\, a_{n-1}\, b_n$

The recursive pattern in these captures leads to the declaration:

```
let rec infixL op q =
  fun p ->
    p <|>
    parser { let! a  = p
             let! f1 = op
             let! b1 = q
             let  a1 = f1 a b1
             let  p1 = parser { return a1 }
             return! p1 |> infixL op q } ;;
val infixL : parser<('a -> 'b -> 'a)> -> parser<'b>
             -> parser<'a> -> parser<'a>
```

The `infixR` combinator is declared as follows:

```
let rec infixR op q = fun p ->
    q <|>
    parser { let! a = p
             let! f = op
             let! b = p |> infixR op q
             return f a b } ;;
val infixR : parser<('a -> 'b -> 'b)> -> parser<'b>
               -> parser<'a> -> parser<'b>
```

It is similar to `infixL` but it builds a tree corresponding to the evaluation of operators associating to the right. Using `infixR` in the above example of addition operators would hence give other expression trees:

```
let psR = numOrVar |> infixR addOp numOrVar ;;
val psR : parser<expr>

psR  "a - b + 5"  0;;
val it : (expr * int) list =
   [(Var "a", 1); (Sub (Var "a",Var "b"), 5);
    (Sub (Var "a",Add (Var "b",Num 5)), 9)]
```

where `Sub(Var "a",Add(Var "b",Num 5))` would define an evaluation of

```
a - b + 5
```

such that 5 is first added to b and the result then afterwards subtracted from a.

Making parsers

The parsers in the examples are based directly on the token parsers and the EBNF grammar:

- A parser is defined for each syntax class.
- Each operator in a syntactic rule in the grammar is translated to a suitable parser combinator.

One should, however, pay attention to the word "suitable": The parser combinators should not only correspond to the syntax but they must also give the right conversion of the textual form to captured value. You will frequently have to write your own parsers for fixed sequence constructs (like `leftPar expr rightPar` in the second example) but is it a good idea to try to design the syntax and the structure (that is, type) of the captured value such that repetitive constructs can be handled using the above parser combinators.

Making the parser in the first example is almost straightforward:

```
let person = pairOf name (listOf number);;
val person : parser<string * int list>

let personData = listOf person;;
val personData : parser<(string * int list) list>
```

```
personData "John 35 2 Sophie 27 Richard 17 89 3" 0;;
val it : ((string * int list) list * int) list =
  [([], 0);
   ([("John", [])], 4);
   ([("John", [35])], 7);
   ...
   ([("John", [35; 2]); ("Sophie", [27]);
           ("Richard", [17; 89; 3])], 35)]
```

The example with expressions is more complex but the required parser combinators have been introduced above, so the grammar can be translated directly into a monadic parser:

```
let rec expr    = term   |> infixL addOp term
    and term    = factor |> infixL mulOp factor
    and factor  = num <|> var
                  <|> parser {let! f = sign
                              let! x = factor
                              return (f x)}
                  <|> parser {let! _ = leftPar
                              let! x = expr
                              let! _ = rightPar
                              return x};;
val expr : parser<Expr>
val term : parser<Expr>
val factor : parser<Expr>
```

The F# compiler issues a warning telling that the above system of mutually recursive declarations may contain cyclic definitions – but the declaration is, nevertheless, accepted by the compiler.

Applying the parser `expr` to the sample string gives the wanted result:

```
expr "-a1 + 2 * (a2 - 3)" 0;;
val it : (Expr * int) list =
  [(Neg (Var "a1"), 3); (Add (Neg (Var "a1"),Num 2), 7);
   (Add(Neg(Var "a1"),Mul(Num 2,Sub(Var "a2",Num 3))), 18)]
```

Parsing the full string

The `personData` and `expr` parsers deliver a match for each matching sub-string. Parsers matching only the full string are made using the `eos` token parser that matches end-of-string (possibly preceded by blank characters):

```
let personDataString = parser {let! dt = personData
                               let! _  = eos
                               return dt };;
val personDataString : parser<(string * int list) list>
personDataString "John 35 2 Sophie 27 Richard 17 89 3" 0;;
val it : ((string * int list) list * int) list =
  [([("John", [35; 2]); ("Sophie", [27]);
      ("Richard", [17; 89; 3])], 35)]
```

```
let exprString = parser { let! ex = expr
                          let! _  = eos
                          return ex };;
val exprString : parser<Expr>

exprString "-a1 + 2 * (a2 - 3)" 0;;
val it : (Expr * int) list =
  [(Add(Neg(Var "a1"),Mul(Num 2,Sub(Var "a2",Num 3))), 18)]
```

Reporting errors

A simple error reporting can be obtained by letting the token parsers update a global variable maxPos. The declarations of token and emptyToken are then preceded by

```
let mutable maxPos = 0
let updateMaxPos pos = if pos > maxPos then maxPos <- pos;;
```

and an extra line is added to the token function

```
let token (reg: Regex) (conv: string -> 'a) : parser<'a> =
  fun str pos ->
    let ma = reg.Match(str,pos)

    match ma.Success with
    | false -> []
    | _     ->
        let pos2 = pos + ma.Length
        updateMaxPos pos2
        [( conv(captureSingle ma 1), pos2)];;
```

and similarly for emptyToken.

Using this set-up we introduce the type ParseResult<'a>

```
type ParseResult<'a> = ParseOk of 'a | ParseError of int;;
```

in order to report an error when an input string cannot be parsed. In the case of such an error, the global variable maxPos identifies the position where the error was detected and this position is reported:

```
let parseString (p: parser<'a>) (s: string) =
    maxPos <- 0
    match p s 0 with
    | (a,_)::_ -> ParseOk a
    | _        -> ParseError maxPos;;
val parseString : parser<'a> -> string -> ParseResult<'a>)

parseString exprString "a - b + c";;
val it : ParseResult<Expr> =
        ParseOk (Add (Sub (Var "a",Var "b"),Var "c"))
```

```
parseString exprString "a - b * (1 + c" ;;
val it : ParseResult<Expr> = ParseError 14
```

where the error in the last case was found at position 14 in the string.

In Exercise 12.8 you are asked to hide the error handling in the builder class for parsers.

Summary

This chapter has introduced the notion of computation expressions of F#. Computation expressions offer a possibility for using special syntactic constructs like `let!`, `return`, etc. with a user-defined meaning through the declaration of so-called builder classes. This concept is based on the theory of monads for functional programming introduced in connection with the Haskell programming language.

The chapter uses sequence expressions (introduced in Chapter 11) and error handling in connection with expression evaluation as examples to show how you may define your own computation expressions. The last section shows how parsers can be constructed in a convenient manner using computation expressions.

Asynchronous computations that will be introduced in Section 13.4 is an important example of computation expressions.

Exercises

12.1 Consider the following "alternative" to the declaration for `bld.Delay` on Page 290:

```
type MaybeClass() =
    ...
    member bld.Delay f:maybe<'a> = delay(start (f()));;
```

This new declaration would not give the desired effect. Explain why.

12.2 Consider the expression evaluation on Page 287. Make a new class declaration for computation expressions that takes care of the evaluation in the environment *env* and simplify the declaration of the function I accordingly. Hint: Consider computations as functions having the type: `Map<string,'a> -> option<'a>`.

12.3 The following grammar for non-empty lists of numbers uses left recursion:

$$numberList \quad ::= \quad number \mid numberList\ number$$

A parser strictly following the structure of this grammar:

```
let rec numberLst = parser {let! n = number
                            return [n] }
                    <|>
                    parser {let! ns = numberLst
                            let! n = number
                            return ns @ [n]};;
```

has a problem. Analyze the parser and explain what the problem is.

12.4 Explain the problem with the grammar for expressions on Page 297 that uses left recursion.

12.5 Consider the formulas of propositional logic introduced in Exercise 6.7. In the string representation of such formulas conjunction $\wedge$ can be written either as & or as and, disjunction either as | or as or and negation either as ! or as not. For example, the formula

$$\neg(P \wedge \neg(Q \vee R))$$

has several string representations. Two of them are:

"neg(P and neg(Q | R))"   and   "!(P & neg(Q or R))"

Write a parser for such formulas that takes care of:

- conjunction and disjunction associates to the left,
- conjunction has higher precedence that disjunction, and
- negation has highest precedence.

12.6 Consider the dating bureau in Exercise 4.23. Make a string representation of the file of the dating bureau and a parser that can convert such strings into the representation of the file used in your solution to Exercise 4.23.

12.7 Declare a parser combinator:

```
pFold : ('a -> 'd -> 'a) ->
            parser<'d> -> parser<'a>  -> parser<'a>
```

such that pFold $f\,t\,p$ captures the values
$$a,\ a_1 = f\,a\,d_1,\ a_2 = f\,a_1\,d_2,\ \ldots,\ a_k = f\,a_{k-1}\,d_k$$
if p first captures the value a and repeated use of t afterwards captures the values $d_1, d_2, \ldots, d_k$. Use this parse combinator to make an alternative declaration of infixL of the form:

```
let infixL op q p = pFold (fun ...) (pairOf op q) p ;;
```

12.8 The report of errors can be hidden in builder class for parsers and in this exercise you shall make a new version of parsers based on the type declarations:

```
type ParseResult<'a> = ParseOk of 'a | ParseError of int
type parser<'a> = string -> int -> ParseResult<('a*int) list>
```

The builder class should not make use of any mutable variable like maxPos, see Page 308, and a value ParseError n should occur when an error is discovered at position n.

- Make a new version of the builder class using the above type declarations.
- Revise the two functions token and emptyToken for generating token parsers accordingly.
- Revise the declaration of the choice operator (<|>) and test your builder class using the examples for parsing person data (see Page 306) and expressions (see Page 307).

13

Asynchronous and parallel computations

This chapter is about programs where the *dynamic* allocation of computer resources like processor time and memory becomes an issue. We consider two different kinds of programs together with programming constructs to obtain the wanted management of computer resources:

1. *Asynchronous, reactive programs* spending most of the wall-clock time awaiting a request or a response from an external agent. A crucial problem for such a program is to minimize the resource demand while the program is waiting.
2. *Parallel programs* exploiting the multi-core processor of the computer by performing different parts of the computation concurrently on different cores.

The construction of asynchronous and parallel programs is based on the hardware features in the computer and software features in system software as described in Sections 13.1 and 13.2. Section 13.3 addresses common challenges and pitfalls in parallel programming. Section 13.4 describes the `async` computation expression and illustrates its use by some simple examples. Section 13.5 describes how asynchronous computations can be used to make reactive, asynchronous programs with a very low resource demand. Section 13.6 describes some of the library functions for parallel programming and their use in achieving computations executing concurrently on several cores.

13.1 Multi-core processors, cache memories and main memory

A typical PC in today's technology (2012) contains two multi-core processor chips, where each processor chip corresponds to Figure 13.1. Programs and data are stored in the main memory while the cache memories contain copies of parts of main memory. Each core gives an independent execution of instructions, and a typical PC offers hence the possibility of four independent executions of instructions. Instructions and data are fetched from the cache memories whenever found there – but have otherwise to be transferred from the main memory. Updating a memory location must always be done in main memory – and in cache if the memory location is cached.

Typical clock frequency of processor is approx. 2 GHz while the clock frequency of main memory is approx. 100 MHz (2012 figures), so cache memory is about 20 times faster than main memory. Maximum speed execution of instructions is hence obtained with instructions and data in cache while the speed may suffer a substantial degradation if there are frequent accesses to main memory. Getting instructions and data in cache may hence give a significant performance gain. Typical memory sizes are 4 GB main memory and 3 MB cache memory

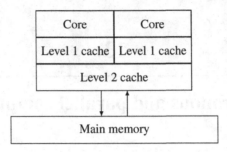

Figure 13.1 A multi-core processor chip in a standard PC

so program and data should fit into the cache unless there is an enormous amount of data –
or some other program is using the cache.

The strategies used in managing the cache memories are outside the scope of this book,
but one should observe that all program activities on the computer are competing for cache.

13.2 Processes, threads and tasks

This section gives a brief survey of the basic features in operating system and run-time system that are used to manage the concurrent execution of several programs on the computer.

Processes

A *process* is the operating system entity to manage an instance of execution of a free-
standing program. The process contains the program and the data of the program execution.
A process may comprise multiple threads of execution that execute instructions concurrently.
A double-click on an icon on the screen will usually start a process to run the program belonging to the icon.

A free-standing F# program comprises the Common Language Runtime System, CLR
(cf. "Interoperating with C and COM" in [13]). The Runtime System manages the memory
resources of the process using a stack for each thread and a common heap as described
in Chapter 9, and it manages the program execution using threads as described below. A
simplified drawing of the memory lay-out of such a process is shown in Figure 13.2.

The `System.Diagnostics.Process` library allows a program to start and manage
new processes. This topic is, however, outside the scope of the present book. The reader may
consult the Microsoft .NET documentation [9] for further information.

Threads

A *thread* is the .NET vehicle for program execution on one of the cores in the computer.
Each thread has its own memory stack and separate execution of instructions. In this chapter
we consider only threads managed via a *thread pool* where *tasks* containing programs can
be enlisted as *work items*. Such a task will be executed when a thread and a core become
available.

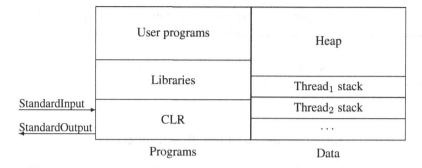

Figure 13.2 Simplified memory lay-out of a process running an F# program

There is a simple example on Page 314 showing creation and start of threads. The reader may consult the description of the `System.Threading` library in [9] for further information.

Tasks

A *task* is a piece of program that can be executed by a thread. When started, a task is *enlisted* as a *work item* in the *thread pool* and it is then executed when a thread becomes available. There are two essentially different ways of executing operations like I/O where the task has to *await the completion* of the operation:

- *Synchronous* operations: The operation is started and the *executing thread* awaits the completion of the operation. The thread continues executing the task when the operation has completed. The standard library I/O functions are synchronous operations.
- *Asynchronous* operations: The operation is started and the task becomes a *wait item* awaiting the completion of the operation. The executing thread is returned to the thread pool to be used by other tasks. The task is again enlisted as a work item when the operation has completed. Asynchronous operations are found in the F# `Async` library and in extensions to the standard I/O libraries.

The continuation of program execution after a *synchronous* operation is done using the stack of the thread where the information is at hand. The mechanism is different in *asynchronous* operations because there is no stack available while the task is waiting. The continuation of the program execution is therefore saved in a special data structure when the asynchronous operations is initiated, and this data structure is then later used to continue the task upon completion of the operation.

A task waiting for completion of an asynchronous operation uses a small amount of memory and no threads and a process may hence run thousands of asynchronous tasks concurrently. The situation is quite different for synchronous tasks where the number is limited by the number of threads available for the program.

These concepts can be illustrated using the "cook-book" metaphor of Section 12.1 where a program is described as a recipe in a cook-book. A process is then described as a restaurant while threads are cooks and tasks are the customer's orders. A synchronous operation corresponds to a cook focussing on the progress of a single order only, while asynchronous operations corresponds to a cook switching between several customer's orders using kitchen stop clocks.

Asynchronous operations are called using `async` computation expressions (cf. Section 13.4).

13.3 Challenges and pitfalls in concurrency

The concurrent execution of tasks gives new challenges and pitfalls for the programmer:

- Management of mutable data shared by several threads.
- Deadlocks caused by threads competing for the same resources.
- Debugging problems where a program failure cannot be reproduced.

Each of these problems is addressed below in a subsection.

Shared mutable data

Updating *mutable* data with a complicated structure may require a number of operations before getting to a well-defined state. The data may hence become garbled if two update operations are intermixed by concurrent execution. This problem is solved by ensuring *mutual exclusion* of updating threads such that two threads do not update the data structure at the same time. The mutual exclusion can be obtained using a `Mutex` object and stipulating the rule that a thread should *acquire* this object before updating the data structure and *release* it after the updating.

The threads `thread1` and `thread2` in the following example both use the mutex object `mutex`. This object is acquired using the `WaitOne` method and released using the `ReleaseMutex` method. The example also illustrates how to create and start threads using F#. The reader may consult the documentation of the `Threading` library in [9] for further details.

```
open System.Threading;;

let mutex = new Mutex();;

let f (n: int) () =
  for k in 1..2 do
    Thread.Sleep 50
    mutex.WaitOne() |> ignore
    printf "Thread %d gets mutex\n" n
    Thread.Sleep 100
    printf "Thread %d releases mutex\n" n
    mutex.ReleaseMutex() |> ignore;;
val f : int -> unit -> unit
```

```
let g() =
  let thread1 = Thread (f 1)
  let thread2 = Thread (f 2)
  thread1.Start()
  thread2.Start();;
val g : unit -> unit

g();;
Thread 2 gets mutex
Thread 2 releases mutex
Thread 1 gets mutex
Thread 1 releases mutex
Thread 2 gets mutex
Thread 2 releases mutex
Thread 1 gets mutex
Thread 1 releases mutex
```

The `System.Collections.Concurrent` library provides thread-safe collections that should be used in place of the corresponding types in the `System.Collections` and `System.Collections.Generic` libraries whenever multiple threads may access the collection concurrently.

These problems of shared mutable data does *not* occur in pure functional programming without mutable data.

Deadlocks

A *deadlock* may occur if two threads $thread_1$ and $thread_2$ are trying to acquire two mutex objects $mutex_1$ and $mutex_2$ simultaneously as follows:

$thread_1$: $thread_2$:

acquire $mutex_1$ acquire $mutex_2$

acquire $mutex_2$ acquire $mutex_1$ ← deadlock

The deadlock occurs because $thread_1$ is waiting for $mutex_2$ that has been acquired and not yet released by $thread_2$ while $thread_2$ is waiting for $mutex_1$ that has been acquired and not yet released by $thread_1$ – both threads are hence stuck and will never proceed.

A problem of this kind can be solved by stipulating a *fixed order* of nested acquirement of mutex objects to be used throughout the program – for instance always acquire $mutex_1$ before acquiring $mutex_2$ in the example. A thread acquiring $mutex_1$ would then always find a free mutex object $mutex_2$ and can proceed acquiring also $mutex_2$. The thread should eventually release both mutex objects – whereupon another thread may proceed acquiring these objects (in the same order).

A program containing a potential deadlock will work most of the time and the deadlock situation will only occur spuriously in special situations where two threads are doing the reservations at exactly the same time. Extensive testing will most likely *not* reveal the problem and you may end up with an unreliable program that occasionally stops working in stressed situations – exactly when a correct function is most needed.

Debugging problems. Logging facilities

A bug in an asynchronous program may have the unpleasant property that it only leads to failure under special courses of external events and special timing conditions (like the above described deadlock). The traditional scheme of receiving error reports from the customer does *not* work for such programs. The programmer receiving the error report will most likely *not* get a relevant description of the course of events and timing conditions leading to the failure and will be *unable to reproduce the failure* – and hence unable to locate the bug.

The solution to this problem is to include *logging facilities* in the program. These facilities should produce a disk file containing a *log of events* occurring while the program is running. The contents of the log file should be part of the error report from the customer sent in case of a program failure. The log file can then be used by the programmer to trace the course of events leading to the failure – and hopefully to find and correct the bug.

Logging facilities should be a part of any serious real-world asynchronous system. This theme will, however, not be pursued further in this book.

13.4 Asynchronous computations

A value of type `Async<'a>` (for some type `'a`) is an *asynchronous computation*. When started it becomes an executing task that either continues the current task or runs as an independent task. A terminating execution of an asynchronous task of type `Async<'a>` delivers a value of type `'a`.

This concept gives a very elegant notation because an asynchronous computation can be used like any other value as argument or result of a function. Simple asynchronous computations are build using the operations in Table 13.1 inside an `async` expression:

$$\text{async } \{ \; asyncExpr \; \}$$

---

stream.`AsyncRead: int -> Async<string>`
   stream.`AsyncRead` n = async.comp. to read n chars from *stream*.
stream.`AsyncRead: byte [] * ?int * ?int -> Async<int>`
   stream.`AsyncRead`(*buf*), *stream*.`AsyncRead`(*buf*, *m*) or
   stream.`AsyncRead`(*buf*, *m*, *n*). Async.comp to read into buf,
   possibly from pos. m and possibly n chars
stream.`AsyncWrite: string -> Async<unit>`
   stream.`AsyncWrite` *str* = async.comp. to write *str* to *stream*
stream.`AsyncWrite: string * int * int -> Async<unit>`
   stream.`AsyncWrite`(*str*, *m*, *n*) = asc.cmp. to write n chars of *str* from pos. m
webClient.`Async.DownloadString: Uri -> Async<string>`
   async.comp. to get WEB source determined by *webClient*.
webRequest.`AsyncGetResponse: unit -> Async<WebResponse>`
   async.comp. to await response on web-request
`Async.Sleep: int -> Async<unit>`
   `Async.Sleep` n = async.comp. sleeping n mS

A question mark (?) signals an optional argument.

Table 13.1 *Selected asynchronous operations*

```
Async.Parallel: Seq<Async<'a>> -> Async<'a []>
  Async.Parallel [c₀; ...; c_{n-1}] = async.comp. of c₀,...,c_{n-1} put in parallel
```

Table 13.2 *Function combining asynchronous computations*

```
Async.RunSynchronously:
  Async<'a> * ?int * ?CancellationToken -> 'a
  Activates async.comp. possibly with time-out in mS and possibly with specified cancel-
  lation token. Awaits completion.
Async.Start: Async<unit> * ?CancellationToken -> unit
  Activates async.comp. possibly with specified canc. token. Does not await completion.
Async.StartChild: Async<'T> * ?int -> Async<Async<'T>>
  Activates async.comp. and gets async.comp. to await result
Async.StartWithContinuations:
  Async<'T> * ('T -> unit) * (exn -> unit)
  * (OperationCanceledException -> unit) * ?CancellationToken
    -> unit
  Activates async.comp. with specified continuation and possibly specified cancellation
  token. Does not await completion of computation.
Async.FromContinuations: (('T -> unit) * (exn -> unit)
  * (OperationCanceledException -> unit) -> unit) -> Async<'T>
  Makes current asynchronous task a wait item. Argument function is called with triple
  of trigger functions as the argument and should save one or more of these closures in
  variables. The task continues as a work item when a trigger function is called.
```

Table 13.3 *Selected functions to activate or deactivate asynchronous computations*

The function `Async.Parallel` in Table 13.2 is used to put asynchronous computations in parallel. The computations are started using the functions in Table 13.3. These tables do only contain a selection of functions – further information can be found in [9].

Simple examples of asynchronous computations

Using the asynchronous operation *webClient*.`AsyncDownloadString` we may build an asynchronous computation to download the HTML-source of the DTU home page:

```
open System ;; open System.Net;;  // Uri, WebClient
let downLoadDTUcomp =
  async {let webCl = new WebClient()
         let! html =
             webCl.AsyncDownloadString(Uri "http://www.dtu.dk")
         return html} ;;
val downLoadDTUcomp : Async<string>
```

This is just a value like any other – but if started, it will run a task to download the HTML-source of the DTU home page. This task will do the following:

1. Create a `WebClient` object. This declaration need actually not be part of the `async` expression and could hence be placed before `async {...}`
2. Initiate the download using `AsyncDownloadString`. This function makes the task an wait item and returns this item in the form of an `Async` value *comp*. The asynchronous computation *comp* will eventually run and terminate when the download has completed.
3. The termination of *comp* re-starts the rest of the computation with the identifier `html` bound to the result of *comp* (which in this case is the result of the download).
4. The expression `return html` returns the value bound to `html`, that is, the result of the download.

Please observe the following

- The computation uses very few resources while waiting for the download – it uses for instance no thread during this time period.
- The `let!` construct is required to make a binding to a value that is later returned at the termination of an asynchronous computation.
- The computation expression does in most cases contain a construct like `return` or `return!` to give a result – and will otherwise give the dummy value "`()`" as the result. Using `return!` yields a new asynchronous computation.

Functions computing asynchronous computations

We may generalize the above example to a function computing the asynchronous download computation for arbitrary URL:

```
let downloadComp url =
    let webCl = new WebClient()
    async {let! html = webCl.AsyncDownloadString(Uri url)
           return html};;
val downloadComp : string -> Async<string>
```

Computations downloading the HTML sources of the DTU and Microsoft home pages may then be obtained as function values:

```
let downloadDTUcomp = downloadComp "http://www.dtu.dk";;
val downloadDTUcomp : Async<string>

let downloadMScomp = downloadComp "http://www.microsoft.com";;
val downloadMScomp : Async<string>
```

A computation downloading the HTML-sources corresponding to an array of URL's in parallel can be made using `Async.Parallel` and `Array.map`:

```
let downlArrayComp (urlArr: string[]) =
    Async.Parallel (Array.map downloadComp urlArr);;
val downlArrayComp : string [] -> Async<string []>
```

and we may hence download the HTML-sources of the DTU and the Microsoft home pages concurrently and compute their lengths:

```
let paralDTUandMScomp =
    downlArrayComp
        [|"http://www.dtu.dk"; "http://www.microsoft.com"|];;
val paralDTUandMScomp : Async<string []>

Array.map (fun (s:string) -> s.Length)
          (Async.RunSynchronously paralDTUandMScomp);;
val it : int [] = [|45199; 1020|]
```

The parallel download of HTML-sources can instead be made using the `StartChild`
function. This gives separated activation and waiting for completion of two child tasks:

```
let parallelChildrenDTUandMS =
    async {let! compl1 = Async.StartChild downloadDTUcomp
           let! compl2 = Async.StartChild downloadMScomp
           let! html1 = compl1
           let! html2 = compl2
           return (html1,html2)};;
val parallelChildrenDTUandMS : Async<string * string>
```

The calls of `StartChild`:

```
let! compl1 = Async.StartChild downloadDTUcomp
let! compl2 = Async.StartChild downloadMScomp
```

start the downloads in two child tasks in parallel. The identifiers `compl1` and `compl2` are
bound to two *asynchronous computations* that *when started* will await the completion of the
child tasks. The main task is hence *not* blocked by the `StartChild` operations. It becomes
blocked when `compl1` is started and awaits the completion of the corresponding child task:

```
let! html1 = compl1
```

The next `let !` construct: `let ! html2 = compl2` will in the same way afterwards await
the completion of the second child task.

Exception and cancellation

Executing `async` computations includes handling *premature termination* caused by an *exception* or a *cancellation*. These concepts can be informally explained using the "cook-book
recipe" metaphor of Section 12.1 by imaging a cook working in a restaurant. The cook
should not only follow the recipe when processing a customer's order but also handle the
following abnormal situations:

- *Exception:* An exception has occurred (like break-down of an oven).
- *Cancellation:* The customer has cancelled the order.

A task executing an `async` computation reacts in case of an *exception* or a *cancellation* by calling the corresponding *continuation*. A cancellation is requested (from outside the task) by setting the *cancellation token* of the execution of the computation (see example below). The cancellation token is polled regularly by the asynchronous library functions and by the member functions of the `async` computation expression. The cancellation is performed with a proper clean-up of resources as soon as the cancellation request has been discovered.

Using the library function `Async.StartWithContinuations` you may supply your own continuations when an asynchronous computation is started. This function requires three continuations among its parameters:

- Normal continuation *okCon* – invoked after normal termination.
- Exception continuation *exnCon* – invoked if an exception is raised.
- Cancellation continuation *canCon* – invoked if the computation is cancelled.

The following example executes the above function `downloadComp` with continuations:

```
open System.Threading;;        // CancellationTokenSource

let okCon (s: string) = printf "Length = %d\n" (s.Length);;
let exnCon _ = printf "Exception raised\n";;
let canCon _ = printf "Operation cancelled\n";;

let downloadWithConts url =
    use ts = new CancellationTokenSource()
    Async.StartWithContinuations
        ((downloadComp url),okCon,exnCon,canCon,ts.Token)
    ts;;
val downloadWithConts : string -> CancellationTokenSource
```

A computation started by a call of `downloadWithConts` may terminate normally:

```
downloadWithConts "http://www.microsoft.com" |> ignore;;
val it : unit = ()
Length = 1020
```

it may be terminated by an exception:

```
downloadWithConts "ppp" |> ignore;;
Exception raised
val it : unit = ()
```

or it may be cancelled:

```
let ts = downloadWithConts "http://www.dtu.dk";;
ts.Cancel();;
val it : unit = ()
Operation cancelled
```

Note the following:

- The task started by `Async.StartWithContinuations` *terminates* when the selected continuation returns the dummy value "`()`". A meaningful program would hence use continuations that initiate some other activity – for instance by sending a message to a queue or activating another task.
- Each *execution* of an asynchronous computation with possible cancellation should have a *fresh* cancellation token source. The above function `downloadWithConts` ensures that by including the allocation in the function declaration.
- Requesting cancellation using `Cancel` on the token source can be followed by a call of one of the *other* continuations if an error occurs or if the operation terminates before the cancellation gets through.

13.5 Reactive programs

A reactive program performs operations using asynchronous waiting and may hence be used to perform many long lasting I/O operations simultaneously while also communicating with the user at the same time. Such a program can be implemented using an *asynchronous event queue*. It is a queue containing events of the following kinds, for example:

- Mouse clicks or key-strokes or other kinds of user input.
- Responses from asynchronous operations.

Asynchronous event queue

An asynchronous event queue from the class `AsyncEventQueue` supports two operations:

```
ev.Post    : 'T -> unit
ev.Receive : unit -> Async<'T>
```

where

- `ev.Post` *msg*: inserts the element *msg* in the event queue *ev*.
- `ev.Receive()`: Awaits the next element in the event queue *ev*.

The event queue class `AsyncEventQueue` is kindly provided by Don Syme, and its implementation is shown in Table 13.4. It is possible that this queue will be included in the F# standard library.

Design of dialogue programs

We shall now consider the design of reactive programs where the system may engage in a dialogue with a user. The systems considered here will have to react to two kinds of events:

- Input from a user.
- Status events from asynchronous computations.

These events are handled by use of an asynchronous event queue.

```
// An asynchronous event queue kindly provided by Don Syme
type AsyncEventQueue<'T>() =
    let mutable cont = None
    let queue = System.Collections.Generic.Queue<'T>()
    let tryTrigger() =
        match queue.Count, cont with
        | _, None -> ()
        | 0, _ -> ()
        | _, Some d ->
            cont <- None
            d (queue.Dequeue())

    let tryListen(d) =
        if cont.IsSome then invalidOp "multicast not allowed"
        cont <- Some d
        tryTrigger()

    member x.Post msg = queue.Enqueue msg; tryTrigger()
    member x.Receive() =
        Async.FromContinuations (fun (cont,econt,ccont) ->
            tryListen cont)
```

Table 13.4 *An implementation of* `AsyncEventQueue` *by Don Syme*

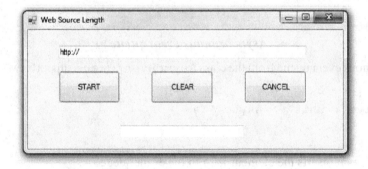

Figure 13.3 Window of asynchronous dialogue program

Consider for example a primitive dialogue program that finds lengths of HTML-sources of web-pages. The program shows a window as in Figure 13.3. The upper text box is used to enter the URL while the lower text box shows the answer from the program. The buttons have the following functions:

Start *url*: Starts the download of the web-page using the URL in the upper text box.
Clear: Clears the text boxes.
Cancel: Cancels a progressing download.

The program we shall construct make use of the asynchronous event queue shown in Table 13.4 and it has three parts:

```
open System
open System.Net
open System.Threading
open System.Windows.Forms
open System.Drawing

// The window part
let window =
    new Form(Text="Web Source Length", Size=Size(525,225))
let urlBox =
    new TextBox(Location=Point(50,25),Size=Size(400,25))
let ansBox = new TextBox(Location=Point(150,150),Size=Size(200,25))
let startButton =
    new Button(Location=Point(50,65),MinimumSize=Size(100,50),
            MaximumSize=Size(100,50),Text="START")
let clearButton =
     new Button(Location=Point(200,65),MinimumSize=Size(100,50),
              MaximumSize=Size(100,50),Text="CLEAR")
let cancelButton =
    new Button(Location=Point(350,65),MinimumSize=Size(100,50),
            MaximumSize=Size(100,50),Text="CANCEL")
let disable bs = for b in [startButton;clearButton;cancelButton] do
                    b.Enabled  <- true
                for (b:Button) in bs do
                    b.Enabled  <- false

// The dialogue part from Table 13.7 belongs here

// Initialization
window.Controls.Add urlBox
window.Controls.Add ansBox
window.Controls.Add startButton
window.Controls.Add clearButton
window.Controls.Add cancelButton
startButton.Click.Add (fun _ -> ev.Post (Start urlBox.Text))
clearButton.Click.Add (fun _ -> ev.Post Clear)
cancelButton.Click.Add (fun _ -> ev.Post Cancel)
// Start
Async.StartImmediate (ready())
window.Show()
```

Table 13.5 *Dialogue program: The Window, Initialization and Start parts*

- The first part contains declarations corresponding to the window shown in Figure 13.3. These declarations are shown in Table 13.5. In this part buttons and text boxes are declared. Furthermore, a function `disable` is declared that controls enable/disable of the buttons in the window. During the download of a web-page, for example, the user should have the option to cancel the ongoing download; but the buttons for clearing the text fields and for starting up a new download should be disabled in that situation.

- The second part (see comments in Table 13.5) contains the dialogue program. We shall focus on this part in the following.
- The third part connects the buttons of the user interface to events, shows the window and starts the dialogue program. This part is shown in the lower part of Table 13.5.

Notice that the program is an event-driven program with asynchronous operations all running on a single thread. The complete program is found at the homepage for the book.

Dialogue automaton

We shall design an event-driven program that reacts to user events and status events from asynchronous operations. The user events are described above. An asynchronous download of a web-page can result in three kinds of status events:

Web *html*: The event containing the html-source of a web-page.
Cancelled: The event signalling a successful cancelling of a download.
Error: The event signalling an unsuccessful download of a web-page possibly due to an
    illegal URL.

The system must perform some *actions* in response to incoming events, for instance: the action corresponding to a Clear event is that the text boxes are cleared, the action corresponding to a Start *url* event is the start of an asynchronous download of the web-page *url*, and the action corresponding to a Web *html* event prints the number of characters in the string *html* in the lower text box.

The possible sequences of events of an reactive program are often conveniently described by a simple automaton. An *automaton* is a directed graph, with a finite number of *vertices* also called called *states* and *edges* also called *transitions*. A specific state is called the *initial state*. A transition is labelled with a set of events. A *path* of the automaton is a sequence:

$$path = s_0 \xrightarrow{e_1} s_1 \xrightarrow{e_2} \cdots \xrightarrow{e_n} s_n$$

where there is a transition labelled e_i from s_{i-1} to s_i, for $1 < i \le n$. The sequence of events $e_1 e_2 \cdots e_n$ is called a *run*.

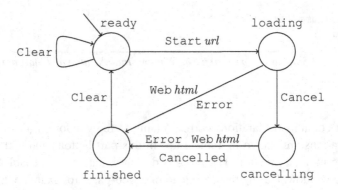

Figure 13.4 A simple dialogue automaton

Consider the automaton in Figure 13.4 with states: `ready`, `loading`, `cancelling` and `finished`, where `ready` is the initial state – it is marked with an incoming arrow, and six events: `Start` *url*, `Clear`, `Cancel`, `Web` *html*, `Cancelled` and `Error`.

The runs starting in the initial state `ready` describe the allowed sequences of events. For example, the sequence

$$\text{Clear Start}(url_1)\ \text{Web}(html_1)\ \text{Clear Start}(url_2)$$

is allowed because it "brings the automaton" from the `ready` state to the `loading` state. Other allowed sequences are:

$$\text{Clear Start}(url_1)\ \text{Web}(html_1)\ \text{Clear Start}(url_2)$$
$$\text{Start}(url_1)\ \text{Cancel Cancelled Clear}$$
$$\text{Start}(url_1)\ \text{Cancel Web}(html_1)$$

while the following sequence is forbidden:

$$\text{Start}(url_1)\ \text{Cancel Clear}$$

because the automaton gets stuck in the `cancelling` state. The two first events:

$$\text{Start}(url_1)\ \text{Cancel}$$

lead to the `cancelling` state and there are no outgoing transition labelled `Clear` from that state.

Notice that the automaton conveys an overview of the interaction in the system. Furthermore, the corresponding dialogue program will systematically be constructed from the dialogue automaton in terms of four mutually recursive functions corresponding to the four states. This leads to the program skeleton in Table 13.6.

The only parts that are missing in this program skeleton relate to the actions for the incoming events of the states. The other parts are systematically derived from the dialogue automaton in Figure 13.4. The function implementing a given state of the automaton, for example, the `ready` state, has three parts:

Part 1: Actions corresponding to the incoming event are performed in the first part. This part is not described in the skeleton because these details are not present in the automaton.

Part 2: Forbidden user input is disabled. By inspection of the events labelling the transitions leaving a state, it can be observed which input the user should be able to provide in that state. The `ready` state has no outgoing transition labelled `Cancel` and the corresponding button is therefore disabled.

Part 3: Wait for incoming events and make a corresponding state transition. In the `ready` state only `Start` and `Clear` events are allowed. A `Clear` event leads back to the `ready` state while a `Start` event leads to the `loading` state.

The program skeleton in Table 13.6 contains a few details not present in Figure 13.4: Answer strings are passed from the `loading` and `cancelling` states to the `finished` state.

```
    let ready() =
        async { .... // actionReady: actions for incoming events
                disable [cancelButton]
                let! msg = ev.Receive()
                match msg with
                | Start url -> return! loading(url)
                | Clear      -> return! ready()
                | _          -> failwith("ready: unexpected message")}

    and loading(url) =
        async { .... // actionLoading: actions for incoming events
                disable [startButton; clearButton]
                let! msg = ev.Receive()
                match msg with
                | Web html ->
                  let ans = "Length = " + String.Format("0:D",html.Length)
                  return! finished(ans)
                | Error      -> return! finished("Error")
                | Cancel     -> ts.Cancel()
                                return! cancelling()
                | _          -> failwith("loading: unexpected message")}

    and cancelling() =
        async { .... // actionCancelling: actions for incoming events
                disable [startButton; clearButton; cancelButton]
                let! msg = ev.Receive()
                match msg with
                | Cancelled | Error
                | Web _ -> return! finished("Cancelled")
                | _     -> failwith("cancelling: unexpected message")}

    and finished(s) =
        async { .... // actionFinished: actions for incoming events
                disable [startButton; cancelButton]
                let! msg = ev.Receive()
                match msg with
                | Clear -> return! ready()
                | _     -> failwith("finished: unexpected message")}
```

Table 13.6 *Skeleton program for automaton in Figure 13.4*

It is now straightforward to complete the whole dialogue program. The type for events (or messages) and an event queue are declared as follows:

```
type Message = | Start of string | Clear | Cancel
               | Web of string | Error | Cancelled;;

let ev = AsyncEventQueue();;
```

and the action parts missing in the skeleton program are declared as follows:

- Actions for incoming event in the ready state: The two text boxes must be cleared:

```
urlBox.Text <- "http://"
ansBox.Text <- ""
```

- Actions for incoming event in the loading state: The text box for the answer is set and an asynchronous download of a web-page is started with continuations as we have seen on Page 320:

```
ansBox.Text <- "Downloading"
use ts = new CancellationTokenSource()

Async.StartWithContinuations
    (async { let webCl = new WebClient()
             let! html = webCl.AsyncDownloadString(Uri url)
             return html },
      (fun html -> ev.Post (Web html)),
      (fun _ -> ev.Post Error),
      (fun _ -> ev.Post Cancelled),
      ts.Token)
```

- Actions for incoming event in the cancelling state: The answer text box is set.

```
ansBox.Text <- "Cancelling"
```

- Actions for incoming event in the finished state: The answer text box is set.

```
ansBox.Text <- s
```

The complete program for the dialogue automaton is found in Appendix C.

A summary of the approach

We have considered the design of reactive systems in terms of a very simple example in order to be able to focus on the principle elements of the approach. Many systems have a similar form where a system is engaging in a dialogue with users and external sources like database servers on the basis of asynchronous communication.

The type Message in the example, provide an abstract notion of the important events in the system that abstracts away the concrete interactions with the user interface. A dialogue automaton provides a convenient technique to define the legal sequences of events in the system. This automaton conveys the essence of the dialogue design in a succinct manner and a dialogue program can systematically be derived from this automaton.

The technical advantage of the approach is that the resulting asynchronous program is executed in a single thread requiring limited computational resources.

13.6 Parallel computations

The Task Parallel Library of the .NET platform provides a powerful framework for exploiting multi-core parallelism. In this section we shall show that functional programming provides an adequate platform for a programmer wanting to exploit this parallelism to speedup the programs. Obtaining a parallel implementation of a side-effect free program makes the correctness problem of the parallel version simple and good library support for parallelism makes the step to the parallel version manageable.

We shall distinguish between two kinds of parallelism: *data parallelism*, where the same function is applied in parallel on distributed data, and *task parallelism*, where a complex problem is solved by combining solutions to simpler problems, that can be solved in parallel. When measuring the effect of multiple cores we consider "big" problems in terms of computation requirements. It does not pay off to parallelize small problems due to the management overhead needed for multiple cores.

In order to experiment with parallelization, we need primitive operations that demands some computation resources in order to make the effect of parallelization visible. Throughout this section a prime number test on randomly generated integers will be used for that purpose. The prime-number test is performed by the function:

```
let isPrime =
    let rec testDiv a b c =
        a>b || c%a <> 0 && testDiv (a+1) b c
    function
    | 0 | 1 -> false
    | n        -> testDiv 2 (n-1) n;;
val isPrime : int -> bool
```

The locally declared function `testDiv` a b c is true if no integer i where $a \leq i \leq b$ divides c. Testing whether n, with $n > 1$, is a prime number, it suffices to test whether no integer between 2 to $\sqrt{n}$ divides n. In order to use more computing resources `isPrime` is inefficiently implemented by performing this test from 2 to $n - 1$.

```
isPrime 51;;
val it : bool = false

isPrime 232012709;;
val it : bool = true
```

A test of a small number is fast whereas a test of a large prime number like the one in the above example takes some observable amount of time.

We shall use randomly generated integers in our experiments. They are generated by the following function gen, where gen *range*, with *range* > 0, generates a number that is greater than or equal to 0 and smaller than *range*:

```
let gen = let generator = new System.Random()
          generator.Next;;
val gen : int -> int
gen 100;;
val it : int = 24
```

```
gen 100;;
val it : int = 53
```

The experiments in the rest of this section are conducted on a 4-core 2.67 GHz Intel I7 CPU with 8GB shared memory.

Data parallelism

The map function on collections is the canonical example for exploiting data parallelism, where a function is applied in parallel to the members of a collection. Parallel implementations of functions on arrays are found in the `Array.Parallel` library as shown in Table 13.7.

```
choose    : ('T -> 'U option) -> 'T [] -> 'U []
collect   : ('T -> 'U []) -> 'T [] -> 'U []
init      : int -> (int -> 'T) -> 'T []
iter      : ('T -> unit) -> 'T [] -> unit
iteri     : (int -> 'T -> unit) -> 'T [] -> unit
map       : ('T -> 'U) -> 'T [] -> 'U []
mapi      : (int -> 'T -> 'U) -> 'T [] -> 'U []
partition : ('T -> bool) -> 'T [] -> 'T [] * 'T []
```

Table 13.7 *Functions in the library:* `Array.Parallel`

We have studied these functions previously in the book, so we just illustrate the advantage of using the function parallel version of the map function on an array with 5000000 numbers:

```
let bigArray = Array.init 5000000 (fun _ -> gen 10000);;
val bigArray : int [] = [|2436; 7975; 2647; 1590; 5959; 3951;
                          430; 1705; 2527; 1004; 2333; ... |]
```

Mapping the `isPrime` function on the elements of `bigArray` will generate a new Boolean array, where an entry is true if and only if the corresponding entry in `bigArray` is a prime number:

```
#time;;

Array.Parallel.map isPrime bigArray;;
Real: 00:00:05.292, CPU: 00:00:20.592,
GC gen0: 0, gen1: 0, gen2: 0
val it : bool [] = [|false; false; true; false; false; false;
                     false; false; false; false; true; ...|]

Array.map isPrime bigArray;;
Real: 00:00:10.220, CPU: 00:00:10.218,
GC gen0: 0, gen1: 0, gen2: 0
val it : bool [] = [|false; false; true; false; false; false;
                     false; false; false; false; true; ...|]
```

The experiment shows a speed-up of approximately 2 in real time when using the parallel version of map. The main point is that achieving this speed-up is effortless for the programmer. Note that the total CPU time (20.218 seconds) used on all cores is approximately double the time needed for a non-parallel version.

In order to use the library for parallel operations on sequences you need to install the F# Power Pack. The PSeq library in that package provides parallel versions of a rich collection of the functions in the Seq library (see Chapter 11). These functions can also be used on lists and arrays as we have seen in Section 11.7. We just show one experiment with the exists function from the PSeq library:

```
#r @"FSHarp.PowerPack.Parallel.Seq"
open Microsoft.FSharp.Collections

let bigSequence = Seq.init  5000000 (fun _ -> gen 10000);;
Real: 00:00:00.001, CPU: 00:00:00.000,
GC gen0: 0, gen1: 0, gen2: 0
val bigSequence : seq<int>

Seq.exists (fun i -> isPrime i && i>10000) bigSequence;;
Real: 00:00:11.557, CPU: 00:00:11.528,
GC gen0: 247, gen1: 3, gen2: 1
val it : bool = false

PSeq.exists (fun i -> isPrime i && i>10000) bigSequence;;
Real: 00:00:05.985, CPU: 00:00:22.183,
GC gen0: 250, gen1: 1, gen2: 0
val it : bool = false
```

In the example we search for the existence of a prime number that do not exists in the generated sequence in order to be sure that the whole sequence is traversed. The speed-up is about 2 and the figures are similar to those for the above experiment using map.

Task parallelism

The problem-solving strategy we have used throughout the book is to solve a complex problem by combining solutions to simpler problems. This strategy, which also is known as *divide and conquer*, fits very well with task parallelism, where a complex problem is solved by combining solutions to simpler problems that can be solved in parallel.

We illustrate the idea on a simple example. Consider the type for binary trees given in Section 6.4:

```
type BinTree<'a> = | Leaf
                   | Node of BinTree<'a> * 'a * BinTree<'a>;;
```

A function to test for the existence of an element in a binary tree satisfying a given predicate is declared as follows:

```
let rec exists p t =
    match t with
    | Leaf                    -> false
    | Node(_,v,_) when p v -> true
    | Node(tl,_,tr)           -> exists p tl || exists p tr;;
val exists: ('a -> bool) -> BinTree<'a> -> bool
```

The divide and conquer strategy is employed in the last clause: In order to check whether an element in a tree satisfies the given predicate, the check is performed in the left and right subtrees and those results are combined.

We shall generate trees using the following function:

```
let rec genTree n range =
    if n=0 then Leaf
    else let tl = genTree (n-1) range
         let tr = genTree (n-1) range
         Node(tl, gen range, tr);;
val genTree : int -> int -> BinTree<int>

let t = genTree 25 10000;;
```

The value of `genTree` n *range* is a balanced binary tree with depth n, where every element v occurring in a node is an integer satisfying $0 \leq v < range$. The generated tree `t`, therefore, has 2^{25} leaves and searching through the whole tree is a time-consuming operation:

```
exists (fun n -> isPrime n && n>10000) t;;
Real: 00:01:22.818, CPU: 00:01:22.727,
GC gen0: 0, gen1: 0, gen2: 0
val it : bool = false
```

The obvious idea for parallelization is to do the search in the left and right subtrees in parallel and combine their results. The function `Task.Factory.StartNew` from the namespace `System.Threading.Tasks` is used to create and start a new task:

```
open System.Threading.Tasks;;
let rec parExists p t =
    match t with
    | Leaf                    -> false
    | Node(_,v,_) when p v -> true
    | Node(tl,_,tr)           ->
      let b1 = Task.Factory.StartNew(fun () -> parExists p tl)
      let b2 = Task.Factory.StartNew(fun () -> parExists p tr)
      b1.Result||b2.Result;;
val parExists: ('a -> bool) -> BinTree<'a> -> bool
```

Evaluation of the declaration

```
let b1 = Task.Factory.StartNew(fun () -> parExists p tl)
```

will create and start a task object of type `Task<bool>` and `b1` is bound to that object (similarly for the declaration of `b2`). The property `Result` gets the result of the task upon its completion.

This parallel version does, however, not give any significant performance gain:

```
parExists (fun n -> isPrime n && n>10000) t;;
Real: 00:01:19.659, CPU: 00:04:43.578,
GC gen0: 2972, gen1: 10, gen2: 1
val it : bool = false
```

The problem with this version is that a huge amount of tasks are created and the administration of these tasks cancels out the advantage with multiple core.

This problem is handled by the introduction of a maximal depth to which new tasks are created:

```
let rec parExistsDepth p t n =
  if n=0 then exists p t
  else match t with
       | Leaf                        -> false
       | Node(_,v,_) when p v -> true
       | Node(tl,_,tr)        ->
           let b1 = Task.Factory.StartNew(
                       fun () -> parExistsDepth p tl (n-1))
           let b2 = Task.Factory.StartNew(
                       fun () -> parExistsDepth p tr (n-1))
           b1.Result||b2.Result;;
val parExistsDepth : ('a -> bool) -> BinTree<'a> -> int -> bool
```

Experiments show that the best result is obtained using depth 4:

```
parExistsDepth (fun n -> isPrime n && n>10000) t 4;;
Real: 00:00:35.303, CPU: 00:02:18.669,
GC gen0: 0, gen1: 0, gen2: 0
```

The speedup is approximately 2.3. At depths starting from about 22 the degradation of performance grows fast. This is not surprising taking the number of subtrees at such depths into account.

Example: Quick sort

A classical algorithm that is based on the divide and conquer problem-solving technique is the Quick sort algorithm that was developed by C.A.R. Hoare. The basic idea is very simple. The array:

To be sorted

Indices :	0	1	. . . . . .	$n-2$	$n-1$
Values :	v_0	v_1		v_{n-2}	v_{n-1}

is sorted by first rearranging the elements $v_1...v_{n-2}v_{n-1}$ such that the resulting elements $v'_1...v'_{n-2}v'_{n-1}$ can be partitioned into two sections with indices $1, \ldots, k$ and $k+1, \ldots, n-1$, respectively, such that all the elements in first section are smaller than v_0 and all the elements in the second section are greater than or equal to v_0:

Indices :	0	1	$\cdots$	$k-1$	k	$k+1$	$\cdots$	$n-2$	$n-1$
Values :	v_0	v'_1		v'_{k-1}	v'_k	v'_{k+1}		v'_{n-2}	v'_{n-1}

$$\underbrace{\phantom{v_{k-1} v_k}}_{\text{All elements } < v_0} \qquad \underbrace{\phantom{v'_{k+1} v'_{n-2}}}_{\text{All elements } \geq v_0}$$

The element v_0 can now be correctly placed in its final position by swapping it with the k's element:

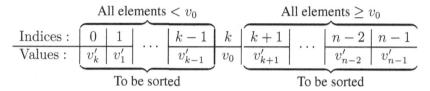

	All elements $< v_0$				All elements $\geq v_0$			
Indices :	0	1	$\cdots$	$k-1$	k	$k+1$	$\cdots$	$n-2$	$n-1$
Values :	v'_k	v'_1		v'_{k-1}	v_0	v'_{k+1}		v'_{n-2}	v'_{n-1}

To be sorted   To be sorted

This array has the property that any element in the first section is smaller than any element in the second section, as the elements in the first section are $< v_0$ while the elements in the second section are $\geq v_0$. The array can hence be sorted by sorting each of the sections separately. This algorithm will have an average run time that is proportional to $n \cdot \log n$ and a worst-case run time proportional to n^2, where n is the length of the array.

The sorting algorithms available in the libraries have a better worst-case run time (proportional to $n \cdot \log n$) and they are using very efficient algorithms. So our recommendation is to use these libraries. We just use the Quick sort algorithm here to illustrate that the above method for parallelizing a divide and conquer algorithm applies to a non-trivial algorithm.

The function `swap` exchanges two elements of an array:

```
let swap (a: 'a[]) i j =
    let v = a.[i]
    a.[i] <- a.[j]
    a.[j] <- v;;
val swap : 'a [] -> int -> int -> unit
```

and the function `partition` can rearrange a section of an array:

Indices :	$\cdots$	k_1	$k_1 + 1$	$\cdots \cdots$	k_2	$\cdots$
Values :		v_{k_1}	v_{k_1+1}		v_{k_2}	

so that the elements in the section which are smaller than a give value v comes before the elements which are greater than or equal to v:

Indices :	$\cdots$	k_1	$k_1 + 1$	$\cdots$	K	$K+1$	$\cdots$	k_2	$\cdots$
Values :		v'_{k_1}	v'_{k_1+1}		v'_K	v'_{K+1}		v'_{k_2}	

All elements $< v$ All elements $\geq v$

The value of the expression `partition` $a\ v\ k_1\ k_2$ is K, that is, the index of the last element in the first section containing elements smaller than v:

```
let rec partition (a:'a[]) v k1 k2 =
    if k2=k1-1 then k2                          //empty section
    else if a.[k2] >= v then partition a  v k1 (k2-1)
        else swap a k1 k2
            partition a v (k1+1) k2;;
val partition : 'a [] -> 'a -> int -> int -> int
                when 'a : comparison
```

The basic Quick sort algorithm is declared as follows:

```
let rec qsort a i j =
    if j-i>1 then let k = partition a a.[i] (i+1) (j-1)
                swap a i k
                qsort a i k
                qsort a (k+1) j;;
val qsort : 'a [] -> int -> int -> unit when 'a : comparison

let sort a = qsort a 0 (Array.length a);;
val sort : 'a [] -> unit when 'a : comparison
```

So far we have just achieved an imperative program that can sort an array:

```
let a1 = [|1; -4; 0; 7; 2; 3|];;
val a1 : int [] = [|1; -4; 0; 7; 2; 3|]

sort a1;;
val it : unit = ()

a1;;
val it : int [] = [|-4; 0; 1; 2; 3; 7|]
```

Even though Quick sort is an imperative algorithm that changes an array, this does not cause any problems for a parallel version since the two recursive calls of qsort work on non-overlapping sections of the array – these two recursive call are independent of each other. Therefore, a parallel version that creates tasks up to a certain depth only is straightforwardly achieved using the same technique as used for the parallel search in a binary tree:

```
let rec pqsort a i j depth =
    if j-i<= 1 then ()
    else if depth=0 then qsort a i j
        else let k = partition a a.[i] (i+1) (j-1)
            swap a i k
            let s1 = Task.Factory.StartNew
                        (fun () -> pqsort a i k (depth-1))
            let s2 = Task.Factory.StartNew
                        (fun () -> pqsort a (k+1) j (depth-1))
            Task.WaitAll[|s1;s2|];;
val pqsort : 'a [] -> int -> int -> int -> unit
                when 'a : comparison
```

```
let parSort a d = pqsort a 0 (Array.length a) d;;
val parSort : 'a [] -> int -> unit when 'a : comparison
```

Since `pqsort` is an imperative algorithm we need to wait for the termination of both of the tasks `s1` and `s2` for the recursive calls. The function

```
Task.WaitAll: Task [] -> unit
```

is used for that purpose. It waits until all the provided tasks have completed their executions. Experiments show a speed-up of approximately 1.7 when sorting an array of size 3200000:

```
let a32   = Array.init 3200000 (fun _ -> gen 1000000000);;
let a32cp = Array.copy a32;;

sort a32;;
Real: 00:00:14.090, CPU: 00:00:14.024,
GC gen0: 1009, gen1: 3, gen2: 0
val it : unit = ()

parSort a32cp 7;;
Real: 00:00:08.352, CPU: 00:00:20.030,
GC gen0: 1016, gen1: 1, gen2: 1
val it : unit = ()
```

It is not surprising that `parSort` gets a smaller speed-up than `parExistsDepth`. The recursive call of `parExistsDepth` requires only that the disjunction `||` is computed on the values of the recursive calls, and this sequential part is a very fast constant-time operation. On the other hand, prior to the two recursive and parallel calls of `parSort`, a partitioning has to be made of the section to be sorted, and this sequential component has a run time that is linear in the size $(j - i)$ of the section.

Summary

In this chapter we have introduced

- asynchronous, reactive programs spending most of the wall-clock awaiting a request or a response from an external agent, and
- parallel programs exploiting the multi-core processor of the computer.

The common challenges and pitfalls in parallel programming are described. The `async` computation expression is introduced and it is shown how asynchronous computations can be used to make reactive, asynchronous programs with a very low resource demand. Library functions for parallel programming are introduced and it is show how they are used in achieving computations executing concurrently on several cores.

Exercises

13.1 Make program producing the deadlocked situation described on Page 315.

13.2 Make a type extension (cf. Section 7.4) of the class `AsyncEventQueue<'T>` with an extra member `Timer: 'T -> int -> unit` such that evaluating

        evnq.Timer evnt n

will start an asynchronous computation that first sleeps n milliseconds and afterwards sends the event `evnt` to the queue `evnq`.

Hint: Apply `Async.StartWithContinuations` to `Async.Sleep` with suitable continuations.

13.3 Consider the dialogue program in Table C.1. Sometimes it is more convenient to let the functions for the state of the automaton communicate using shared variables rather than using function parameters. Revise the program so that `loading` and `finished` become parameterless functions. Is this revision an improvement?

13.4 Make a quiz program where a user should guess a number by asking the following questions:

- Is the number $< n$?
- Is the number $= n$?
- Is the number $> n$?

where n is a integer. The program can give the following answers:

- Yes
- No
- You guessed it!

The program must fix a random number between 0 and 59 to be guessed before starting the dialogue, and each run of the program should give a new number to be guessed.

13.5 Make a geography program guessing a country in Europe. The program asks questions to the user who answers `yes` or `no`. The program should use a binary tree with country names in the leaves and with a question in each node, such that the left subtree is chosen in case of answer `yes` and the right in case of answer `no`.

The program can be made to look more "intelligent" by inserting some random questions in between the systematic questions taken from the tree. The random questions should be of two kinds: Silly questions where the answer is not used by the program, and direct questions guessing a specific country where the answer is used by the program in case it gets answer `yes`.

13.6 The game of Nim is played as follows. Any number of matches are arranged in heaps, the number of heaps, and the number of matches in each heap, being arbitrary. There are two players A and B. The first player A takes any number of matches from a heap; he may take one only, or any number up to the whole of the heap, but he must touch one heap only. B then makes a move conditioned similarly, and the players continue to take alternately. The player who takes the last match wins the game.

The game has a precise mathematical theory: We define an operator xorb for non-negative integers by forming the *exclusive or* of each binary digit in the binary representation of the numbers, for example

$$109 \;=\; 11011101_2$$
$$70 \;=\; 10001110_2$$
$$109 \text{ xorb } 70 \;=\; 01010011_2 \;=\; 43$$

The xorb operator in F# is written `^^^`, for example:

```
109 ^^^ 70;;
```

```
val it : int = 43
```

The operator xorb is associative and commutative, and 0 is the unit element for the operator. Let the non-negative integers $a_1, \ldots, a_n$ be the number of matches in the n heaps, and let m denote the integer:

$$m = a_1 \text{ xorb } a_2 \text{ xorb } \cdots \text{ xorb } a_n$$

The following can then be proved:

1. If $m \neq 0$ then there exists an index k such that $a_k \text{ xorb } m < a_k$. Replacing the number a_k by $a_k \text{ xorb } m$ then gives a new set of a_i's with $m = 0$.
2. If $m = 0$ and if one of the numbers a_k is replaced by a smaller number, then the m-value for the new set of a_i's will be $\neq 0$.

This theory gives a strategy for playing Nim:

1. If $m \neq 0$ before a move, then make a move to obtain $m = 0$ after the move (cf. the above remark 1).
2. If $m = 0$ before a move, then remove one match from the biggest heap (hoping that the other player will make a mistake, cf. the above remark 2).

Use this strategy to make a program playing Nim with the user.

13.7 In this exercise we shall use data and task parallelism in connection with computation of Fibonacci numbers.

- Consider your solution to Exercise 1.5. Make an array containing the integers from 0 to 40 and apply `Array.map` to compute the first 41 Fibonacci numbers. Measure the run time of this operation. Make a data parallel solution using `Array.Parallel.map` and compare the solutions.
- Make a task-parallel solution to Exercise 1.5 and measure the obtained speedup when computing big Fibonacci numbers.
- Compare the obtained results with a sequential solution using accumulation parameters (Exercise 9.7). Note that the linear speedup obtained using multiple cores does not replace the use of good algorithms.

13.8 In this exercise you shall make a list-based version of the Quick sort algorithm. Note that you can use `List.partition` in your solution. Make a sequential as well as a task-parallel version and measure the speedup obtained by using the parallel version. The speedup for the list-based version should be smaller than that for the array-based version due to garbage collection (that is a sequential component) and due to the sequential operation that appends two sorted sub-lists.

Appendix A

Programs from the keyword example

This appendix provides complete programs of the keyword program from the Chapter 10. It consists of

- a section introducing the basic HTML concepts,
- a section containing the complete `IndexGen` program, and
- a section containing the complete `NextLevelRefs` program.

The remaining program for the keyword example: `MakeWebCat`, appears in Table 10.19. The source can also be found on the homepage of the book.

A.1 Web source files

The source of a web-page is a file encoded in the HTML (Hyper Text Mark-up Language) format. This section gives a brief introduction to HTML using the library documentation web-page as an example.

An HTML file is an ordinary text file using a special syntax. Certain characters like <, >, & and " are delimiters defining the syntactical structure. The file consists of *elements* of the form <...> intermixed with text to be displayed. The following construction will for instance make a button with a link to a web-page:

```
<a href="http://msdn.microsoft.com/en-us/library/ee353439.aspx">
active pattern</a>
```

The text:

```
active pattern
```

is displayed in the button and a click will cause the browser to select the web-page given by the URI:

```
http://msdn.microsoft.com/en-us/library/ee353439.aspx
```

A link is hence defined by a pair of elements: a *start element* <a...> and an *end element* </a> surrounding the text to be displayed. The construction:

$$href="..."$$

defines the `href` *attribute* of the element <a...>. Attributes have special uses and are not displayed text.

Elements in HTML appear in pairs of start and end elements, and some elements may contain attributes. The line break element `<br />` is considered a (degenerated) pair of start and end element `<br></br>`.

Text to be displayed is *encoded* in the HTML encoding with certain characters *encoded* using HTML *escape sequences* like `&lt;` and `&amp;` encoding < and &. The internet browser performs the corresponding *decoding* when displaying a text.

The HTML notation has developed over time and web-pages around the world follow different standards. The standard is now controlled by the World Wide Web Consortium (W3C) and more recent standards define HTML as a specialization of the XML notation.

The HTML-source of the library keyword index page starts with the *Document type definition* that is an XML `<!DOCTYPE...>` element:

```
<!DOCTYPE html PUBLIC "-//W3C//DTD HTML 4.01//EN"
    "http://www.w3.org/TR/html4/strict.dtd">
```

The start of the HTML part is signalled by:

```
<html>
```

The heading starts with the *title* to be displayed on the boundary of the browser window:

```
<head>
<title>F# Program Library Documentation Keyword Index</title>
```

It is followed by the *style* section:

```
<style type = "text/css">
h1 {color: purple; font-size: x-large; font-family: Verdana}
p  {font-family: Verdana; font-size: large; color: maroon}
a  {font-family: Verdana; text-decoration: none;
    font-size: medium}
</style>
</head>
```

This section defines the appearance of different parts of the web-page:

h1 : Level 1 heading in purple with x-large Verdana font.
p : Paragraphs in large Verdana font in maroon colour
a : Links in medium-sized Verdana font without the default underlining.

The reader may consult a Cascading Style Sheet (CSS) manual for further information about styles in HTML.

The *body* starts with a level 1 heading `<h1>...</h1>` and a paragraph `<p>...</p>`:

```
<body>
<h1>F# Program Library Documentation Keyword Index</h1>
<p>Version date: Saturday, August 27, 2011</p>
```

Each link is followed by a line break `<br />`:

```
<a href="http://msdn.microsoft.com/en-us/library/ee353439.aspx">
active pattern</a><br />
```

A empty keyword line is just an extra line break:

```
<br />
```

Document body and entire HTML document are terminated by end elements:

```
</body></html>
```

HTML-sources may contain links with an abbreviated reference. The web-page with URI:

```
http://msdn.microsoft.com/en-us/library/ee353439.aspx
```

do for instance contain a link with a *path* instead of a full URI:

```
href="/en-us/library/ee370230"
```

This path is interpreted relative to the *base URI*:

```
http://msdn.microsoft.com/
```

as pointing to the web-page with URI:

```
http://msdn.microsoft.com/en-us/library/ee370230
```

The reader may consult an HTML (or XHTML) manual for further information.

A.2 The `IndexGen` program

This section contains the complete `IndexGen` program. For the documentation of the program, we refer to Section 10.8. The source code is split into an input and an output parts, that are shown in following the two tables.

```
open System;;
open System.IO;;
open System.Globalization;;
open System.Text.RegularExpressions;;
open Microsoft.FSharp.Collections;;
open System.Web;;
open TextProcessing;;


// Input part

type resType = | KeywData of string * string list
               | Comment
               | SyntError of string;;
let reg = Regex @"\G\s*\042([^\042]+)\042(?:\s+([^\s]+))*\s*$";;
let comReg = Regex @"(?:\G\s*$)|(?:\G//)";;
let tildeReg = Regex @"~";;
let tildeReplace str = tildeReg.Replace(str," ");;
let getData str =
  let m = reg.Match str
  if m.Success then
    KeywData(captureSingle m 1,
             List.map tildeReplace (captureList m 2))
  else let m = comReg.Match str
       if m.Success then Comment
       else SyntError str;;

let enString = orderString "en-US";;

let keyWdIn() =
  let webCat = restoreValue "webCat.bin"
  let handleLine (keywSet: Set<orderString*string>) str =
    match getData str with
    | Comment          -> keywSet
    | SyntError str    -> failwith ("SyntaxError: " + str)
    | KeywData (_,[])  -> keywSet
    | KeywData (title,keywL) ->
        let uri = Map.find title webCat
        let addKeywd kws kw = Set.add (enString kw, uri) kws
        List.fold addKeywd keywSet keywL
  let keyWdSet = Set.empty<orderString*string>
  fileFold handleLine keyWdSet "keywords.txt";;
```

Table A.1 *The* `IndexGen` *program: Input part*

```
// Output part

let preamble =
  "<!DOCTYPE html PUBLIC \"-//W3C//DTD HTML 4.01//EN\"
   \"http://www.w3.org/TR/html4/strict.dtd\">
<html>
<head>
<title>F# Program Library Documentation Keyword Index</title>
<style type = \"text/css\">
h1 color: purple; font-size: x-large; font-family: Verdana
p  font-family: Verdana; font-size: large; color: maroon
a  font-family: Verdana; text-decoration: none;
    font-size: medium
</style>
</head>
<body>
<h1>F# Program Library Documentation Keyword Index</h1>
<p>Version date: "
   + (String.Format(CultureInfo "en-US","0:D",DateTime.Now))
   + "</p>" ;;

let postamble = "</body></html>" ;;

let webOut (keyWdSet) =
  use webPage = File.CreateText "index.html"
  let outAct oldChar (orderKwd: orderString,uri: string) =
    let keyword = string orderKwd
    let newChar = keyword.[0]
    if (Char.ToLower newChar <> Char.ToLower oldChar
       && Char.IsLetter newChar)
    then webPage.WriteLine "<br />"
    else ()
    webPage.Write "<a href=\""
    webPage.Write uri
    webPage.WriteLine "\">"
    webPage.Write (HttpUtility.HtmlEncode keyword)
    webPage.WriteLine "</a><br />"
    newChar

  webPage.WriteLine preamble
  Set.fold outAct 'a' keyWdSet |> ignore
  webPage.Close()

[<EntryPoint>]
let main (param: string[]) =
  let keyWdSet = keyWdIn()
  webOut keyWdSet
  0;;
```

Table A.2 *The* IndexGen *program: Output part*

A.3 The NextLevelRefs **program**

This section contains the complete NextLevelRefs program. For the documentation of the program, we refer to Section 10.9.

```
open System      ;;
open System.IO   ;;
open System.Net ;;
open System.Collections.Generic ;;
open System.Text.RegularExpressions ;;
open System.Web ;;
open System.Xml ;;
open TextProcessing ;;

type infoType = StartInfo of int | EndDiv of int
                | RefInfo of string * string | EndOfFile;;

let rec nextInfo(r:XmlReader) =
  match r.Read() with
  | false -> EndOfFile
  | _       ->
  match r.NodeType with
  | XmlNodeType.Element ->
    match r.Name with
    | "div" when (r.GetAttribute "class" =
                     "toclevel2 children")
         -> StartInfo (r.Depth)
    | "a" -> let path = r.GetAttribute "href"
             ignore(r.Read())
             RefInfo(r.Value,path)
    | _ -> nextInfo r
  | XmlNodeType.EndElement when r.Name = "div"
         -> EndDiv (r.Depth)
  | _       -> nextInfo r ;;

let rec anyRefs(r:XmlReader) =
  match nextInfo r with
  | StartInfo n -> Some n
  | EndOfFile   -> None
  | _             -> anyRefs r ;;

let regQuote = Regex @"\042"  ;;
let quoteReplace str = regQuote.Replace(str,"'") ;;
let cStr s = quoteReplace(HttpUtility.HtmlDecode s) ;;
```

```
let getWEBrefs(uri: string) =
  let baseUri = Uri uri
  let webCl = new WebClient()
  let doc = webCl.DownloadString baseUri
  use docRd  = new StringReader(doc)
  let settings =
      XmlReaderSettings(DtdProcessing = DtdProcessing.Ignore)
  use reader = XmlReader.Create(docRd,settings)
  let rec getRefs(n) =
    match nextInfo reader with
    | RefInfo(t,path) ->
      let pathUri = Uri(baseUri,path)
      (cStr t, pathUri.AbsoluteUri) :: getRefs(n)
    | EndDiv m         ->
      if m <= n then [] else getRefs n
    | p               -> failwith ("getRefs error: " + (string p))
  match anyRefs reader with
  | None   -> []
  | Some n -> getRefs n

open System ;;
open System.IO ;;

let outputRef (output:StreamWriter) (title:string, uri:string) =
  output.WriteLine title
  output.WriteLine uri;;

let expandUri (output:StreamWriter) uri =
  let lst = getWEBrefs uri
  List.iter (outputRef output) lst  ;;

let handleLinePair (output:StreamWriter) (rdr: StreamReader) =
  ignore(rdr.ReadLine())
  expandUri output (rdr.ReadLine()) ;;

[<EntryPoint>]
let main (args: string[]) =
  if Array.length args < 2 then
    failwith "Missing parameters"
  else
  if File.Exists args.[1] then
    failwith "Existing output file"
  else
    use output = File.CreateText args.[1]
    fileXiter (handleLinePair output) args.[0]
    output.Close()
    0 ;;
```

Table A.3 *The* NextLevelRefs *program*

Appendix B

The `TextProcessing` **library**

This appendix contains the source code of the `TextProcessing` library that was introduced in Chapter 10. It consists of a signature file `TextProcessing.fsi` and an implementation file `TextProcessing.fs`. This library is organized into four groups:

- A group on regular expressions. This group is documented on Page 224. See Table 10.4.
- A group on file functions. This group is documented on Page 230. See Table 10.6.
- A group on file handling. This group is documented on Page 230. See Table 10.8.
- A group on culture-dependent string ordering. This group is documented in Section 10.6. See Table 10.9.

The interface file `TextProcessing.fsi` is given in Table B.1. The listing of the implementation file `TextProcessing.fs` is split into four tables: Table B.2 – B.5, one for each of the above-mentioned groups. The source can also be found on the homepage of the book.

```
module TextProcessing

// Regular expressions

open System.Text.RegularExpressions

val captureSingle : Match -> int -> string
val captureList : Match -> int -> string list
val captureCount : Match -> int -> int
val captureCountList : Match -> int list

// File functions

open System.IO

val fileXfold : ('a -> StreamReader -> 'a) -> 'a -> string -> 'a
val fileXiter : (StreamReader -> unit) -> string -> unit
val fileFold : ('a -> string -> 'a) -> 'a -> string -> 'a
val fileIter : (string -> unit) -> string -> unit

// File handling

open System.IO

val saveValue:      'a -> string -> unit
val restoreValue:   string -> 'a
```

```
// Culture-dependent string ordering

open System

exception StringOrderingMismatch

[<Sealed>]
type orderString =
  interface IComparable

val orderString : string -> (string -> orderString)
val orderCulture : orderString -> string
```

Table B.1 *The file* TextProcessing.fsi

```
module TextProcessing

// Regular expressions

open System.Text.RegularExpressions

let captureSingle (ma:Match) (n:int) =
   ma.Groups.[n].Captures.[0].Value

let captureList (ma:Match) (n:int) =
  let capt = ma.Groups.[n].Captures
  let m = capt.Count - 1
  [for i in 0..m -> capt.[i].Value]

let captureCount (ma:Match) (n:int) =
  ma.Groups.[n].Captures.Count

let captureCountList (ma:Match) =
  let m = ma.Groups.Count - 1
  [for n in 0..m -> ma.Groups.[n].Captures.Count]
```

Table B.2 *The file* TextProcessing.fs – *Regular expression*

```
// File functions

open System
open System.IO

let fileXfold f e0 path =
  use s = File.OpenText path
  let rec fld e =
    if s.EndOfStream then e
    else fld (f e s)
  let res = fld e0
  s.Close()
  res

let fileXiter g path =
  use s = File.OpenText path
  while not(s.EndOfStream)
    do g s
  s.Close()

let fileFold f e s =
  fileXfold (fun e s -> f e (s.ReadLine())) e s

let fileIter g s =
  fileXiter (fun s -> g (s.ReadLine())) s
```

Table B.3 *The file* TextProcessing.fs *– File functions*

```
// File handling

open System.IO
open System.Runtime.Serialization.Formatters.Binary

let saveValue v path =
  use fsOut = new FileStream(path,FileMode.Create)
  let formatter = new BinaryFormatter()
  formatter.Serialize(fsOut,box v)
  fsOut.Close()

let restoreValue path =
  use fsIn = new FileStream(path,FileMode.Open)
  let formatter = new BinaryFormatter()
  let res = formatter.Deserialize(fsIn)
  fsIn.Close()
  unbox res
```

Table B.4 *The file* TextProcessing.fs *– File handling*

```
// Culture-dependent string ordering

open System.Globalization
open System

exception StringOrderingMismatch

[<CustomEquality;CustomComparison>]
type orderString =
  {Str: string; Cult: string; Cmp: string->string->int}
  override s.ToString() = s.Str
  interface System.IComparable with
    member s1.CompareTo sobj =
      match sobj with
      | :? orderString as s2 ->
        if s1.Cult <> s2.Cult then raise StringOrderingMismatch
        else
        match s1.Cmp s1.Str s2.Str with
        | 0 -> compare s1.Str s2.Str
        | z -> z
      | _ ->
        invalidArg "sobj"
                   "cannot compare values with different types"
  override s1.Equals sobj =
    match sobj with
    | :? orderString as s2 -> s1 =  s2
    | _                    -> false
  override s.GetHashCode() = hash(s.Str)

let orderString (cult: string) =
  let culInfo = CultureInfo cult
  let comp s1 s2 =
    String.Compare(s1,s2,culInfo,CompareOptions.None)
  fun s -> {Str = s; Cult = cult; Cmp = comp}: orderString

let orderCulture s = s.Cult
```

Table B.5 *The file* TextProcessing.fs *– Culture-dependent string ordering*

Appendix C

The dialogue program from Chapter 13

This appendix contains the complete program for the skeleton program shown in Table 13.6.
The reader should consult Section13.5 for further information.

```
type Message = Start of string | Clear | Cancel
             | Web of string | Error | Cancelled

let ev = AsyncEventQueue()

let rec ready() =
  async {urlBox.Text <- "http://"
         ansBox.Text <- ""

         disable [cancelButton]
         let! msg = ev.Receive()
         match msg with
         | Start url -> return! loading(url)
         | Clear     -> return! ready()
         | _         -> failwith("ready: unexpected message")}

and loading(url) =
  async {ansBox.Text <- "Downloading"
         use ts = new CancellationTokenSource()
         Async.StartWithContinuations
             (async {let webCl = new WebClient()
                     let! html = webCl.AsyncDownloadString(Uri url)
                     return html},
              (fun html -> ev.Post (Web html)),
              (fun _    -> ev.Post Error),
              (fun _    -> ev.Post Cancelled),
              ts.Token)

         disable [startButton; clearButton]
         let! msg = ev.Receive()
         match msg with
         | Web html ->
             let ans = "Length = " + String.Format("0:D",html.Length)
             return! finished(ans)
         | Error    -> return! finished("Error")
         | Cancel   -> ts.Cancel()
                       return! cancelling()
         | _        -> failwith("loading: unexpected message")}
```

```
and cancelling() =
  async
    {ansBox.Text <- "Cancelling"

     disable [startButton; clearButton; cancelButton]
     let! msg = ev.Receive()
     match msg with
     | Cancelled | Error | Web  _ -> return! finished("Cancelled")
     | _                -> failwith("cancelling: unexpected message")}

and finished(s) =
   async {ansBox.Text <- s

          disable [startButton; cancelButton]
          let! msg = ev.Receive()
          match msg with
          | Clear -> return! ready()
          | _        -> failwith("finished: unexpected message")}
```

Table C.1 *Dialogue program for automaton in Figure 13.4*

References

[1] Harold Abelson, Gerald Jay Sussman, *Structure and Interpretation of Computer Programs*, second edition, The MIT Press, Cambridge, MA, USA, 1996.

[2] Alfred Aho, Monica S. Lam, Ravi Sethi, Jeffrey D. Ullman, *Compilers: Principles, Techniques and Tools*, second edition, Pearson Addison-Wesley, Boston, MA, USA, 2006.

[3] Guy Cousineau, Michel Mauny, *The Functional Approach to Programming*, Cambridge University Press, Cambridge, United Kingdom, 1998.

[4] Maarten M. Fokkinga, Functioneel programmeren in een vogelvlucht, *INFORMATIE*, vol. 27, pp. 862–873, Kluwer b.v., Deventer, The Netherlands, 1985.

[5] Michael R. Hansen, Hans Rischel, *Introduction to Programming using SML*, Addison-Wesley Longman, Harlow, England, 1999.

[6] Peter Henderson, Functional Geometry, *Proceedings of the 1982 ACM Symposium on LISP and Functional Programming*, pp. 179–187, ACM, Pittsburgh, PA, USA, 1982.

[7] Graham Hutton, Erik Meijer, Monadic Parsing in Haskell, *Journal of Functional Programming*, vol. 8, pp. 437–444, Cambridge University Press, Cambridge, United Kingdom, 1998.

[8] Robin Milner, Mads Tofte, Robert Harper, David MacQueen, *The Definition of Standard ML*, revised edition, The MIT Press, Cambridge, MA, USA, 1997.

[9] Microsoft Development Network *MSDN*, on the internet.

[10] L.C. Paulson, *ML for the Working Programmer*, second edition, Cambridge University Press, Cambridge, United Kingdom, 1996.

[11] Peter Sestoft, Henrik I. Hansen, *C# Precisely*, second edition, The MIT Press, Cambridge, MA, USA, 2012.

[12] Peter Sestoft, *Programming Language Concepts for Software Developers*, Springer, London, England, 2012.

[13] Don Syme, Adam Granicz, Antonio Cisternino, *Expert F# 2.0*, Apress, New York, NY, USA, 2010.

[14] Simon Thompson, *Haskell. The Craft of Functional programming*, third edition, Addison-Wesley Longman, Harlow, England, 2011.

[15] Philip Wadler, Monads for functional programming, *Advanced Functional Programming*, Proceedings of the Båstad Spring School, May 1995, Lecture Notes in Computer Science 925, Springer, Berlin, Heidelberg, Germany, 1995.

The URL of [9] is found on the home page of the book (see Page x).

Index

Printed in the United States
by Baker & Taylor Publisher Services